Marriage, Law and Modernity

Marriage, Law and Modernity

Global Histories

Edited by Julia Moses

BLOOMSBURY ACADEMIC
LONDON • NEW YORK • OXFORD • NEW DELHI • SYDNEY

BLOOMSBURY ACADEMIC
Bloomsbury Publishing Plc
50 Bedford Square, London, WC1B 3DP, UK
1385 Broadway, New York, NY 10018, USA

BLOOMSBURY, BLOOMSBURY ACADEMIC and the Diana logo
are trademarks of Bloomsbury Publishing Plc

First published 2018
Paperback edition first published 2019

Copyright © Julia Moses and Contributors, 2018

Julia Moses and Contributors have asserted their rights under the Copyright,
Designs and Patents Act, 1988, to be identified as Authors of this work.

For legal purposes the Acknowledgements on p. xi constitute
an extension of this copyright page.

Cover image: Westernized wedding parties of Zulu tribespeople
with their attendants, circa 1910 © Popperfoto/Getty Images

All rights reserved. No part of this publication may be reproduced or
transmitted in any form or by any means, electronic or mechanical,
including photocopying, recording, or any information storage or retrieval
system, without prior permission in writing from the publishers.

Bloomsbury Publishing Plc does not have any control over, or responsibility for,
any third-party websites referred to or in this book. All internet addresses given
in this book were correct at the time of going to press. The author and publisher
regret any inconvenience caused if addresses have changed or sites have
ceased to exist, but can accept no responsibility for any such changes.

A catalogue record for this book is available from the British Library.

Library of Congress Cataloging-in-Publication Data
Names: Moses, Julia, editor.
Title: Marriage, law and modernity : global histories / edited by Julia Moses.
Description: London : New York, NY : Bloomsbury Academic, 2017. | Includes
bibliographical references and index.
Identifiers: LCCN 2017020739| ISBN 9781474276108 (hb) | ISBN 9781474276115
(epub)
Subjects: LCSH: Marriage–History. | Marriage law–History.
Classification: LCC HQ515 .M386 2017 | DDC 306.8109–dc23 LC record available at
https://lccn.loc.gov/2017020739

ISBN: HB: 978-1-4742-7610-8
PB: 978-1-3501-1238-4
ePDF: 978-1-4742-7612-2
ePub: 978-1-4742-7611-5

Typeset by Deanta Global Publishing Services, Chennai, India

To find out more about our authors and books visit
www.bloomsbury.com and sign up for our newsletters.

Contents

List of Figures   vii
List of Contributors   viii
Acknowledgements   xi

Introduction: Making Marriage 'Modern' *Julia Moses*   1

Part 1   Marriage and Forms of the Family

1. From Liberalism to Human Dignity: The Transformation of Marriage and Family Rights in Brazil *Sueann Caulfield*   27
2. From Toleration to Prosecution: Concubinage and the Law in China *Lisa Tran*   54
3. The Birth of Mistresses and Bastards: A History of Marriage in Siam (Thailand) *Tamara Loos*   71
4. Royal Marriage in Europe: An Inherently Conservative System *Helen Watanabe-O'Kelly*   90

Part 2   Marriage, Religion and the State

5. 'Till Death Do You Part': Catholicism, Marriage and Culture War in Austria(-Hungary) *Ulrike Harmat*   109
6. Modernizing Marriage in Egypt *Kenneth M. Cuno*   129
7. 'A Babel of Law': Hindu Marriage, Global Spaces and Intimate Subjects in Late-Nineteenth-Century India *Leigh Denault*   149
8. English Exports: Invoking the Common Law of Marriage across the Empire in the Nineteenth Century *Rebecca Probert*   168

Part 3   Marriage, Kinship and Community

9. Finding the Ordinary in the Extraordinary: Marriage Norms and Bigamy in Canada *Mélanie Méthot*   187
10. Equality before the Law? The Intermarriage Debate in Post-Nazi Germany *Julia Woesthoff*   204

11 Customary and Civil Marriage Law and the Question of
    Gender Equality in Twentieth- and Twenty-First-Century
    Gabon and Africa *Rachel Jean-Baptiste*   222

Postscript: How History mattered in Same-Sex Marriage Rights *Nancy F. Cott*   243

Select Bibliography   255
Index   263

List of Figures

1.1	2014 LGBT Pride Parade in São Paulo. Source: Wikimedia Commons	39
3.1	Photograph of King Chulalongkorn, Queen Saowapha and Royal Sons, 1890s. Source: U-M Library Digital Collections. Trans-Asia Photography Review Images.	80
3.2	Portrait of King Chulalongkorn, Queen Saowapha and their Sons, ca. 1900. Courtesy Maurizio Peleggi.	80
4.1	The Marriage of Crown Prince Friedrich of Brandenburg-Prussia and Elisabeth Christine, Duchess of Braunschweig-Bevern, 1733. Source: Ullsteinbild.	93
4.2	Memento of the Wedding of the German Crown Prince Friedrich Wilhelm of Prussia and Cecilie, Duchess of Mecklenburg-Schwerin, 1905. Source: Deutsches Historisches Museum, Berlin /I. Desnica.	102
6.1	Khedive Tawfiq and Khediva Amina Ilhami, mid-1880s. Source: The Bibliotheca Alexandrina Memory of Modern Egypt Digital Archive.	137
6.2	Family Portrait, probably 1920s. Courtesy of the Rare Books and Special Collections Library, The American University in Cairo.	142
9.1	Number of Prosecuted Cases of Bigamy in Quebec and Nova Scotia.	193
11.1	Map of Gabon. Source: Rachel Jean-Baptiste, *Conjugal Rights: Marriage, Sexuality, and Urban Life in Colonial Libreville, Gabon* (Athens, OH, 2014).	227
11.2	Bridewealth Payment, 2002. Courtesy Rachel Jean-Baptiste.	232

List of Contributors

Nancy F. Cott is Jonathan Trumbull Professor of American History at Harvard University. Most of Nancy Cott's work in nineteenth- and twentieth-century US history focuses on gender questions. Her interests also include social movements, political culture, law and citizenship. She is the author of *Public Vows: A History of Marriage and the Nation* (2000), *A Woman Making History: Mary Ritter Beard through Her Letters* (1991), *The Grounding of Modern Feminism* (1987), *The Bonds of Womanhood:* (1977) as well as numerous path-breaking articles in the *American Historical Review* and elsewhere. Since writing *Public Vows*, Professor Cott has participated in writing historians' *amici* briefs on the same-sex marriage question in several states, including challenges to the federal Defense of Marriage Act, and she testified as an expert witness in the federal case against Proposition 8 in California.

Kenneth M. Cuno is professor of history at the University of Illinois at Urbana-Champaign. He is the author of *Modernizing Marriage: Family, Ideology, and Law in Nineteenth- and Early Twentieth-Century Egypt* (2015), which received the Albert Hourani Book Award from the Middle East Studies Association. Other recent books include *Race and Slavery in Nineteenth-Century Egypt, Sudan, and the Ottoman Mediterranean: Histories of Trans-Saharan Africans*, co-edited with Terence Walz (2010); and *Family, Gender, and Law in a Globalizing Middle East and South Asia*, co-edited with Manisha Desai (2009). He also contributed the chapter on nineteenth-century Egypt in *The New Cambridge History of Islam*, vol. 5 (2010).

Leigh Denault is fellow of Churchill College, Cambridge, where she directs studies in history. She lectures in modern South Asian history, and offers MPhil option courses covering both the colonial and postcolonial periods. Her research interests include colonial legal history, the history of the family, gender and sexuality, and the politics of identity and personhood.

Ulrike Harmat is a research associate at the Institute for Modern and Contemporary Historical Research at the Austrian Academy of Sciences, Vienna. She is an expert in Austrian legal and social history in the nineteenth and twentieth centuries and edits the series *Die Habsburgermonarchie 1848-1918*. Her books include *Ehe auf Widerruf? Der Konflikt um das Eherecht in Österreich 1918-1938* (Max Planck Institut für Europäische Rechtsgeschichte: Frankfurt a.M. 1999) and *Die Habsburgermonarchie 1848-1918*, vol. 9/1 (Österreiche Akademie der Wissenschaften: Vienna, 2010) and vol. 11/3 (Vienna, 2017). Her articles have appeared in the *Austrian History Yearbook*, *Beiträge zur Österreichischen Rechtsgeschichte*, *L'Homme* and a number of edited collections.

Rachel Jean-Baptiste is associate professor in the Department of History at the University of California Davis. Her research focuses on the history of gender, sexuality and marriage and family law, racial thought and colonialism in francophone West and Equatorial Africa. She is the author of *Conjugal Rights: Marriage, Sexuality, and Urban Life in Colonial Libreville, Gabon.* (Athens: Ohio University Press, 2014) and has published articles in *The Journal of Women's History, The Journal of African History, Cahiers d'Études Africaines* and *The Journal of the History of Sexuality.*

Tamara Loos is professor of history at Cornell University and former director of the Southeast Asia Program. Her most recent book, *Bones around My Neck: The Life and Exile of a Prince Provocateur* (Ithaca: Cornell, 2016), narrates the story of Prince Prisdang Chumsai (1852–1935), a provocateur whose dramatic life reveals the subjective experience of global imperialism. Her first book, *Subject Siam: Family, Law, and Colonial Modernity in Thailand* (Ithaca: Cornell, 2006) considered Siam's place as a colonized and colonizing power in Southeast Asia. Her articles include studies of sex and politics, transnational sexualities, comparative law, sodomy, the family, suffrage, intimate violence, rape and notions of liberty in Thailand.

Mélanie Méthot is associate professor of history at the Augustana Campus of the University of Alberta. She has published on Canadian social reformers at the turn of the twentieth century, female police magistrates and bigamy in Canada. She is currently working on two research projects: on the administration of justice in Alberta in the first part of the twentieth century, and on bigamy in Australia. Her work has appeared in journals including the *Journal of Family History, History of the Family: An International Quarterly* and the *Urban History Review.*

Julia Moses is senior lecturer in modern history at the University of Sheffield and Marie Curie Fellow at the Institute of Sociology at the University of Göttingen. Her research focuses on social problems and policy in Western Europe in the late nineteenth and early twentieth centuries, with a particular focus on the welfare state and ideas about risk; private law on the family and torts; and, the global diffusion of legal and social norms. She has co-edited (with Michael Lobban) *The Impact of Ideas on Legal Development* (Cambridge: Cambridge University Press 2012) and special issues of *The Journal of Global History* (with Martin Daunton) and *Social Science History* (with Eve Rosenhaft). Her books *The First Modern Risk: Workplace Accidents and the Origins of European Social States* (Cambridge/New York: Cambridge University Press, 2018) and *Civilizing Marriage: Family, Nation and State in the German Empire* are forthcoming.

Rebecca Probert is professor of law at the University of Exeter, where she teaches family law and legal history. She has published a number of books on the history of marriage and cohabitation, including *Marriage Law and Practice in the Long Eighteenth Century: A Reassessment* (CUP, 2009) and *The Changing Legal Regulation of Cohabitation: From Fornicators to Family, 1600-2010* (CUP, 2012). She has also written widely on all aspects of modern family law.

Lisa Tran is professor of history at California State University, Fullerton, in the United States. Her research focuses on women and the law in twentieth-century China. She has published numerous articles and a book, *Concubines in Court: Marriage and Monogamy in Twentieth-Century China* (Lanham, MD: Rowman & Littlefield, 2015).

Helen Watanabe-O'Kelly is professor of German literature at the University of Oxford. Among her books are *Triumphal Shews. Tournaments at German-Speaking Courts in their European Context 1560-1730* (1992) and *Court Culture in Dresden from Renaissance to Baroque* (2002). She has edited *The Cambridge History of German Literature* (1997), *Spectaculum Europaeum. Theatre and Spectacle in Europe, (1580-1750)* with Pierre Béhar (1999) and *Europa Triumphans. Court and Civic Festivals in Early Modern Europe* with J. R. Mulryne and Margaret Shewring (2004). Her most recent books are *Beauty or Beast? The Woman Warrior in the German Imagination from the Renaissance to the Present* (2010) and *Queens Consort, Cultural Transfer and European Politics 1550-1750* with Adam Morton (2016). She is a fellow of the British Academy and leader of the HERA-funded project: "Marrying Cultures. Queens Consort and European Identities 1500-1800".

Julia Woesthoff is associate professor of history at DePaul University, where she specializes in modern Germany. Her current research investigates questions of ethnicity, migration and gender after 1945. The chapter in this book is part of a broader project on intermarriage in Germany, portions of which have appeared in *Contemporary European History* and the *Journal of Family History*. She has also published on the sham marriage discourse in Austria in *Contemporary Austrian Studies*.

Acknowledgements

This book builds on the findings of an international network of researchers who met at the 2013 conference *Ties that Bind: Marriage, Cultural Norms and the Law, c. 1750 to the Present* that was held at the University of Sheffield and at a series of conferences, including those held by the Social History Society (2013), the Social Science History Association (2013), the German History Society (2015), the German Studies Association (2016) and the European Network in Universal and Global History (2017). The contributors are grateful to participants at these events for feedback on early drafts of the papers. The initial conference was generously funded by the University of Sheffield and the Arts and Humanities Research Council UK (Grant J00751X/1), and the volume benefited from the editor's stay at the Free University Berlin with a German Academic Exchange fellowship. Thanks to Oliver Janz for acting as host at the FU and to Nancy Cott for her excellent keynote lecture at the conference and support of this initiative, and thanks to the anonymous reviewers at Bloomsbury for their careful and detailed comments on the manuscript.

Introduction: Making Marriage 'Modern'*

Julia Moses

This collection calls for a global perspective on the modern history of marriage. Widespread recent debate has focused on the changing nature of families, characterized by both the rise of unmarried cohabitation and the legalization of same-sex marriage. Some have pointed to the increasing fragility of marriage, which seems to have become both more optional, as individuals prioritize self-fulfilment or love instead, and decoupled from both procreation and familial expectations.[1] Others have pointed to the growing variety of new marital arrangements, with transnational couples living in different countries, and international migration and the internet facilitating courtship and marriage across the world.[2] And, some have gone as far as arguing that marriage no longer makes sense as an analytical category.[3] Despite extensive discussion, historical understanding of these developments remains limited. How has marriage come to be the target of national legislation? Are recent policies on same-sex marriage part of a broader transformation? And, has marriage come to be similar across the globe despite claims about national, cultural and religious difference? The contributions to this book suggest that the period since the eighteenth century saw common debates about 'policing the family',[4] with marriage as its linchpin, through the state. It also witnessed the creation of global marital norms that, to a certain extent, became enshrined in international law. This transformation reflected ideas about making marriage a 'modern' social institution that denoted civil status. The move to modernize marriage had contradictory effects, enabling love to thrive in various forms, yet discouraging or outright banning certain types of relationships. Not least, despite globalization – through improved communications technologies, travel and trade, the rise and fall of vast new empires, and new international organizations – marriage continued to exist in a variety of configurations and remained imbued with diverse meanings.

With its focus on modernity, this book suggests that there have been a number of broad transformations since the eighteenth century that have marked out this era as different from those preceding it, and these transformations mattered for the composition and understandings of marriage around the world. However, to contemporaries, whether in the eighteenth century or in the present, 'modernity' also frequently served as an organizing concept for social life, including understandings of the family.[5] To some, 'modernity' meant the quality of being 'civilized', and was denoted by monogamous marriage based on love involving an adult man and woman. And, civil marriage, conducted by the state rather than through religious authorities, and available as a civil right to all rather than as a privilege for those of the same confession, seemed to go hand in hand with the quality of civility.[6] In this respect, it seemed that there was a 'singular' way of being modern, and it was European and referred to a particular point in time, with 'progress' towards the future as its hallmark. To others, however, perhaps due to its peculiarly European and colonial associations, 'modernity' was something to be avoided, and it was frequently seen as an imposition on local or private traditions, even if those traditions were, to a certain extent, invented.[7] And for still others, 'modernity' meant casting off the legal regulation of marriage, making it a private matter separate from the rule of law under political authorities. Removed from the aegis of the state, marriage could again return to an emphasis on love or to a grounding in religious tenets.[8] In the context of marriage, 'modernity' became a powerful – and internationally portable – argument for and against different laws and practices, encouraging some to diffuse (usually in piecemeal form) across regional and national borders and others to fade out as bygone relics or to find a new following in the name of 'tradition'.[9]

By focusing on the intersection of marriage, law and modernity, the chapters in this book highlight a twin paradox. As Nancy Cott argues in her postscript to this book, 'marriage is both essentially private and essentially public. It signifies both a private, intimate relationship and a public status, validated by public witness and civil law. Marriage requires free will – consent given freely – but amounts to a fixed obligation'.[10] In this sense, the history of marriage forces us to question the separation between the state, civil society and the family described by G. W. F. Hegel in 1820 and taken up by various theorists since.[11] Instead, as the contributions to this book show, individuals, communities, religious authorities and public officials worked together, and against each other, to define, recognize and regulate marriage.

This tension between public and private has worked in tandem with another paradox in the modern history of marriage. The period examined in this book saw new global connections forged through war, empire, trade and international organizations, leading to the mass migration of people, ideas and social practices.[12] It also witnessed the redrawing of local and regional maps, as new nation-states took form and laid claim to marriage in the name of the 'nation',[13] and industrialization brought vast swathes of the new working classes from the countryside to the city and consumers to growing marketplaces, resulting in the breakdown of extended family networks in rural communities and the role of the family as a producer through cottage industries and farming.[14] Moreover, a boom in global communication facilitated by rising literacy rates, the invention of the telegraph and the spread of affordable books and periodicals as well as the internet fostered the flow of new ideas about love, marriage and family life.[15] Not least, this period saw the growth of a new culture of claiming social, political and civic rights that fundamentally questioned the meaning and nature of marriage, including the growth and spread of feminism; lesbian, gay, bisexual, transgender and queer movements; and, cases put forward by ethnic and religious minorities.[16] Against this backdrop, some have argued that societies around the globe became more similar in the face of modernity, and marriages around the world have come to resemble each other. They are monogamous and companionate: based on love, with the conjugal couple as the focus of the family.[17] Nonetheless, marriage law and practices have varied, and continue to vary, in the face of these global connections.[18]

This book brings together scholars from across the world in order to address these issues. It unites legal, political and social history, and seeks to draw out commonalities and differences by exploring connections through empire, international organizations and international migration as well as through common experiences in legislating on and reforming marriage law. In this way, contributors trace the law as a means to create common norms about marriage, as well as to underline differences in marital forms and practices. With this perspective, the collection contributes to a new and growing field of study focused on the global history of marriage.[19] It also builds upon a rich historical tradition of writing on the social history of the family.[20] Moreover, it complements numerous recent works that have sought to understand the complex landscape of modern families by examining the conceptions and practices of love,[21] kinship,[22] singleness,[23] cohabitation,[24] and gender and sexuality.[25] Not least, it builds upon studies that have focused in particular on the historical role of law and legal reform in marriage and divorce.[26] Of course, this book does not aim to, and cannot attempt to, address all aspects of marriage law across the globe since the eighteenth century. Instead, it uses a careful selection of case studies from the Americas, the Middle East, Europe, East Asia and Southeast Asia and offers insights into three key areas in order to understand how marriage has been the object of legal regulation and reform in efforts to make it, in the eyes of contemporaries, 'modern'. These key areas include the changing rules and expectations about who can marry and what constitutes a 'marriage'; the role of religion in governing marriage and its dissolution; and the relationship between marriage and broader kinship networks and communities. The collection has been structured around these topics, which form three distinct, but naturally related, parts that build on the two overarching themes of law and modernity.

Marriage, Law and the State

Marriage has, of course, been the subject of written legal rules for millennia. Guidelines on the family could be found in the ancient Babylonian Code of Hammurabi and, later, in ancient Roman law as well as various forms of religious law, such as Muslim guidelines on spousal roles outlined in the Qu'ran and Christian canon law rules on marriage rituals that were outlined in 1215 and updated in the wake of the Protestant Reformation in the sixteenth century.[27] And, unwritten rules on marriage have abounded for just as long, governing family formation around the world in the past and into the present, evidenced for example by African customary marriage and the practice of non-marriage among the matriarchal Mosuo community in southwest China.[28] As Mélanie Méthot shows in Chapter 9 of this book, for example, tacit consent to bigamy was widespread in Canada in the late nineteenth and early twentieth centuries, despite its status as a criminal offence, because local communities frequently accepted the decisions of bigamous couples to marry.

From the eighteenth century onwards, however, in various places around the world, marriage increasingly came into the fold of the state as part of a broader movement to create modern polities bound by constitutions and the rule of law and removed from the seemingly arbitrary rule of local notables and religious authorities. For example, in 1792, in the wake of revolution, France declared that marriage needed to be made civil and performed by the state, not the church, in order to be legal. Two years later, in 1794, the Prussian Civil Code outlined rules for marriage, defining it an institution for the purpose of mutual protection and procreation. The impetus behind many of these legislative reforms on marriage was making it more accessible to various population groups, regardless of social class or confession. By making marriage an institution of the seemingly neutral, secular state, it could be turned into a kind of civil right. For example, in 1836, Britain introduced a law that made civil marriage available for Catholics, Hindus, Muslims and other religious minorities, including atheists. The policy meant that members of these confessions could marry in a way recognized by the state without having to undergo an Anglican ceremony, which had previously been the only route to legal marriage in England and Wales.[29] Similarly, Mexico (1860), Chile (1884), Uruguay (1885) and Argentina (1888) adopted laws on civil marriage both to render authority from the Catholic Church and to give non-Catholics easier access to marriage. In Chile, Uruguay and Argentina, the shifting of authority over marriage to the state was also seen as a means to grant women greater rights within marriage. However, these laws were not grounded only in concerns about civil rights. For example, the English reform built on an earlier policy from 1753 that had banned the practice of 'clandestine marriage'. To be legal, marriage in England and Wales – but not in Scotland, which had its own legal system – had to be brought into the open and conducted in a way recognized by the state. Similarly, in Brazil, civil marriage was introduced in 1891, shortly after the deposition of the monarchy, as a signal of both the liberties guaranteed by the new republic and its authority.[30]

Behind these legal initiatives was, to a certain extent, the idea that the family – and, by extension, marriage – mattered to the state. In the eighteenth century, a number of early economists and demographers began counting populations and advocating how to manage population growth. Various proposals for reforms emerged from this thinking. While the British clergyman Thomas Malthus saw that starvation might help to stave off a social crisis due to the vast population growth in the wake of industrialization, the Prussian King Frederick II sought to encourage reproduction in order to foster both a strong military and a healthy economy that could export its goods to the world.[31] Despite different opinions about how to manage populations, many in the late eighteenth and early nineteenth centuries agreed that regulating marriage was central. However, they saw that marriage mattered to the state not only because of its implications for economic growth and military might but also because it was intimately linked to political and social power.[32] It could create alliances and vast networks of wealth; determining who could marry whom, therefore, could define political maps and the distribution of property. This was especially the case, of course, for dynastic elites, as Helen Watanabe-O'Kelly shows in Chapter 4 of this book, which throws light on marriage practices among European monarchies.

It was perhaps, in part, for this reason that the Protestant reformer Martin Luther had argued two centuries earlier that marriage was a task for the state and a part of everyday life, and not something that should be subject to divine rules alone. From this perspective, marriage could be viewed as effectively a contract rather than a sacrament, which had been the predominant Christian view prior to the Reformation.[33] However, the political implications of marriage transcended the creation and maintenance of powerful dynasties and wealth. Marriage was, in the eyes of many, part of a broader metaphor about the family and the state that was epitomized by the language of fraternity in the American and French revolutions and the creation of new republics.[34] And, for some, marriage was a relationship analogous to that which bound citizens and the state, with the family seen as a kind of commonwealth or republic in miniature. By implication, divorce was discouraged.[35] For others, the family was the means through which social solidarism could be secured, and this fostered movements to legislate on it as well as to analyse it through various social sciences.[36] By the nineteenth century, the family, with marriage as its axis, became so central to the state, argued historian Jacques Donzelot for France, that it would need to be 'policed' through new legislation and a host of social services and social workers.[37] The policing of families, and marriage in particular, continued into the twentieth century, as Julia Woesthoff shows in Chapter 10 on West Germany, as local charities and churches worked together with political authorities to advise German women against marrying non-German, and especially Muslim, men.

The history of marriage in modernity has been bound up with the history of the state. As part of a broader practice that Lynne Haney and Lisa Pollard have called 'familialism', marriage policy has been the outcome of 'power relations [that] are imagined, secured and reformed through techniques of rule based on the family'.[38] And, marriage law has defined socially accepted norms on specific gender roles, sexual practices and behaviour according to one's social status. As Margot Canaday has shown, therefore, social and employment policies in the United States intersected with marriage in order to establish that heterosexuality provided the basis for the family in the twentieth century.[39] Yet, views on sexuality frequently operated in conjunction with other values that guided marriage policy. In Chapter 1 on the long history of marriage in Brazil, for example, Sueann Caulfield reveals that heterosexual norms mitigated against the movement for same-sex marriage. However, due to Brazil's heritage of colonialism and slavery, there was a degree of acceptance of various kinds of familial formations that sat outside the 'traditional' nuclear family based on husband and wife.

In interwar Europe, by contrast, not only was heterosexuality regarded as the basis for marriage, reproduction was its primary goal. Following the loss of a generation of young men at war, alongside declining birth rates, pro-natalist movements targeted single people to marry and procreate and elevated men as husbands and fathers. Fascist Italy implemented a 'bachelor tax' in 1927, while France, Germany and the Soviet Union offered couples financial incentives to have large families.[40] The Soviet Union had been founded on the basis of creating new forms of equality through communism, yet the promise to revolutionize gender roles and the family, which had been articulated already by nineteenth-century and early-twentieth-century socialists like Friedrich Engels and Lenin, fell flat by the late 1920s.[41] In the Soviet Union, as in a number of other countries, the family became a protected category in the interwar period, and its special status was enshrined in new constitutions from the Republic of Ireland to the Weimar Republic and, later, Egypt. As the Spanish Constitution of 1931 put it, 'The family is under the special care of the State.'[42]

In the eyes of many at the time, the family should not only be legally protected, but it should also be cultivated in particular ways. Various federal state and national policies used marriage law as a means to keep ethnic groups separate and to ban certain populations from procreating. National Socialist Germany, with its ideal of a 'racial state', is often seen as the hallmark of eugenic marriage policies, having banned marriage involving the 'genetically ill', including epileptics, alcoholics, the mentally disabled and others, in 1935. The same year, marriage between non-Jews and 'full Jews' was also outlawed.[43] However, Denmark had placed restrictions on access to marriage for the mentally ill in 1923, and several US states, from California to Maine, had banned interracial marriage in the nineteenth century. By 1860, 23 of the 33 US states banned ethnically mixed marriages. These policies continued into the twentieth century as fears about interracial relationships between African Americans and whites were joined by new concerns about the influx of Chinese immigrants.[44] These kinds of marriage prohibitions were not unique to the United States and mainland Germany. In 1905 and 1906, interracial marriage was banned in the German colonies of East Africa (later broken into Burundi, Rwanda and Tanzania) and Southwest Africa (Namibia), while interracial relationships were increasingly frowned upon in the British Empire from the mid-nineteenth century, as British women began to settle and establish households in the colonies.[45] By contrast, however, interracial marriage in imperial Japan was not officially banned; it was condoned as a means to spread Japanese genes abroad and, in the case of Koreans living in mainland Japan, culture at home.[46] In any case, marriage prohibitions were by no means a potential burden for interracial couples alone. In Prussia, for example, marriage involving elite men and women from lower classes had required special dispensations under Christian canon law and, later, by the state.[47] And, one of the most widespread state prohibitions on marriage targeted another kind of 'mixed marriage' – that between different denominations of the same religion. Until civil marriage laws enabled couples from different confessions to marry, interdenominational couples were often forced to end their relationships, cohabit or have one of the partners convert. For some, as Ulrike Harmat shows in Chapter 5 on Austria–Hungary, the only alternative was to move home and take up the citizenship of a country with less restrictive marriage laws.

In contrast to received wisdom, therefore, many of the legal norms associated with modern marriage reflect broader religious tenets and confessional practices. Across the globe, through laws on civil marriage, divorce, inheritance and the family, marriage increasingly came within the remit of the state's activities from the eighteenth century. Nonetheless, marriage was not secularized nor did it shift clearly from the private domain of belief and communal practices to the shared realm of public and political life. In countries with civil marriage laws, for example, religious marriage remains an option after a civil ceremony has taken place. Moreover, many national legislative reforms on the family either tacitly or explicitly enshrined beliefs or practices related to or ascribed to religion. For instance, in 1804, France enacted a civil code that retained civil marriage but reformed some of the more radical ideas of the French Revolution in order to return to what was seen as more traditional family practices. As a consequence, divorce was banned, and, by law, marriage in France came to be defined in patriarchal terms based on the rule of men as husbands, fathers and sons.[48] From this perspective, which was widespread across Europe during the nineteenth century, the husband was not only seen as the head of the family. He also became legally responsible for his family, and especially for the protection of his wife, who lost her independent legal status upon marriage in a practice known as coverture.[49] Similarly, as Kenneth M. Cuno shows in Chapter 6 of this book and elsewhere, Egypt in the nineteenth century targeted marriage and family law as part of its reform of the legal system. Marriage was brought into the auspices of state law in new ways that seemed, on the surface, to be a return to traditional Muslim jurisprudence that emphasized patriarchal authority as a means to protect the family.[50]

Moreover, in several empires, the problem of accommodating different ethnic and religious groups led to allowing each group to undertake its own practices in family law, including marriage, in a form of legal pluralism. This was the approach in the Ottoman Empire as well as in imperial Britain, France, Germany and the Netherlands.[51] And, in many countries in the late twentieth and twenty-first centuries, including South Africa, the UK and Canada, couples have been able to choose to undertake religious divorces either instead of or in tandem with civil divorce procedures through recourse to Sharia councils and Jewish tribunals. Moreover, customary marital practices, including polygamy, are allowed in South Africa as well as Kenya. Elsewhere, such as Israel, India and Egypt, marriage law is governed by religious courts or rules as a matter of course, with each confession following its own precepts, which are sanctioned by state law.[52]

Therefore, despite various attempts to bring marriage within the immediate fold of the state, marriage law has retained direct or indirect links with religion. As Nancy Cott discusses in her postscript to this book, marriage in the United States has been far from a private experience alone, and the underlying assumptions behind many marriage policies often echo the views of the majority, including religious beliefs. As a consequence, for example, much of the antipathy towards the movement for same-sex marriage around the world has stemmed from religious doctrine about the basis of marriage in the union of a man and a woman (or women) for the purposes of procreation. On similar grounds, the Mormon practice of polygamy in the United States became the subject of intense criticism and was outlawed through a Supreme Court ruling in 1878. To many observers at the time, Mormon polygamy not only went against the theological views of the majority, it was also 'uncivilized'; it had no place in modern, American society.[53]

Civility, Modernity and the Family

Undergirding discourses about 'modernity' related to marriage has been an awareness of cultural difference: through trade, mass migration and growing empires in the eighteenth and nineteenth centuries, individuals encountered new cultures that seemed vastly divergent from their own. To make sense of difference, some marital customs were cast as uncivilized or barbaric. For example, in 1748, the French philosopher Montesquieu declared that 'in despotic states princes have always abused marriage. They usually take several wives, especially in that part of the world, Asia, where despotism is, so to speak, naturalized. They have so many children that they can scarcely have any affection for them nor can the children have any for their brothers'. Not least, he noted, 'Women are marriageable in hot climes at eight, nine and ten years of age. ... They are old at twenty,' leading their husbands to find attractive new wives.[54] As Ann Laura Stoler and others have shown, this emphasis not only on difference but also on inferiority in family practices and forms of sexuality later served as both a justification for and a tool of empire building.[55] In various ways, this trope of contrasting marital practices continued from the nineteenth into the twentieth century, as colonial officials as well as feminist movements and international organizations increasingly called for new 'civilized' norms related to marriage, including bans on polygamy, child marriage and widow burning (*sati*), as well as demands for legal and property rights for wives.[56] In response to these movements, some anti-colonial reformers pushed to preserve 'local traditions' such as child marriage in Bengal and female genital mutilation in Kenya in the face of marital and familial customs that seemed to have been imposed by colonial and Western elites.[57]

As Lata Mani has argued with regard to *sati*, it is important to recognize the 'modernity of ... discourse on tradition'.[58] And, many of the 'local practices' and 'traditions' recorded by colonial governments, missionaries and travellers were exaggerated or, to a certain extent, invented by European observers as part of a broader process of codifying religions, languages and peoples abroad.[59] For example, critiques about polygyny under Islam in the Ottoman Empire and colonial Egypt neglected the reality that the practice was relatively infrequent and in any case on the decline, especially in cities and among the upper classes.[60] Similarly, arguments about the prevalence of child marriage and widow burning in India ignored the fact that the practices were primarily the preserve of the Hindu elite, as well as those who wished to emulate their customs. Moreover, the main British analysis of Hindu family law stemmed from the early nineteenth century, rendering it, in part, irrelevant for later decisions by colonial authorities. Nonetheless, when ruling in favour of child marriage in India, British jurists argued that they were upholding Hindu traditions.[61] Rather than instituting a single system of family law, therefore, colonial regimes often encouraged local practices to continue, creating legal regimes in which 'personal status law' derived from one's religion or ethnic group determined how marital matters and related aspects of family life, including inheritance and adoption, were adjudicated and carried out.[62] For European settlers, by contrast, marriage matters continued to be determined by European laws even in colonial outposts. Where it proved difficult to conduct marriages according to European legislation, imperial authorities, following international law, allowed couples to marry legally following local practices – as long as they accorded with European morality. As a consequence, as Rebecca Probert shows in Chapter 8 on the British Empire, 'common law' marriage was practised and accepted for colonial settlers as a convenient means to uphold a semblance of British family life when local marriage laws and customs proved unappealing.

In part, this movement to uphold local traditions stemmed from anthropological and sociological research in the nineteenth century which suggested that societies developed over time, from primitivism to civility, and that the family was the key to this transformation. For example, from different perspectives, both the Swiss anthropologist Johann Jakob Bachofen and the British lawyer Henry Sumner Maine wrote about the rise of patriarchy as the basis for contemporary marriage, and the American anthropologist Lewis Henry Morgan evaluated the evolution of five different kinds of families over time, concluding that the 'monogamian', or monogamous, family was the current, but by no means final, form.[63] By the 1890s, sociologists like Emile Durkheim followed Morgan in emphasizing monogamy and, in particular, companionate, affectionate and consensual relationships as the hallmark of modern marriage. With this emphasis, Durkheim to a certain extent echoed a widespread view that modern marriage was characterized by the conjugal couple, headed by the male patriarch, rather than a broader group of kin. By contrast, as Morgan, Maine and others argued, marriage based on kinship relations, for example, by prioritizing the keeping of property within the family or the forging of an alliance between families, was typical of premodern societies. Not least, these familial expectations for sons and daughters to marry into a specific group or within their own extended family seemed, to many nineteenth-century Europeans, but certainly not all, 'incestuous'.[64]

In order to cast off the shackles of tradition, whether real or ascribed, colonial reformers and new post-imperial republics often sought to reform marriage as part of a broader nationalist project. As Leigh Denault shows in Chapter 7, the 'Hindu traditions' identified by colonial officials and feminist critics were not uniformly accepted by Indians, let alone Indian legal reformers, who sought to reform family law in order to transform India. And, in the movement towards national independence as well as in the wake of decolonization, India instituted the Child Marriage Restraint Act in 1929, followed by a new Hindu Marriage Act in 1955 that banned polygamy.[65] Similarly, republican China targeted concubinage and promoted women's equal rights within marriage in its civil code of 1929/30, as Lisa Tran shows in Chapter 2. And, as Tamara Loos shows in Chapter 3, Siam (later, Thailand) clamped down on polygyny in 1935, in part, as a means to stave off critiques from infringing European governments. By the same token, in the new Republic of Turkey, the Swiss civil code was appropriated in 1926 in an attempt to create what was perceived as a modern, secular form of the nation-state by restructuring family relations in emulation of European norms. An important consequence of the new code was the ban on polygyny in Turkey.[66] While the new code addressed concerns about women's equal rights within marriage, it ultimately aimed to replace an older form of patriarchy from the Ottoman era with a 'new patriarchy' that drew on European values.[67]

The new language of human rights of the mid-twentieth century helped to legitimate some of these reform movements but also fostered paradoxical results. Following the global breakdown of empires, nation-states and economies after the First World War, the protection of minority rights and the guarantee of some form of citizenship, alongside the protection of the family, became the focus of international legal debates. For example, the 1930 Conference for the Codification of International Law considered whether women should be allowed the right to retain their own citizenship after marrying a person with another nationality. To feminists, changing citizenship law in this way would be another victory in the long-standing battle against coverture. However, the conference ultimately decided that each family should have the same, single citizenship, meaning that a woman's legal status was subsumed under her husband's unless a country's own laws dictated otherwise. Of course, married women found other ways in which to articulate and negotiate their citizenship, for example, by taking to the streets or writing petitions in protest.[68] Nonetheless, in many countries, women married to foreign nationals were only allowed to retain their original citizenship after various legislative reforms were implemented, as was the case in the United States in 1934 and in the Netherlands in 1964.[69]

These tensions within human rights discussions continued after the Second World War and held important implications for the legal treatment of marriage around the world. Partly in response to National Socialist restrictions on marriage, the 1948 United Nations Universal Declaration of Human Rights (UDHR) marked out the family as an institution in merit of special protection by the state, with the majority of signatories in favour of the right 'to marry and to found a family'. However, the UDHR also emphasized the importance of equality between the sexes, including the equal right to initiate a divorce and to consent to marriage, also across confessional lines. While protection of the family received widespread approval, the extent of the freedoms to found and dissolve a marriage proved unacceptable to some participants in the convention such as Saudi Arabia.[70]

Thirty years later, at a UN conference in Mexico City in 1975, the international 'Decade of Women' inaugurated events around the world advocating the education of women and, especially, their inclusion in the workforce as a means to foster economic development. One outcome of these endeavours was the 1979 Convention on Elimination of All Forms of Discrimination against Women (CEDAW), which was rapidly ratified across the world. In part, ratification was a conscious decision to symbolize that one's country was 'modern' in its understanding of women's roles in society.[71] However, despite the sweeping language of the convention, states were given permission to ratify it with reservations 'on the ground that national law, tradition, religion or culture are not congruent with Convention principles'. Ultimately, countries including Saudi Arabia and Pakistan ratified CEDAW with reservations, while the United States and the Islamic Republic of Iran have yet to sign the convention, even if they have addressed concerns about women's rights within and beyond marriage in other ways.[72] Moreover, these international efforts to address women's rights within marriage also led to debates about the erosion of 'traditional' norms and practices. For some critics, especially when debating family law in Muslim countries, it appeared impossible to reconcile the competing pulls of liberalism enshrined within these international endeavours: it seemed that one could either protect women's rights within marriage or protect the rights of religious and other minority communities to carry out their marital practices irrespective of norms on gender equity. As a consequence, it proved increasingly difficult to determine which marriage laws counted as valid when married couples travelled across international borders, testing the marital norms in their new country of residence.[73] Moreover, individuals often ignored new national policies adopted in response to changing international norms and debates, as Rachel Jean-Baptiste shows in Chapter 11 on colonial and independent Gabon.[74] When the customary practice of giving bridewealth (a payment to the bride or her family) upon marriage was outlawed, not only was there public outcry, individuals also simply carried on with the tradition in order to honour the expectations of their families and communities.

Family, Religion and Community

In the three parts of this book, contributors emphasize the contingent and contested nature of regulating marriage and the family – in part, due to reformers' own sense of needing to 'modernize' or to preserve 'traditions'. By employing a global perspective, the chapters reveal how marriage has been developed, nuanced and challenged in various ways since the eighteenth century, through individual choices, imperialism and new forms of nationalist ideologies, alongside reforms to religions and legal systems as well as international rights movements and transformations in international law. In this sense, the global history of marriage points to what Frederick Cooper has called the 'lumpiness of cross-border connections', in which 'structures and networks penetrate certain places and do certain things with great intensity, but their effects tail off elsewhere'.[75] Accordingly, as Judith Stacey has argued in her ethnographic research on marriage, various modernization theories about the family, which have been intimately connected to ideas about globalization, fail to account for the diversity of family arrangements in the past and into the present.[76] This book sheds light on these tensions by focusing on three areas in which they emerge especially clearly.

Part 1, on marriage and forms of the family, explores who was seen in particular contexts as capable of marrying or forming part of a marriage. In Chapter 1, on the transformation of marriage and family rights in Brazil, Sueann Caulfield reveals how the legalization of same-sex marriage in 2011 drew on long-standing discussions about the composition of the family dating to the early nineteenth century. The Brazilian Supreme Court ruled unanimously in favour of 'homoaffective unions' as legal families, which resulted in rights to marry and adopt children. In part, as Caulfield shows, the ruling stemmed from a twenty-year process of democratization following the collapse of dictatorship in 1985 and the introduction of a new constitution in 1988 that declared 'human dignity' a guiding principle. In this context, Lesbian, Gay, Bisexual and Transgender (LGBT) and feminist movements worked together, successfully drawing on both international human rights discourse and international law in pushing for the legalization of same-sex marriage. However, the ruling also reflected how legal principles grounded in liberalism gradually replaced Catholic precepts on family law over the nineteenth century, in the wake of independence from Portugal in 1822, and how those nineteenth-century reforms came to be challenged in the twentieth century, as single mothers made new demands for family rights.

The movement in Brazil to expand the legal scope of marriage contrasted sharply with developments in China and Siam at the turn of the twentieth century. As Lisa Tran shows in Chapter 2, concubinage had been regarded as a 'semi-marital' union under the Qing dynasty (1644–1911). In late imperial China, concubinage was justified as a form of filial piety following Confucian principles, according to which 'continuing the family line [was] the principal duty of every man'.[77] However, by the early twentieth century, the practice increasingly came into question in the wake of the New Culture movement (1915–25) and a growing women's movement that embraced Western ideas on the family, often introduced by way of Japan. As a consequence, the 1929 civil code enacted by the republican Guomindang government shifted the focus of family law from the patrilineal family to the conjugal family, with the monogamous couple as its centre. In this context, concubinage came to be seen as a form of adultery that could be prosecuted under the criminal code. By 1950, under a new Marriage Law enacted by the Chinese Communist Party, concubinage came under renewed attack, now as a form of de facto marriage that could be prosecuted for bigamy. As Tran argues, these changes in legal interpretations of concubinage not only reflected transforming views about monogamy as the basis of marriage in early-twentieth-century China, but they also held crucial implications for the legal status of the concubine in relation to her master and his family.

In Siam, like in China, legal forms of marriage narrowed in the early twentieth century partly as an outgrowth of interactions with and ideas from the West. Prior to new codification efforts in the twentieth century, Siam's main legal source was the Laws of the Three Seals, which were based on religious and legal texts from the Theravada tradition of Buddhism. They did not establish a system of family law, but rather understood family as a 'man's entire entourage of people', and condoned polygyny as the foundation of the monarchical system. Accordingly, as Tamara Loos shows, polygyny was primarily an elite practice in Siam that enabled ruling families to create interregional political alliances, garner authority and emphasize virility. However, 'Siam's ruling elites, in full awareness of the strategic nature of imperial discourse … defended polygyny as a source of their kingdom's cultural authenticity'. Siam retained its independence from colonialism, but it came under pressure from imperial powers who opposed the practice and its associated 'harems' as 'uncivilized'. As a consequence, extraterritoriality clauses were imposed on Siam that exempted foreigners from its laws from 1855 until 1935, when the section on marriage in the new civil code cited monogamy as the legal norm. However, polygyny was not banned. Paradoxically, as Loos shows, when it came to be uncoupled from its historical role as a means to create political alliances, polygyny was 'democratized to include non-elite men', creating Siam's first 'mistresses' and 'illegitimate children' as a result of the new civil code's rules on monogamy as the foundation of the family.[78]

The historical use of marriage as a means to create powerful political alliances also emerges in Chapter 4 on the case of royal marriage in Europe, which has connected various regions and countries and has also ensured the stability of existing monarchies. As Helen Watanabe-O'Kelly argues, 'though royal marriage adapted to new ideas about romantic love in the nineteenth century and to modern mores relating to social class and to divorce in the last few decades, its purpose is to ensure monarchical succession and is one of the reasons for "monarchical durability".[79] To this end, rules on royal marriage have been based on the equality of descent between husband and wife and the bloodline of each spouse. As a consequence, the practice of royal marriage in Europe has been relatively constant over hundreds of years, and its continuities have transcended many of the changes to marriage law that occurred between the eighteenth and twentieth centuries in the wake of state-building efforts, religious reforms, legal codifications, imperialism and mass migration, and movements for social and civil rights.

The chapters on marriage and forms of the family are connected in a number of ways with Part 2 of the book, which emphasizes the tension between religious norms on the family and state laws. The contributions in this part engage with a web of related questions, including: How did the confessional regulation of marriage interact with secular law? Under which circumstances did religious law clash with secular law? How did processes of state building shape the treatment of marriage as a secular or faith-based institution? As Ulrike Harmat shows in Chapter 5, the battle between church and state over marriage law in Austria, the core of the expansive and ethnically diverse Habsburg Empire, lasted more than a hundred and fifty years. In the context of the Enlightenment, the absolutist monarch Joseph II issued a marriage policy in 1783 that initiated the gradual process of separating civil law from canon law, drawing a clear line between marriage as a sacrament and marriage as a contract. When conducting a wedding ceremony, clerics no longer acted as servants of the church; they effectively became civil servants. Despite this dramatic secularization of marriage in Austria, for Catholics – the majority of the empire's population – canon law continued to dictate not only how marriage was carried out but also how it was governed on a daily basis. The close alliance between the monarchy and the church stood in the way of a fundamental transformation of marriage law in imperial Austria and continued under Dualism, when the empire was formally split between Hungarian and Austrian rule (1867–1918), as well as into the First Republic, after revolution and imperial collapse in 1918. Conflict over marriage law centred on the ban on remarriage for Catholics, which had been laid down in the Civil Code of 1811 and sparked various forms of popular as well as political resistance. The ban led some Austrian Catholics to shop for a new forum in which to marry by choosing to convert to Protestantism or to take up Hungarian citizenship, as the law was less restrictive in the Hungarian part of the empire. It was only under National Socialist rule in Austria that the conflict over marriage, church and state was finally resolved.

In Egypt, as in Austria, religion and the state were intertwined in the regulation of marriage. However, as Kenneth M. Cuno argues in Chapter 6, on Egypt in the late nineteenth and early twentieth centuries, 'This construction of the conjugal family as the basis of society, its stability as a social good, and women's dependency and domesticity is an artefact of colonial modernity, although it is widely understood by Egyptians to come from their own traditions and Islam'. After 1841, when it became an autonomous province of the Ottoman Empire, Egypt introduced a civil law system based on the French model but left Muslim personal status law, including marriage matters, to be administered by Sharia courts. Separate religious courts handled Christian and Jewish personal law, also under British rule from 1882, until the judicial system was unified in 1955. Cuno shows how Egyptians reformed their marriage system and family law at the turn of the twentieth century, including the abandonment of polygyny and slave concubinage. The shift was partly a result of the model set by the ruling khedival family, which favoured monogamous marriage, but also a response to books and essays by marriage reformers who wrote favourably on companionate marriage and monogamy. Over time, marital norms began to shift among the upper and middle classes, who married later, advocated higher education – also for women – prior to marriage and started to set up households based on the conjugal family. In this sense, Cuno argues, a 'hybrid of European ideas and precolonial Muslim norms regarding marriage and marital relations' shaped the reform of family law in Egypt.[80] However, the results were paradoxical. The reorganization of the Sharia court system enhanced the role of the courts in family life, but it also denied married women rights they had enjoyed historically, in part due to the newfound emphasis on the maintenance–obedience relationship between husband and wife following presumed Muslim marital traditions. Ultimately, the codification of Muslim family law in the 1920s addressed most of these disadvantages, while also reaffirming the managerial role of the state in family life.

In colonial India, as in Egypt, the reform of marriage law was influenced simultaneously by reformers who looked to Europe in order to demand change and, in particular, bring marriage within the fold of the state, and those who sought to change marriage and family law from a position of new religious orthodoxy. Also as in Egypt, in India, marriage was governed by personal status law, meaning that Hindus, Muslims, Sikhs and religious minorities including Christians and Jains would turn to different legal fora to adjudicate their cases. In Chapter 7, Leigh Denault shows how legal reformers in colonial India grappled with this system as they attempted to address child marriage, widow remarriage, divorce and other practices that had come under scrutiny by British colonial authorities and Indian nationalist leaders alike. As Denault argues, 'Debates over marriage ultimately defined a new Hindu conservative position, with far-reaching consequences: the marginalization of lower-caste and non-Brahmin perspectives, the use of Muslim law as foil, and the establishment of the protection and policing of rituals concerning female sexuality and autonomy as critical to maintaining the integrity of Hindu law and Hindu identity'.[81]

As the example of colonial India shows, personal status law in the British Empire was characterized by religious authority over marriage. However, personal status law was not used throughout the British Empire to govern families. In fact, as Rebecca Probert discusses in Chapter 8, no unified legal system governed the whole of the empire. As a consequence, there were a variety of rules on marriage and the family throughout. Some colonies made their own rules on marriage, as was the case in Australia, while others continued to apply law established under earlier colonial rule, as in St Lucia, which had been acquired from the French. Elsewhere, as in India, personal status law based on one's confession determined how marriage and family matters were handled. In this diverse and global context, as Probert argues, British courts in the nineteenth century ruled that Britons 'took the "common law" of marriage with them' in their journeys throughout the empire, and they 'could rely on it in situations where they could not be expected to comply with the local law'. The underlying assumption behind the informal policy 'reflected broader ideas about the place of the British in the world, in particular the idea of a "Greater Britain" united by a common Christianity'.[82] As such, Britons in the empire were expected to preserve British culture, including religious practices associated with it, rather than adhere to local customs.

Behind this idea of 'Greater Britain' was, to a certain extent, an understanding of community. For those native Britons abroad, upholding British marital traditions – for example, by marrying through an Anglican missionary – meant that individuals could maintain a sense of combined national and imperial identity. The final part (Part 3) of this book continues the theme of community by reflecting on how expectations about communal connections and culture shaped marital practices in various contexts. As Mélanie Méthot shows, marriage has stood consistently as a pillar of society for colonial settlers and, later, citizens of independent Canada in the transition from frontier society to nation-state. In this context, responses to bigamy – a duplicitous second marriage that was prosecutable as a crime – were surprisingly diverse. By focusing on cases in Quebec and Nova Scotia, a predominantly Catholic former French colony and a largely Protestant British colony, Méthot reveals a range of different norms about marriage across Canada from the mid-eighteenth to the mid-twentieth century. Nonetheless, marriage laws aimed to protect primarily the wife and children. In this context, judges showed lenience towards female bigamists who remarried to escape a difficult family life or the economic hardships following abandonment by a previous husband. Even clergymen seldom denounced female bigamists when called to testify in civil courts, and bigamy was often tolerated by families and local communities when it was seen as a necessity – even though it remained a crime throughout this period.

In contrast to the experience with bigamy in Canada, in West Germany, strong communal pressure militated against certain kinds of unions: interracial marriages. As Julia Woesthoff shows in Chapter 10, from the late 1950s, the authorities and the press cited growing concerns about marriage as an institution in West Germany. It seemed that divorce rates were skyrocketing, while some were preferring simply not to marry at all. Against this backdrop, marriages involving Germany's small minority of Muslim students became the subject of national debate, involving not only religious and secular authorities but also various periodicals, including a number of magazines targeted at young women readers. As Woesthoff shows, 'particular visions of race and gender relations guided policy makers and emigration experts', 'reflect[ing] the inability to envision the central institution of marriage as a union between German women and foreign men'. Nonetheless, in light of Germany's recent history of National Socialism, 'officials in the Federal Republic astutely worked to avoid any association with Nazi-era racialized social policy'.[83] Moreover, couples often ignored guidance against intermarriage, arguing that a spouse from another country was preferable to a German mate.

As in West Germany, in colonial and postcolonial French West Africa, individuals frequently pursued their own agendas in marrying and, in the process, flouted new state regulations on marriage. However, as Rachel Jean-Baptiste shows in Chapter 11 on Gabon, those who decided to subvert official marital practices often did so with the approval of their communities. Jean-Baptiste focuses on the example of bridewealth. As she notes, 'The remittance of goods, money or varied forms of wealth or labour from the groom's kin to the bride's father or other male kin was a customary practice across sub-Saharan Africa that legitimized a heterosexual relationship as a marriage.' The practice had come under attack by Christian missionaries and colonial authorities as the effective sale of wives to their husbands. And, shortly after independence in 1960, the president of Gabon declared the year of the woman and targeted bridewealth as an antiquated custom. Not only did the practice seem to undermine women's equality; it also meant that marriages could be solemnized between families without the involvement of the state. In this sense, bridewealth seemed to point to the ongoing power of clans in postcolonial Gabon. By 1963, it was banned. However, the ban sat uneasily within the legal landscape in Gabon, which was characterized by plurality and involved the input of 'a plethora of kin, community and neighbourhood fora, religious figures, and NGOs' rather than 'just one hegemonic sector of society or the state'. In the wake of Gabon's signing of CEDAW, new rights groups began to call for the simplification of the civil code in order to make marriage and family law accord better with the practices of ordinary people. Accordingly, some critics cited 'the disconnect between the letter of the law and everyday practice [because] the Gabonese state wish[ed] to model itself on Western norms of marriage rather than the traditional values and cultures of Gabon's varied ethnicities'.[84] As a result of this disjuncture, some argued, women, in particular, were prone to suffer. Despite the gulf between official law and everyday practices, however, the ban on bridewealth has remained in place.

By taking the long view, going back to the sixteenth century with Chapter 4 and up to the twenty-first century with Chapter 11 the contributions to this book reveal a number of the continuities in marital practices: concerns about kinship and community; the various forms of familial arrangements within marriage; the role of religion; the changing emphasis on love as a basis for marriage; and, the reach of the law as well as demands for its reform. In her postscript, Nancy Cott takes up these themes as she reflects on perhaps the most significant change to marriage law across the globe in the late twentieth and early twenty-first centuries: the legalization of same-sex marriage. She considers the movement for same-sex marriage in the United States that began in the 1980s and continued until 2015, when the US Supreme Court ruled in favour of the policy. As Cott shows, the reform of marriage law in the United States has been especially shaped by the changing political landscape, which previously saw legislators across the political spectrum agree to policies to 'defend' marriage and to consider declaring it an institution 'between a man and a woman'. This final chapter in the book lays emphasis on the importance of history as a discipline for understanding why and how marriage law has changed over time, and how legal reforms can build on that past. Cott is particularly well placed to reflect on these issues. Having written extensively on the history of marriage as a public institution in the United States, she has been called upon in many state-level and federal marriage cases to contribute declarations, amicus briefs and expert reports about the history of marriage. As Cott argues here, marriage is fundamentally a public institution, guided by law, and subject to change out of impulses to modernize it or return to presumed traditions. However, marriage is not a universal practice. Despite legal reforms that have made it more accessible, in some ways, marriage has become the preserve of the few.

In this way, the postscript by Cott, like the other contributions to this book, points to the two central and connected paradoxes that have defined marriage in modernity: the tension between public vows and private relations and the strain between global connections and local, national and personal experiences of marriage. The tensions within these two paradoxes have fostered the transformation of marriage law across the world since the eighteenth century. And, yet, as the contributors show here, marriage has also been characterized by various sources of constancy over the last three hundred years, from the role of power and kinship networks in forging new families to the function of religion in governing married life. And, perhaps the greatest source of constancy has been the role of emotions, including (but certainly not only) love, in marriage, both on paper, hidden behind the sometimes wooden language of legal doctrines, and in person, between those who married, their families and associates. While marriage may have been a legal matter, it nonetheless sparked strong reactions, including the will to transform it.

Notes

* I am grateful to Kenneth M. Cuno and Bodo Nehring for their careful reading of and helpful suggestions on this chapter.
1 Andrew Cherlin, *The Marriage-Go-Round: The State of Marriage and the Family in America Today* (New York: Vintage, 2009); Stephanie Coontz, *Marriage, a History: From Obedience to Intimacy, or How Love Conquered Marriage* (New York: Viking, 2005); Ulrich Beck and Elisabeth Beck-Gernsheim, *The Normal Chaos of Love*, trans. Mark Ritter and Jane Wiebel (Cambridge: Polity, 1995); Anthony Giddens, *The Transformation of Intimacy: Sexuality, Love & Eroticism in Modern Societies* (Stanford: Stanford University Press, 1993).
2 Ulrich Beck and Elisabeth Beck-Gernsheim, *Distant Love* (Cambridge: Polity, 2014).
3 Heather Brook, *Conjugality: Marriage and Marriage-like Relationships before the Law* (Basingstoke: Palgrave Macmillan, 2007).
4 Jacques Donzelot, *The Policing of Families*, trans. Robert Hurley (New York: Pantheon Books, 1979).
5 On grappling with this duality, see Carol Gluck, 'The End of Elsewhere: Writing Modernity Now', *American Historical Review* 116, no. 3 (2011): 676–87.
6 Nandini Chatterjee, 'English Law, Brahmo Marriage, and the Problem of Religious Difference: Civil Marriage Laws in Britain and India', *Comparative Studies in Society and History* 52, no. 3 (2010): 524–52.
7 Zvi Ben-Dor Benite, 'Modernity: The Sphinx and the Historian', *American Historical Review* 116, no. 3 (2011): 638–52; Kathleen Davis, *Periodization and Sovereignty: How Ideas of Feudalism and Secularization Govern the Politics of Time* (Philadelphia: University of Pennsylvania Press, 2008); Dipesh Chakrabarty, *Provincializing Europe: Postcolonial Thought and Historical Difference* (Princeton: Princeton University Press, 2000); Bernard Yack, *The Fetishism of Modernities: Epochal Self-Consciousness in Contemporary Social and Political Thought* (Notre Dame, IN: University of Notre Dame Press, 1997); Vanessa Ogle, *The Global Transformation of Time, 1870-1950* (Cambridge, MA: Harvard University Press, 2015).
8 Tamara Metz, *Untying the Knot: Marriage, the State and the Case for their Divorce* (Princeton: Princeton University Press, 2010).
9 On these issues, see David A. Westbrook, 'Keynote Address: Theorizing the Diffusion of Law: Conceptual Difficulties, Unstable Imaginations, and the Effort to Think Gracefully Nonetheless', *Harvard Law Journal* 47, no. 2 (2006): 489–506; Takao Tanase, 'The Empty Space of the Modern in Japanese Law Discourse', in *Adapting Legal Cultures*, ed. David Nelken and Johannes Feest (Oxford: Oxford University Press, 2001), 187–98.
10 Nancy F. Cott, 'How History Mattered in Gaining Same-Sex Marriage Rights in the United States', in this book, 242. See also Nancy F. Cott, *Public Vows: A History of Marriage and the Nation* (Cambridge, MA: Harvard University Press, 2000), 1.
11 G. W. F. Hegel, *Elements of the Philosophy of Right*, ed. Allen W. Wood, trans. H. B. Nisbet (1820; Cambridge: Cambridge university Press, 1991), 624. An elaboration

on this division: Quentin Skinner (ed.), *Families and States in Western Europe* (Cambridge: Cambridge University Press, 2011); Jürgen Nautz, Paul Ginsborg and Ton Nijhuis (eds), *The Golden Chain: Family, Civil Society and the State* (New York: Berghan, 2013).

12 Akira Iriye (ed.), *Global Interdependence: The World after 1945* (Cambridge, MA: Harvard University Press, 2014); Emily S. Rosenberg (ed.), *A World Connecting, 1870-1945* (Cambridge, MA: Harvard University Pres, 2012); Jürgen Osterhammel, *The Transformation of the World: A Global History of the Nineteenth Century*, trans. Patrick Camiller (2009; Princeton: Princeton University Press, 2014).

13 Kristin Celello and Hanan Kholoussy (eds), *Domestic Tensions, National Anxieties: Global Perspectives on Marriage, Crisis and the Nation* (Oxford: Oxford University Press, 2016); Etienne Balibar, 'The Nation Form: History and Ideology', trans. Immanuel Wallerstein and Chris Turner, *Review* 13, no. 3 (1990): 329–61.

14 Peter N. Stearns, 'The Family in Modern World History', in *The Cambridge World History*, vol. VII: *Production, Destruction and Connection, 1750-Present*, Part 2: *Shared Transformations?*, ed. J. R. McNeill and Kenneth Pomeranz (Cambridge: Cambridge University Press, 2015), 58–83.

15 For example: Ann Heilmann and Margaret Beetham (eds), *New Woman Hybridities: Femininity, Feminism, and International Consumer Culture, 1880-1930* (London: Routledge, 2004); The Modern Girl Around the World Research Group (ed.), *The Modern Girl Around the World: Consumption, Modernity and Globalization* (Durham, NC: Duke University Press, 2008); Purnima Mankekar and Louisa Schein (eds), *Media, Erotics and Transnational Asia* (Durham, NC: Duke University Press, 2012).

16 For example: Mary Lyndon Shanley, *Feminism, Marriage and the Law in Victorian England* (Princeton: Princeton University Press, 1989); Kelly Kollman, *The Same-Sex Unions Revolution in Western Democracies: International Norms and Domestic Policy Change* (Manchester: Manchester University Press, 2013); Johannes A. van der Ven, *Human Rights or Religious Rules?* (Leiden: Brill, 2010), 226–62.

17 For example: William J. Goode, *World Revolution and Family Patterns* (New York: Free Press, 1963); Coontz, *Marriage, a History*. On the rise of companionate marriage, alongside love for children: Edward Shorter, *The Making of the Modern Family* (New York: Basic Books, 1975); Lawrence Stone, *The Family, Sex and Marriage in England, 1500-1800*, abridged edn (Harmondsworth: Penguin, 1979).

18 A point emphasized by Edward Westermarck in his path-breaking work that initially sought to chart a universal history of marriage patterns: *The History of Human Marriage* (London: Macmillan, 1891), 549–50. See also related observations by John Hajnal and Jack Goody in their groundbreaking demographic and anthropological research: Jack Goody, *The European Family: An Historico-Anthropological Essay* (Malden, MA: Blackwell, 2000); John Hajnal, 'European Marriage Patterns in Perspective', in *Population in History*, ed. D. V. Glass and D. E. C. Eversley (London: Edward Arnold, 1965), 101–46.

19 For example: Kristin Celello and Hanan Kholoussy (eds), *Domestic Tensions*; Christer Lundh and Satomi Kurosu (eds), *Similarity in Difference: Marriage in Europe and Asia, 1700-1900* (Cambridge, MA: MIT Press, 2014); Kenneth M. Cuno, *Modernizing Marriage: Family, Ideology and Law in Nineteenth and Early Twentieth-Century Egpyt* (Syracuse: Syracuse University Press, 2015); Emily S. Burrill, *States of Marriage: Gender, Rights and Justice in Colonial Mali* (Columbus: Ohio University Press, 2015); Rachel Jean-Baptiste, *Conjugal Rights: Marriage, Sexuality and Urban Life in Colonial*

Libreville, Gabon (Columbus: Ohio University Press, 2014); Katie Barclay, *Love, Intimacy and Power: Marriage and Patriarchy in Scotland, 1650-1850* (Manchester: Manchester University Press, 2014); Angela Wanhalla, *Matters of the Heart: A History of Interracial Marriage in New Zealand* (Auckland: Auckland University Press, 2013); Elizabeth Abbott, *A History of Marriage* (London: Duckworth Overlook, 2011); Rochona Majumdar, *Marriage and Modernity: Family Values in Colonial Bengal* (Chapel Hill: Duke University Press, 2009).

20 For example: David Kertzer and Marzio Barbagli, *The History of the European Family*, 3 vols. (New Haven: Yale University Press, 2001–3); André Burguière, et al. (eds), *A History of the Family*, 2 vols. (Cambridge, MA: Belknap, 1996).

21 For example: Alana Harris and Timothy Jones (eds), *Love and Romance in Britain, 1918-1970* (Basingstoke: Palgrave Macmillan, 2015); Claire Langhamer, *The English in Love: The Intimate Story of an Emotional Revolution* (Oxford: Oxford University Press, 2013).

22 For example: Leonore Davidoff, *Thicker than Water: Siblings and their Relations, 1780-1920* (Oxford: Oxford University Press, 2011).

23 For example: Katherine Holden, *The Shadow of Marriage: Singleness in England, 1914-60* (Manchester: Manchester University Press, 2010); Catherine Dollard, *The Surplus Woman: Unmarried in Imperial Germany, 1871-1918* (New York: Berghahn, 2009).

24 For example: Rebecca Probert, *The Changing Legal Regulation of Cohabitation: From Fornicators to Families* (Cambridge: Cambridge University Press, 2012); Elizabeth Pleck, *Not just Roommates: Cohabitation after the Sexual Revolution* (Chicago: University of Chicago Press, 2012).

25 For example: Matt Houlbrook, *Queer London: Perils and Pleasures in the Sexual Metropolis, 1918-1957* (Chicago: University of Chicago Press, 2005); Dagmar Herzog, *Sex after Fascism: Memory and Morality in Twentieth-Century Germany* (Princeton: Princeton University Press, 2005).

26 For example: Xiaoping Cong, *Marriage, Law and Gender in Revolutionary China, 1940-1960* (Cambridge: Cambridge University Press, 2016); Mark Seymour, *Debating Divorce in Italy: Marriage and the Making of Modern Italians, 1860-1974* (Basingstoke: Palgrave Macmillan, 2006); Roderick Phillips, *Putting Asunder: A History of Divorce in Western Society* (Cambridge: Cambridge University Press, 1988).

27 Mary Jo Maynes and Ann Waltner, *The Family: A World History* (Oxford: Oxford University Press, 2012), 32; Mary Ann Glendon, *The Transformation of Family Law: State, Law and Family in the United States and Western Europe* (Chicago, 1989), 17–31; Knut S. Vikør, *Between God and the Sultan: A History of Islamic Law* (Oxford: Oxford University Press, 2005), 299–25.

28 However, various laws, such as South Africa's 1998 Recognition of Customary Marriages Act, have sought to acknowledge and, in the process, to regulate these practices. See Judith Stacey, *Unhitched: Love, Marriage and Family Values from West Hollywood to Western China* (New York: New York University Press, 2011), 95–102, 152–87.

29 However, Jews and Quakers in Britain had been allowed to marry according to their own traditions prior to the enactment of the 1836 law. Glendon, *The Transformation of Family Law*, 29–34, 59; Suzanne Desan, *The Family on Trial in Revolutionary France* (Berkeley: University of California Press, 2004), 49–67.

30 John Lynch, 'The Catholic Church', in *Latin America: Economy and Society, 1870-1930*, ed. Leslie Bethell (Cambridge: Cambridge University Press, 1989), 301–70, at 338–43, 354–5; Asunción Lavrin, *Women, Feminism and Social Change in Argentina,*

Chile and Uruguay, 1890-1940 (Lincon, NE: University of Nebraska Press, 1995), 197–227.
31 Some scholars like Michel Foucault have seen this movement as part of the development of a new way of thinking linking biology and politics, or 'biopolitics'. See Michel Foucault, *The Birth of Biopolitics: Lectures at the Collège de France, 1978-1979*, ed. Michel Senellart, trans. Graham Burchell (Basingstoke: Palgrave Macmillan, 2008), 21–2. Others have expanded on this analysis by placing the family at the intersection of sex and power. See Göran Therborn, *Between Sex and Power: Family in the World, 1900-2000* (London: Routledge, 2000), 1.
32 For example, see Julia Adams, *The Familial State: Ruling Families and Merchant Capitalism in Early Modern Europe* (Ithaca: Cornell, 2005).
33 Steven Ozment, *When Fathers Ruled: Family Life in Reformation Europe* (Cambridge, MA: Harvard University Press 1983), 32; John Witte, Jr. *From Sacrament to Contract: Marriage, Religion and Law in the Western Tradition*, 2nd edn (Louisville, KY: Westminster John Knox Press, 2012), 6–14.
34 Lynn Hunt, *The Family Romance of the French Revolution* (Berkeley: University of California Press, 1992).
35 Ozment, *When Fathers Ruled*, 8; John Demos, *A Little Commonwealth: Family Life in Plymouth Colony* (Oxford: Oxford University Press, 1970); Karen Harvey, *The Little Republic: Masculinity and Domestic Authority in Eighteenth-Century Britain* (Oxford: Oxford University Press, 2012); Cott, *Public Vows*, 9–10.
36 Camille Robcis, *The Law of Kinship: Anthropology, Psychoanalysis, and the Family in France* (Ithaca: Cornell University Press, 2013), 18.
37 Donzelot, *The Policing of Families*.
38 Lynne Haney and Lisa Pollard, 'Introduction: In a Family Way: Theorizing State and Family Relations', in *Families of a New World: Gender, Politics and State Development in a Global Context*, ed. eadem (New York: Routledge, 2003), 1–14, at 5.
39 Margot Canaday, *The Straight State: Sexuality and Citizenship in Twentieth-Century America* (Princeton: Princeton University Press, 2011).
40 Patrizia Albanese, *Mothers of the Nation: Women, Families and Nationalism in Twentieth-Century Europe* (Toronto: University of Toronto Press, 2006), 38, 54–6, 74; Kristen Stromberg Childers, *Fathers, Families, and the State in France, 1914-1945* (Ithaca: Cornell, 2003), 174.
41 See, for example, Engels' *The Origins of the Family: Private Property and the State* (1884; London: Penguin, 1972). See also Paul Ginsborg, *Family Politics: Domestic Life, Devastation and Survival, 1900-1950* (New Haven: Yale University Press, 2014), 21–7.
42 Quoted in Ginsborg, *Family Politics*, 229. See also 337–9.
43 Michelle Mouton, *From Nurturing the Nation to Purifying the Volk: Weimar and Nazi Family Policy, 1918-1945* (Cambridge: Cambridge University Press, 2007), 34–68, 88.
44 Cott, *Public Vows*, 40–1. See also Peter Wallenstein, *Tell the Court I Loved my Wife: Race, Marriage and Law – An American History* (Basingstoke: Palgrave Macmillan, 2002).
45 Lora Wildenthal, *German Women for Empire, 1884-1945* (Durham, NC: Duke University Press, 2001), 86–121. On Britain, including the legacies of this project, see Barbara Bush, 'Gender and Empire: The Twentieth Century', in *Gender and Empire*, ed. Philippa Levine (Oxford: Oxford University Press, 2004), 77–111.
46 Yukiko Koshiro, 'East Asia's "Melting-Pot": Reevaluating Race Relations in Japan's Colonial Empire', in *Race and Racism in Modern East Asia: Western and Eastern Constructions*, ed. Rotem Kowner and Walter Demel (Leiden: Brill, 2013), 475–98, at 477–80.

47 Monika Wienfort, *Verliebt, Verlobt, Verheiratet: eine Geschichte der Ehe seit der Romantik* (Munich: C. H. Beck, 2014), 45–8.
48 Ute Gerhard, *Debating Women's Equality: Towards a Feminist Theory of Law from a European Perspective*, trans. Allison Brown and Belinda Cooper (New Brunswick, NJ: Rutgers University Press, 2001), 140, 158.
49 Rachel G. Fuchs and Victoria E. Thompson, *Women in Nineteenth-Century Europe* (Basingstoke: Palgrave Macmillan, 2005), 53; Shanley, *Feminism, Marriage and the Law*; Claire Goldberg Moses, *French Feminism in the Nineteenth Century* (Albany: SUNY Press, 1984), 19.
50 Kenneth M. Cuno, *Modernizing Marriage: Family, Ideology and Law in Nineteenth- and Early Twentieth-Century Egypt* (Syracuse: Syracuse University Press, 2015), chs. 4 and 5, especially at 125–41.
51 See, for example, Lauren Benton and Richard J. Ross, *Legal Pluralism and Empires, 1500-1850* (New York: New York University Press, 2013); Emmanuelle Saada, *Empire's Children: Race, Filiation and Citizenship in the French Colonies* (Chicago: University of Chicago Press, 2012), 69; George Steinmetz, *The Devil's Handwriting: Pre-coloniality and the German Colonial State in Qingdao, Samoa and Southwest Africa* (Chicago: University of Chicago Press, 2007), 63.
52 Joel A. Nichols, 'Multi-tiered Marriage: Reconsidering the Boundaries of Civil Law and Religion', in *Marriage and Divorce in Multicultural Context: Multi-tiered Marriage and the Boundaries of Civil Law and Religion*, ed. Joel A. Nichols (Cambridge: Cambridge University Press, 2012), 11–59; John Bowen, *On British Islam: Religion, Law, and Everyday Practice in Shari'a Councils* (Princeton: Princeton University Press, 2016).
53 Sarah Barringer Gordon, *The Mormon Question: Polygamy and Constitutional Conflict in Nineteenth-Century America* (Durham, NC: Duke University Press, 2002), 4–8; Cott, *Public Vows*, 73–4, 105–20.
54 Montesquieu, *The Spirit of the Laws*, ed. Anne M. Cohler, et al. (1748; Cambridge: Cambridge University Press, 1989), 63, 264.
55 Ann Laura Stoler, *Carnal Knowledge and Imperial Power: Race and the Intimate in Colonial Rule* (Berkeley: University of California Press, 2002); Julia Ann Clancy-Smith and Frances Gouda (eds), *Domesticating the Empire: Race, Gender and Family Life in French and Dutch Colonialism* (Charlottesville: University of Virginia Press, 1998); Frederick Cooper and Ann Laura Stoler, 'Between Metropole and Colony: Rethinking a Research Agenda', in *Tensions of Empire: Colonial Cultures in a Bourgeois World*, ed. Frederick Cooper and Ann Laura Stoler (Berkeley: University of California press, 1997), 1–57.
56 For example: Mrinalini Sinha, *Specters of Mother India: The Global Restructuring of an Empire* (Durham, NC: Duke University Press, 2006); Brett L. Shadle, 'Debating "Early Marriage" in Colonial Kenya, 1920-50', in *Marriage by Force? Contestation over Consent and Coercion in Africa*, ed. Annie Bunting, et al. (Athens, OH: Ohio University Press, 2016), 89–108.
57 For example: Penelope Hetherington, 'The Politics of Female Circumcision in the Central Province of Colonial Kenya, 1920-30', *Journal of Imperial and Commonwealth History* 26, no. 1 (1998): 93–126; Tanika Sarkar, 'A Prehistory of Rights: The Age of Consent Debate in Colonial Bengal', *Feminist Studies* 26, no. 3 (2000): 601–22.
58 Lata Mani, *Contentious Traditions: The Debate on Sati in Colonial India* (Berkeley: University of California Press, 1998), 77. For a related observation, see Rachel Sturman, *The Government of Social Life in Colonial India: Liberalism, Religious Law and Women's Rights* (Cambridge: Cambridge University Press, 2012), 150–1.

59 For example: Edmund Burke III, *The Ethnographic State: France and the Invention of Moroccan Islam* (Berkeley: University of California Press, 2014); Karuna Mantena, *Alibis of Empire: Henry Maine and the Ends of Liberal Imperialism* (Princeton: Princeton University Press, 2010); Nicholas B. Dirks, *Castes of Mind: Colonialism and the Making of Modern India* (Princeton: Princeton University Press, 2001); Mahmood Mamdani, *Citizen and Subject: Contemporary Africa and the Legacy of Late Colonialism* (Princeton: Princeton University Press, 1996).

60 Lisa Pollard, *The Family Politics of Modernizing, Colonizing, and Liberating Egypt, 1805-1923* (Berkeley: University of California Press, 2005), 10; Alan Duben and Cem Behar, *Istanbul Households: Marriage, Family and Fertility, 1880-1940* (Cambridge: Cambridge University Press, 1991), 149-58, 213-14.

61 Mani, *Contentious Traditions*; Flavia Agnes, 'Patriarchy, Sexuality and Property: The Impact of colonial State Policies on Gender Relations in India', in *Family, Gender & Law in a Globalizing Middle East & South Asia*, ed. Kenneth M. Cuno and Manisha Desai (Syracuse: Syracuse University Press, 2009), 19-39.

62 Colonial administrators were not, however, always in agreement on this policy. See, for example, Majumdar, *Marriage and Modernity*, 177.

63 J. J. Bachofen, *Das Mutterrecht: eine Untersuchung über die Gynaikokratie der alten Welt nach ihrer religiösen und rechtlichen Natur* (Stuttgart: Krais & Hoffmann, 1861); Sir Henry Maine, *Ancient Law: Its Connection to the History of Early Society* (1861; London: J. M. Dent and Sons, 1917), 91-4; Lewis Henry Morgan, *Ancient Society, or Researches in the Lines of Human Progress from Savagery through Barbarism to Civilization* (London: Macmillan, 1877), ch. 5. On the context and connections between these analyses, see Ann Taylor Allen, 'Feminism, Social Science, and the Meanings of Modernity: The Debate on the Origin of the Family in Europe and the United States, 1860-1914', *The American Historical Review* 104, no. 4 (1999): 1085-1113.

64 Adam Kuper, *Incest & Influence: The Private Life of Bourgeois England* (Cambridge, MA: Harvard University Press, 2009); David Warren Sabean, *Kinship in Neckarhausen, 1700-1870* (Cambridge: Cambridge University Press, 1998).

65 On the complex rationale behind reforms to Hindu family law during this period, see Narendra Subramanian, *Nation and Family: Personal Law, Cultural Pluralism, and Gendered Citizenship in India* (Stanford: Stanford University Press, 2014), 100-5 and Sinha, *Specters of Mother India*, 152-96.

66 Duben and Behar, *Istanbul Households*, 149-58.

67 Thanks to Kenneth M. Cuno for drawing my attention to this important point. On 'old' and 'new patriarchy', see Partha Chatterjee, *The Nation and Its Fragments: Colonial and Postcolonial Histories* (Princeton: Princeton University Press, 1993), 116-34. See also: Judith E. Walsh, *Domesticity in Colonial India: What Women Learned when Men Gave them Advice* (Lanham, MD: Rowman and Littlefield, 2004), 52-4. It is important to note that concerns about women's rights within marriage had already been addressed in various ways in the 1917 Ottoman family law code and in the earlier Muslim jurisprudence from which it was derived.

68 Geoff Eley, 'Some General Thoughts on Citizenship in Germany', in *Citizenship and National Identity in Twentieth-Century Germany*, ed. Geoff Eley and Jan Palmowski (Stanford: Stanford University Press, 2008), 233-49, at 242-4.

69 Nitza Berkovitch, *From Motherhood to Citizenship: Women's Rights and International Organizations* (Baltimore: Johns Hopkins University Press, 1999), 80; Candice Lewis Bredbenner, *A Nationality of Her Own: Women, Marriage and the Law of Citizenship*

(Berkeley: University of California Press, 1998); Betty de Hart, 'The Morality of Maria Toet: Gender, Citizenship and the Construction of the Nation-State', *Journal of Ethnic and Migration Studies* 32, no. 1 (2006): 49–68.
70 Johannes Morsink, *The Universal Declaration of Human Rights* (Philadelphia: University of Pennsylvania Press, 1999), 24–5, 88–9, 120–4. Although Saudi Arabia opposed aspects of the convention on the grounds of protecting Islam through the family, other predominantly Muslim countries did not object, including Syria, Iran, Turkey and Pakistan. See also Mary Ann Glendon, *A World Made New: Eleanor Roosevelt and the Universal Declaration of Human Rights* (New York: Random House, 2001), 93, 141–2, 153–4.
71 Berkovitch, *From Motherhood to Citizenship*, 107–10, 142–54.
72 Thanks to Kenneth M. Cuno and Bodo Nehring for highlighting these issues. The wording of the convention can be found here: http://www.un.org/womenwatch/daw/cedaw/reservations.htm, accessed on 20 January 2017. This stipulation to respect cultural difference can also be found in related international reforms, such as the UNESCO Universal Declaration on Cultural Diversity of 2001.
73 On these complex questions, see, for example: Ayelet Shachar, 'Faith in Law? Diffusing Tensions between Diversity and Equality', in *Marriage and Divorce in Multicultural Context*, ed. Nichols, 341–56; Pascale Fournier, *Muslim Marriage in Western Courts: Lost in Transplantation* (Farnham: Ashgate, 2010); Lisa Fishbayn Joffe and Sylvia Neil (eds), *Gender, Religion, and Family Law: Theorizing Conflicts between Women's Rights and Cultural Traditions* (Waltham, MA: Brandeis University Press, 2012); Susan Moller Okin, *Is Multiculturalism Bad for Women? Susan Moller Okin with Respondents*, Joshua Cohen, et al. (eds) (Princeton: Princeton University Press, 1999).
74 States, too, sometimes flouted implementing the international conventions related to marriage that they signed. For example: Bala Saho, 'Challenges and Constraints: Forced Marriage as a Form of "Traditional" Practice in the Gambia', in Bunting, et al. (eds), *Marriage by Force?*, 178–98.
75 Frederick Cooper, 'What Is the Concept of Globalization Good for? An African Historians' Perspective', *African Affairs* 100, no. 399 (2001): 189–213, at 190, 194. For a related observation, see Geoff Eley, 'Historicizing the Global, Politicizing Capital: Giving the Present a Name', *History Workshop Journal* 63 (2007): 154–88, at 157–8.
76 Stacey, *Unhitched*, 8–9, 189–91.
77 Lisa Tran, 'From Toleration to Prosecution: Concubinage and the Law in Modern China', in this book at 55.
78 Tamara Loos, 'The Birth of Mistresses and Bastards: A History of Marriage in Siam (Thailand)', in this book at 74, 71 and 84.
79 Helen Watanabe-O'Kelly, 'Royal Marriage in Europe: An Inherently Conservative System', in this book, 90.
80 Kenneth M. Cuno, 'Modernizing Marriage in Egypt', in this book, at 129–30.
81 Leigh Denault, '"A Babel of Law": Hindu Marriage, Global Spaces and Intimate Subjects in late-nineteenth-century India', in this book, at 161.
82 Rebecca Probert, 'English Exports: Invoking the Common Law of Marriage across the Empire', in this book, at 179.
83 Julia Woesthoff, 'Equality before the Law? The Intermarriage Debate in Post-Nazi Germany', in this book, at 217.
84 Rachel Jean-Baptiste, 'Customary and Civil Marriage Law and the Question of Gender Equality in twentieth and twenty-first-century Gabon and Africa', in this book, 222, 224 and 236–7.

Part One

Marriage and Forms of the Family

1

From Liberalism to Human Dignity: The Transformation of Marriage and Family Rights in Brazil*

Sueann Caulfield

On 5 May 2011, the Brazilian Supreme Court (Supremo Tribunal Federal, STF), in a unanimous binding decision, recognized 'homoaffective unions' (same-sex unions) as legal family entities, paving the way for conferral of same-sex partners' right to marry and adopt children. The court's recognition of same-sex couples as 'family entities' deserving of equal protection was made possible by profound social and cultural changes that took place over several decades, leading to the growing normalization of 'sexual diversity' and recognition of Lesbian, Gay, Bisexual and Transgender (LGBT) rights as human rights. These changes had resulted from various processes that coalesced in the decades of democratization that followed Brazil's 21-year dictatorship (1964–85), including local and international political activism, publicity in the Brazilian media, and national and international legal scholarship and jurisprudence. Yet the twenty-first-century transformation of marriage and family in Brazil is also part of a much deeper history of debate over legal regulation of marriage and family.

Brazilian legal scholars tend to view the history of marriage as marked by two major paradigm shifts. The first, consolidated by the 1916 Civil Code, saw the repudiation of colonial-era religious canons and patriarchal clans and their replacement by liberal principles and a 'bourgeois' family model. This transformation mirrored similar processes of liberal secularization taking place over the nineteenth century in various Western societies, as illustrated in this book by Chapter 5 on the introduction of civil marriage in nineteenth-century Austria. The second paradigm shift was marked by the 1988 Constitution, which replaced liberalism with human dignity, a concept defined by a much broader set of social and civil rights, which led to the embrace of a 'plurality' of family forms. LGBT[1] activists' successful deployment of the international human rights framework that had unified diverse social movements in the 1980s played an important role in the latter transformation. From a legal historical perspective, however, their struggle was a continuation of efforts begun half a century earlier by feminists who worked within a liberal paradigm to achieve gender equality within marriage and to extend family rights to unmarried women.

In both periods, the work of activists helped to empower women and men whose families were not recognized by positive law. Ultimately, it was these individuals' demands for rights that led the courts to expand the legal definition of family. Ironically, as these individuals presented themselves in ways that fit within the norms of the 'bourgeois' family, they eroded its patriarchal and heteronormative foundations.

Colonial Society and the Long Shadow of the 'Traditional Brazilian Family', 1500–1889

Legal discussions of marriage in modern Brazil invariably reference its evolution away from Roman and canon law traditions implanted by Portuguese colonizers. These traditions included the establishment of patriarchy as a foundational principle of political authority and social organization that entailed extreme forms of heteronormative discipline. Control of women's sexuality was considered a measure of male power, and sex acts between two men were considered among the most abominable of crimes: akin to treason, they were punishable by death at the stake and loss of social identity.[2] Historians have shown, however, that although 'the nefarious sin' was considered anathema to the family and persecuted as heresy by the Inquisition, responses by church and crown varied, and the most severe punishment seems to have been uncommon.[3] What might seem more surprising, since Portugal's efforts to colonize Brazil over the late sixteenth and early seventeenth centuries was partly fuelled by the Catholic counter-reformation, is that colonial-era social norms and legal practice supported a variety of family forms. Although the Council of Trent (1545–63) defined marriage as a sacrament and determined that its consummation must follow a ceremony performed by a priest, royal ordinances compiled in 1604 continued to 'presume marriage' when unimpeded couples[4] cohabited publicly as 'husband and wife', considering the spouses equal co-owners of family property, and their 'natural' children (illegitimate, but not adulterous, incestuous, or sacrilegious) full heirs of both parents.[5] The Church condemned the general state of 'lasciviousness' and widespread concubinage in the colony, but its attempts to disseminate Tridentine doctrine through a 1707 edict made relatively little headway.[6]

Exacerbating the inconsistency in royal and ecclesiastical rulings, neither church nor crown was able to communicate doctrine or even establish a consistent presence in the family lives of most of the colonial population. Unable to dispatch sufficient numbers of civil or religious officials to administer its claims in the New World, the Crown 'donated' vast territories to men charged with settling and governing the land and creating productive enterprises. Few Portuguese women accompanied the men who sought fortune in the colony. In a pattern that would endure over the centuries that followed, higher-status men (generally Portuguese colonists or their descendants) commonly formed lasting conjugal relationships and raised children with lower-status indigenous and, later, mixed-race and African women, enslaved or freed. Formal marriage between un-equals, however, was uncommon. Instead, missionaries petitioned the Crown to send marriageable Portuguese women to Brazil – including even prostitutes for the poorer colonists – arguing that marriage would provide a moralizing and stabilizing force.[7]

As Brazil's multi-ethnic slave society developed complex layers of social stratification over nearly 400 years (slavery was abolished only in 1888), legitimate marriage continued to be most common among the 'white' elite (which by the second generation incorporated mixed-race individuals). Few slaves had access to marriage.[8] Among the freed or free poor population, marriage was often pursued by couples who had amassed some property or who saw it as a means of formalizing fictive kinship networks through godparentage (*compadrio*).[9] Many slaves and former slaves preserved elements of marriage rituals and spousal expectations from their African cultures of origin, whether in addition to or in lieu of Catholic marriage. Studies of marital separation among African-born freed people suggest that wives expected mutual economic and emotional support within marriage, rarely depending solely on a husband's earnings.[10] Female-headed households were an accepted social norm, and, as was true in many other cultures where formal marriage was largely restricted to elites,[11] non-elite couples who cohabited, and especially those who had children, were 'presumed' married by their communities as well as the state.

For elite families, legitimate marriage was an indispensable mark of honour and a means of consolidating economic and political power. As slave-based plantation agriculture spread in the seventeenth century, rural clans, whose alliances and wealth were held together by strategically arranged marriages, came to dominate large regions of colonial territory. With royal and religious authority at a distance, many heads of plantation households ruled over sizeable populations of slaves, free or freed dependents, neighbouring smallholders and their own extended family. This enhanced the authority that Portuguese ordinances, following Roman and Canon law antecedents, invested in husbands. Charged with maintaining family order and honour, husbands held 'marital power' that at its most extreme included the prerogative to murder an adulterous wife, but more commonly entitled them to demand obedience and sexual modesty and administer marital property.[12] Yet even among the colonial elite, the marriage and kinship system was not entirely patriarchal, and wives were far from powerless. Social recognition of descent and transmission of family wealth were bilateral, which signalled women's continued ties to their family of origin and offset their dependence on husbands. Bilateral descent was reflected in naming patterns, with girls commonly receiving both the Christian names and surnames of their female kin, and boys, the names of male kin. Wives did not adopt their husbands' surnames until the late nineteenth century.[13] The protection of elite women's property served as the most important counterweight to their husband's 'marital power'. Spouses were equal partners in parenthood and in ownership of common marital property, which the husband could not alienate without the wife's consent. The wife's dowry, though administered by the husband, remained solely hers.[14]

After Brazil's independence from Portugal, in 1822, the 'traditional Brazilian family' of the colonial era became a target of liberal attempts to shape the new Brazilian Empire – a constitutional monarchy – into a modern nation based on individual rights, equality and dynamic free markets. The 1830 Criminal Code, extolled internationally as a model compendium of liberal law, decriminalized sodomy along with other 'sins', and did not permit husbands to physically punish (much less murder) their wives.[15] This was followed by campaigns to reform marriage and inheritance laws, including reducing husbands' 'marital power', expanding the rights of illegitimate children and their access to patrimony, ending clerical celibacy and lowering the age of majority.[16] These efforts, however, were stymied by the state's recognition of the Catholic Church as the nation's official religion, the persistence of slavery and political instability, which resulted in the empowerment of conservatives by the 1840s.

Much to the dismay of liberals – both those who attempted to enact these changes in the nineteenth century and those who looked back on this history in order to understand the failure of liberalism in the early twentieth century – colonial rural clans did not give way to state institutions.[17] Instead, they evolved into more sophisticated, but still kin-based, regional oligarchies. The Church retained its authority over marriage, although the state reiterated late-eighteenth-century laws that required parental consent for the marriage of children under twenty-one years old.[18] The only significant changes to family law after independence represented losses for liberal reformers: an 1827 decree[19] ordered the observation of Tridentine dispositions regarding marriage (liberals had argued for secularization), and, in 1847, natural children lost the right to sue for paternal support and inheritance.[20] The nation's first compendium of family law, written by the politician and jurist Lafayette Rodrigues Pereira in 1869, addressed only families formed through legitimate marriage, ignoring couples whom the Philippine Ordinances had 'presumed married'.[21]

As marriage and family law became more exclusive under the empire, the gendered balance of power within elite marriages seems to have shifted dramatically in favour of husbands. The change resulted in part from the decline of the dowry and the expansion of commercial capitalism (as the courts increasingly refused to protect women's property from their husbands' creditors[22]), and in part from the spread of liberal discourses of individualism and marriage in the West as a whole, which extolled romantic love and free will. Increasingly, men were expected to have independent means to establish nuclear households and fully support their wives.[23] Perhaps as a signal of wives' increased dependence on husbands, they began to adopt their husbands' surname, adding it to their own, at the end of the nineteenth century.[24] By the time the empire was replaced by a republican regime in 1889, an idealized 'bourgeois' model of the nuclear family had been disseminated throughout the country. Although marriage rates seem to have increased over the second half of the nineteenth century, as slavery was gradually abolished and the urban population grew, the bourgeois ideal remained out of reach for most families.

The Struggle to Modernize Marriage Law, 1889–1988

The first Brazilian republic (1889–1930) was established through a military coup, not a revolution. The regime's inspiration in an authoritarian form of liberalism that was taking hold across Latin America, and its general disregard of the popular will, was reflected in the decree that secularized marriage just two months after the coup. The move was resisted by the Church and ignored by masses of Brazilians who continued to marry only in the Church, if at all: six decades later, census bureau studies showed that over half of Brazilian couples remained officially unmarried, including 25 per cent who contracted solely religious marriages.[25] Notwithstanding what seemed to be a growing distance between law and social practice, however, the republic's separation of church and state, together with the abolition of slavery (one of the last acts of the imperial government), finally freed liberal jurists and legislators to elaborate normative laws that reflected what they saw as society's natural evolution towards rational scientific principles.[26]

Clovis Beviláqua, the idealistic young jurist contracted to draft a comprehensive civil code in 1899, defined marriage as a bilateral civil contract among free and equal parties. Although he agreed that some degree of women's subordination to men within marriage was both natural and necessary to family harmony, he sought 'to be as liberal as he was permitted to be' in defining the rights of wives.[27] Legislators did not permit much. In the final draft of the civil code, promulgated in 1916, a wife could not, without her husband's permission, make decisions regarding her children, represent herself in court, work outside the home or accept any position of authority, administer property or accept or decline an inheritance or gift. For the first time, women were required to adopt their husband's surname.[28] These limitations on married women's civil capacity mirrored the republican regime's interpretation of the 1890 constitution in a way that defined women as 'inactive' citizens, denying them the right to vote or hold elected office.

From the beginning of the republic, women writers and activists deployed liberal principles of equality and citizenship in vigorous women's rights campaigns. In the late 1920s, some women voted and even ran for office in scattered local elections after winning lawsuits that convinced a few judges and the governor of the state of Rio Grande do Norte that the exclusion of women was unconstitutional.[29] Feminist demands for an end to women's subordination in civil law gained traction after 1930, when the republican government was overthrown by a diverse coalition headed by Getúlio Vargas. In the early 1930s the new regime leaned leftward as Vargas decreed various labour and social welfare reforms, recruited progressive social reformers to staff new ministries, and called a Constituent Assembly. As a result of intense lobbying by feminists, most notably the Brazilian Federation for Feminine Progress (FBPF) headed by biologist Bertha Lutz, the 1932 Electoral Code and the 1934 Constitution guaranteed women's right to vote and hold office, and Lutz became a member of congress in 1936. Among her most notable efforts was to draft the Women's Legal Statute, a bill that aimed to eliminate women's inequality from all aspects of civil law, with particular emphasis on women's equality within marriage and patrimonial rights for women living in consensual unions.[30]

Vargas's revolution, however, had also brought into the political arena a new generation of Catholic social conservatives who were explicitly anti-liberal. These men successfully lobbied for a provision that protected a particular family model – 'the family formed by indissoluble marriage' – in the text of the 1934 Constitution. This provision, reiterated in subsequent constitutions over the next three decades, made legitimate marriage the defining feature of the family for the first time.[31] Vargas's sharp turn to the right in 1937, when he closed congress and created the authoritarian Estado

Novo (New State, 1937–45), muted public debate over how to interpret this provision and killed Lutz's bill.

Struggles over civil and constitutional law were mirrored by debates within the fields of psychology and legal medicine in the late 1930s, most notably regarding the definition and punishment or medical treatment of sexual 'deviance'. For the first time since the colonial period, serious consideration was given to proposals to penalize homosexuality, some of which were inspired by fascist policies underway in Nazi Germany and justified by the argument that the 'contagion' of homosexuality threatened the family. These proposals were considered, but finally rejected by the team of jurists and legislators who prepared the new penal code in 1940, and homosexuality continued to be addressed privately as a disease and publicly through the discretion of the police, whose authority was enhanced under the Estado Novo.[32] Homosexual relationships were not discussed in the realm of family or even civil law until the 1980s.

After the return of democracy in 1945, in a new context of post-war international human rights, feminist lawyers and their allies in congress, most importantly Congressman Nelson Carneiro, reinvigorated the campaign for equality within marriage, divorce and rights for companions (including an unsuccessful 1947 bill that 'equated the companion to the wife' for purposes of alimony, shared property and social security benefits[33]). These activists pointed out that Brazil's civil code perpetuated patriarchal traditions that were incompatible with liberal democracy and explicitly violated Brazil's international obligations. Conservative politicians countered with Cold War rhetoric, warning that reducing husbands' authority or liberalizing marriage would open the door to communism. Change came only in 1962 with the Statute of the Married Woman, a watered-down version of Lutz's 1937 bill. Marriage remained formally patriarchal, with husbands retaining their authority over property and children, but wives gained the right to accept paid employment and inheritance without their husband's permission, as well as enhanced rights regarding child custody after a separation.[34]

No-fault divorce legislation, which required a constitutional amendment, would take another fifteen years, partly because a military coup in 1964 restricted political debate and pushed parliament to the right. The military was still in power when Carneiro re-launched the divorce campaign in 1975. The regime, however, had become less inclined to throw its weight behind the Catholic Church, which over the previous decade had condemned its human rights violations. Under the presidency of General Ernesto Geisel, a Protestant, Congress finally amended the Constitution and passed a divorce law in 1977.[35]

The most significant change leading up to the expanded definition of family in the 1988 Constitution involved not the rights of married women, but those of unmarried companions. Legislative efforts by activists such as Lutz and Carneiro in favour of 'companion's rights' made some headway in the social welfare laws of the 1930s, only to be turned back by the mid-1940s. Individual women, however, continued to pursue these rights through the courts. Over the next half century, their cases produced jurisprudence that supported the inclusion of new family forms in the 1988 Constitution as well as the subsequent replacement of the 'bourgeois' family norm by the 'pluralistic' model in twenty-first-century jurisprudence and doctrine. This process paved the way for the legalization of same-sex marriage.

Brazilian statutory sources that supported companions' claims date to the first accident law of 1912 (specifically regarding railway accidents), which defined potential beneficiaries simply as those dependent on the victim. In 1919, a broader worker's compensation law specified that beneficiaries could include the worker's 'family' or *cônjuge* (a term that could be interpreted as legitimate spouse or conjugal partner) or, in the absence of immediate family, 'other persons' dependent on the worker. Similarly opaque language appeared in 1930s social welfare legislation. Most notably, the pension law of 1931 used the popular term 'woman' (*mulher*), which could mean either legitimate wife or consensual partner.[36] Claims by companions multiplied as a result, moving the debate over 'companions' rights' from the public forum into labour law jurisprudence. Between 1931 and 1935, the National Labour Council, which oversaw labour and social welfare policy, issued decisions regarding companions that the Council's own governing board characterized as 'diametrically opposed to one another', contributing to the 'divergent jurisprudence' produced by the courts it administered.[37] While the Labour Council struggled to resolve the discrepancy, the term 'companion' appeared in legislation for the first time in 1934, when a revised workers' compensation law equated 'the companion supported by the victim' to 'the wife'.[38] The following year, a Labour Council resolution ordered judges to 'equate the companion to the wife' when determining pension beneficiaries.[39]

Progressive influence waned after 1937, and the 'situation of the companion' became increasingly ambiguous in the morass of additional state and federal provisions regarding new public–private enterprises and syndicates.[40] In 1944, the conservative Estado Novo regime removed the term 'companion' from worker's compensation regulations.[41] Nonetheless, social security policy and labour court jurisprudence of the early 1930s continued to serve as sources for labour and civil court judges, who faced a steady stream of cases involving companions and a lacuna regarding their rights.

When the Labour Council ordered its judges to 'equate the companion to the wife' in 1935, it cited the jurisprudence of its own chambers as well as that of the civil courts in a few progressive state jurisdictions (São Paulo and, though not specifically mentioned in the resolution, Rio Grande do Sul), which had 'equated companions to wives for the purpose of inheritance and division of property … recognizing reality [and applying] the principles of humanity and equity'.[42] Like the social welfare legislation discussed above, however, the jurisprudence regarding 'concubinage' (the legal term for unions of unmarried partners, whether adulterous or not[43]) was inconsistent over the 1940s and 1950s.

Jurists who supported concubines' patrimonial rights, citing European (especially French and Italian) sources as well as Brazilian cultural and legal traditions, argued that concubinage was a 'social fact' (*fato social*). This term was used to designate an entity recognized by society but not regulated by law, in contrast to a 'juridical fact' (*fato jurídico*) or something to which the law attributes specific legal consequences.[44] Since the civil procedural code of 1939 did not allow judges to dismiss cases by 'alleging legal obscurity or lacunae', they were obliged to adjudicate such entities. In 1942, a new law instructed them to rule 'by analogy, customs, and the general principles of law' and to attend to the 'social purpose of the law and the common good'.[45] Some jurists discussed 'social fact' in the Durkheimian sense (though without citing Durkheim), as a cultural norm or institution that guided individual behaviour: concubinage was a social reality for most poor Brazilian women, who 'accepted concubinage in good faith', and 'society' did not consider concubines 'dishonourable or immoral'.[46]

In the legal sense, jurists generally agreed that whereas marriage was a de jure partnership (*sociedade de direito*), created by a contract that generated specific family rights, concubinage was a de facto partnership (*sociedade de fato*) in which there was no legal contract. For some, this meant that the two were analogous and should be treated similarly. If the relationship was stable, public and 'similar to marriage', especially as evidenced by the woman's 'honesty' (sexual fidelity, modesty and domesticity), the court 'should presume the communion of life and property'.[47] A 1947 appeals decision, for example, applauded the 'extensive, increasingly humane jurisprudence' that recognized these women's family rights, pointing out that many concubines were 'heroic, exemplary mothers' who formed 'happy, dignified, and respectable families'.[48] Citing an opposing jurisprudential trend in 1955, however, another São Paulo appeals court supported the argument that 'concubinage, a situation contrary to morality, can never be a source of rights'. A concubine's claims could be recognized not through family law but only through commercial contract law, or the law of obligations: 'the concubine's right does not result from her status as lover (*amasia*) but instead from either contributing to building her lover's patrimony, or from working for him as a maid'.[49]

It was up to a judge to determine whether or how much a concubine had contributed to building patrimony during their relationship, and whether to consider her a family member, business partner or employee. In some cases, judges viewed the 'honest' concubine's domestic work as a full or partial contribution to her partner's wealth and awarded her a proportional share; in others, they considered it as simply unremunerated labour and required payment of back wages.[50] In some cases, a woman's paid work was evidence of her contribution to building patrimony[51]; in others, it evidenced 'the absence of the honesty element'.[52] Mutual care was frequently cited as evidence of the couple's 'communion', but in at least one case, a woman's illness in the final few years of a thirty-year relationship was evidence that she did not deserve a share of her companion's wealth, since his economic fortune improved while she was no longer able to work.[53] Cases in which one or both partners were married, whether or not legally separated, generated especially complex and inconsistent considerations. Court battles between the former wife and the companion often hinged on the judge's determination of whether the former wife had been the guilty party in the separation.[54]

The lack of clear legal guidelines or jurisprudence resulted in mountains of litigation and many dissenting appeals opinions from the 1930s to the 1960s, leading the Supreme Court to issue two resolutions recognizing 'concubine's rights': in 1963 it recognized the concubine's right to indemnification for her companion's death under worker's compensation laws; and in 1964, it ordered the courts to proceed with 'legal separation and division of patrimony acquired through mutual effort' in cases of '*de facto* partnership between concubines', as though they were married.[55] This validation of what was then referred to as 'concubine's rights' was accompanied by a gradual shift in legal language: 'companion' began to replace 'concubine'; 'irregular familial partnership' or 'stable union' began to appear in place of 'concubinage'.[56] In 1973, the 'companion' reappeared in new statutory laws: women companions who could not marry their partners because one or both of them was already married, though legally separated (since divorce was not permitted until 1977) were permitted to adopt their partners' surname, and the 'companion' was once again 'equated to the wife' as a beneficiary in a new federal social security law.[57] Many jurists began to distinguish 'pure concubinage', comprising two unmarried 'companions' who 'lived maritally' for a period of time (usually five years[58]), a relationship they saw as analogous to marriage and customary in Brazilian society, from 'impure concubinage', involving adulterous concubines or 'irregular' relationships – which still might generate valid claims of unremunerated domestic service or property rights. In practice, the distinctions were frequently unclear and terminology was used inconsistently.[59] Debates over whether a wife or a companion/concubine, or both, could claim pension or other benefits continued to generate jurisprudential debate at least up to 2015.[60] Still, jurisprudence shifted decisively towards recognition of companions' rights in the realm of family law in the 1970s, leading Bittencourt, in 1975, to characterize Brazilian jurisprudence as 'among the most advanced in the world'.[61]

The uneven development of jurisprudence that recognized companions' family rights paved the way for the 1988 Constitution's recognition of 'stable unions' (the new legal designation for consensual unions) as 'family entities', alongside and equal to families formed by married couples or single parents.[62] This expanded definition of family was the direct result of a well-orchestrated campaign against patriarchy led by a new generation of feminists, who began organizing as part of a broad movement for democracy and social justice during the final years of the military dictatorship (1964–85). Feminists also won constitutional guarantees of equality between women and men, both as citizens and family members, and equal rights for adopted and biological children, regardless of their parents' marital status.[63] According to jurists charged with interpreting the new provisions, the changes amounted to a revolution in family law, a transformation that was consistent with the Constitution's radical expansion of citizenship rights and commitment to equality, social justice and pluralism.[64]

Marriage, the Construction of Homosexuality and LGBT Rights Activism

Same-sex relationships were not included among the 'family entities' named by the 1988 Constitution. Yet in a process that paralleled the expansion of family rights to include heterosexual companions, same-sex couples increasingly, though unevenly, won family rights through civil law jurisprudence over the two decades that followed. And as was true in regard to the expansion of family law to include unmarried heterosexual couples, individual struggles to gain rights through the courts were made possible by an even longer history of political activism. Although most of this activism was not focused on the right to marry – 'homosexual liberation' groups of the late

1970s, in fact, rejected sexual possessiveness, monogamy and marriage as instruments of patriarchal repression – the promotion of visibility and celebration of sexual diversity helped to influence a cultural shift that, thirty years later, made it possible to persuade judges that same-sex relationships were among Brazil's pluralistic social customs and could be considered analogous to heterosexual stable unions.

After 1830, homosexuality was never again criminalized in Brazil. Instead, men and, to a lesser extent, women who were perceived to be sexually deviant were subject to harassment, internment in mental asylums and incarceration under public indecency laws, which frequently allowed the police wide discretionary powers. Outlets for expression of non-normative sexuality nonetheless grew, though unevenly, in a variety of leisure spaces in urban centres, particularly over the first half of the twentieth century. In fact, sensuality and sexual transgression played (and continue to play) a prominent role in the construction of Brazil's national identity, as is illustrated most explicitly in its iconic carnival celebrations. Even under the military dictatorship of the 1960s and 1970s, the police 'tolerated' increasingly open expressions of non-heteronormative sexuality that began to appear in circumscribed areas of Brazil's major cities, as the military considered homosexuality an aspect of Brazilian culture.[65] Coinciding with similar developments in other Western cities in the 1960s, the commercialization of sexuality in increasingly vibrant urban 'homosexual ghettos' emboldened challenges to heteronormativity. Police 'toleration', however, alternated with moralization campaigns consisting of arbitrary raids, mass arrests and harassment, while military censors stymied the politicization of the developing sexual subculture, particularly after the regime entered its most repressive phase in 1969.[66] When the military eased political repression in the late 1970s, a multitude of grass-roots movements began to mobilize in a cascade that turned into a broad-based struggle against the authoritarian regime and its repressive social and cultural underpinnings. Among these movements were at least twenty-two groups calling for homosexual affirmation and sexual liberation.[67]

'New social movements', as the diverse grass-roots movements came to be known, were linked to one another, and to similar movements taking place all over Latin America and elsewhere in the world, by their common discourse stressing universal human rights. This discourse, which as we have seen was mobilized by feminist activists in the post-war period, took on special resonance in Latin America during the intense political repression that swept the region in the early 1970s. Universal human rights were evoked as Christian dogma by social activists within the Catholic Church when theologians inspired by the Vatican's 'preferential option for the poor' sought religious grounds for their criticism of state violence as well as the inhumane social and economic effects of military rule.[68] Human rights also offered international legitimation and a legal framework for condemnation, on secular grounds, of the regimes' crimes against humanity.

Homosexual liberation groups of the late 1970s rarely counted more than a few dozen core activists, but, together with feminists, they played a fundamental role in incorporating the struggle against patriarchy and sexual oppression within the broader human rights movement.[69] The radical anti-authoritarianism of some of these groups sparked vibrant and productive intellectual debates regarding, for example, institutional hierarchy, sexual practices and identification, and political alliances (most importantly, whether to ally with left-wing groups, including the Worker's Party [*Partido dos Trabalhadores*, PT] which was formed in 1980). Yet constant debate also led to high attrition, and some radical strategies, such as sexual experimentation as a political act and the rejection of monogamy, distanced some potential allies.[70] By the time the dictatorship finally came to an end in 1985, few of the 'first wave' groups had survived. The AIDS crisis, which coincided with the end of the dictatorship, put a final end to the exuberant but fragmented liberationist phase of the struggle for LGBT rights.[71]

As many former homosexual liberation militants shifted their focus to health advocacy, grass-roots liberation groups of the anti-authoritarian era gave way to a small number of more conventionally structured organizations such as the Grupo Gay da Bahia (GGB), founded in 1980, which became the nation's first legally recognized gay rights non-governmental organization (NGO) in 1983, and led a successful campaign that year to persuade the Federal Council of Medicine to recognize that homosexuality is not a disease.[72] By focusing on anti-discrimination and civil rights, forming alliances with feminist and other national and international NGOs, and publicizing the idea that gay rights were human rights, these organizations positioned themselves to take part in the re-democratization process that was underway in the late 1980s.

In 1987, as in the early 1930s, the Constituent Assembly presented an opportunity for activists not only to shape the nation's charter but also to invigorate their movements and gain national attention. Lobbying efforts by activists affiliated with new gay rights groups, led by lawyer João Antônio Mascarenhas of the Triângulo Rosa (Pink Triangle), persuaded delegates to include 'sexual orientation' in the Constitution's anti-discrimination clauses and to create an inclusive 'stable union' law, worded in a way that did not exclude same-sex couples.[73] These proposals sparked virulent attacks by a new, rapidly growing group of conservative Pentecostal activists, and were ultimately defeated by large margins. While the final draft of the Constitution granted 'special protection' to 'the family', without any modifying clause, a bishop from the most politically active of the new Pentecostal churches, the Igreja Universal do Reino de Deus (formed in 1977), drafted the paragraph regarding 'stable unions', with the specific intention of excluding same-sex unions: 'stable union[s] between a man and a woman are recognized as family entities'.[74]

Despite the defeat of pro-LGBT proposals during the Constituent Assembly, the lobbying effort by LGBT and feminist activists had succeeded in pushing the left, particularly the PT, whose delegates had sponsored the original proposals, to voice commitment to LGBT rights. This, in addition to broad media coverage of the discussions, lent unprecedented credibility to the gay rights struggle, situating it within the broad social movement that placed human dignity, equality and anti-discrimination at the centre of the 'Citizen's Constitution', as the 1988 document came to be known.

In the decade that followed, anti-AIDS activism solidified the association of LGBT rights with human rights and invigorated the LGBT civil rights movement. When the government responded to the crisis with inadequate and stigmatizing programmes, proponents of LGBT rights worked through NGOs, using international ties and financing to create alternatives through a 'human rights approach'. After 1995, cooperation between the state and hundreds of AIDS-relief NGOs dramatically curbed the spread of HIV. The following year, Brazil won international acclaim for defending, on human rights grounds, its policy to produce anti-retroviral drugs in order to provide free, quality treatment to every HIV-AIDS patient in the country, over the protest of US-backed patent holders in the pharmaceutical industry. The episode produced heightened domestic support for Brazil's anti-AIDS programme, as well as ever-increasing visibility and normalization of people living with HIV, including gay men.[75]

The alliance between LGBT organizations and the state expanded dramatically after the PT gained power in 2003.[76] Most notably, gay rights NGOs helped design and implement the federal government's 'Brazil Without Homophobia' programme in 2003–4, which developed a range of visibility, education, health and anti-violence initiatives, as well as a series of LGBT conferences that culminated in a national meeting in 2008, where President Luís Inácio 'Lula' da Silva (2003–11) donned a rainbow cap and voiced his commitment to LGBT rights. PT support also helped to pass various municipal and state-level laws and policies, including anti-homophobia legislation in 13 of Brazil's 26 states between 2000 and 2013.[77]

Many LGBT leaders, however, became increasingly concerned with what they feared was the co-optation and bureaucratization of the LGBT movement in the 1990s, pointing out that the PT was an unreliable ally. Although the party's platforms supported LGBT rights, this commitment was often strategically abandoned, both during campaigns and after the PT took office, as it formed governing alliances with some of the most homophobic elements of the right.[78] As a result, the 'evangelical bloc' in the federal Congress has obstructed every pro-LGBT bill submitted from the time of the Constituent Assembly to the present, including three separate bills to legalize same-sex unions. Observing this situation in 2008, anthropologist Peter Fry argued that the PT used the rainbow banner in support of its 'ideology of diversity', promoting the image of Brazil as a multicultural democracy while failing to guarantee equal rights. Brazil's egalitarianism, in this view, like its gay pride parades, is just a show.[79] Omar Encarnación observed in 2016 that this criticism has continued, despite major federal policy initiatives and victories over the preceding five years, including the legalization of same-sex marriage. Pointing to the persistence of widespread homophobic attitudes and high levels of violence, a number of scholars and activists from both within and outside of the Brazilian LGBT movement suggest that the movement erred by casting its lot with international NGOs and the state rather than creating a mass movement by 'reaching out directly to society, with the aim of influencing hearts and minds'.[80]

Yet as LGBT rights activists worked to pressure the state to create pro-LGBT legislation and institutions, their work continued to strengthen the public discourse that linked LGBT rights to human rights, which reverberated powerfully in the arenas of culture and everyday life. The 1990s and early 2000s saw a surge in the creation and marketing of 'gay' culture, both for gay and non-gay consumers. The best example is the boom of annual pride parades, which today number around 300 and are important tourist attractions (Figure 1.1). The largest, in São Paulo, grew from about 2,000 marchers/spectators in 1997 to three million by 2006. The parades share the goal of celebrating Brazil's distinctive sensuality and sexual diversity and are sometimes characterized as 'carnival out of season'. Yet complementary events and parade themes channel LGBT cultural politics towards political militancy and policy. In 2005, for example, the São Paulo parade theme was 'Civil Unions, now!', publicizing the parade association's campaign for marriage equality.[81] The following year, the association filed suit with the Supreme Court, demanding revocation of the discriminatory wording in the stable union law. Although the Court did not agree that the law could be proclaimed unconstitutional (and therefore declined to hear the law suit), it voiced support for future challenges to exclusionary interpretations of the stable union law.[82]

The most surprising realm where cultural production significantly 'influenced hearts and minds' in favour of LGBT rights is mainstream television, particularly Brazil's famous *novelas* (soap opera-type dramas). Several screenwriters, including Aguinaldo Silva, who in the late 1970s was a founding editor of Brazil's most celebrated LGBT journal before joining the staff of Brazil's major TV network (TV Globo), have promoted LGBT visibility and rights from within a conventional genre that reaches tens of millions.[83] Comic, effeminate and generally likeable gay male characters have been staples since the 1970s, but increasingly, sub-plots have revolved around mainstream, monogamous, white, upper-middle-class couples grappling with homophobia and legal inequality. The pioneering work was aired when the Constituent Assembly was still underway in 1988. As the media reported on debates in the Assembly over the rights of homosexuals, a fictional lesbian couple won the public's sympathy in 'Vale Tudo', while religious conservatives demanded censorship ('Anything Goes', 1988–9). When one of the lesbian partners in the drama was killed by a bomb, the screenwriters (who included Silva) depicted the surviving partner's struggle to inherit the property her deceased partner had accumulated through their joint effort.[84] TV Globo did little to build on this momentum over the decade that followed, which coincided with the AIDS crisis and conservative ascendance in national politics. Gay rights discussions returned to *telenovelas* when national politics turned leftward. Beginning with *Senhora*

Figure 1.1 2014 LGBT Pride Parade in São Paulo. Source: Wikimedia Commons.[85]

do Destino ('Lady of Destiny', 2004–5), and *Páginas da Vida* ('Pages of Life', 2006–7), screenwriters created sub-plots that evoked viewers' sympathy for sophisticated and beautiful same-sex couples (one female, the other male) who struggled against prejudice, formed families and sought to adopt children. Although other *novelas* drew viewers with the promise of 'the first gay kiss' (finally delivered in *Amor e Revolução* ['Love and Revolution', SBT network] in 2011 by two women), *novelas* did not place same-sex couples in steamy sex scenes that were standard fare for heterosexual couples, nor did they challenge monogamy or middle-class decorum. Instead, they portrayed same-sex couples as upstanding citizens, loyal family members, and responsible and loving parents: precisely the social roles that real-life LGBT individuals were struggling to occupy in their appeals to the courts.[86]

Winning Marriage Equality through the Courts, 1988–2013

Real-life dramas involving same-sex couples' family matters began to play out in the Brazilian courts in the late 1980s. As we have seen, this was a moment when the human rights focus of LGBT activism dovetailed with the 1988 Constitution's establishment of human dignity, based in equality, diversity and social justice, as the foundational principle of the Brazilian state. Although the Constitution was silent on the question of same-sex unions, advocates of marriage equality argued that the principle of dignity, together with the constitution's recognition of 'the plurality of families that exist in reality', had 'revolutionized' family law in ways that demanded their inclusion.[87]

As jurists interpreted the 1988 Constitution's motives in granting 'special protection' to the family within a dignity framework in the 1990s, particularly in cases regarding children's rights, they consolidated a concept that would later provide doctrinal grounding for marriage equality: the 'socio-affective family'.[88] They reasoned that family law could no longer be based in moral traditions or the right to property – the fundamental liberal principle that had justified protection of the 'patrimonial family' through legitimate marriage and patriarchy. Instead, the law protected 'family entities' that were bonded through love and affection, fundamental human values and essential building blocks of dignity. The 'socio-affective' family not only nurtured constitutionally protected human rights, including solidarity, health and education, but it was also the instrument for the development of personhood and identity, and thus the capacity to possess and fully exercise rights. By the start of the twenty-first century, standard civil law textbooks described 'affection' as an 'implicit juridical principle' of family law, derived from the explicit principle of dignity, and explained that 'socio-affective' bonds were the primary constituent elements of family relationships, above legal documents or biological ties.[89]

As the concept of the 'socio-affective' family was emerging in jurisprudence regarding adoption and contested paternity, same-sex couples gradually won certain state benefits and patrimonial rights on the basis of their 'de facto partnerships', in a process that mirrored the development of 'concubines' rights' in the 1930s. Early victories included the right to state insurance and social security benefits. In 1990, representing a same-sex couple, the gay rights group Nuances, in the state of Rio Grande do Sul, petitioned the National Social Security Institute (INSS) to provide benefits to 'homosexual companions'. When they were denied, the State Public Ministry (which the 1988 Constitution charged with public prosecution and defence of constitutional rights) successfully sued the INSS, forcing it to offer such benefits throughout the country. The INSS repeatedly appealed, losing each time, which resulted in federal jurisprudence that supported similar suits against other federal and state employee benefit agencies. As was true of the cases brought by female companions before the 1980s, however, the outcomes of these suits were inconsistent.[90]

During the same period, LGBT partners began winning recognition of their unions for patrimonial purposes such as struggles over inheritance (like the one depicted fictionally in 'Anything Goes' in 1989) and establishment or separation of common property. Led by appeals courts within one of the jurisdictions that had first recognized 'concubine's' rights, Rio Grande do Sul, courts around the country increasingly, though unevenly, recognized same-sex unions as de facto partnerships in the 1990s, based on their existence as a 'social fact'. Like the rulings involving heterosexual companions' rights, judges increasingly cited civil procedural law to argue that the partnerships were analogous to stable unions and that 'the evolution of customs' had led to their acceptance by society.[91] Most judges nonetheless insisted that the law could recognize same-sex partnerships as analogous only to commercial, not family entities, again reproducing the reasoning of their predecessors regarding heterosexual unions.

A turning point came in 1999, when the Rio Grande do Sul Court of Appeals ruled that a same-sex couple's separation should be resolved by the family court because the relationship had been based on affection.[92] Over the following year, the appeals courts issued similar decisions in several other cases regarding patrimonial rights and the right to legally register a same-sex relationship.[93] Reviewing the state's recent jurisprudence in a 2000 book, Appeals Court Justice Maria Berenice Dias coined the phrase 'homoaffective union' and in a 2004 appeals court decision, Dias insisted that homoaffective unions constituted 'family entities' under constitutional law: 'Unions of love are what characterize family entities ... it is affection that is the purest expression of being and living, such that marginalization of same sex relationships is a type of violation of the right to life, as well as the principles of human dignity and equality.'[94] In the same year, the Rio Grande do Sul Court of Appeals ordered state notaries to accept registries from same-sex couples who wished to document their unions.[95] These legal documents could be used for an increasing variety of purposes as different institutions, public and private, slowly began to recognize same-sex families.[96]

By 2010, arguments developed in Rio Grande do Sul's appeals courts, along with the term 'homoaffective union', were incorporated into national doctrine on 'the socio-affective family'.[97] Sympathetic media coverage of notable cases also occasionally influenced the direction of jurisprudence. Examples include the custody battle over rock star Cassia Eller's son after her death in 2001 and LGBT activist Toni Reis's struggle to stop the deportation of his British partner of fourteen years in 2003. In a celebrated decision, Eller's female partner won custody when Eller's father relinquished his claim. Reis's relationship was recognized as a 'stable union' by a federal court in 2003, which made it possible for his partner to request a permanent visa.[98] Finally, the case of Maria da Penha, a (heterosexual) victim of domestic violence who won a suit against Brazil at the Inter-American Commission on Human Rights in 2001, resulted in the only federal law that explicitly addressed sexual orientation. The 2006 domestic violence law, named for Maria da Penha and redacted in consultation with feminist and human rights organizations, defines the family as 'the community formed by individuals who are or consider themselves to be related', specifying that its provisions applied to family members 'regardless of sexual orientation'.[99]

These and other highly publicized cases contributed to growing cultural normalization of same-sex relationships and growing jurisprudence favouring recognition of 'homoaffective unions' as 'family entities'. As was true in the United States during this period, however, the jurisprudence remained extremely uneven, both within the judiciaries of each state and among different states. In Rio Grande do Sul, most family courts followed the state appeals court jurisprudence, recognizing same-sex unions for civil purposes, but individual judges and Public Ministry officials often did not. In other states such as São Paulo, Minas Gerais and Rio de Janeiro, lawyers began to specialize in 'homoaffective' family law, sharing strategies for documenting their clients' relationships and intent to 'constitute a family' and increasing the likelihood of having their cases heard by a sympathetic family court judge. Many lawyers and judges, and countless law professors and master's and doctoral students, contributed to the growing legal scholarship, significantly influencing the Brazilian Association of Family Law and other major legal associations, as well as their states' appeals jurisprudence, in favour of same-sex family rights. A growing scholarship in the social sciences documented the phenomenon of changing patterns of family formation, with the increase in what came to be known as 'homoaffective families'.[100] Yet as late as 2008, when the Supreme Court requested that each of Brazil's 26 state judiciaries submit a report on their jurisprudence regarding same-sex relationships, several states replied that there was none.[101]

The cases that met the greatest resistance throughout Brazil involved child custody and adoption. As late as 2000, although same-sex couples commonly raised children, they rarely did so openly, and the two partners were rarely equal parents. Usually, children in these families were the biological or, less frequently, adopted children of one of the partners. In some cases, a parent adopted through a fraudulent process that was so common (among heterosexual couples) that jurists refer to it as 'Brazilian-style adoption': the parent simply registered a child as though she or he were the biological parent.[102] The case of Cassia Eller and her partner, who had openly raised Eller's son together, represented a landmark because it came at the moment (2002) when this was changing. In Brazil's major cities, the change was happening very rapidly.

As same-sex couples began to gain the confidence to publicly assume roles as co-parents, more and more couples approached the courts to seek legal protection for their existing families as well as to jointly adopt. In 2006, the first two cases of joint adoption by same-sex parents were approved. In São Paulo, a family court approved the adoption of a four-year-old girl by two fathers, although one was required to adopt first, then add the other father after a few months.[103] In Rio Grande do Sul, the first parent had adopted the two children a few years earlier, and a family court judge approved a second-parent adoption by her partner. Unlike the São Paulo case, the Rio Grande do Sul case was repeatedly appealed by the state's Public Ministry, resulting in a landmark decision by the Federal Superior Court of Justice (STJ – Superior Tribunal de Justiça, the highest court of appeal) in 2010 confirming same-sex couples' right to adopt. The STJ cited the Maria da Penha law along with what it considered 'strong jurisprudential trends' in favour of 'homoaffective families' and emphasized that judges' obligation to apply principles of dignity and well-being was especially critical in cases involving the best interest of a child.[104]

Anticipating accusations that this 2010 decision represented unconstitutional judicial activism, STJ minister[105] João Otávio de Noronha issued a 'clarification', explaining that 'Brazilian family law has always been created through jurisprudence. The law always comes afterwards. This was the case with concubinage, and with stable unions'.[106] His statement was a thinly veiled criticism of a federal adoption law passed one year earlier.[107] The original bill, submitted in 2003, had included a clause recognizing 'homoaffective couples' as potential parents, but evangelical legislators blocked its passage until this clause was struck. The bill's author was Congresswoman Laura Carneiro, daughter of Senator Nelson Carneiro, who had led the campaign for companions' rights, married women's equality and divorce from the 1940s to the 1980s. In her vigorous defence of adoption by homoaffective couples, Carneiro cited emerging international and national jurisprudence and pointed out that there were 'innumerable cases of children already living in homoaffective families, whose existing affective relationships with both parents are not protected by law' – a clear violation of these children's constitutional rights.[108]

The outcome of the congressional debates over adoption between 2003 and 2009 was similar to that of the Constituent Assembly of 1987–8: the evangelical bloc succeeded in halting the explicit recognition of same-sex companions' rights, but it was not able to create explicitly discriminatory legislation. Like the 1988 Constitution, the final adoption law of 2009 did not mention same-sex couples, but limited joint adoption to couples joined through marriage or stable union.[109] This 'legal lacuna' produced contradictory jurisprudence and facilitated discrimination by local judges and other adoption officials around the country, both before and after the STJ confirmed the adoption by the two mothers from Rio Grande do Sul in 2010. It would take another five years for the Supreme Court to resolve the issue in favour of joint adoption by same-sex couples. By then – 2015 – the Supreme Court had already recognized 'homoaffective unions' as family entities, yet couples continued to encounter discriminatory adoption procedures.[110]

Multiple cases were thus already making their way to the STJ and the Supreme Court in 2008, when Rio de Janeiro governor Sérgio Cabral, frustrated by his inability to offer equal benefits to LGBT state employees' families, filed the suit that resulted in the Supreme Court's 2011 decision to recognize 'homoaffective unions' as families, extending to them 'the same rights and responsibilities as stable unions between a man and a woman'.[111] Since the Constitution requires the state to 'facilitate the conversion' of stable unions into marriage, same-sex couples around the country approached public notaries to convert their unions into marriage, receiving mixed responses. In 2013, the National Judicial Council, which oversees legal procedure throughout Brazil, responded by ordering public notaries to issue marriage certificates irrespective of the gender of the prospective spouses.[112] Two separate decisions of the STJ, in 2015 and

2016, respectively, reinforced the Judicial Council's resolution, confirming same-sex couples' right to marry.[113]

The ministers of the Supreme Court and Supreme Tribunal of Justice, in their respective decisions to recognize 'homoaffective' couples' rights to constitute families and to marry, relied on arguments that had recently become dominant in national legal scholarship and jurisprudence and were presented by LGBT and feminist organizations in numerous amicus briefs. The ministers cited an array of specific individual constitutional rights that the state violated by not recognizing homoaffective families: dignity, freedom, privacy, equality, non-discrimination, well-being, the pursuit of happiness and the right to family planning. They ruled that the Constitution's explicit recognition of stable unions 'between a man and a woman' did not preclude recognition of other potential family forms, as the Constitution itself stipulated that explicit conferral of certain rights 'does not exclude others that are derived from its regime and principles'.[114]

Both courts' main argument, however, was that in addition to protecting individual civil rights, the Constitution had transformed the legal conception of the family and the purpose of marriage:

> The Federal Constitution of 1988 inaugurated a new phase of family law and thus of marriage ... in which multifaceted arrangements are equally capable of constituting the domestic nucleus called 'family'... . Now, the constitutional conception of marriage – in contrast to previous constitutions – must be necessarily plural, because families are plural and, moreover, marriage is not the object of protection, but merely the means of protecting a greater good, which is the protection of the human person and his/her inalienable dignity.[115]

Interpreted through this lens, the explicit recognition of stable unions of a man and a woman was 'intended to more efficiently combat the remnants of patriarchy in Brazilian customs' by guaranteeing equality within and among different family forms.[116] It was not intended to exclude other possible arrangements.

Yet if constitutional principles made it possible to interpret family law in ways that promoted pluralistic and egalitarian family forms, the legal construction of new modalities – whether 'stable unions of a man and a woman' in 1988 or 'homoaffective unions' in 2011 – resulted from decades of public and private struggle. As an appeals court justice from Bahia remarked in a 2006 interview, explaining why there was virtually no jurisprudence regarding same-sex families in her state, 'we can only rule on the cases that reach our courts, on the arguments made by lawyers about the values and situations lived by those individuals who seek justice'.[117] And a family court judge from Rio de Janeiro, who refused in 2008 to accept a case involving a same-sex couple, said in 2010 that she hoped to have a second chance soon: 'It wasn't possible then, although I feel badly about it. But if I had accepted it, I would have been overturned on appeal. I can interpret things differently now; you can see in the cases that some of my colleagues have judged, and in doctrine, and in the stories that you see in the media – these are families like any other family and they deserve equal rights.'[118] 'Homoaffective' family members, like unmarried heterosexual 'companions', won recognition of their constitutional right to 'special protection' by convincing the court that their behaviour conformed to social customs, not by attacking marriage or moral conventions. Yet the conventions that had defined previous family paradigms had been radically transformed by their individual and collective struggles.

Notes

* The author thanks Julia Moses, Paulina Alberto, Valerie Kivelson, Susan Juster, Helmut Puff, Paolo Squatriti and Leslie Pincus for their helpful comments on earlier versions of this chapter.
1 I am using 'LGBT' here to stand in for a variety of movements. For discussion of the shifting nomenclatures and acronyms used by different groups from the 1970s to the 2000s, see Regina Facchini, *Sopa de letrinhas?: Movimento homossexual e produção de identidades coletivas nos anos 90* (Rio de Janeiro: Editora Garamond, 2005).
2 Cândido Mendes de Almeida, *Codigo Philippino, ou, Ordenações e Leis do Reino de Portugal* Book 5, Title 13 (Rio de Janeiro: Inst. Philomatico, 1870), 1162.
3 The Inquisition stopped prosecuting lesbian relationships in the sixteenth century after deciding that although immoral, they were not cardinal crimes because the 'sacred seed' was not spilled. Ligia Bellini, *A coisa obscura: mulher, sodomia e inquisição no Brasil colonial* (São Paulo: Brasiliense, 1989). For discussion of the varying patterns of homosexual relationships, and church responses to them, see the chapters by David Higgs and Luiz Mott in *Infamous Desire: Homosexuality in Colonial Latin America*, ed. Peter Segal (Chicago: University of Chicago Press, 2003), 152–67, 168–96; Luiz Mott, *Sexo proibido: virgens, gays e escravos nas garras da Inquisição* (Campinas: Editora Papirus, 1989).
4 Those whose unions were not prohibited by canonical impediments to marriage such as consanguinity, prior marriage to a still-living spouse or religious vows of chastity.
5 Book 4, Title 46, par. 2, Almeida, *Codigo Philippino*, 834. Almeida and other nineteenth-century jurists insist that the compilers of the ordinances had 'inadvertently' contradicted Tridentine doctrine, which superseded these laws. They argued that the state therefore should not recognize couples who lived together as though they were married. This opinion inspired an 1827 law (see note 19). Therefore, at least in the nineteenth century, the courts apparently did not treat consensual partners' property as marital property. The inheritance rights of natural children, however, were reinforced by other laws. See Augusto Teixeira de Freitas, *Consolidação das leis civis*, 3rd rev. edn (Rio de Janeiro: B. L. Garnier, 1876), 109.
6 Sebastião Monteiro da Vide, *Constituições primeiras do arcebispado da Bahia* (1707; São Paulo: Editora da Universidade de São Paulo, 2010). See discussion in Ronaldo Vainfas, *Trópico dos pecados: moral, sexualidade e Inquisição no Brasil* (Rio de Janeiro, RJ, Brasil: Editora Campus, 1989), 285–339.
7 Stuart B. Schwartz, *Sovereignty and Society in Colonial Brazil: The High Court of Bahia and Its Judges, 1609-1751* (Berkeley: University of California Press, 1973), 30–31n14; Vainfas, *Trópico dos pecados;* Maria Beatriz Nizza da Silva, *Sistema de casamento no Brasil colonial* (São Paulo: T.A. Queiroz, Editora da Universidade de São Paulo, 1984), 18. Foundational myths of Brazil's national identity (created in the early twentieth century) view the propensity of Portuguese colonists and their male descendants to mix with native and African women as a stark contrast to practices in British settler colonies. The role of marriage in maintaining distinctions between the colonists and

the rest of the colonial population, however, was common to various settler societies (c.f. Chapter 8 in this book).
8   Slave marriage rates varied widely over time and region. See Robert W Slenes, *Na senzala, uma flor: esperanças e recordações na formação da família escrava: Brasil Sudeste, século XIX* (Rio de Janeiro: Editora Nova Fronteira, 1999).
9   Baptism was an even more important Catholic ritual for creating godparentage ties. See Stuart B. Schwartz, 'Opening the Family Circle: Godparentage in Brazilian Slavery', in *Slaves, Peasants and Rebels: Reconsidering Brazilian Slavery* (Chicago: University of Chicago Press, 1992), 137–76; Moacir Maia, 'Tecer redes, proteger relações: portugueses e africanos na vivência do compadrio' (Minas Gerais, 1720–50), *Topoi (Rio de Janeiro)*, 11, no. 20 (June 2010): 36–54.
10 Most studies of marriage among enslaved and freed Africans focus on the eighteenth and nineteenth centuries. See Slenes, *Na senzala, uma flor*; Sandra Lauderdale Graham, 'Honor Among Slaves', in *The Faces of Honor: Sex, Shame, and Violence in Colonial Latin America*, ed. Lyman L Johnson and Sonya Lipsett-Rivera (Albuquerque: University of New Mexico Press, 1998), 201–28; Juliana Barreto Farias, 'Sob o governo das mulheres: casamento e divórcio entre africanas e africanos minas no Rio de Janeiro no século XIX', in *Mulheres negras no Brasil escravista e do pós-emancipação*, ed. Giovana Xavier, Juliana Barreto Farias, and Flávio dos Santos Gomes (São Paulo: Selo Negro, 2012), 112–133; Graham, 'Being Yoruba in Nineteenth-Century Rio de Janeiro', *Slavery and Abolition* 32, n. 1 (2011): 1–26; Maria Odila Leite da Silva Dias, 'Escravas: resistir e sobreviver', in *Nova história das mulheres*, ed. Carla Beozzo Bassanezi and Joana Maria Pedro (São Paulo: Contexto, 2012), 366–9.
11 C.f. Chapter 3 in this book.
12 See the discussion of 'marital power' in the 1604 Philippine Code by nineteenth-century jurist and politician Lafayette Rodrigues Pereira, *Direitos de família* (Rio de Janeiro: B. L. Garnier, 1869), 68–96.
13 Linda Lewin, *Politics and Parentela in Paraiba: A Case Study of Family-Based Oligarchy in Brazil* (Princeton, NJ: Princeton University Press, 1987), 134–41; Muriel Nazzari, *Disappearance of the Dowry: Women, Families, and Social Change in São Paulo, Brazil (1600-1900)* (Stanford, CA: Stanford University Press, 1991), 140–1, 167–8.
14 Nazzari, *Disappearance of the Dowry*; Teresa Cristina de Novaes Marques, 'Mulheres e seus direitos de propriedade: o dote versus o poder marital', *Revista de História Econômica & Economia Regional Aplicada* 7, no. 13 (December 2012): 115–28.
15 Américo Jacobina Lacombe, 'A cultura jurídica', in História geral da civilização brasileira, ed. Sérgio Buarque de Holanda (São Paulo: Difusão Europeu do Livro, 1967), vol. 2, pt. 3, 357. Pereira, *Direitos de família*, 70n2.
16 Linda Lewin, *Surprise Heirs, Vol. II: Illegitimacy, Inheritance Rights, and Public Power in the Formation of Imperial Brazil, 1822-1889* (Stanford, CA: Stanford University Press, 2003).
17 The most influential of these twentieth-century critiques is Sérgio Buarque de Holanda, *Raízes do Brasil* (Rio de Janeiro: J. Olympio, 1936). See the discussion of his critique of 'patriarchalism' and Brazilian character in Sueann Caulfield and Cristiana Schettini, 'Gender and Sexuality in Brazil since Independence', in *The Oxford Research Encyclopedia of Latin American History*, ed. William Beezley (New York: Oxford University Press, forthcoming).
18 Pereira, *Direitos de família*, 5. Those older than twenty-one were required to request paternal consent 'only out of the duty of obedience and filial respect, although denial of [paternal] permission does not prevent them from being married'. The Criminal

Code penalized 'clandestine marriage', or marriage without prior permissions and announcements, with punishment for both the officiating priest and the couple. Arts. 247 and 248 *Código Criminal do Império do Brasil*, Lei 16 de dezembro de 1830, *Coleção de Leis do Império do Brasil* [hereafter CLBR], 1830.
19 Decreto 3 de novembro de 1827, *CLBR, 1827*, vol. 1 pt. I, 83; Freitas, *Consolidação*, 103-4.
20 Decreto n° 463, de 2 de setembro de 1847, *CLBR, 1847*, vol. 9 pt I, 48; Lewin, *Surprise Heirs, Vol. II*, 297-315.
21 Pereira, *Direitos de família*, 216 n. 5.
22 Marques, 'Mulheres e seus direitos'.
23 Nazzari, *Disappearance of the Dowry*, chaps. 10-11.
24 Ibid., 140-1.
25 Decreto 181 de 24 de janeiro de 1890; Thales de Azevedo, "Família, casamento e divórcio no Brasil," *Journal of Inter-American Studies*, 3, no. 3 (April 1961): 213-37, 230. The first republic's experience with marriage law was similar to church-state struggles in the rest of Latin America, whereas the failure of liberal laws to change popular marriage practices was even more widespread. See for example Chapter 11 on postcolonial Gabon in this book.
26 For discussion of liberals' conviction that slavery was incompatible with modern civil law, see Keila Grinberg, *Código civil e cidadania* (Rio de Janeiro: Jorge Zahar, 2001).
27 Clóvis Beviláqua, *Em defeza do Projecto de Codigo Civil Brazileiro* (F. Alves, 1906), 96.
28 Art. 186, 233, 240, 242, *Código Civil dos Estados Unidos do Brasil, lei 3.071 de 1 de janeiro de 1916, Diário Oficial da União* [hereafter DOU], 5 January 1916.
29 Branca Moreira Alves, *Ideologia e feminismo: a luta da mulher pelo voto no Brasil* (Petrópolis, RJ, Brasil: Vozes, 1980); June Edith Hahner, *Emancipating the Female Sex: The Struggle for Women's Rights in Brazil, 1850-1940* (Durham: Duke University Press, 1990).
30 'Commissão Especial de Elaboração do Estatuto da Mulher, Acta da reunião realizada em 14 de outubro de 1937', *Diário do Poder Legislativo, Câmara dos Deputados* 4, no. 745 (19 October 1937): 46781-807; Teresa Cristina de Novaes Marques and Hildete Pereira de Melo, 'Os direitos civis das mulheres casadas no Brasil entre 1916 e 1962. Ou como são feitas as leis', *Revista Estudos Feministas* 16, no. 2 (August 2008): 463-88.
31 Art. 144, *Constituição da República dos Estados Unidos do Brasil* (de 16 de julho de 1934); Art. 124, *Constituição dos Estados Unidos do Brasil* (de 10 de novembro de 1937); Art. 163, *Constituição dos Estados Unidos do Brasil* (18 de setembro de 1946); Art. 167, *Constituição do Brasil* (24 de janeiro de 1967). Official publications appear in *DOU* on 16 July 1934; 10 November 1937; 19 September 1946; and 20 October 1967, respectively.
32 James Naylor Green, *Beyond Carnival: Male Homosexuality in Twentieth-Century Brazil* (Chicago: University of Chicago Press, 1999), 129-31; João Silvério Trevisan, *Devassos no Paraíso: a homossexualidade no Brasil, da colônia à atualidade*, 5° ed (Rio de Janeiro: Ed. Record, 2002), 192.
33 Projeto de lei 122, de 1947, *Diário do Congresso*, 30 April 1947, 1354.
34 Lei 4.121 de 27 de Agosto de 1962, *DOU*, 3 September 1962; Marques and Melo, "Os direitos civis das mulheres casadas".
35 Nelson Carneiro, *A luta pelo divórcio: a síntese de uma campanha em defesa da família* (São Paulo: Editora Lampião, 1977).
36 Art. 22, Decreto 2.681, de 7 de dezembro de 1912, *CLBR*, 1912; Par. 3, Decreto 3.72434, de 15 de janeiro de 1919, *DOU*, Section 1, 18 January 1919; Paragraph 1, Decreto 20.465, de 1 de outubro de 1931, *DOU*, Section 1, 3 October 1931.

Female spouses and minor children, and in some laws, adult unmarried daughters, were generally presumed to be dependents. Male spouses could benefit only if 'invalid'. See also Eugenia Carla de Araújo Mendes, 'A situação da companheira na previdência social', *Revista de Ciência Política* 28, no. 3 (1985): 52–60; Alipio Silveira, 'A Companheira e a nova lei de acidentes do trabalho', *Revista do Trabalho* 13, no. 10 (1945): 5–24. Similar worker protection legislation, and similar discussions regarding women companions, emerged in turn-of-the-century France and Italy and were followed closely by Brazilian jurists. See Edgard de Moura Bittencourt, *Concubinato* (São Paulo: Livraria Editora Universitária de Direito, 1975), 89–96.

37 Resolução do Conselho Nacional de Trabalho de 28 de março de 1935, Processo n. 13.719, de 1934, *DOU*, 9 May 1935, 9211–12, quotation on 9211.
38 Decreto 24.637, de 10 de julho de 1934, *DOU*, Seção 1, 12 July 1934, 14001. The law also equated natural and legitimate children.
39 Resolução do Conselho Nacional de Trabalho, 9212.
40 Mendes, 'A situação da companheira na previdência social'.
41 The new worker's compensation law of 1944 still allowed a worker to designate 'other persons dependent on the victim' as beneficiaries in the absence of a wife or invalid husband and dependent children. Decreto-lei 7.036, de 10 de novembro de 1944, *CLBR*, 31 December 1944.
42 Resolução do Conselho Nacional de Trabalho, 9212.
43 'Concubine' referred to both partners (*concubina* [f]/*concubino* [m]), but the male form was rarely used and there was no jurisprudential debate regarding male concubines' rights.
44 In 1975, jurist and family law specialist Edgard Bittencourt argued that concubinage is both a social and juridical fact, since it is mentioned in accident law, but he cited only foreign jurists. Bittencourt, *Concubinato*, 45.
45 Art. 113, *Código de Processo Civil*, Decreto-lei 1.608 de 18 de setembro de 1939, *CLBR*, 1939; Art. 4–5, Lei 4657 de 4 de setembro de 1942, Lei de Introdução ao Código Civil Brasileiro, *DOU*, 9 September 1942. These instructions are reiterated in Art. 126, Lei 5.869 de 11 de janeiro de 1973, *Código de Processo Civil*, *DOU*, 17 January 1973.
46 Acórdão, Embargos, 53.752, Terceiro Grupo de Câmaras, São Paulo, 10 de agosto de 1951, *Revista dos Tribunais*, 194 (1951): 748; Acórdão, Apelação 37.656, 5a Câmera de Apelação de São Paulo, 4 de junho de 1948, *Revista dos Tribunais* 175 (1948): 649.
47 Acórdão, Apelação 98.173, 4a Câmara, Tribunal de Justiça, 22 de abril de 1960, *Revista dos Tribunais*, 300 (1960), 191–4, 192; Edgard de Moura Bittencourt, *O concubinato no direito* (Rio de Janeiro: Ed. Jurídica e Universitária, 1969), vol. 1, 69; Bittencourt, *Concubinato*, ch. 4.
48 Tribunal de Justiça de São Paulo, Acórdão, 6 de março de 1947, cited in Bittencourt, *O concubinato no direito*, vol. 1, 43.
49 The sentence was confirmed on appeal: Acórdão, Apelação 71.780, 4a Câmara, Tribunal de Apelação de São Paulo, 5 de dezembro de 1955, *Revista dos Tribunais* 427 (1956): 133–7, 134. See also *Revista dos Tribunais* 210 (1953): 217.
50 See the decision and dissenting opinion in Acórdão, Apelação 98.173, 4a Câmara, Tribunal de Justiça, 22 de abril de 1960, *Revista dos Tribunais*, 300 (1960), 191–4.
51 Ibid., 193.
52 Acórdão, Apelação 63.215, 1a Câmara Civil do Tribunal de Alçada, *Revista dos Tribunais*, 352 (1965): 350–3, 351.
53 Acórdão, Apelação 71.780.

54 See Supremo Tribunal Federal [hereafter STF], 2ª Turma, RE nº 7182/47, *Revista Forense*, (August 1947): 422; Bittencourt, *Concubinato*, 109–11, 277–9, 375.
55 STF, Súmula 55, 13 de dezembro de 1963, *Súmula da Jurisprudência Predominante do STF*, Imprensa Nacional, 1964, p. 45.; Súmula 380, 4 de março de 1964, *Diário da Justiça*, 8 May 1964, 1237.
56 Rodrigo da Cunha Pereira, *Concubinato e união estável*, 6th edn (Belo Horizonte: Del Rey, 2001), 57.
57 Art. 57, paragraphs 2 and 3, Lei 6015 de 31 de dezembro de 1973, *DOU*, 31 December 1973 (adoption of surname) Art. 11, paragraph 3, Lei 5.890, 8 de junho de 1973, *DOU*, 8 September 1973 (social security law). The companion could be recognized only if the worker was single or legally separated and had no alimony obligation. Similar qualification of the companion appeared in the military pension law: Art. 3, paragraph d, Lei 4.297 de 23 de dezembro de 1963, *DOU*, 14 January 1964. These and other laws continued to discriminate against male dependents of female workers: husbands could only benefit if they were 'invalid' and there was no provision for male companions. A new accident compensation law in 1974 was the first to recognize both the *companheiro* and *companheira* as potential beneficiaries. Lei 6194 de 19 de dezembro de 1974, *DOU*, 31 December 1974.
58 The five-year period first appeared in the 1963 military pension law.
59 Bittencourt, *Concubinato*, 49. In the 1970s, some argued that 'companion' referred to the honest concubine. After 1988, 'concubine' was generally used to refer to an adulteress/adulterer (although the male form was rarely used), whereas the companion (*companheiro/a*) was a partner in a now legalized 'stable union'. The lack of clarity in jurisprudence continues to generate confusion: see the discussion of legal doctrine and jurisprudence regarding the difference between companion and concubine in the federal Supreme Court case, STF Mandado de Segurança 33.404, Distrito Federal, 11 February 2015, n. 7808086 http://www.stf.jus.br/portal/autenticacao/ (accessed on 20 March 2017).
60 STF Mandado de Segurança 33.404.
61 Bittencourt, *Concubinato*, 39.
62 Art. 226 paragraph 4, Constituição da República Federativa do Brasil, *DOU*, Anexo, 5 October 1988 [hereafter 1988 Constitution].
63 Art. 5 paragraph 1 and Art. 226 paragraph 5, Art. 227, paragraph 6, 1988 Constitution.
64 Paulo Luiz Netto Lobo, 'Entidades familiares constitucionalizadas: para além do numerus clausus', 2007, http://www.mundojuridico.adv.br/sis_artigos/artigos.asp?codigo=264 (accessed on 20 March 2017).
65 Green, *Beyond Carnival*, 128–31; Trevisan, *Devassos no Paraíso*, 187–92.
66 Edward MacRae, 'Em defesa do gueto', in *Homossexualismo em São Paulo e outros escritos*, ed. James N. Green and Ronaldo Trindade (São Paulo: Unesp, 2005), 291–308; Green, *Beyond Carnival*.
67 Elaine Marques Zanatta, 'Documento e identidade: o movimento homossexual no Brasil na década de 80', *Cadernos Arquivo Edgard Leuenroth*, no. 5/6 (1996–7): 193–220; Edward Macrae, *A construção da igualdade: identidade sexual e política no Brasil da abertura* (Campinas: Editora da Unicamp, 1990); Green, *Beyond Carnival*; Trevisan, *Devassos no Paraíso*; Facchini, *Sopa de letrinhas*.
68 Clara Amanda Pope, 'Human Rights and the Catholic Church in Brazil, 1970-1983: The Pontifical Justice and Peace Commission of the São Paulo Archdiocese', *Journal of Church and State* 27, no. 3 (1985): 429–52.
69 Trevisan, *Devassos no paraíso*, 335–64; Facchini, *Sopa de letrinhas?*
70 See especially the discussion of lesbian participation in Trevisan, *Devassos no paraíso*, 340.

71 Green, *Beyond Carnival*, 76-7; Trevisan, *Devassos no paraíso*, 353-72; Facchini, *Sopa de letrinhas*.
72 Luiz Mott, 'História da homossexualidade no Brazil: cronologia das principais destaques', *Grupo Gay da Bahia*, 25 October 2001, http://www.ggb.org.br/cronologia_movimento_homossexual.html; Luiz Mello, 'Da diferença à igualdade: os direitos humanos de gays, lésbicas e travestis', in *Direitos Humanos e Cotidiano*, ed. Ricardo Barbosa Lima (Goiânia: Bandeirante, 2001), 159-77.
73 João Antônio de Souza Mascarenhas, *A tríplice conexão: machismo, conservadorismo político e falso moralismo, um ativista guei versus noventa e seis parlamentares* (Rio de Janiero: 2AB Editora, 1997). 'Atas da Subcomissão dos Negros, Populações Indígenas, Pessoas Deficientes e Minorias', *Diário da Assembléia Nacional Constituinte*, Suplemento, 20 May 1987, 165-68.
74 Comissão de Sistematização, Ata da 32 reunião extraordinária', *Diário da Assembléia Nacional Constituinte*, Suplemento C, vol. 2, 1988, 97-98; 'Comissão de Redacção', *Diário da Assembléia Nacional Constituinte*, Suplemento B, 1988, 109; Art. 126 paragraph 3, 1988 Constitution. Later civil legislation that defined 'stable union' retained this language: Art. 5, Lei 9.278, de 10 de maio de 1996, *DOU*, 13 May 1996; Art. 1.723, Lei 10.406, de 10 de janeiro de 2002, *Código Civil*, *DOU*, 11 January 2002. See Antônio Flávio Pierucci, "Representantes de Deus em Brasília: a bancada evangélica na Constituinte," in *A realidade social das religiões no Brasil*, ed. Reginaldo Prandi and Antônio Flávio Pierucci' (São Paulo: Hucitec, 1996), 165-91.
75 Jane Galvão, *AIDS in Brazil* (São Paulo: Editora 34, 2000); Jane Galvão, 'Brazil and Access to HIV/AIDS Drugs: A Question of Human Rights and Public Health', *American Journal of Public Health* 95, no. 7 (July 2005): 1110-16; Francisco Inácio Bastos et al., 'Treatment for HIV/AIDS in Brazil: Strengths, Challenges, and Opportunities for Operations Research', *AIDScience* 1, no. 15 (27 November 2001), http://www.aidscience.org/Articles/aidscience012.pdf (accessed on 20 March 2017); Amy Stewart Nunn et al., 'AIDS Treatment In Brazil: Impacts And Challenges', *Health Affairs (Project Hope)* 28, no. 4 (2009): 1103-13; Adriana R. B. Vianna and Sérgio Carrara, 'Sexual Politics and Sexual Rights in Brazil: A Case Study', in *Sex Politics: Reports from the Frontline*, ed. Richard Parker, Rosalind Petchesky and Robert Sember (Sexual Policy Watch, 2008), 27-51.
76 The party remained in power until 2016.
77 Toni Reis, 'Avanços na promoção da cidadania de gays, lésbicas, bissexuais, travestis e transexuais', in *Constituição 20 anos: estado, democracia e participação popular: caderno de textos* (Brasília: Câmara dos Deputados, Edições Câmara, 2009), 227-30.
78 Omar Encarnación, *Out in the Periphery: Latin America's Gay Rights Revolution* (New York: Oxford University Press, 2016), 177-81.
79 CLAM (Programa de Estudos e Pesquisas em Gênero, Sexualidade e Saúde do Instituto de Medicina Social da Universidade do Estado do Rio de Janeiro), 'Movimiento LGBT em debate', 18 June 2008, http://www.clam.org.br/noticias-clam/conteudo.asp?cod=4327 (accessed on 20 March 2017).
80 Encarnación, *Out in the Periphery*, 186.
81 'Quem somos', Associação da Parada do Orgulho LGBT de São Paulo, http://paradasp.org.br/quem-somos/ (accessed on 20 March 2017).
82 STF, ADI: 3300 Distrito Federal, Relator: Min. Celso de Mello, 3 de fevereiro de 2006, *Diário da Justiça*, 9 February 2006.
83 Silva insists that he is not a political militant, but depicts 'reality' in a way that does not alienate his audience. See 'Aguinaldo Silva diz que não pretende mostrar beijo gay em novela sua e que pensa na mãe na hora de escrever', *Folha de São Paulo*, 12

July 2016, online edition, http://f5.folha.uol.com.br/televisao/2016/07/10003055-aguinaldo-silva-diz-que-nao-pretende-mostrar-beijo-gay-em-novela-sua-e-que-pensa-na-mae-na-hora-de-escrever.shtml (accessed on 20 March 2017); 'Não confiavam em mim no jornalismo porque sou gay, diz Aguinaldo Silva', *UOL Livraria da Folha*, 6 May 2010, http://www1.folha.uol.com.br/folha/livrariadafolha/ult10082u731304.shtml (accessed on 20 March 2017).

84 According to journalist James Cimino, there was public outcry over the network's apparent caving in to conservative demands, but the character's death had been written into the original script because the screenwriters wanted to address the issue of patrimonial rights, which had just begun to appear in the courts. James Cimino, 'Em "Vale Tudo," censura vetou falas de lésbicas, mas liberou maconha', *UOL*, 15 de janeiro de 2013, online edição, http://televisao.uol.com.br/noticias/redacao/2013/01/15/em-vale-tudo-censura-vetou-dialogos-de-lesbicas-mas-liberou-cena-de-maconha.htm (accessed on 20 March 2017).

85 https://commons.wikimedia.org/w/index.php?title=Special:Search&limit=20&offset=20&profile=default&search=gay+pride+parade+sao+paulo&uselang=en-gb&searchToken=3oucb7reak10cm9jx8klnpbpb#/media/File:S%C3%A3o_Paulo_LGBT_Pride_Parade_2014_(14105070102).jpg (accessed on 10 September 2016).

86 TV Globo's website section on *novelas* contains information on screenwriters and *novelas*: http://memoriaglobo.globo.com/mostras/frases-no-ar/entretenimento/entretenimento-dramaturgia.htm (accessed on 20 March 2017). On censorship of Silva's *novelas*, see Cimino, 'Em "Vale Tudo".' For a detailed analysis of gay characters in *telenovelas*, Fernanda Nascimento, *Bicha (nem tão) má: LGBTs em telenovelas* (Rio de Janeiro: Editora Multifoco, 2015).

87 Luiz Edson Fachin, 'Aspectos jurídicos da união de pessoas do mesmo sexo', *Revista dos Tribunais* 85, no. 732 (1996): 47–54.

88 See the discussion of jurisprudence regarding contested paternity in Sueann Caulfield, 'The Right to a Father's Name: A Historical Perspective on State Efforts to Combat the Stigma of Illegitimate Birth in Brazil', *Law and History Review* 30, no. 1 (February 2012): 1–36, 16–21.

89 Paulo Luiz Netto Lobo, *Código Civil comentado* (arts. 1591 a 1993), vol. 16 (São Paulo: Atlas, 2003), 55–59; Paulo Luiz Netto Lobo, *Direito Civil: famílias* (Saraiva, 2012), 20–27; Maria Berenice Dias, *Manual de direito das famílias* (São Paulo: Revista dos Tribunais, 2007), 66–69; Maria Helena Diniz, *Curso de direito civil brasileiro*, vol. 5 (Sao Paulo: Saraiva, 2011), 38; Luiz Edson Fachin, *Comentários ao novo Código Civil*, vol. 18 (Rio de Janeiro: Forense, 2003), 27; Rodrigo da Cunha Pereira, *Princípios fundamentais norteadores para o direito de família* (Belo Horizonte: Del Rey, 2005), 179; Rolf Madaleno, *Curso de direito de família* (Rio de Janeiro: Forense, 2011), 95; Carlos Roberto Gonçalves, *Direito civil brasileiro*, vol. 6 (São Paulo: Saraiva, 2011), 24.

90 Ação civil pública nº 2000.71.00.009347; Instrução Normativa 25/2000, Instituto Nacional de Seguridade Social (INSS). http://www.inss.gov.br/conteudoDinamico.php?id=87 (accessed on 29 March 2017). See Shawn Schulenberg, 'Policy Stability without Policy: The Battle for Same-Sex Partnership Recognition in Brazil', in *Same-Sex Marriage in the Americas: Policy Innovation for Same-Sex Relationships*, ed. Jason Pierceson, Adriana Piatti-Crocker and Shawn Schulenberg (Lanham, Md: Lexington Books, 2010), 93–127.

91 See note 45.

92 Tribunal de Justiça do Rio Grande do Sul [hereafter TJRS], AI 599 075 496, 8ª Câmara Cível, Rel. Des. Breno Moreira Mussi, 17 June 1999.

93 TJRS, Apelação Civil 599348562, Rel. Des. Antônio Carlos Stangler Pereira, 25 November 1999; TJRS, Confl. Comp. 70000992156, 8ª Câmara Cível, Rel. Des. José Ataídes Siqueira Trindade, 29 June 2000; TJRS, Apelação Civil 70002355204, 7ª Câmara Cível, Rel. Des. Sérgio Fernando de Vasconcellos Chaves, 11 April 2001.

94 Maria Berenice Dias, *União Homossexual: O Preconceito & a Justiça* (Porto Alegre, RS: Livraria do Advogado, 2000); Apelação Cível Nº 70009550070, Sétima Câmara Cível, Tribunal de Justiça do RS, Relator: Maria Berenice Dias, 17 November 2004. See also Maria Berenice Dias, *Homoafetividade: o que diz a justiça! As pioneiras decisões do Tribunal de Justiça do Rio Grande do Sul que reconhecem direitos às uniões homossexuais* (Porto Alegre, Livraria do Advogado Editora, 2003).

95 Art. 215, Consolidação Normativa Notarial Regional (Provimento nº 06/4-CGJ). See Schulenberg, 'Policy Stability'.

96 Lawyers with experience in same-sex couples' legal issues in Rio Grande do Sul, São Paulo and a few other states advised clients to create affidavits confirming their union and their 'intent to constitute a family' and identifying scattered registrars' offices that would accept them. The Grupo Gay da Bahia also created its own registry, which is held at its main office in Bahia Mott, 'Historia da homossexualidade'.

97 See Gerivaldo Alves Neiva, 'A união homoafetiva na jurisprudência', *Revista Jus Navigandi*, February 2009 http://jus.uol.com.br/revista/texto/12409/a-uniao-homoafetiva-na-jurisprudencia (accessed on 20 March 2017).

98 'Companheira de Cássia Eller fala sobre maternidade', *Diário de Pernambuco*, 10 May 2015. As a result of publicity surrounding Reis's case in 2003, the National Immigration Council passed a resolution to allow same-sex partners of Brazilian citizens to immigrate, but bureaucratic requirements, including the need for proof of a stable union, limited the number of visas conceded. *Estadão*, 26 November 2003.

99 Art. 5, Lei 11340 of 7 August, 2006, *DOU* 8 August 2006.

100 Anna Paula Uziel, Miriam Grossi and Luiz Mello, *Conjugalidades, parentalidades e identidades lésbicas, gays e travestis* (Rio de Janeiro: CLAM/Editora Garamond, 2007); Luiz Mello, *Novas famílias: conjugalidade homossexual no Brasil contemporâneo* (Rio de Janeiro: Garamond, 2005); Miriam Grossi, 'Gênero e parentesco: famílias gays e lésbicas no Brasil', *Cadernos Pagu* 21 (2003): 261–80; Anna Paula Uziel, *Homossexualidade e adoção* (Editora Garamond, 2007).

101 See responses from Roraima, Mato Grosso, Paraná, Sergipe, Tocantins, and Amazonas. Several others reported that there was no consensus on the issue in their state's jurisprudence. STF, Argüição de Descumprimento de Preceito Fundamental ADPF/132, 25 Febuary 2008. http://redir.stf.jus.br/estfvisualizadorpub/jsp/consultarprocessoeletronico/ConsultarProcessoEletronico.jsf?seqobjetoincidente=2598238 (accessed on 22 March 2017).

102 Caulfield, 'The Right to a Father's Name', 20–1.

103 'Casal de homens autorizado a adotar menina em SP', *Terra*, 22 November 2006 http://noticias.terra.com.br/brasil/noticias/0,,OI1262455-EI306,00-Casal+de+homens+e+autorizado+a+adotar+menina+em+SP.html (accessed on 22 March 2017); 'Casal gay adota 2ª filha e descobre que ela é irmã biológica da primeira', *Fantástico*, 30 December 2012, http://g1.globo.com/fantastico/noticia/2012/12/casal-gay-adota-2-filha-e-descobre-que-ela-e-irma-biologica-da-primeira.html (accessed on 22 March 2017).

104 STJ, Recurso Especial Nº 889.852 – RS (2006/02091374), Documento: 966556 – Inteiro Teor do Acórdão, *Diário da Justiça*, 10 August 2010. This decision confirmed

the Rio Grande do Sul appeals court decision, which was written by Maria Berenice Dias: Apelação Cível 70013801592, Sétima Câmara Cível do Tribunal de Justiça do Estado do Rio Grande do Sul, Porto Alegre, 05 de abril de 2006, http://jij.tjrs.jus.br/paginas/docs/jurisprudencia/Adocao_casal_formado_duas_pessoas_mesmo_sexo.html (accessed on 22 March 2017).
105 Jurists on the Brazilian Supreme Court and Superior Court of Justice hold the title of minister.
106 STJ, Recurso Especial Nº 889.852, *Diário da Justiça*, 10 August 2010, 29.
107 Lei 12.010, de 3 de agosto de 2009, *DOU* 4 August 2009.
108 Projeto de Lei 1766, de 2003 (Da Sra. Laura Carneiro), *Diário da Câmara dos Deputados*, Sup 'A', 9 May 2007, 178–9, 256–9, 256. On page 258, Carneiro cites the 2006 Rio Grande do Sul appeals decision that would later result in the 2010 STJ decision.
109 Art. 42, paragraph 2, lei 12.010, de 3 de agosto de 2009.
110 The 2015 Supreme Court case was initiated by activist Toni Reis and his partner, who had encountered discriminatory adoption policies in their home state of Paraná. STF RE 846102/Paraná, Relatora Ministra Cármen Lúcia, 5 de maio de 2015, *Diário da Justiça*, March 18, 2015. See interview of Reis in "'Ninguém pode falar que não somos família,' diz casal gay', *BBC Brasil.com*, 9 April 2015, https://noticias.terra.com.br/brasil/ninguem-pode-falar-que-nao-somos-familia-diz-casal-gay,7b9f76b3c4f9c410VgnVCM3000009af154d0RCRD.html (accessed on 20 March 2017).
111 STF, ADI 4.277/ADPF 132, Plenário, 5 de maio de 2011, *Diário da Justiça*, 14 October 2011.
112 Conselho Nacional de Justiça, Resolução 175, de 15 de maio de 2013.
113 The marriage cases are STJ, AREsp 408276, 28 de agosto de 2015, *Diário da Justiça Eletrónico*, 3 September 2015; STJ, REsp 1516484, 22 de março de 2016, *Diário da Justiça Eletrónico*, 13 April 2016.
114 Ementa, STF, ADI 4.277/ADPF 132, paragraph 5.
115 STJ, REsp 1516484, 22 de março de 2016, *Diário da Justiça Eletrónico*, 13 April 2016, 5.
116 Ementa, STF, ADI 4.277/ADPF 132, paragraph 4.
117 Informal communication with the author, 20 June 2008.
118 Marise Cunha de Souza (Juíza de Direito da 2ª Vara de Família Regional da Ilha do Governador), interview with the author, 26 July 2010.

2

From Toleration to Prosecution: Concubinage and the Law in China

Lisa Tran

In 1829, the prefect of Henan confronted three widowed concubines, each seeking to claim the privileges of the main wife after the first main wife had passed away years ago. The prefect based his decision on timing: the first concubine who entered the household after the death of the first main wife was declared the new main wife.[1] In 1942, a main wife charged her husband with adultery and bigamy on the basis of his seven-year relationship with his concubine. The bigamy charge was later dropped, and the Shanghai District Court dismissed the adultery charge on the grounds that the wife had consented to her husband's relationship with the concubine for years.[2] In 1950, a man and his newly acquired concubine appeared before the People's Court in Qingdao. The man already had a wife and a concubine, but his acquisition of a second concubine after the implementation of the 1950 Marriage Law led him and his new concubine to be convicted of bigamy.[3] What do these three cases, tried under different legal systems in China, reveal about the nature of concubinage and its relationship to marriage?[4]

The case of the three concubines indicates that late imperial law regarded a concubine as a secondary wife who could be promoted to main wife status after the death of the first main wife. The second case shows that under Guomindang (GMD) law, concubinage was considered adultery but not bigamy, and that exceptions to the law weakened its full force. And the third case highlights the Chinese Communist Party's (CCP) prosecution of concubinage as bigamy. The three cases, then, show that in the Qing dynasty (1644–1911), concubinage was regarded as a semi-marital union, and in the twentieth century, it was treated either as an extramarital relationship or as a bigamous marriage, depending on the laws in force at the time. These changes in the legal conception of concubinage signal important shifts in the meaning and purpose of the family in early-twentieth-century China, which witnessed an assault against the multigenerational family structure and a promotion of the nuclear family model.[5] Susan Glosser links the emergence of the 'small family' (*xiao jiating*) ideal in public discourses to the social reform campaigns of male intellectual elites, the spread of urban consumer culture and the state-building projects of the GMD and the CCP.[6] Central to this shift from the extended family to the 'small family' model was the new importance of monogamy as both a social and a legal ideal, as Kathryn Bernhardt and

Harriet Evans have shown.[7] For obvious reasons, the commitment to monogamy held important implications for concubinage.

On the face of it, Chinese law – whether in the Qing dynasty or in the twentieth century – prohibited bigamy. Whether concubinage constituted bigamy depended on how the law defined the nature of a man's relationship with his concubine. Qing law considered a concubine to be a minor, but not a legal, wife. Hence, concubinage did not fall within the purview of the law that punished a man for having more than one legal wife at a time.[8] The GMD, the nominal head of China for most of the Republican era (1912–49), ignored the semi-marital features of concubinage, focusing exclusively on the sexual nature of a man's relationship to his concubine. Consequently, concubinage was placed under the laws on adultery. After the CCP's promulgation of the 1950 Marriage Law, concubinage came to be treated as de facto marriage, which was considered legally valid; hence, concubinage now constituted bigamy. What does the shift from legal tolerance to public prosecution of concubinage suggest about changes in the meaning and purpose of marriage, in the eyes of both state and society in twentieth-century China?

In many respects, the story of concubinage reflects the legal and social transformations that marked China's transition from endorsing a late imperial ideology centred on Confucianism to embracing a Western-inspired set of beliefs that the majority of Chinese intellectuals viewed as 'modern'. Since the Han dynasty (206BCE–220CE), Confucianism, a secular political philosophy and ethical code, had defined Chinese civilization. In politics, it strengthened imperial authority and was the basis of the civil service examination system that produced government officials. In law, it informed legal statutes and the administration of justice. In society, it governed interpersonal and family relations. Confucianism defined orthodoxy; other belief systems, including Buddhism and popular religions, were considered heterodoxy and were tolerated provided they did not challenge the established Confucian order. By the late nineteenth century, however, a new generation of leaders influenced by Western ideas began to do precisely that. The Hundred Days of Reform in 1898 introduced political, administrative, educational and legal reforms that expressed a distinctive Chinese modernity.[9] Although squashed by conservatives, these reforms paved the way for the sweeping changes of the twentieth century. In the realm of law, what began as a reform of the Qing Code culminated in the promulgation of new criminal and civil codes that reflected the influence of the various European legal systems that inspired them.[10]

A parallel development unfolded in the social realm. In the late imperial era, Confucianism made concubinage legally permissible, socially acceptable and even morally justifiable. The Confucian value of filial piety made continuing the family line the principal duty of every man. Concubinage offered a married man an opportunity to sire a son with a woman other than his wife.[11] In this way, concubinage in China reflected the related practice of polygyny in Siam and Egypt in the same period.[12] Although regarded as socially inferior to a son of the legal wife, a concubine's son was a legitimate heir. By the turn of the twentieth century, however, the introduction of Western notions of monogamy and equality between men and women challenged the system of concubinage and the Confucian family model it supported, particularly in the cities. In this sense, too, the transformation of family practices in China at the turn of the twentieth century reflected that in Egypt and Siam, where European marital norms also proved influential, as Kenneth M. Cuno and Tamara Loos show in their chapters in this book. Keith McMahon's analysis of late Qing literary texts demonstrates 'how the dominant sexual regime of polygamy met its first stage of paradigmatic change in the nineteenth century'.[13] By the early twentieth century, the definition of family came to centre on husbands and wives.[14] As a consequence, marriage came to be viewed less as a joining of two families than as a union between a man and a woman. Conjugal happiness now replaced patrilineal succession as the goal of marriage and family, as seen in the new laws and regulations promulgated by the GMD and the CCP. Both espoused the principles of monogamy and equality as the pillars of marriage; not surprisingly, both the GMD and the CCP targeted concubinage, if in different ways.

The redefinition of concubinage by the GMD and the CCP as adultery and bigamy, respectively, aimed to eliminate the custom, reflecting the increasing power of the state over private family matters. The GMD's eventual criminalization of concubinage as adultery reflected the state's concern with regulating sexuality, both male and female.[15] The CCP's criminalization of concubinage as bigamy reflected the state's goal to eliminate 'feudal customs' through the marriage registration system. In so doing, the CCP made government approval rather than social convention the basis of a valid marriage.[16] In short, GMD and CCP efforts to end concubinage reflected the growth of state power at the expense of patriarchal authority.[17]

The Confucian Marriage System

In the Qing era, as in earlier dynasties, the influence of Confucianism led the state to link political and social stability to family harmony. Confucian ideology held that maintenance of proper hierarchical family relationships was the basis for social and political order; filial children who obeyed their parents made loyal subjects who obeyed their emperor.[18] The system of marriage reflected the Confucian principles which privileged the family over the individual, the elderly over the young and men over women. Three of the five cardinal relationships in Confucianism called for wifely obedience, filial piety towards parents and respect towards older brothers.[19] Marriage practices throughout Qing China reflected this deference to patriarchal authority. Parents (or in their absence, senior relatives) arranged marriages for their children.

The purpose of marriage was to continue the patriline; thus, producing sons was the main task of the couple. Without a son to marry and have sons of his own, there would be no descendants to pay homage to the ancestors.[20] Although the custom of ancestor reverence predated Confucianism, it became associated with the Confucian value of filial piety. Every man's filial obligation was to beget sons to ensure that there would be descendants to perform the ancestral sacrifices. A household without sons was considered extinct. Having a son also secured a couple's means of support when they were no longer able to take care of themselves. Given that marriage was patrilocal, a woman was not considered a permanent member of her birth family and was not expected to take care of her parents in their old age. Upon marriage, she usually moved into the man's household, was incorporated into his family line and was expected to provide loyal service to her parents-in-law.[21] Indeed, the selection of a wife was sometimes described as finding a daughter-in-law. To not have a son, then, was to be left destitute in one's old age and to commit the most unfilial of acts by allowing the patriline to end.

To avoid such a fate, a sonless couple could turn to the husband's brothers. If a man had a brother who had at least two sons, one son would continue his father's family line, and the other son would continue his uncle's family line. In cases where there was only one son to be shared among brothers, the son could marry two wives: one to carry on his father's line, the other to continue his uncle's line. Although the wives married in the practice of combined succession (*jiantiao*) were regarded as having equal status, the Board of Rites, the judicial arm of the Qing state, only recognized the first woman married as the legal wife; the subsequent wife was considered to have the status of a concubine. In the 1814 case that established this legal precedent, the Board of Rites acknowledged that She Dusheng was 'simultaneously married to two wives' (*erqi bingqu*).[22] Qing law required that the second marriage be dissolved, but by a legal sleight of hand, the Board of Rites left intact both marriages concluded in the practice of combined succession by categorizing any wife married after the first wife as a concubine.[23]

However, the wives married in the practice of combined succession were different from concubines. Their legal status notwithstanding, the wives were equal in rank. Their sons represented different branches of the patriline, and neither wife had any legal claim to the other woman's children.[24] In contrast, a woman who entered the household as a concubine was in a subordinate position to the main wife. By law and custom, the main wife held the same rights over a concubine's children as she did over her own children. Regardless of which woman gave birth, the children sired by the man belonged to the main wife. In this respect, concubinage fulfilled a similar function to the modern practice of surrogacy. In both, the couple had a legal claim to the baby. Both viewed a woman's womb as a space that could be borrowed, leased or owned.[25] When the Qing official Xu Yingkui wished to honour his concubine mother when she passed away, the main wife of his father told him, 'You were an embryonic dragon, nurtured temporarily in a dog's belly.'[26] By comparing him to a dragon, a traditional symbol of power, strength and luck, the main wife acknowledged the greatness of Xu's achievements and character. However, by comparing his birth mother to a dog and describing his connection with her as temporary, the main wife denigrated and minimized the biological link he had to his birth mother.

Although the birth mother held no rights over her child, she could expect maintenance; both a concubine in Qing China and a surrogate in today's world were entitled to support during their tenure of service. Of course, there were important differences, the most obvious one being the means of conception. A concubine was impregnated through the act of sexual intercourse while a modern-day surrogate would be artificially inseminated with the man's sperm.[27] And while a couple's relationship with the surrogate usually ended after the birth of the child, a couple's relationship with a concubine could last a lifetime. While both surrogacy and concubinage served a reproductive purpose, the latter also fulfilled other aims.

Concubinage offered benefits to both husband and wife. Since marriages were arranged, concubinage offered the husband a way to meet needs he was unable to satisfy with his wife, both sexual and emotional. The writings of the Song dynasty (960–1279) poet Su Shi reflect his enduring affection for his favourite concubine, Morning Cloud.[28] A concubine was also a status symbol, both of the man's wealth and of his virility. Su Shi composed a famous poem describing how his friend, Zhang Xian, was still purchasing concubines at the age of eighty-five.[29] Edward Henderson, a physician living in Shanghai in the early 1870s, made the following generalization about men who purchased concubines: 'Many rich Chinamen regard the payments of these large sums as public proofs of their superior wealth, and will shew (*sic*) wives so obtained with pride, boasting of the money they have cost.'[30] Furthermore, wives sometimes selected a concubine for their husbands. In his autobiography, Shen Fu, a member of the lower gentry who lived during the height of the Qing dynasty, described how his wife 'was obsessed with the idea of finding me a concubine'.[31] A concubine could fulfil the sexual, reproductive and domestic duties of marriage on the wife's behalf without undermining the wife's legal or social position.[32]

To be sure, a wife could feel threatened by or jealous of her husband's relationship with a concubine, although these feelings were minimized when a main wife 'managed' her husband's relationship with a concubine by either establishing an alliance with the concubine or selecting the concubine herself.[33] Although a concubine could replace a wife in the husband's heart or even run the household, a concubine could not usurp the wife's status as legal wife as long as the wife was alive. The law punished any attempt to do so.[34] To blur the status distinction between wife and concubine would rupture the kinship and ritual ties between the families of the husband and wife, thereby creating chaos in a social universe defined by Confucian ideals.

Concubinage as a Semi-Marital Union in the Qing

Although the law never recognized concubinage as a valid marriage, it did acknowledge the similarities between wife and concubine. Numerous statutes in the Qing Code mentioned the wife and concubine together, often making both equally liable for the same crimes. In light of the fact that liability and punishments were determined on the basis of the nature of the relationship between the parties involved, the treatment of a concubine as a wife in these statutes indicates the law's concession that a concubine's relationship with certain members of the household mirrored a wife's relationship with those members. This was particularly true in crimes categorized as illicit sex because a wife or concubine who engaged in sex with another man injured the husband.

The statutes on adultery and incest suggest that Qing law viewed the concubine as a carrier of a man's family line. Consequently, a concubine was held to the same standard of sexual fidelity as a wife; for both wife and concubine, sex with another man polluted the patriline. For this reason, the concubine was included in the statute on adultery. The statutes on incest evinced a similar logic. Sex with the concubine of one's father, paternal grandfather or other male relative was categorized as incest.[35] By punishing such acts as incest, Qing law implicitly acknowledged the kinship relationship between a concubine and the male relatives of her master.

While a concubine faced the same punishment as a wife for giving herself to another man, she could also enjoy the same benefits as a wife for remaining faithful to her master. The law protected a widowed concubine's right to reside in and be supported by her deceased master's household for as long as she remained faithful to his memory.[36] In addition, the Qing cult of chastity offered a widowed concubine who refused to remarry and devoted her life to taking care of her master's family the opportunity to earn imperial honours. A widowed concubine who committed suicide out of grief or to avoid remarriage could also gain recognition as a virtuous widow. For example, in 1903, the concubine Wang née Zhu received imperial recognition after she committed suicide following her master's death.[37] Local gazetteers also featured widowed concubines in stories honouring chaste wives. The biography of a concubine surnamed Zhang, who was widowed when she was in her early twenties and remained faithful to her master her entire life, reported the concubine to have said, 'Wives and concubines are different [in status], but their duty is the same.'[38] For widowed concubines, chastity offered a way to access the privileges of the legal wife, in both life and death.

Naming practices also reflected the semi-marital status of concubines, as evidenced in the frequency with which the words for wife (*taitai, laopo*) appeared in popular phrases for concubine. A concubine was called a minor wife (*xiao taitai, xiao laopo*) or second wife (*er taitai*).[39] These terms of address highlight society's recognition of the concubine as a wife of some sort, as further evidenced in the use of terms for marriage for concubinage as well. The gender-specific words for 'marry' (*qu* for men and *jia* for women) were often used to describe the acquisition of a concubine. The character *qu* can be translated as 'to take a woman as wife'; when applied to a concubine, it was understood as 'to take a woman as concubine'. The character *jia* conveys the meaning of transfer of authority over the woman from her father to her husband/master. In this respect, the application of the words for marry to concubinage reaffirmed patriarchal authority by making the man the active agent who did the 'taking' and the woman a passive being that was 'handed over' from one man to another.

Although concubinage shared many features with marriage, Qing law and society never mistook one for the other. On the one hand, a concubine fulfilled many of the same roles as a wife, the most important one being producing sons to carry on the patriline. Hence, a concubine, just like a wife, could not have the same surname as the man to ensure that the two did not share any ancestors, however distant.[40] On the other hand, a concubine was subordinate to the wife in every respect. A concubine who usurped a wife's position while the wife was still living and able to carry out her duties faced legal sanction and public criticism.[41] Although the line separating concubinage from marriage was fine, it was strictly guarded by law and custom. In the Qing dynasty, concubinage was part of a Confucian family system strengthened and perpetuated by Qing law.[42] When Confucianism came under attack in the early twentieth century, so too did concubinage and the set of laws that protected it. With the introduction of Western notions of monogamy and equality, the meaning and purpose of marriage came to centre on the conjugal unit, which held important implications for the custom of concubinage.

Concubinage as Adultery under GMD Law

Defeat in a series of wars with foreign powers throughout the nineteenth century resulted in the division of China into spheres of influence that undermined Chinese sovereignty. In an attempt to regain control of their country, reformers introduced changes that transformed Chinese politics, economics, society, culture and law, although the effects of most of these changes were limited to the areas in eastern China controlled by the GMD. In the realm of law, the codes promulgated by the GMD represented the culmination of decades of legal reform that had begun in the late Qing dynasty. The criminal code (promulgated in 1928 and revised in 1935) and the civil code (issued in parts in 1929 and 1930) were based on earlier versions that had existed in provisional or draft form since the late nineteenth century.

The civil code marked a departure from Chinese legal tradition in a number of ways. To start with, it was the first of its kind. Although the Qing Code contained provisions that dealt with civil matters, there was not a clear separation between civil and criminal law.[43] In its approach to the law, the civil code also broke from late imperial practice, which looked to the circumstances in each case to determine the nature of the crime and the appropriate sentence. Instead, the civil code began with a set of Western-inspired principles that informed specific laws.[44]

The civil code introduced a new conception of marriage and family based on monogamy and equality. Driving this change were the New Culture movement (1915–25), also referred to as the May Fourth movement, and a burgeoning women's movement.[45] Dominated by young men and women from elite families and inspired by Western ideas, many of them introduced via Japan, these movements railed against a Confucian family system now perceived as oppressive and criticized sexual norms that only demanded chastity from women.[46] As a result of expanded educational opportunities, women's voices entered the public discourse on an unprecedented scale, and women from the middle and upper classes established organizations and magazines to actively campaign for such issues as female suffrage and legal equality.[47] Increased literacy rates and the proliferation of periodicals combined with the weakness of state controls over the media created a growing urban readership that influenced public policy.[48] To a great extent, lawmakers' decision to make the conjugal unit rather than the patriline the centre of family law reflected the role of public opinion in shaping legal reform.

This shift in the law's focus robbed concubinage of its patrilineal justification. Lawmakers agreed the custom had to end, but they believed it would eventually disappear on its own as social attitudes changed. In the meantime, they treated concubinage as adultery. Since adultery was listed as one of the grounds for divorce in the civil code, a wife could now divorce her husband for having a concubine. Exceptions, however, weakened the force of the law. If the wife had consented to her husband acquiring a concubine or tolerated his concubine after the fact, then she forfeited legal cause. The courts' liberal interpretation of consent and tolerance more often than not resulted in a denial of divorce suits initiated by wives who only had as legal grounds their husband's relationship with his concubine.[49] The treatment of concubinage as adultery under civil law, then, largely left concubinage arrangements intact. When lawmakers decided to treat concubinage as adultery in the civil code, husbands were not criminally liable for adultery. The criminal code promulgated in 1928 had retained the Qing provision on adultery, which punished wives and their lovers. A married man would only be punished if he had sex with another married woman, and even then, his punishment was for abetting the woman in her crime of adultery, not for committing adultery himself. The Qing understanding of adultery as sexual activities that could potentially pollute the patriline continued to influence the 1928 criminal code; defined in this way, adultery continued to be a crime for wives only, while husbands who had sex with unmarried women were not punished.

In light of lawmakers' avowed commitment to the principle of equality, this glaring example of legal inequality did not go unnoticed. When lawmakers set to the task of revising the criminal code in the early 1930s, women's groups launched a public campaign to pressure lawmakers into either making husbands equally liable for adultery or expunging the adultery law altogether. In the previous decade, women's groups had been unsuccessful in getting lawmakers to criminalize concubinage as bigamy in the 1928 criminal code; they did not want to lose this next legal battle.[50] The Society of Women's United Voice (*Funü gongmingshe*), the Shanghai chapter of the Young Women's Christian Association of China (*Zhonghua jidujiao nü qingnianhui*) and the Shanghai Women's Circle (*Funü jie*) used the journals they published to pressure lawmakers to uphold equality for men and women.[51] Guo Qingbai, a contributor to one of the many women's magazines covering the issue, reasoned, 'The spirit of national legislation lies in equality. Under the law, men and women should have equal opportunities and rights. It cannot permit men to engage in illicit sex but restrict women [from the same].'[52] After extensive debate, lawmakers revised the adultery law to include husbands. The adultery provision in the 1935 revised criminal code read, 'Whoever, being married, commits adultery with any person, shall be punished with imprisonment for not more than one year. The other party to such adultery shall be liable to the same punishment.'[53] For the first time in Chinese history, men faced both civil and criminal sanctions for being unfaithful to their wives, at least in theory. As noted above, loopholes in the law made it difficult for wives to take advantage of the civil provisions on adultery to attack their husbands' relationships with concubines, and the absence in the case records of any husband being convicted of adultery for having a concubine attests to the weakness of the new adultery law in the criminal code.

In many respects, GMD law's categorization of concubinage as adultery gave legal force to the new value of conjugal fidelity that now replaced the patriline as the foundation of the institution of marriage. The 'small family' replaced the 'five generations under the same roof' as the ideal family structure. In the latter, the patriline determined degrees of kinship; consequently, paternal relatives mattered more than maternal relatives and a wife's relatives. In the former, a new conception of kinship emerged that centred on the conjugal unit; spousal relations were now important in their own right, and relatives were categorized as either by blood or through marriage.[54] The new emphasis on the conjugal unit in legal conceptions of marriage erased the space concubinage had occupied within the patrilineal kinship structure. Despite the concubine's social identity as minor wife, GMD lawmakers continued the Qing practice of denying legal status as wives to concubines. But unlike their Qing predecessors, GMD jurists had no category of 'concubine' they could use since they had eliminated it from the legal codes. Early Republican judges had considered the concubine a household member; the GMD Supreme Court followed suit, placing the concubine in the category of household members who were not related by either blood or marriage.[55]

As household members, concubines could no longer be expelled from the household without just cause, and they were legally entitled to maintenance for as long as they remained in the household.[56] However, the discretion judges enjoyed in determining what constituted just cause weakened a concubine's claim to the rights of household membership. In a 1937 case, the Supreme Court accepted as evidence of adultery love letters that a widowed concubine had exchanged with another man.[57] Since the court did not refer to any actual evidence of sexual relations between the widowed concubine and her male correspondent, the love letters appear to have constituted just cause in this case. A concubine's claim to maintenance was also weakened by the residency requirement attached to household membership. In 1933, the Supreme Court rejected a concubine's suit demanding maintenance on the grounds that she had moved out of the household the previous summer.[58] However limited, the recognition of concubines as household members did give concubines a new legal basis upon which they could claim rights and protections.

To a great extent, the recognition of concubines as household members reflected the lawmakers' goal of distancing concubinage from marriage. However, legal intent notwithstanding, the requirements for marriage specified in the civil code sometimes led judges to grant legal wife status to a woman whom they conceded was a concubine. Article 982 listed only two criteria for a valid marriage: an open ceremony and two witnesses. That opened the door for a concubine to argue that the ceremony marking her entry into the household met the legal criteria for marriage. A ceremony was sometimes performed to mark a concubine's entry into the household, reflecting the semi-marital nature of concubinage. Qing law did not invest the ceremony with any legal meaning; Article 982 did.[59] As long as there was evidence of a ceremony, then in the eyes of the law if not society, a concubine was a legal wife.[60] In such cases, the court had no choice but to issue a guilty verdict if a bigamy charge had been lodged.

The majority of bigamy cases were instigated by the concubine or her parents to wrest from the man a financial settlement. In 1943, the concubine Sun Shumin charged Wang Shoushan with bigamy. Satisfied with the evidence that a ceremony had occurred, the Beijing District Court convicted Wang of bigamy, which he promptly appealed. In the meantime, Wang agreed to pay his concubine compensatory damages as well as child support if she agreed to recant her story when the case appeared before the Hebei Superior Court, which she obligingly did. However, the court saw through the scheme, remarking in its judgement that the concubine changed her story after Wang agreed to a financial settlement, and that her new story that they had been merely living together was to 'exonerate' Wang.[61] The court upheld the conviction, although in light of the circumstances, it did commute the sentence from six to three months of imprisonment.

In bigamy cases, the concubine and her parents claimed to be victims of marriage fraud; they denied knowledge of the man's true marital status when the ceremony had been performed. However, if the concubine refused to go along with that story, then she too could be convicted of bigamy. Such was the case with the concubines Li Erbao and Zhao Meibao who in two unrelated cases were both convicted of knowingly entering into a bigamous marriage when they refused to corroborate their respective mothers' stories of marriage fraud.[62] The bigamy law only worked to the advantage of concubines when they convinced the court that they believed themselves to have been married as wives. However, a bigamy conviction in these cases should not be misinterpreted as de jure recognition of concubinage as marriage. The legal framework within which GMD judges operated required them to recognize as a valid marriage any union that met the ceremony and witness requirements of Article 982. Not all cases of concubinage met the criteria; a concubine who failed to convince the court that a ceremony had been performed when she entered the household had no other legal grounds to prove marriage. Judges issued bigamy convictions in cases that were clearly concubinage because the legal requirements for marriage had been met, not because the woman was a concubine.

Concubinage as Bigamy under CCP Law

While the recognition of concubinage as bigamy was an exception under GMD law, it eventually became the rule under CCP law. The legal rationale for the treatment of concubinage as bigamy first appeared in handbooks on the 1950 Marriage Law and was elaborated in judicial interpretations. CCP law considered concubinage to be de facto marriage, defined as a union that resembled marriage in all respects but that had not been officially registered with the government. Unions categorized as de facto marriage were distinguished from other forms of cohabitation, which the law did not consider to be marriage. In recognizing concubinage as de facto marriage rather than cohabitation, the CCP gave legal force to the semi-marital features of concubinage and legally recognized what women's groups since the 1920s had been saying: concubinage constituted bigamy. Although the CCP treated concubinage as de facto marriage, the two were not the same. By definition, de facto marriage referred to a marriage that had not been formally registered with the government. Since the marriage registration system was still being rolled out across the country, most marriages fell into this category. The legal recognition of such unions as legally valid was a short-term strategy to deal with the current situation; the long-term goal was to instil in the populace the habit of registering their marriages with the vast network of marriage bureaus to be established.

Cases of concubinage, however, would have never been registered as marriage. For all that concubinage resembled marriage, no man would have sought official recognition of his relationship with a concubine as marriage. Even in the unlikely scenario that a man and his concubine tried to register their union with the government, their request would have been denied since concubinage was prohibited under the Marriage Law. The identification of concubinage as de facto marriage – and more broadly the legal recognition of de facto marriage as a valid marriage – was intended to be a temporary measure. The permanent solution was to prevent such unions from forming in the first place. To this end, the CCP focused its efforts on raising public awareness of the provisions in the 1950 Marriage Law and the new legal requirement to register marriages with the government.

The CCP soon realized that many of its cadres had a poor grasp of the Marriage Law or simply ignored it, resulting in a number of mishandled cases. In 1951, Zhang Xueyan, chief judge of the Chuanbei People's Court in Sichuan province, circulated a bulletin reviewing the errors in a number of cases in an effort to educate judges on the principles of the Marriage Law. In one case, a concubine's multiple requests for divorce were not only denied but also resulted in her being locked up each time; the entire village was also mobilized to struggle against her. In another case, a concubine who cited abuse from her husband and the main wife as grounds for divorce was informed that she needed to have twenty-four reasons before a divorce could be granted.[63] In both of these cases, the requests for divorce should have been automatically granted simply because the women were concubines.[64]

To prevent miscarriages of justice, the CCP launched the Marriage Law Campaign in the early spring of 1953. CCP officials regarded the campaign as a critical step in the creation of a marriage system that would be regulated and protected by the state. The Directive of the Government Administrative Council Concerning the Thorough Implementation of the Marriage Law, issued in February 1953, compared marriage reform to 'thought struggle' and identified 'propaganda' and 'education' as the main tools in this endeavour aimed at both 'the broad masses and the cadres' to root out 'feudal' influences and establish 'the new democratic marriage system'.[65]

Not surprisingly, many men with concubines panicked, fearing that their concubines would be 'confiscated' just as their property had been.[66] Towards concubinage, however, the CCP adopted a preventive rather than punitive approach. Existing relationships were left alone unless one of the parties made a request for divorce. Courts were to grant the divorce if the wife or concubine requested it. If the husband wanted the divorce, or if the wife demanded that her husband divorce the concubine, then the court based its decision on its assessment of the 'emotional relationship' (*ganqing*) of each marriage, decreeing divorce in the one the court deemed to have the weakest foundation, which did not always correspond with the litigant's original request.[67] In a model case from 1950, the main wife Jia Changxiu asked the court to divorce her husband Zhang Huashu from his concubine Wu Zhixiu. While the husband professed his undying love for his concubine, his concubine agreed to the divorce, provided that she receive an exorbitant sum for her living expenses. At this point, the wife asked that *she* be the one divorced from the husband, apparently preferring to be a well-compensated divorcée than a woman stuck in a marriage with a man who had openly professed his love for another woman. The court investigated the family situation to determine which marriage had the strongest chance of surviving. After taking into consideration the husband's attachment to his concubine, the concubine's willingness to remain married to him and the wife's last-minute request to be the one divorced, the court decreed divorce between the husband and wife.[68] The court's decision was based less on what the litigants wanted than on which marriage the court deemed to have the weakest foundation, reflecting the interventionist role of the state in the family. According to the letter of the law, new cases of concubinage, which were now defined as those occurring after the close of the Marriage Law Campaign in 1953 rather than the promulgation of the Marriage Law in 1950 as had originally been the case, were to be prosecuted as bigamy. The inaccessibility of court cases after 1949 makes it impossible to ascertain how vigorously the state pursued reports of new cases of concubinage. With the exception of a handful of show trials conducted immediately after the promulgation of the Marriage Law, the model cases featured in the state-controlled media indicate a preference for handling concubinage cases through the civil provisions on divorce rather than through criminal prosecution as bigamy.

With the passage of a new Marriage Law in 1980, the provision on concubinage disappeared, leaving only the prohibition against bigamy. Speaking on behalf of the national procurator's office in Beijing, Ma Yaqing explained that 'because of the last 30 years of carrying out propaganda after the promulgation of the [1950] Marriage Law, monogamy has deeply penetrated popular feeling; the conduct of taking concubines basically does not exist in society'.[69] To be sure, concubinage as it had been practised in the Qing dynasty and in the first half of the twentieth century no longer exists in China today. But one wonders to what extent 'propaganda' deserves all the credit for its disappearance.

Conclusion

When viewed over the course of the last four centuries, the treatment of concubinage under Qing, GMD and CCP laws reflects important changes in the meaning and purpose of marriage. In the Qing era, patrilineal and patriarchal values prevailed; marriage was viewed as the means to continue the male line and it served the interests of the parents rather than the married couple. Qing law tolerated the custom of concubinage because it supported the Confucian family system endorsed by the state. By the late Qing era, however, Western ideas found a receptive audience among many Chinese reformers who blamed Confucianism for holding their country back. They envisioned a new family system centred on the conjugal couple and sought to create a legal framework based upon what they identified as the 'modern' ideals of monogamy and equality. After the collapse of the Qing dynasty, the GMD completed this task with the promulgation of new legal codes that defined marriage as a union entered into freely by a man and a woman. The concubine was now regarded as an interloper, and GMD law provided the wife with legal recourse if she was unhappy with her husband's relationship with the concubine. If the wife made no complaint, GMD jurists, like their Qing predecessors, continued to tolerate concubinage.

The CCP also espoused the principles of monogamy and equality in their marriage laws, but in contrast to the GMD, the CCP treated concubinage as de facto marriage, which was accepted as legally valid; hence concubinage constituted bigamy. By categorizing concubinage as bigamy, the CCP transformed what had been a crime against an individual into a crime against society. Yet, although the state held the prerogative to prosecute men for taking a concubine, in most cases, if the wife or concubine made no complaint, the CCP opted to not prosecute, preferring instead to apply the laws on divorce to cases of concubinage. In this respect, the CCP's handling of cases of concubinage resembled that of the GMD; both left intact existing concubinage arrangements unless an involved party (the wife under GMD law, and the wife or the concubine under CCP law) filed charges with the court. To be sure, the last century has witnessed the decline and eventual disappearance of concubinage. The legal and social landscape of early-twentieth-century China proved hostile to a custom associated with a Confucian tradition now under attack. As conjugal fidelity replaced patrilineal obligations as the foundation of marriage, concubinage came to be seen as undermining rather than strengthening the institution of marriage. The principles of monogamy and equality, now codified as law, transformed concubinage from a custom tolerated by the state into a prosecutable offence.

Notes

1. Kathryn Bernhardt, *Women and Property in China, 960–1949* (Stanford: Stanford University Press, 1999), 173–4.
2. Shanghai Municipal Archives (hereafter SMA) Q185.2.6492.
3. Wang Naicong, *Hunyinfa wenti jieda huibian* (Compendium of questions and answers on the Marriage Law) (Beijing: Wenhua gongyingshe, 1951), 21–2.
4. This chapter addresses concubinage as a popular custom; royal or imperial concubinage is not considered. Literature, gazetteers and court cases suggest that concubinage was a regular feature of marriage patterns well into the twentieth century. Although more prevalent among the elite (about 10 per cent of households), concubinage also existed in some peasant households. See Keith McMahon, *Polygamy and Sublime Passion: Sexuality in China on the Verge of Modernity* (Honolulu: University of Hawaii, 2010), 2; Matthew H. Sommer, *Polyandry and Wife-Selling in Qing Dynasty China: Survival Strategies and Judicial Interventions* (Berkeley: University of California Press, 2015). The practice of concubinage was also generally consistent throughout China, although regional and class differences contributed to variations in the way a concubine was acquired.
5. Anthropological studies draw attention to the female-centred spaces of the Chinese family, its corporate features and the private realms of family life. For representative works, see Margery Wolf, *Women and the Family in Rural Taiwan* (Stanford: Stanford University Press, 1972); Myron L. Cohen, *House United, House Divided: The Chinese Family in Taiwan* (New York: Columbia University Press, 1976); Yunxiang Yan, *Private Life Under Socialism: Love, Intimacy, and Family Change in a Chinese Village, 1949-1999* (Stanford: Stanford University Press, 2003).
6. Susan L. Glosser, *Chinese Visions of Family and State, 1915-1953* (Berkeley: University of California Press, 2003).
7. Bernhardt, *Women and Property*; Harriet Evans, *Women and Sexuality in China: Female Sexuality and Gender Since 1949* (New York: Continuum, 1997).
8. Xue Yunsheng, *Duli cunyi* (Doubts remaining after perusing the substatutes), ed. Huang Tsing-chia (1905; Taibei: Chinese Materials and Research Aids Service Center, 1970), vol. 5, statute 103.3.
9. Rebecca E. Karl and Peter Zarrow (eds), *Rethinking the 1898 Reform Period: Political and Cultural Change in Late Qing* (Cambridge, MA: Harvard University Press, 2002).
10. For representative works, see Philip C. C. Huang, *Code, Custom, and Legal Practice in China: The Qing and the Republic Compared* (Stanford: Stanford University Press,

2001); Xu Xiaoqun, *Trial of Modernity: Judicial Reform in Early Twentieth-Century China, 1901–1937* (Stanford: Stanford University Press, 2008).

11 The Qing Code, which was an amalgamation of previous dynastic legal codes dating back to the Tang dynasty (618–907), included a law that only permitted men over the age of forty who still had no sons to have a concubine; however, the law was deleted in 1740 (Bernhardt, *Women and Property*, 161–2, n.1).

12 See Tamara Loos, 'The Birth of Mistresses and Bastards: A History of Marriage in Siam (Thailand)' and Kenneth M. Cuno, 'Modernizing Marriage in Egypt'.

13 McMahon, *Polygamy and Sublime Passion*, 1.

14 Glosser, *Chinese Visions*; Lisa Tran, 'Adultery, Bigamy, and Conjugal Fidelity: The ABC's of Monogamy in Republican China', *Twentieth-Century China* 36, no. 2 (May 2011), 99–118; Margaret Kuo, *Intolerable Cruelty: Marriage, Law, and Society in Early Twentieth-Century China* (Lanham, MD: Rowman & Littlefield, 2012).

15 Female sexuality had always been regulated. See Matthew Sommer, *Sex, Law, and Society in Late Imperial China* (Stanford: Stanford University Press, 2000); Lisa Tran, 'Sex and Equality in Republican China: The Debate over the Adultery Law', *Modern China* 35, no. 2 (March 2009): 191–223.

16 Although most marriages were recorded by a 'marriage document', it held no legal validity. The GMD considered a marriage legally valid when a wedding ceremony in accordance with local custom had been performed; a marriage document could be used as supporting evidence, but it held no legal force (Vermier Y. Chiu, *Marriage Laws and Customs of China* (Hong Kong: Chinese University of Hong Kong, 1966); Lisa Tran, *Concubines in Court: Marriage and Monogamy in Twentieth-Century China* (Lanham, MD: Rowman & Littlefield, 2015), 103–28.

17 Glosser, *Chinese Visions*; Judith Stacey, *Patriarchy and Socialist Revolution in China* (Berkeley: University of California Press, 1983).

18 For an exemplary study of the relationship between the Qing state's regulation of sexuality and the maintenance of social and political order, see Sommer, *Sex, Law, and Society*.

19 The other two relationships were emperor and subject, and friend and friend.

20 Before marriage, women participated in the ancestral sacrifices of their natal family. After marriage, they were incorporated into their husband's family line and paid homage to his ancestors.

21 An exception to this general rule was an uxorilocal marriage, in which the husband assumed residence in his wife's parents' household. This kind of marriage offered couples who only had a daughter to continue the patriline as the children of uxorilocal marriages took the mother's rather than the father's surname. See Patricia Buckley Ebrey, *The Inner Quarters: Marriage and the Lives of Chinese Women in the Sung Period* (Berkeley: University of California Press, 1993), 235–49; Arthur P. Wolf and Chieh-shan Huang, *Marriage and Adoption in China, 1845–1945* (Stanford: Stanford University Press, 1980), 94–101.

22 Bernhardt, *Women and Property*, 183–4.

23 The change in their mother's legal status, however, did not change the children's relationship to the patriline; the children of the wife the law deemed a concubine still belonged to the junior branch.

24 In general, both wives lived in the same household; however, if the wives did not get along and if the husband could afford it, they lived in separate households.

25 For the various customs that supported surrogate motherhood among the poor, see Sommer, *Polyandry and Wife-Selling*.

26 As cited in Francesca Bray, *Technology and Gender: Fabrics of Power in Late Imperial China* (Berkeley: University of California, 1997), 354.
27 Technology offers couples today a variety of options, including in vitro fertilization in which the embryo is placed in the uterus of the surrogate. In this case, the surrogate carries the embryo to term but has no genetic link to the baby. This type of surrogacy would not be comparable to concubinage as the concubine was the biological mother of the child.
28 Beverly J. Bossler, *Courtesans, Concubines, and the Cult of Female Fidelity* (Cambridge, MA: Harvard University Asia Center, 2013), 93–9.
29 Ibid., 84.
30 As cited in Sommer, *Polyandry and Wife-Selling*, 178.
31 Shen Fu, *Six Records of a Floating Life* (Harmondsworth: Penguin, 1983), 48.
32 Ebrey, *The Inner Quarters*, 217–34; Bray, *Technology and Gender*, 351–8.
33 McMahon, *Polygamy and Sublime Passion*, 141–3.
34 The demotion of a wife to concubine status was punished with 100 strokes of heavy bamboo, and the promotion of a concubine to wife status during the wife's lifetime was punished with 90 strokes of heavy bamboo (Xue, *Duli cunyi*, statutes 103.1 and 103.2).
35 Xue, *Duli cunyi*, statutes 367, 368.3, 368.4. The definition of incest was based on the male line, so a man who had sex with his concubine's sisters, for example, did not commit incest.
36 Ibid., statute 105.3.
37 Bernhardt, *Women and Property*, 170–2.
38 As cited in ibid., 171.
39 If there was more than one concubine, then the other concubines were referred to as third wife, fourth wife and so on. The formal term for wife, *qi*, was generally reserved for the legal wife (as in *diqi, zhengqi, faqi*). Although pronounced differently in the various dialects spoken in China, the written characters were the same across the country and held the same meaning.
40 Patricia Buckley Ebrey, *Women and the Family in Chinese History* (New York: Routledge, 2003), 42. The prohibition of single-surname marriage was based on the assumption that two people who shared the same surname also shared a male ancestor. In the eyes of Chinese society, marriage between two people with the same surname constituted incest.
41 After the death of the legal wife, the man had the prerogative to promote a concubine to legal wife status.
42 Ch'u T'ung-tsu, *Law and Society in Traditional China* (Paris: Mouten, 1961).
43 The civil provisions in the Qing Code were concentrated in the 'Household Law' section, which in the early-twentieth-century compilation comprised 300 of the 1,907 substatutes in the code (Philip C. C. Huang, *Civil Justice in China: Representation and Practice in the Qing* (Stanford: Stanford University Press, 1996). Magistrates routinely referred to these substatutes in their adjudication of civil cases.
44 Huang, *Code, Custom, and Legal Practice*, 49–68.
45 Wang Zheng, *Women in the Chinese Enlightenment: Oral and Textual Histories* (Berkeley: University of California Press, 1999).
46 See, for instance, Ba Jin [Pa Chin], *Family* (Long Grove, IL: Waveland Press, 1972).
47 Xiaoping Cong, *Teachers' Schools and the Making of the Modern Chinese Nation-State, 1897–1937* (Vancouver: University of British Columbia Press, 2007); Louise Edwards, *Gender, Politics, and Democracy: Women's Suffrage in China* (Stanford:

Stanford University Press, 2008); Elizabeth R. VanderVen, *A School in Every Village: Educational Reform in a Northeast China County, 1904-31* (Vancouver: University of British Columbia Press, 2012).
48 Eugenia Lean, *Public Passions: The Trial of Shi Jianqiao and the Rise of Popular Sympathy in Republican China* (Berkeley: University of California Press, 2007).
49 Kathryn Bernhardt, 'Women and the Law: Divorce in the Republican Period', in *Civil Law in Qing and Republican China*, ed. Kathryn Bernhardt and Philip C. C. Huang (Stanford: Stanford University Press, 1994), 187-214.
50 Tran, 'Adultery, Bigamy, and Conjugal Fidelity', 110-12.
51 Tran, 'Sex and Equality', 198.
52 Guo Qingbai, 'Funüjie lizhengzhong zhi xianfa cao'an xingfa fuyi wenti' (Women's circles argue strongly for a re-evaluation of the provisional constitution and the criminal code issue), *Nüzi yuekan* (Ladies' monthly) 2, no. 12, 1 December 1934, 3419-20.
53 *Zhonghua minguo xingfa* (The criminal code of the Republic of China), English title: The Chinese Criminal Code and Special Criminal and Administrative Laws, Bilingual edition. Tr. Legal Department of the Shanghai Municipal Council (Shanghai: Commercial Press, 1935), 86.
54 Bernhardt, *Women and Property*, 107.
55 Guo Wei and Zhou Dingmei (eds), *Zuigao fayuan minshi panli huikan* (Collected publications of Supreme Court judgements in civil law) (Shanghai: Faxue shuju, 1934), vol. 17, 60.
56 Bernhardt, 'Women and the Law', 210-1; Bernhardt, *Women and Property*, 191-5.
57 Fu Bingchang and Zhou Dingyu (eds), *Zhonghua minguo liufa liyou pan jie huibian* (Compendium of the six laws of the Republic of China, with rationales, judgements and explanations) (Taibei: Xinlu shudian, 1964), vol. 2, 1149.
58 Guo and Zhou, *Zuigao fayuan*, vol. 17, 58-61.
59 Qing law accepted as marriage a union that had been formalized by completion of the Six Rites, only one of which was the ceremony (Chiu, *Marriage Laws and Customs*, 4-10). The German, French, Swiss and Japanese codes that had been used as models for the civil code all identified marriage registration as a requirement for a legal marriage. Drafts of the Chinese civil code also contained provisions on marriage registration, but they did not appear in the civil code promulgated in 1929 and 1930. Documentary evidence shows that the GMD experimented with marriage registration in Beijing, but did not make it a requirement for a legal marriage (Zhao Ma, *Runaway Wives, Urban Crimes, and Survival Tactics in Wartime Beijing, 1937-1949* (Cambridge, MA: Harvard University Asia Center, 2015), 206-17).
60 *Xingfa shiyong fenze* (Application of the specific provisions of the criminal code) (Publication of the Sifa xingzhengbu faguan xunliansuo (Bureau of Judicial Administration training institute for judges), n.d.), 124.
61 Beijing Municipal Archives (hereafter BMA) 65.7.12404.
62 BMA 65.8.4981; SMA R43.2.4401.
63 Zhang Xueyan, 'A bulletin regarding incidents of violations of freedom of marriage occurring in various locales in Cangxi, in hopes that People's Courts at all levels will pay attention and self-criticize' (Guanyu Cangxi dengdi fasheng fanghai hunyin ziyou shijian xi geji renmin fayuan zhuyi jiancha de tongbao), *Chuanbei zhengbao* (Chuanbei political bulletin) 2, no. 18 (31 October 1951), 36.
64 *Zhonghua renmin gongheguo minfa cankao ziliao* (Reference materials on civil law of the People's Republic of China) (Beijing: Zhongguo renmin daxue, 1956-7), vol. 3, 576.

65 Marinus J. Meijer, *Marriage Law and Policy in the Chinese People's Republic* (Hong Kong: Hong Kong University Press, 1971), 304–5.
66 Neil Diamant, *Revolutionizing the Family: Politics, Love, and Divorce in Urban and Rural China, 1949–1968* (Berkeley: University of California Press, 2000), 54.
67 For the role of 'emotional relationship' in the CCP's mediation of divorce cases, see Philip C. C. Huang, *Chinese Civil Justice: Past and Present* (Lanham, MD: Rowman & Littlefield, 2010), 87–123.
68 *Dangdai Zhongguo de shenpan gongzuo* (Trial work in contemporary China) (Beijing: Dangdai Zhongguo chubanshe, 1993), 51.
69 Ma Yaqing, *Xin hunyinfa: tiaowen jingshi* (The new marriage law: explanations of the essence of the articles) (Beijing: Zhongguo jiancha chubanshe, 2001), 13.

3

The Birth of Mistresses and Bastards: The History of Modern Marriage in Siam (Thailand)[1]

Tamara Loos

In 1935, Siam's lawmakers adopted monogamy as the kingdom's legal marital standard in place of a range of culturally acceptable conjugal arrangements, including polygyny. The stakes for maintaining polygynous marriage were high for countries like Siam, Egypt, China, India and other non-Western states in the nineteenth century, as explicated by Cuno, Tran and Denault in this book, because imperial countries regularly justified colonization on the basis of social practices considered backward or harmful to native women.[2] In Siam, which maintained its formal independence throughout the colonial era, the government's legitimation of polygyny up to 1935 had legal repercussions. Over a dozen foreign countries hampered Siam's legal sovereignty by imposing extraterritoriality clauses, which exempted foreigners and their Asian subjects from the laws and courts of Siam, from 1855 until 1935, when Siam finally passed the section on marriage in its civil code.[3] Even domestically, polygyny had its detractors, which made the costly decision to maintain this form of marriage until 1935 even more remarkable. Domestic debates over a marital standard – polygyny or monogamy – polarized Siamese along class lines, with segments of the emerging middle class condemning polygyny as a debauched practice of officialdom. Others worried that formally adopting polygyny would harm Siam's reputation internationally, and therefore wished to adopt monogamy in law but allow polygyny in practice.

Despite these imperial and domestic pressures to adopt monogamy over polygyny, Siam's ruling elites, in full awareness of the strategic nature of imperial discourse, initially defended polygyny as a source of their kingdom's cultural authenticity. In fact, Siamese elites, like the royals and dynasts in Europe discussed by Watanabe in Chapter 4 in this book, were reluctant to change their marital practices because it enabled their continued political domination. Paradoxically, polygyny, which was an elite practice that most Siamese did not engage in, came to be seen as *the* representative marital norm for Siam as a consequence of imperial pressures to abolish it. The barrage of moral discourse against polygyny as a sexual vice spouted by imperialists joined with structural transformations in Siam's political economy to render polygyny indefensible except in nativist terms, as a Buddhist tradition. As revealed in this chapter, at the same moment that polygyny's place as a cornerstone of the Siamese political system began to crumble, the elite defence of polygyny intensified, outlasting one of its original political and social functions of integrating the kingdom.[4]

Within a few years of the passage of the monogamy law, the remaining extraterritorial clauses were rescinded by foreign powers. Siam became a legal equal in the international system of nations. Although domestically polygynous unions continued in practice, the myriad paths by which a couple could legally 'marry' narrowed to one. The 1935 law, however, delegitimized existing polygynous unions and their progeny, transforming minor wives into mistresses and producing out-of-wedlock children or bastards for the first time in Siam's history. The law on monogamy ironically created new legal categories of women and children without legal protections, and further empowered men who could engage in polygynous unions with impunity. These ironic reversals that developed as a consequence of imperialist demands for liberal legal reform are explicated below.

Nineteenth-Century Imperialism and the Politics of Polygyny in Siam

Western imperialism in Southeast Asia brought with it both opportunities and perils for Siam's leaders. Since the early sixteenth century, the Portuguese, the Spanish, the Dutch, the British, the French and the Americans arrived in successive and overlapping waves to the shores and then the interiors of the Philippine islands, the Indonesian archipelago, the Malay Peninsula, Borneo, Burma, Vietnam, Cambodia and eventually Laos. Britain expanded gradually beyond India to Singapore and the Malay Peninsula, and into Burma on Siam's western flank, while France claimed areas on Siam's east that became known as French Indochina. By the mid-nineteenth century, a question mark loomed over Siam's head demanding to know for how long Siam would remain sovereign.

Siam's leaders confronted the very real possibility that their kingdom would be carved up by the world's two strongest imperial powers: France and Britain. In the hope of staving this off, a group of Siamese officials and King Mongkut (r. 1851–1868) invited British envoy Sir John Bowring to negotiate a treaty with Siam.[5] Bowring had such strong faith in the alleged mutual benefits of free trade that he militarily forced it upon the Qing dynasty when they refused his offering. After shelling Chinese forts, he headed to Bangkok to negotiate and sign the Bowring Treaty in 1855. The treaty opened Siam to foreign trade, abolished royal monopolies and promised legal protection to foreigners who were not subject to Siamese law.[6] Siam's king proceeded to sign similar treaties with over a dozen additional countries. These treaties would not be rescinded until Siam radically transformed its court system and laws, except for those laws regarding the family that foreign powers considered sacrosanct sources of a people's unique cultural identity.[7]

In the nineteenth century, colonial ethnographic discourse considered family structures the source of a society's uniqueness, which would be protected, in theory, from modern legal change. In colonized countries as well as in independent Siam, foreign powers required drastic legal reforms in the civil and penal codes as part of their 'civilizing' process, but they sought to shield from change family and personal (religious) law. In practice, family and religious codes changed as dramatically as the penal and commercial codes. Nonetheless, the ideology behind the process of modernizing law in colonial and semi-colonial states made family and its marital form overdetermined sites for the creation of Siam's authentic national identity.[8]

By signing the treaties, Siam obviated empire's rationale for colonizing the kingdom. Britain dominated Siam's export trade through such measures, while foreign and Asian subjects of treaty powers could break Siamese law without repercussions. So while Siam alone among its Southeast Asian neighbours maintained its formal political independence, it suffered instead a form of indirect colonization. In return for these concessions to foreign nations, Siam's king and his coterie of supporters maintained their positions at the helm of an imperfectly independent Siam, whose administration they began to centralize and modernize. The kingdom opened to new markets, new technologies and an imperial context that continued to threaten Siam's independence through myriad accusations of backwardness and incivility.

One practice above all provoked foreign judgement: the practice of polygyny, in which most of Siam's ruling elites engaged. The Siamese did not interpret polygyny narrowly as a sign of sexual depravity or Oriental despotism, as many Westerners believed it to be. Instead, polygyny performed three kinds of political work. First, it integrated geographically disparate settlements into the kingdom. Siam's king built personal alliances with heads of provincial settlements through marriage with the latter's daughters. Up to the late nineteenth century, dynastic rule was made possible by the institution of the Inner Palace – the 'harem' – founded upon the gifting of women, which cemented bonds among powerful men. Polygyny differed from other forms of political networking because it, as marriage, was a relationship in process rather than a single event: it enabled political alliances that could be negotiated, altered and deepened over time. The presentation of female relatives by provincial and elite families to the king provided a concrete and continuous connection of blood, communication and loyalty between the monarch and his subordinates. By sending a daughter to the king, fathers in outlying regions proved their allegiance to the king and in return, the monarch would assist the family in various ways such as by conferring gifts appropriate to the rank of the father's position in the government.

As a consequence, the Inner Palace was the residence for up to several thousand women connected to the king through blood, marriage or service (as maids-in-waiting, cooks, slaves and others), or as officials who helped run the all-female city within the palace walls. Not all of these women were the king's consorts and, in fact, the majority of women in the Inner Palace were either servants or female royal family members with retinues of their own. Some of the servant women had husbands and families living outside the palace walls. The women who became queens and consorts were subject to a complex ranking system dictated by their family's status as royal, noble or commoner; their personal appearance, social skills and charisma; and their reproduction of royal children, which typically entailed a promotion in rank.[9] Within the class categories of royal, noble and commoner consorts, women were further ranked within an elaborate hierarchy that was not rigid. For example, of the four royal queens that a king could have, the highest-ranking queen could be demoted should her eldest son die. Consorts were ranked as well and only those who gave birth to a royal child were listed in the royal family genealogy lists.

It is likely that not all women gifted as consorts became the king's sexual partners, but the gifting itself remained important. This form of vertical alliance-making through the gifting of women was replicated down the sociopolitical hierarchy such that many royal and aristocratic men had multiple wives and dozens of children. By contrast, most commoners engaged in monogamy for economic reasons – one had to be of some means to support multiple wives. Also, because many commoner men moved in with their wife's family, the likelihood that they would obtain another wife decreased.[10] In other words, both monogamous and polygynous unions had for long existed in Siam. Polygyny, however, had historically played an essential political role. Far from being an institution parasitical or peripheral to political history, polygyny was a system that helped integrate the kingdom's disparate geographic settlements through the exchange of women.

Polygyny served a second function as well. It enabled the royal family to reproduce sufficient numbers of male elite to fill the highest posts in the government, which they did until the overthrow of the absolute monarchy in 1932. This process helped maintain sociopolitical hierarchies by ensuring that royal and aristocratic men remained in lucrative and powerful positions of rule. Staffing officialdom with royalty was possible only because of polygynous procreation, which provided over three hundred children to the first five kings of the Jakri dynasty (1782–1910). Related to this reproductive capacity is polygyny's third historic function: it was central to the notion of masculine authority, which was expressed through the number of a man's wives, the reproduction of children and his ability to control the sexuality of the women in his household.[11] Polygyny's political purpose dovetailed with its sexual function, at least for heterosexual monarchs. Aside from the king and his prepubescent sons, no men, not even eunuchs, lived in Siam's Inner Palace.

Siam's single most important legal text prior to the overhaul of the legal system was the Laws of the Three Seals (*Kotmai tra samduang* or KTSD), a collection of religious and legal scriptures based in the Theravada Buddhist tradition.[12] The KTSD supported a monarchical political system founded on polygynous ties, but did not require state intervention into or sanctioning of marriages. The KTSD rarely used the term *family* (khropkhrua), and when it did, it referred to a man's entire entourage of people, cows, horses, gems and other material goods, not necessarily to blood relations.[13] There was no family law per se, and the laws on husbands and wives (*Laksana phua mia*) rarely mentioned children. Instead, the laws delineated three types of wives: a wife given by the woman's parents was a major wife; if a man directly requested to marry a woman without using a go-between, she was considered a minor wife; and those obtained through purchase were slave wives.[14] Forty of the 134 laws on marriage considered instances in which a man or woman did not follow the traditional exchanges and negotiations characteristic of a proper marriage – which entailed employing an intermediary to request a woman as a wife from her parents, negotiating bridewealth, performing marital ceremonies and so on – suggesting that many broke with the custom. For example, if a suitor could not afford the bridewealth or if he desired a woman who was already betrothed to another, he could abduct her and have intercourse with her, after which he would send a go-between to apologize and beg her guardians' permission to wed. The degree to which the desired woman consented to either process varied, and class relations were considered in interpretations of consent.[15] For instance, the male owner of an unmarried slave woman could not be prosecuted for raping her. Instead, the act of intercourse transformed her into his slave wife. However, as explained below, the law penalized unions between elite women and non-elite men.

Aside from arranged marriages and elopement, couples could also be considered married in the eyes of their community if they cohabited or gave birth to a child. Procreation automatically and retroactively conferred marital legitimacy to a couple, which also meant that illegitimate children were a legal impossibility. In cases of blended families, it was not uncommon for non-biological parents to informally adopt their spouses' children from previous relationships. All of these paths to marriage demonstrate that religious, state and legal forms of marital legitimacy were not particularly significant. Instead, community and parental acknowledgement was sufficient to bestow legitimacy to a union as a marriage, particularly for non-elites. Although gender inequities clearly existed in the polygynous system of Siam, non-elite women could obtain divorce and remarry easily and without stigma. While wealth and status often dictated the degree of formality in marriage rituals, the 'state' did not require registration of marriage.

Given the theoretically limitless numbers of wives associated with one man, children derived their rank from their mother's social status rather than that of the father alone. Consequently, the legal system reflected this principle by regulating the sexuality of women as a way to preserve her social rank, which was in turn important for the prestige of her entire family. This standard applied to laws on marriage for royal and aristocratic women, prohibiting them from marrying below their status.[16] One of the most reprehensible sex crimes in Siam before the Laws of the Three Seals were replaced entailed the sexual union between an elite woman and a lower-status man, an act that stripped her and their children of rank since she married down, as it were.[17] Until the creation of the Penal Code in 1908, marrying below one's status was explicitly criminalized for aristocratic and royal women. The act of transgressing social status lines by marrying down for women, or marrying up for men, was considered adultery (*chu*), a fact that suggests the enormity of the crime. Liaisons between elite men and lower ranking women, by contrast, were encouraged.

Commoner women generally exercised more latitude in their choice of a spouse, particularly after 1865 when new laws granted greater choice of marital partners to commoner women but withheld it from women born into high status families. A famous case from the 1860s involved an arranged marriage between a wealthy man and a commoner woman named Amdaeng Muan, who escaped by running away with her commoner lover. Despite the repeated efforts of her parents and local judges to force her to marry the wealthy suitor, including beating Amdaeng Muan and sending her to prison where she performed hard labour, Amdaeng Muan successfully appealed to King Mongkut (r. 1851–1868). He ruled that in future cases involving women from non-elite families, judges must follow the wishes of the woman rather than her family because he thought it 'natural' for poor parents 'to think only of money and gold' and to coerce the sale of their children.[18] The same legal decree, however, reinforced the control of the parents from elite families over the marriage of their daughters because otherwise an elite woman might marry a commoner husband, thus 'upsetting' the woman's family and catalysing them to withdraw their support from the throne.[19]

The legal, geographic and cultural rationales that supported the institution of polygyny, linked as intimately as it was to Siam's political structure, gradually changed as a consequence of the treaties signed with foreign powers from the 1850s on, which deepened Siam's integration into the world trading system. This in turn affected structural shifts in the economy and in the political relationship between subjects and rulers. King Mongkut, who had presided over the Bowring Treaty and other similar treaties, later issued a proclamation that revealed the unravelling of political threads woven by marital ties. He informed government officials that the tradition of 'gifting' daughters was gradually dying out and that officials could have their daughters returned to them. Familial ties alone were no longer as reliable a source of political power. In addition, criticism of the 'harem' and the sheer number of 'concubines' obtained by Siam's kings increased in tandem with the rise in numbers of foreigner visitors. Orientalist references to the monarch's flagrant dereliction of official duty, resulting from such 'past times', litter the accounts written by foreign observers, from missionaries to officials. In 1856, the American consul to Japan, Townsend Harris, visited Siam to negotiate a treaty with King Mongkut. The meeting was, however, postponed which may account for some of the vitriol behind Harris's conclusion that 'His Majesty is pedantic beyond belief, and that too on a very small capital of knowledge. Add to this the fact that he is much given to women, and a solution is found for the delay of all useful business. It may be said that [he] resembles Solomon only in the chapter of wives and concubines.'[20] Most famous among the Western observers was Anna Leonowens, who cemented the interpretation of polygyny as slavery in the popular imagination of Westerners. Monogamy was, in Leonowens's writings, the next step towards freeing women from enslavement as minor wives. Her friendship with Harriet Beecher Stowe undoubtedly influenced her treatment of polygyny as a form of bondage. The narrow castigation of polygyny as a sexual perversion, an injustice to women and a sign of an uncivilized nation reframed it within Western imperial discourses of civilization. They thereby denied the political functions served by polygyny in Siam up to the late nineteenth century.

These same discourses, however, considered the institutions of family and marriage to be sources of cultural authenticity.[21] The belief that familial and religious norms opened windows onto the authentic character of a people is a fundamental component of civilizing, modernizing rhetoric and capitalist forms of modernity. All theories about the origins and nature of human society written by nineteenth-century ethnologists – Lewis H. Morgan, Sir Henry Maine, Johann Bachofen, John F. McLennan and Numa Denis Fustel de Coulanges – understood kinship structures and marital institutions as the source of each society's governmental organization and of its relative degree of civilization.[22] Seeking to explain what they saw as the evolutionary transformation from primitive to civilized society, they deployed the language of science to categorize human communities: family, gentes, phratries, tribes, clans and so on.[23] Kinship and family constituted *the* primary objects of study for early ethnologists because kinship and family indicated where a given society would be placed on an evolutionary scale that located primitive societies at one end and modern societies at the other. By privileging the family as an object of study, late-nineteenth-century ethnographic discourse overdetermined the significance of the family as the litmus test of a society's place on the evolutionary scale of progress. Accusations by colonizers of degenerate and barbaric familial practices, such as polygyny in Siam and child marriage in India, as revealed in Chapter 7 on India, sanctioned Western colonization of so-called primitive societies.[24]

To varying degrees, British, French and Dutch colonial powers in Asia treated family and its marital form as windows onto the specificity of local communities. In European colonies, pre-existing non-monogamous arrangements were understood as culturally authentic and therefore in need of preservation, even as such practices were condemned as lower on the civilizational scale. In short, the imposition of a civilizational hierarchy based on family norms helped justify imperial intervention into and control over their colonial populations. Heterosexual, Christian monogamous marriage anchored the nuclear family as the most civilized familial form: other types of sexual union found their place lower down on the evolutionary scale of progress. European colonial regimes the world over divided their populations based on marital form. By the late nineteenth century in the Netherlands East Indies, for example, the legal category of 'Foreign Orientals' included all non-Europeans and non-natives who observed polygyny, whereas the category of 'Europeans' included 'Japanese and other peoples ... who came from states in which substantially the same family law was observed as that which held good in Holland'.[25]

Non-colonized countries such as Siam found themselves in a slightly different position than directly colonized areas: they could choose to pass a law on monogamy or maintain pre-existing marital norms. Siam's leaders experimented with colonial models in Malay Muslim areas in the southern parts of the kingdom, where they set up Muslim family courts in colonial competition with the British next door in Malaya.[26] They sought to prove that they too could treat their colonial natives with paternalistic respect rather than impose 'foreign' (Siamese Buddhist) family law. But these same leaders agonized over the decision with regard to Siam's own code on the family, prolonging the promulgation of the kingdom's modern civil code.

Treaties between Siam and foreign powers explicitly excluded family law from the requirement of general legal reform. As a consequence, the treaties opened up a space for domestic debate and limited control over marriage law within the asymmetrical global system of imperialism and its condemnatory civilizational ideology. Even the foreign advisers hired by Siam to help 'modernize' Siam's legal code refused to weigh in on the issue of marital norms. For example, Frenchman Georges Padoux, Siam's legislative adviser from 1904 to 1913, stated that 'I was – and I am still – strongly of [the] opinion that the initiative of fundamental reforms in questions of marriage, divorce, parentage, inheritance, must lie only with the Siamese Statesmen and legal men. ... We would have been of course quite prepared to substitute monogamy for polygamy in the draft [of the civil law code], if instructed by the Government to do so. But it would have been mere presumption on our part even to simply raise the point. It seems very difficult for a man who has been born and brought up in one of the systems to form an independent opinion as to whether monogamy is superior to polygamy or not'.[27] Padoux's privileging of Siamese epistemological insight – the Siamese know best based on their experiences – and the fact that the Siamese initiated the reforms in family law raise the question of why Siamese reformers did not adopt monogamy sooner if it would have helped end the unequal treaty system. The reasons why are more complicated and have to do with arguments about Siam's alternative path to modernizing both its political and familial systems.

Siam's Alternative Marital Modernity: Buddhist Defence of Polygyny

Polygyny's intimate association with Siam's absolute monarchical system arguably made it impossible to discard until a coup in 1932 established a constitutional monarchy. However, Siam's last two absolute monarchs were either indifferent to heterosexual marriage altogether or practised monogamy. They would have been amenable to passing a monogamy law, but they, along with earlier rulers, were anxious that this would amount to a confession that Christianity and monogamy were indeed morally superior. Siamese elites consciously challenged the Christian West's view of Siamese polygyny and Buddhism as backward and unequal.

Although kings and statesmen of Siam from the 1850s to the early 1930s refused to abolish polygyny in favour of monogamy, they intensely debated the issue. Among Siam's political elites, few could envision an end to polygyny. Instead, they worried about Siam's international reputation should they officially adopt polygyny and about domestic repercussions for women and children should they adopt monogamy in law without penalizing the practice of polygyny. In addition, a newly emerging middle class chastened traditional elites over the issue of polygyny, which became symbolic of the excesses of the old order. These debates began in the 1860s among ruling elites who defended polygyny as a practice sanctioned by Buddhism. Initially, polygyny was discussed as a religiously justified form of marriage, parallel to Christian monogamy. But by the early twentieth century, when a broader segment of society participated in the conversation, polygyny belonged within a national cultural frame as a core Siamese tradition. As such, it was harder to abolish.

One of Siam's highest-ranking officials, Jao Phraya Thiphakorawong (Kham Bunnag), first articulated Siam's differences from Christianity and Islam through a Buddhist defence of polygyny. Thiphakorawong's involvement in the Bowring Treaty and other interactions with foreign officials, missionaries, envoys and travellers prompted him to write *A Book Explaining Various Things* (Nangsu sadaeng kichanukit), which he published in 1867.[28] The book argues that Buddhism sanctioned polygyny by not explicitly forbidding it. Unlike Islam, which allowed polygyny for the irreligious reasons of a man's sexual convenience, he explained that Buddhism allowed polygyny because it prevented a man from forcing a woman to have intercourse against her will, which would cause him to lose merit.[29] His comparison offered the first publicly articulated distinction between Islamic and Buddhist rationales for legitimating polygyny: Buddhist men had putatively purer reasons for requiring sexual access to multiple women based in maintaining merit rather than in sexual desire.[30] Siam's national identity and distinct route to modernity were articulated against that of the normative family forms of both the Christian West and Muslims.

Even as Siam's political and economic conditions changed, the associations between polygyny, political power and virility remained intact. It was crucial for Mongkut, whose power was based on the support of key factions among the elite, to contain the seismic shifts occurring not just in Siam's economy and foreign relations, but in its domestic political hierarchy as well. Domestically, keeping polygyny meant maintaining the existing political hierarchy and appeasing other elites whose positions and domestic alliance-making strategies relied on polygyny. The families of women who became consorts of the king or high-ranking officials and princes benefitted from the marriages as well. Hence, to preserve the good will of the officials he relied on, King Mongkut maintained a rigid conservatism with regard to his kingdom's social hierarchy and norms concerning polygynous marriage.

Preservation of the social hierarchy became one of the major reasons why kings continued to support the institution of polygyny despite its high legal and political costs in relations with foreign powers. This remained true for Mongkut's son and successor, King Chulalongkorn (r. 1868–1910), the man given credit for reforming Siam's state machinery along modern lines. His reforms, known later as the Jakri Reformation, created a territorially based, functionally differentiated, centralized administrative bureaucracy. He hired hundreds of foreigners to reform Siam's fiscal, legal, cartographic and telecommunications systems. Siam's cartographers mapped the kingdom's boundaries, which signified political inclusion in the kingdom.[31] It was no longer necessary for provincial elites to send a proxy, in the form of a daughter, to the king to establish political affiliation. The king's subjects no longer 'belonged' to him based on personalized ties cemented through marriage alliances, but were instead based on cadastral maps and lines of longitude and latitude. Moreover, after the introduction of the rule of primogeniture in 1886, individual monarchs were no longer as beholden to elite families, which had traditionally determined kingly successors.[32]

Yet, contrary to the logic of the modern state, which would have spelt the end of polygynous institutions such as the 'harem', the size and political significance of the Inner Palace increased under Chulalongkorn, Siam's most famous 'modernizing' monarch.[33] He preserved this aspect of Siamese political culture because it served to maintain a class hierarchy. Yet even while King Chulalongkorn amassed a large number of consorts, he was sensitive to his public image abroad as a polygynous king, as indicated in a photo taken in the Lentz studios in Bangkok in the 1890s (see Figure 3.1). The photo of the king, his highest-ranking Queen-Consort Saowapha, three of their sons, and two sons by the king and other consorts was used as the basis for a royal family painting by Italian portraitist, Odoardo Gelli. The king commissioned Gelli, famous for his paintings of European kings, to render the photo into a portrait. However, he had Gelli switch the two half-sons, Chiraprawati and Sommatiwong, with the king and queen's two other full sons, Crown Prince Vajiravudh and Prince Chakrabongse, suggesting his desire to represent an image of his family as nuclear and monogamous (see Figure 3.2).[34]

80   *Marriage, Law and Modernity*

Figure 3.1 Photograph of King Chulalongkorn, Queen Saowapha and Royal Sons. The two princes standing, Princes Chiraprawati and Sommatiwong, were sons of the king and Consort Mother Thapthim and Queen Sawangwatana, respectively. Lenz Studio, Bangkok, late 1890s. Source: U-M Library Digital Collections. Trans-Asia Photography Review Images.[35]

Figure 3.2 Portrait of King Chulalongkorn, Queen Saowapha and their Sons. Crown Prince Vajiravudh (future Rama VI) stands between his parents, and Prince Prajadhipok (future Rama VII) stands to the right of the queen. Odoardo Gelli, circa 1900. Courtesy Maurizio Peleggi.

Within Siam it became almost impossible to openly critique polygyny at the time when its integrative function had become obsolete. The example of Prince Prisdang Chumsai demonstrates this point. He belonged to a cohort of the king's closest reform-minded supporters who had submitted a proposal to the king in 1885 that outlined reforms they thought necessary to implement in order to avoid colonization.[36] The petition daringly advocated replacing the absolute monarchy with a constitutional monarchy, which King Chulalongkorn dismissed as untimely for Siam. However, these same reform-minded men, most of whom had spent time in Europe, found it easier to request that the king end absolutism than to ask him to terminate the custom of polygyny.[37] They feared upsetting the king, who had over 150 consorts.

Prince Prisdang was not against polygyny because he understood it as inimical to women or gender equality, but because it enabled the operation of influence outside formal institutions of political power through appeal to the queens, consorts, their families and children of the king and through treacherous rumours fed into and spun within this network. 'The immense power and influence of the favourite Queens works wonders and plays an important part, though indirectly, in political and social affairs of the country. It can make and unmake a man, and can frustrate … those who devote their life to public affairs.'[38] According to Prisdang, to gain favour, officials had to 'vie with one another to give costly presents and offer their services' to the king's consorts and children, which detracted attention and funding away from the public good.[39] As a consequence, nearly all officials were personally indebted, and the Treasury was not treated as distinct from the king's personal coffers. The king was in charge of the funds, which had grown under his rule as the various ministries came under his control. By the time he died, he was allegedly one of the richest monarchs in the world.[40] Prisdang ended up fleeing into exile in 1890 as a consequence of myriad damning rumours about him that spread throughout officialdom. His case demonstrates the feared penalties for critiquing polygyny even in an era of modern political reform. This abruptly changed when King Chulalongkorn died in 1910, at which point arguments about the merits and demerits of polygyny resurfaced.

It is important to note that the debates questioning the continued relevance of polygyny began before the overthrow of the absolute monarchy in 1932, when a coup established a constitutional monarchy. In fact, the Inner Palace drastically declined in numbers and political significance much earlier, in 1910, when Chulalongkorn's son and successor, King Vajiravudh (Rama VI, 1910–25), all but abolished it. Immediately after he ascended the throne, he dispersed the inhabitants of the Inner Palace.[41] Within five years, there were only about twenty-five royal wives and princesses (of King Chulalongkorn) remaining. Moreover, King Vajiravudh refused to participate in polygynous politics by declining to marry the daughters of his princely elders. Instead of building personal alliances through marriages, he surrounded himself with a group of young men and gradually replaced many government officials who had been the previous king's loyal subjects. He thereby failed to procreate the official body through the prodigious reproduction of children, and no longer evinced masculine virility through the accumulation of wives. He was likely homosexual. These factors caused the monarch's precipitous decline in popularity among the ruling class. Ultimately, while it is tempting to explain the cessation of polygyny as a political institution by resorting to King Vajiravudh's sexual preference for men, this is an insufficient explanation. He did not uphold the sociopolitical hierarchy, which he could have easily done by marrying the daughters of elites regardless of his personal sexual preferences, as had some European homosexual kings treated in Chapter 4.

Connubial Ambivalence: Siam's Law on Monogamy

Perhaps King Vajiravudh's self-proclaimed indifference to all types of marriage – whether polygynous or monogamous – explains the eruption of robust debates about adopting a marital standard in the 1910s and 1920s. 'For myself, I shall neither gain nor lose by the adoption of either the system of monogamy or polygyny, so that I feel I am competent to state a disinterested opinion on the subject.'[42] This comment, expressed in front of men who had multiple wives, may not have endeared him to other princes and elites in the Cabinet Council where they discussed the dire need for a law on Siam's marital standard. Memoranda written in the mid-1910s passed between the king and council member Prince Svasti Sobhon, the half-brother of King Chulalongkorn. They reveal the nature of the controversy that stumped the process of legal reform on the family.[43] In essence, Prince Svasti, who had multiple consorts, advocated adopting a law on monogamy because otherwise foreigners would criticize Siam's law as substandard.[44] He argued that polygyny was a class issue, even in the West, where wealthy foreigners practice a form of polygyny by maintaining mistresses. In Siam, he claimed, only the upper classes engaged in polygyny, so the law should be in keeping with the majority, who practice monogamy, rather than the minority.[45]

In response, Rama VI wrote a lengthy memo in 1913 outlining the immorality of adopting monogamy in Siam and the severe repercussions it would have on women and children. 'The making of Law to deceive the world, i.e., the appearance of a Law that is not true in reality, appears to me to be a downright cynical lie. Therefore, if we are going to have a lot of wives, I do not think it right that we should state that we are adopting the monogamous system as a principle of our Marriage Law.'[46] King Vajiravudh argued instead that should polygyny continue, then the law should reflect this and require that all wives and their children be registered 'in order to regulate the promiscuity of irregular unions, since I have noted that in our country people so easily become "Man and Wife" that it is sometimes difficult to get evidence of such a union'. Registration could protect minor wives, particularly if their husbands deserted them, and would prevent men from deceiving women into 'marriage' by requiring him to prove his seriousness by registering the marriage rather than simply engaging in sexual intercourse.[47] He aimed to protect Siamese women who would operate according to customary norms only to find that they had no legal standing vis-à-vis the man they considered their husband.

The king also worried about the impact of a monogamy law on children born to women other than the registered wife. 'When we have *no illegitimate children in our Laws, it is not desirable to provide for their coming into being*… . Should, however, the monogamous system be adopted as the principle of our Marriage Law, a father who does not wish to acknowledge the children of a minor wife would simply take refuge behind the Law.'[48] In the case of adopting a monogamy law, the king advocated a provision that would compel a man to acknowledge his children regardless of who was the mother. Even so, he could see potential problems with this provision. 'If we are to hold that all children acknowledged by a man become legally the children of his wedded wife, will the Europeans believe that we are really monogamists? Supposing a man had 20 or 30 children, could anyone be made to believe that they are all born from the same mother?'[49] Like Prince Svasti, the king believed that polygyny was related to class. Elsewhere he noted that Siamese farmers had for long practised sexual equality in the form of monogamous marriage. 'We don't have to look as far as any country of white Westerners. I invite you Thai nobles to go to the villages of Siam itself, where you will see examples of monogamous families. … Our Thai villagers are genuinely closer to being civilized than people in Bangkok or large cities!'[50]

In the end, the king took the moral and practical high ground: if the Siamese are going to practice polygyny no matter what, then adopt polygyny as the marital standard which would at least give women and children some form of protection. The Buddhist defence of polygyny was raised in the discussion but played a much smaller role. King Vajiravudh maintained that 'It cannot be said that the Siamese who has several wives is on a lower moral plane than the European with only one wife, because to admit such a proposition would mean that we shall have also to admit that the Buddhist Religion itself is on a lower moral plane than the Christian Religion, which naturally I for one *cannot* admit.'[51] More importantly, however, polygyny was increasingly discussed as a cultural institution rather than a religious one. Unable to come to a decision, the council members once again failed to promulgate a law on marriage. The backlog of inheritance and divorce cases continued to mount as did pressure to reform the law that would ultimately rid Siam of the remaining unequal treaty clauses. Under Rama VI's successor, King Prajadhipok (Rama VII, 1925–35), who personally practised monogamy, discussions among the highest-ranking elites consistently backed polygyny as Siam's marital standard. Just as they were about to promulgate a polygyny law, the Depression hit, and a coup by a group of commoner civilian and military officials overthrew the absolute monarchy in 1932, replacing it with a constitutional one.

Some urban intellectuals voiced their opposition to polygyny as part of a broader critique of the state abuse of power, especially under the absolutist regime.[52] In stark contrast to the masculinist elite political culture that linked polygyny to membership in the ruling class, members of the middle class writing for the popular press held absolutism and its political administration responsible for Siam's backward ways, symbolized by polygyny, and questioned their moral fitness to rule. They deployed earlier imperial discourses condemning polygyny against Siamese royalty and officialdom. By doing so, they exposed the Buddhist defence of polygyny, cloaked in the discourse of 'tradition', as an elitist rationale that was not so relevant to members of the lower and middle classes. Once polygyny was uncoupled from its political function of integrating the state, it could be used against elites as a sign of the unmodern, and relegated to the past. Marriage had become a lightning rod for domestic politicking and polygyny served to dis-integrate the state.

A common critique against the practice held that polygyny was economically wasteful, harmful to a man's health and debauched.[53] Novels and newspaper articles railed against licentious elite men and their sexual peccadilloes. Female writers blamed the government as well for sanctioning polygyny, allowing men to abandon their wives and children for younger women and promoting related forms of gender inequality.[54] Many critics linked polygyny to the increase in prostitution in Bangkok, where men lured women under the guise of customary marriage, only later to abandon them.

Although members of the middle class writing for the popular press held absolutism responsible for Siam's backward ways, symbolized by polygyny, they frequently attached the practice to officialdom more broadly. As a consequence, even after the overthrow of the absolute monarchy, critiques of polygyny as a debauched practice of officials, regardless of their royal or non-royal background, continued unabated. The practice of polygyny did not map onto one's class position alone, but onto officialdom as well.

As the number of men from commoner backgrounds who worked in the administration increased, so too did the practice of having multiple wives. Not only did this threaten to blur the distinction between traditional elites and the middle class, but it also suggested that polygyny had paradoxically become democratized.[55] The bureaucracy had expanded sevenfold in size between 1892 and 1925, which meant that non-elite men began to fill official posts where they earned a salary that afforded them more opportunities to engage in polygyny and pay for commercial sex.[56] No statistics are available to reveal the expansion of polygynous unions to non-elites, but the number of court cases involving middling officials who had more than one wife is indicative of the continued connection between polygyny and masculine official power. Perhaps it is no coincidence that the moment that polygyny became democratized to include non-elite men, the parliament passed the monogamous marriage law. Lawmakers finalized the draft of the Civil and Commercial Code's outstanding books on family and inheritance, which the newly established parliament passed in 1935. The law on monogamy enshrined in the new code recognized couples as married only if they registered with their local district officials, which brought the state squarely into their marital affairs. The law did not recognize the former multiplicity of paths to marriage: traditional marriage ceremonies, parental consent, elopement, cohabitation and birth of a child no longer conferred legal conjugality.

Once married, the law declared the husband the head of the family with the right to choose place of residence and to control a wife's property, which merged with that of the husband unless they made a prenuptial agreement. Divorce remained relatively easy to obtain if both parties consented, but if they did not, then certain inequalities crept into the process. For example, a husband could divorce his wife if she committed adultery – which could mean a single act of sexual intercourse with another man – but not vice versa. For men, adultery meant his financial support of another woman, not sexual relations with a woman other than his wife.[57] The new law also favoured the father in the awarding of custody of children, even in a mutual divorce.

Clause 1451 of the law weakly advocates monogamy as Siam's marital standard. It states that if an individual has already registered a marriage, he or she cannot register another marriage unless the first has ended by death, divorce or annulment by the court.[58] A man could only register one wife with the state, which fell short of criminalizing polygyny. In fact, there remains no punishment for registering more than one wife, which happens when officials fail to verify whether either spouse is already registered. According to some observers, 'Such a departure of law from custom has created added social problems of unmarried mothers and consequently of illegitimate children to a degree unknown under the ancient polygamous law.'[59] To avoid the creation of bastards, the law allowed men to legitimate children born outside of wedlock by legally acknowledging them, but few men pushed for legitimization of their children in practice. The law also created a class of women unprotected by law and ineligible for inheritance. These were exactly the concerns identified as potential problems with a toothless monogamy law by King Vajiravudh in 1913.

Conclusion

Modern, codified law, even when promulgated with ethical motives, created perverse incentives and unintended outcomes in Siam. The 1935 Civil Code endorsed monogamy as the country's new marital standard, after eight long decades of acrimonious debate. These debates began in the encounter between Siamese elites and representatives from the Christian imperial West who regarded polygyny as backward, in part because it treated women as unequal to men. This provoked a defence of polygyny within Siam as an integral part of their Buddhist traditions. As a consequence, even though monogamy and polygyny each had long histories in Siam as two of many types of marital unions, polygyny became symbolic of Thai 'tradition'. By highlighting family and marriage as the foundation of a country's cultural identity, imperial powers understood polygyny as Siam's singular cultural form of marriage, ignoring a multiplicity of marital practices.

The adoption of a law on monogamy in 1935 enabled Siam's leaders to abolish the final vestiges of the remaining unequal treaties that hampered the kingdom's sovereignty. However, ironically, rather than protecting women and children from the perils of polygyny, the monogamy law increased their vulnerability. It produced two illegitimate categories that had not existed before: mistresses and bastards. Polygyny did not vanish, though the generation that overtly practised it did. The practice of polygyny has continued into the twenty-first century, as has the development of political alliances through arranged marriages between powerful political dynasties that are no longer exclusively of noble or royal blood. Even though most polygynous men maintain a public silence about their multiple families, the number of women obtained by a man still indexes his virility and masculinity. Polygyny persists in practice today and remains central to Siam's masculine culture of political authority.[60]

Notes

1. Thailand was referred to as Siam until 1939–41.
2. Examples of exemplary scholarship in this vein include Gayatri Spivak, 'Can the Subaltern Speak?' in *Marxism and the Interpretation of Culture*, ed. Cary Nelson and Lawrence Grossberg (London: Macmillan, 1988), 24–8; Lata Mani, 'Contentious Traditions: The Debate on SATI in Colonial India', *Cultural Critique* (Fall 1987): 119–56; and Richard W. Lariviere, 'Justices and *Panditas*: Some Ironies in Contemporary Readings of the Hindu Legal Past', *Journal of Asian Studies* 48 (1989): 757–69.
3. Foreign nations considered Siam's existing legal system backward and incapable of meting out justice. It also greatly restricted foreign economic access to Siam's trade and natural resources. As a consequence, Siam had to radically reform its legal system

and codes along Western lines before the unequal treaties were lifted. See Tamara Loos, *Subject Siam: Family, Law, and Colonial Modernity in Thailand* (Ithaca: Cornell University Press, 2006).
4   This chapter is informed by earlier work I have written about gender and sexuality in Thailand's history, including *Subject Siam* (2006) and 'Sex in the Inner City: The Fidelity between Sex and Politics in Siam', *The Journal of Asian Studies* 64, no. 4 (November 2005): 881–909.
5   Pasuk Phongphaichit and Chris Baker, *A History of Thailand* (Cambridge: Cambridge University Press, 2005), 45.
6   Sir John Bowring, *The Kingdom and People of Siam* (Kuala Lumpur: Oxford University Press, 1969 [1857]); Philip Bowring, *Free Trade's First Missionary: Sir John Bowring In Europe and Asia* (Hong Kong: Hong Kong University Press, 2014).
7   Loos, *Subject Siam*.
8   This process is discussed at length in Loos, *Subject Siam*.
9   Leslie Woodhouse, 'A "Foreign" Princess in the Siamese Court: Princess Dara Rasami,the Politics of Gender and Ethnic Difference in Nineteenth-Century Siam', PhD diss., Department of History, University of California-Berkeley (2009), 113–15.
10 Nidhi Eoseewong, 'Khlum thung chon' (Arranged Marriage), in *Khwam yung khong kan yu* (Difficulties of Living), ed. Mukhom Wongthes (Bangkok: Matichon, 2005), 18, cited in Chalidaporn Songsamphan, 'Private Family, Public Contestation: Debates on Sexuality and Marriage in the Thai Parliament', 89.
11 Craig J. Reynolds, 'A Nineteenth Century Thai Buddhist Defense of Polygamy and Some Remarks on the Social History of Women in Thailand', paper presented for the 7th Conference of the International Association of Historians of Asia, Chulalongkorn University, Bangkok, 1977, 936–9.
12 The KTSD's origins have been traced to the fourteenth century, with a major revision occurring in 1805. Robert Lingat, *Prawatisat kotmai thai* (The History of Thai Law), vol. 2, ed. Charnvit Kasetsiri and Wikal Phongphanitanon (Bangkok: 1983), 58; Yoeno Ishii, 'The Thai Thammasat (with a note on the Lao Thammasat)', in *Laws of South-East Asia*, vol. 1, *The Pre-Modern Texts*, ed. M. B. Hooker (Singapore: Butterworth and Co.,), 154–7.
13 Supaporn Shigetomi, 'The Concept of Family and its Meaning in Thai History', in *The Family in Flux in Southeast Asia: Institution, Ideology, Practice*, ed. Yoko Hayami, et al. (Kyoto: Kyoto University Press, 2012), 29–36.
14 'Laksana phu mia', Vol. 2, *Kotmai tra samduang* (Thammasat Edition), 2.
15 See Loos *Subject Siam*, 136–44.
16 Women with the rank of 400 sakdina marks or above in Siam's legal system.
17 Tamara Loos 'Issaraphap: The Limits of Individual Liberty in Thai Jurisprudence', *Crossroads: An Interdisciplinary Journal of Southeast Asian Studies* 12, no. 1 (1998): 51; Hong Lysa, 'Of Consorts and Harlots in Thai Popular History', *The Journal of Asian Studies* 57, no. 2 (May 1998), 333–53; and Hong Lysa, 'Palace Women at the Margins of Social Change: An Aspect of the Politics of Social History in the Reign of King Chulalongkorn', *Journal of Southeast Asian Studies* 30, no. 2 (September 1999): 310–24.
18 King Mongkut, 'Prakat phraratchabanyat lakpha, j.s. 1227 (1865)' (Royal Proclamation on Abduction, 1865), in *Khruangmai haeng khwam runk ruang khu saphap haeng satri* (A Symbol of Civilization: The Status of Women), ed. Khunying Suphatra Singloka (Bangkok: Samakhom banthit satri thang kotmai haeng prathet thai, 1991), 66.

19 Ibid., 68-9.
20 Townsend Harris, *The Complete Journal of Townsend Harris*, intro. Mario Emilio Cosenza, with preface by Douglas MacArthur II (Rutland, Vermont: Charles E. Tuttle Co., rev. edn, 1959), 145.
21 My discussion about family law as the window into a country's unique cultural identity stems from Loos, 'The Imperialism of Monogamy in Family Law', in *Subject Siam*, ed. Loos (Ithaca: Cornell University Press, 2006), 100-29.
22 Elman R. Service, 'Introduction', *A Century of Controversy: Ethnological Issues from 1860 to 1960* (Orlando: Academic Press, Inc., 1985), 3-12. Sir Henry Maine, *Ancient Law* (1861); Johann Bachofen, *Das Mutterrecht* (1861); John F. McLennan, *Primitive Marriage* (1865); Numa Denis Fustel de Coulanges, *The Ancient City* (1864); Lewis H. Morgan, *Systems of Consanguinity and Affinity of the Human Family* (1870) and *Ancient Society* (1877).
23 Morgan, perhaps the most famous of the early ethnologists, based the distinction between modern and primitive society on its governmental foundation in either kin relations or territorial and property relations. He is also well known for linking technological changes to various stages of social organization and inspired, in part, works on this point written by Marx and Engels. *Gentes* is the plural for *gens*, which referred to a Roman clan that traced family lineage through the male line. Maine and others who wrote before Morgan espoused to an ascending order of kinship institutions: 'families proliferate into the *gens*, which are then allied to one another in the *phratry*, then into *tribe*, and finally into *city*'. All but the *city* were formed by a proliferation of kin groups. Service, 'Introduction', 9, 36.
24 Mani, 'Contentious Traditions'. Partha Chatterjee, 'The Nation and Its Women', *The Nation and Its Fragments: Colonial and Postcolonial Histories* (Princeton: Princeton University Press, 1993), 116-34.
25 Peter Burns, 'The Netherlands East Indies', in *The Laws of South-East Asia*, vol. 2, ed. M. B. Hooker (Singapore: Butterworth and Co., 1988), 261, 246.
26 Tamara Loos, 'Competitive Colonialisms: Siam and Britain on the Malay Muslim Border', in *The Ambiguous Allure of the West: Traces of the Colonial in Thailand*, ed. Rachel Harrison and Peter Jackson (Hong Kong: Hong Kong University Press, 2009), 75-91.
27 Padoux wrote this in a memo to King Vajiravudh on 9 May 1913, cited in Adul Wichiencharoen and Luang Chamroon Nitisastra, 'Some Main Features of Modernization of Ancient Family Law in Thailand', *Family Law and Customary Law in Asia: A Contemporary Legal Perspective*, ed. David C. Buxbaum (The Hague: Martinus Nijhoff, 1968), 97.
28 Henry Alabaster summarized the book in English in a chapter on 'The "Modern Buddhist," or the Ideas of a Siamese Minister of State on his own and other Religions', which he published in his 1871 book, *The Wheel of the Law: Buddhism Illustrated from Siamese Sources* (London: Trubner & Co., 1871), 1-73. Reynolds, 'A Nineteenth Century Thai Buddhist Defense', 945.
29 Jao Phraya Thiphakorawong, *Nangsu sadaeng kitchanukit*, 220-2, 226; Reynolds, 'A Nineteenth Century Thai Buddhist Defense', 947-8, 962-3.
30 Eventually, Siam modelled the legal reform and rule over its Malay Muslim minority in southern Siam on imperial Britain's legal treatment of its Malay Muslim population. Siam's leaders similarly reformed the courts and codes in its Malay areas so as to integrate them into Siam's centralizing legal system, but created distinct Islamic family courts and laws for the local population. By so doing, Siam's leaders

hoped to demonstrate that they treated 'their' colonized Muslim natives as well as Britain's managed their subject populations. See Loos, 'Competitive Colonialisms'.
31 Thongchai Winichakul, *Siam Mapped: A History of the Geo-Body of a Nation* (Honolulu; University of Hawaii Press, 1994); and Tej Bunnag, *The Provincial Administration of Siam from 1892 to 1915: the Ministry of the Interior under Prince Damrong Rachanuphap* (London: Oxford University Press, 1977).
32 Stephen Greene, *Absolute Dreams: Thai Government under Rama VI, 1910-1925* (Bangkok, Thailand: White Lotus Press, 1999), 2.
33 Tamara Loos, 'Sex in the Inner City: The Fidelity between Sex and Politics in Siam', *The Journal of Asian Studies* 64, no. 4 (November 2005): 881–909.
34 Maurizio Peleggi, *Lords of Things: The Fashioning of the Siamese Monarchy's Modern Image* (Honolulu: University of Hawai'i Press, 2002), 66–7.
35 Accessed on 14 August 2016.
36 The king eventually adopted many of the remaining reforms when he initiated the Chakri Reformation.
37 Prisdang Chumsai, 'Confidential. Notes on Siamese Administration, Relations with Foreign Powers and Life in the King's Palace at Bangkok, Written for me/Mr. Swettenham (British Resident in Perak in October 1891 by a Siamese Gentleman of Rank – Now in Disgrace (1891)', in *Two Views of Siam on the Eve of the Chakri Reformation: Comments by Robert Laurie Morant and Prince Pritsdang*, ed. and intro. Nigel Brailey (Whiting Bay, Scotland: Kiscadale Publications, 1989), 71. See also, Loos, *Bones around My Neck: The Life and Exile of a Prince Provocateur* (Ithaca: Cornell University Press, 2016).
38 Prisdang, 'Confidential', 53.
39 Ibid., 54–5.
40 This is according to Malcolm Smith, *A Physician in the Court of Siam* (Kuala Lumpur: Oxford University Press, 1982 [1947], 86. Under Chulalongkorn, Siam's revenue increased from 8,000,000 ticals in 1868 to 63,000,000 in 1910 (about 12,000,000 pounds). The Bunnag family, for example, lost control of the Kalahom in 1886 after heading that lucrative ministry for over one hundred years, and they lost control of the Phrakhlang in 1885, after having run it more or less from 1822 to 1885. These were two of the three most powerful ministries that controlled the administration of the southern and western provinces, foreign trade and foreign affairs, and the gulf provinces. See David K. Wyatt, 'Family Politics in Seventeenth and Eighteenth Century Siam', *Studies in Thai History* (Chiang Mai: Silkworm Books, 1994), 119.
41 Smith, *A Physician in the Court of Siam*, 98.
42 King Vajiravudh cited in Adul and Chamroon, 'Some Main Features of Modernization of Ancient Family Law in Thailand', 92.
43 The memoranda are reproduced in part in Adul and Chamroon, 'Some Main Features of Modernization of Ancient Family Law in Thailand'.
44 He had eight wives according to Petcharat Promnart, 'Modern Woman, Modern Man: the Discursive Construction of Sexual Property in Sixth-Reign Siam (1910-1925)', MA thesis, National University of Singapore, 2015, 61n237.
45 These points are summarized from Adul and Chamroon, 'Some Main Features of Modernization of Ancient Family Law in Thailand', 96, 97.
46 Vajiravudh cited in Adul and Chamroon, 'Some Main Features of Modernization of Ancient Family Law in Thailand', 92.
47 Ibid., 92–3.
48 Emphasis in original. Ibid., 94.

49 Ibid., 95.
50 King Vajiravudh in *Khruangmai haeng khwamrungruang khu saphap haeng satri* (A Symbol of Civilization: The Status of Women), ed. Supatra Singloka (Bangkok: Somakhom banthit satri thang kotmai haeng prathet thai, 1992), 1, 3–4.
51 Emphasis in original. King Vajiravudh in Adul and Chamroon, 'Some Main Features of Modernization of Ancient Family Law in Thailand', 94.
52 Scot Barmé studied the use of print media by middle-class intellectuals to voice anti-monarchical and anti-polygynous sentiment. See especially, 'A Question of Polygamy', in his *Woman, Man, Bangkok* (Lanham, MD: Rowman & Littlefield Pubs. Inc., 2002), 157–78.
53 See Loos, 'The Imperialism of Monogamy in Family Law', 124–9; and Barmé, *Woman, Man, Bangkok*.
54 Barmé, *Woman, Man, Bangkok*, 165.
55 This is also discussed at length in Loos, *Subject Siam*, 127–9.
56 Benjamin Batson, *The End of the Absolute Monarchy in Siam* (Singapore: Oxford University Press, 1984), 45, n40.
57 Childaporn Songsamphan, 'Private Family, Public Contestation: Debates on Sexuality and Marriage in the Thai Parliament', in *The Family in Flux*, ed. Hayami, et al., 96, 98–9.
58 Phrarachabanyat jot thabian khropkhrua (Royal Act on Registering Families), September 1935, 48 pt. 1, PKPS 354-93.
59 Adul and Chamroon 1968, 105).
60 Katja Rangsivek, 'Trakun, Politics and the Thai State', PhD diss., University of Copenhagen, 2013.

4

Royal Marriage in Europe: An Inherently Conservative System

Helen Watanabe-O'Kelly

Royal marriage in Europe exists to preserve the monarchy, an ancient system of government which was in force in every European territory with the exception of France up to the twentieth century and which is still in force, in spite of constitutional developments, in a surprising number of European states. Belgium, Britain, Denmark, the Netherlands, Norway, Spain and Sweden all still have a monarch as actual or titular head of state. Though royal marriage adapted to new ideas about romantic love in the nineteenth century and to modern mores relating to social class and to divorce in the last few decades, its purpose is to ensure monarchical succession, and this is one of the reasons for 'monarchical durability'.[1] To a certain extent, this emphasis on stability and succession resembled that in Siam at the turn of the twentieth century, as discussed in Chapter 3.

Dynasty and Royal Marriage

In contrast to developments in Siam, however, this chapter discusses a marriage system which of its very nature is conservative and inimical to change. Royal marriage, till very recently, was dynastic marriage; that is, it united members of two different royal houses or dynasties.[2] Dynasties, writes Daniel Schönpflug, are 'cross-generational alliances of individuals constituted by land ownership and sovereign rights, and whose members married partners of equal rank and social standing to maintain and expand their existing social and power-political position'.[3] The monarch is chosen not by election but because he (or more rarely she) is a member of the ruling dynasty. Prominent European dynasties in the early modern period were the Tudors and Stuarts in Britain, the Habsburgs in Spain and the Holy Roman Empire, and the Valois and Bourbons in France.[4] Among the German-speaking states the Guelphs in Braunschweig and Hanover, the Hohenzollerns in Brandenburg and Prussia, the Wittelsbachs in Bavaria and the Wettins in Saxony are other notable examples. The Guelphs, the dynasty from which the current reigning queen of Britain and Northern Ireland Elizabeth II is descended, are the oldest dynasty in Europe, in existence since the eighth century.

Apart from territories such as Poland, which had an elective monarchy, or eighteenth-century Russia, where Peter the Great decreed that a ruler could designate whomever he considered the most suitable person to be his successor, in most of these dynasties the principle was established that the eldest son should succeed to the throne and title or, failing a son, the closest male relative. This is known as agnatic succession or patrilineal primogeniture. Males from a secondary branch of the family were preferred under this system over daughters in the direct line, since women were not allowed, according to the Salic Law, to inherit their father's title. Britain did not adhere to the Salic Law, and so, where there was no direct male heir, women could inherit. Notable examples are Mary Queen of Scots, who succeeded her father James V of Scotland in 1542, Mary I and Elizabeth I, who succeeded their father Henry VIII in 1553 and 1558, Victoria, who ascended the throne in 1837, and Elizabeth II, the present queen, who succeeded to the throne in 1953. Some of the German houses divided their territories among all the sons of a deceased ruler, thus establishing side-branches of the dynasty and leading to ever smaller territories with hyphenated names such as Saxe-Coburg-Gotha and Schleswig-Holstein-Sonderburg-Glücksburg. Whether the prevailing system is patrilineal primogeniture or one in which all the sons are allowed to inherit, whether the Salic Law is in force or not, it is essential for the survival of a dynasty to have strict control of its marriage policy in order to eliminate any doubt about the legitimacy of the heirs and to ensure that its power and wealth are maintained and, ideally, increased.

Since providing healthy male offspring was the most important task that the royal couple had to fulfil, one might expect that their robust good health would be the primary criterion before a marriage was arranged. The system of primogeniture meant, however, that the suitability of the ruler as a breeding partner was the outcome of biological chance. He might be a strong and virile prince, or he might be unable to procreate at all, as was the case with Charles II (1661–1700), the last Habsburg king on the Spanish throne. He was the offspring of an uncle and a niece, for his father Philip IV of Spain (1605–66) took as his second wife his niece Mariana of Austria, with the result that the product of this union, Charles, was physically and mentally disabled and, even worse, infertile.[5] As the legitimate only son, he ascended the throne regardless of his severe physical and mental disabilities and, though he married twice, it is thought that he was impotent. Certainly neither of his unfortunate wives ever became pregnant.

There might be other impediments on the husband's side. The dynastic system demanded that not only the direct heir to the throne but also his nearest male relatives should procreate, so they had to marry for the sake of the dynasty as an insurance policy in case the heir presumptive did not father sons. A prince might, for instance, be a practising homosexual, as was the case with Philippe, duc d'Orléans (1640–1701), the brother of Louis XIV, king of France. In spite of his many relationships with men, Philippe did his dynastic duty and married twice, fathering six children. Three were by his first wife, three by his second, who was none other than the famous letter-writer Elisabeth Charlotte of the Palatinate (1652–1722). None of the children of his first marriage survived, but two of his children with Liselotte, as she is often called, lived to adulthood: a son and a daughter. After Elisabeth Charlotte's third pregnancy the couple agreed to put an end to their sex life and he returned to his male partners.⁶ Another impediment preventing the conception of offspring might be that a prince did not feel affection for his bride and so had no desire to consummate the marriage. The Spanish princess Anne of Austria (1601–66) married Louis XIII, king of France (1601–43), in 1615, as part of the double marriage that also saw the union of her brother Philip IV of Spain and his sister Elisabeth of France. The marriage was not consummated for many years and Anne did not give birth to a son until 1638, when she herself was thirty-seven years old. She produced a second son, Philippe, duc d'Anjou, in 1640.

It also happened surprisingly often that a prince was not interested in sex or was ignorant about it, as appears to have been the case with Louis XVI, king of France, who did not consummate his marriage with Marie Antoinette (Maria Antonia of Austria, 1774–91) for seven years after their marriage.⁷ Sophie Friederike Auguste of Anhalt-Zerbst-Dornburg (1729–96), better known as Catherine the Great, empress of Russia, slept in the same bed as her husband Peter III for nine years without his being able to consummate the marriage.⁸ Elisabeth Christine of Braunschweig-Wolfenbüttel (1715–97) was married for fifty-three years to Frederick II (the Great) of Prussia, who not only did not sleep with her but hardly ever even saw her (Figure 4.1). The extent to which this was due to Frederick's supposed homosexuality is still a matter for debate. Frederick the Great, therefore, did not have any children himself and instead designated his nephew Friedrich Wilhelm as his heir.

If the health and virility of the bridegroom in a dynastic marriage could not be taken for granted, it might be thought that the bride would be chosen for her breeding qualities, since her primary task was to produce at least the proverbial 'heir and a spare' and as many marriageable daughters as might be useful as future political bargaining counters. However, in her case political and confessional considerations trumped any notions of physical suitability and she was most often chosen to forge a political alliance or to seal a peace treaty. This was the case when Philip IV, king of Spain (1605–65), married Elisabeth of France (1602–44) in 1615 in the double marriage between the Spanish Habsburgs and the Bourbons mentioned above. The bridegroom was only ten years old and his bride thirteen, even though they had been betrothed at that point for three years. They were, therefore, too young to procreate. Maria Amalia of Saxony (1724–60) was only thirteen on her marriage in 1738 to Carlo di Borbone, king of the Two Sicilies.⁹ This marriage also sealed a peace between the Habsburgs, from whom she was descended on her mother's side, and the Bourbons, the dynasty to which her husband belonged. Maria Amalia was so young that she needed a Papal Dispensation to marry in the first place and she did not reach puberty until a year and a half after her marriage. Sometimes marriages were forged between couples who might have been thought too old to procreate. The Polish princess Zofia Jagiellonka (1522–7) did not marry Heinrich II, Duke of Braunschweig-Wolfenbüttel, until she was thirty-four and her husband seventy-seven, while her sister Katarzyna (1526–83) was thirty-six when she married Johan Vasa, Duke of Finland, later Johan III, king of Sweden. Katarzyna bore him a son when she was forty and a daughter at the age of forty-two, but this was a fortunate outcome that no one can have expected.¹⁰

If the Spanish Habsburgs condemned themselves to extinction through their consanguineous marriage policy, other dynasties used their marriage alliances to

Figure 4.1 The Marriage in 1733 of Crown Prince Friedrich of Brandenburg-Prussia and Elisabeth Christine, Duchess of Braunschweig-Bevern. Friedrich, later Frederick II, king of Prussia, was pressured into this marriage, and it took place in the palace among the courtiers. Source: Ullsteinbild.

create a Europe-wide network. This was the policy of the Wettins of Saxony. Friedrich August I, Elector of Saxony (1670–1733), known to posterity as August the Strong, converted to Catholicism in 1697 in order to have himself elected to the Polish throne as August II. Thereafter members of his dynasty were able to intermarry with the great Catholic houses of Europe. August II arranged a marriage for his son Friedrich August II, Electoral Prince of Saxony (1696–1763), with the Habsburg princess Maria Josepha (1699–1757), the elder daughter of Emperor Joseph I. August III and Maria Josepha married their eldest daughter Maria Amalia to the Bourbon Carlo, king of the Two Sicilies, as mentioned above. He succeeded to the throne of Spain in 1759, so she was queen of Spain during the last year of her life. Her sister Maria Josepha became the second wife of the Dauphin, while another sister married the Elector of Bavaria and, in a double marriage, her brother the sister of the Elector of Bavaria. Frederick the Great pursued quite a different strategy in the marriages he arranged for the various members of the Hohenzollern dynasty, constructing a web of German dynastic alliances, none of which could threaten his own dominance.[11]

Two other factors were important in the choice of a royal bride. One was the bridegroom's desire to extend his territory. Thanks to the inheritance of Anna of Prussia (1576–1625), who married Elector Johann Sigismund of Brandenburg (1572–1619), the territory of Prussia was added to that of Brandenburg, thereby doubling it in size. Anna also inherited the territories of Cleves, Mark and Ravensberg in the Lower Rhineland.[12] Uniting two of the territories belonging to different branches of the Guelph dynasty was the reason for the incompatible and ultimately disastrous marriage between Georg Ludwig, electoral prince of Hanover (later George I, king of Great Britain, 1660–1727), and his cousin Sophie Dorothea of Celle (1666–1726) discussed below. The territorial enlargement that resulted from the marriage was seen as a necessary step towards the creation of the new electorship of Hanover.

An equally powerful factor when arranging a dynastic marriage was the confessional acceptability of the bride to the dynasty and the territory she was about to marry into. Once mainland Europe had been split after the Reformation into the three confessional blocs, Catholic, Lutheran and Reformed, marriage alliances had to be made within the boundaries of whichever confessional bloc a dynasty belonged to. The Catholic Habsburgs intermarried with the Catholic houses of France, Spain and Italy. Lutheran Electoral Saxony most often chose marriage partners from the Lutheran houses of Denmark and Württemberg.[13] Before the Reformation it was possible for a Hohenzollern such as Barbara of Brandenburg-Kulmbach (1455–1503), granddaughter of the first Elector of Brandenburg, to marry a Gonzaga. After the Reformation and the conversion of the Hohenzollerns to Calvinism the dynasty intermarried most often with other Calvinist dynasties such as the Palatine branch of the Wittelsbachs, the House of Orange-Nassau and the Brandenburg-Ansbach branch of the Hohenzollerns. They also intermarried, on occasion, with Lutheran dynasties such as the Guelphs of Braunschweig-Wolfenbüttel, the Wettins of Saxony and the House of Oldenburg – that is, Denmark, Schleswig-Holstein and, after 1762, Russia. It would have been as impossible for them as for the Wettins in Saxony, before their conversion to Catholicism in 1697, to intermarry with a Catholic house. If, for political reasons, a bride who belonged to another confession was, exceptionally, chosen, she was usually required to convert to that of her husband. Elisabeth Christine of Braunschweig-Wolfenbüttel (1691–1750) converted from Lutheranism to Catholicism in order to marry Emperor Charles VI (1711–40), for instance. Elisabeth Charlotte of the Palatinate also had to convert to Catholicism in order to become the duchesse d'Orléans, while Luise Ulrike of Prussia converted from Calvinism to Lutheranism in 1744 before becoming queen of Sweden. Other considerations had to come into play – a large dowry or a vital military alliance – before a consort, that is, the official spouse of a monarch, could negotiate in her marriage contract for permission to continue to practise her own religion after her marriage. Examples are Catherine of Braganza (1638–1705), consort of Charles II of Great Britain (1630–85), who was allowed to remain a Catholic at the Protestant (Anglican) English court, and Charlotte Amalie of Hesse-Kassel (1650–1714), who was given permission to remain a Calvinist at the Lutheran Danish court.

Britain in the seventeenth century was an exception to the strict confessional congruity practised by other European dynasties. All its seventeenth-century Protestant Stuart monarchs were married to Catholics, from James I of England and VI of Scotland, whose consort Anna of Denmark converted to Catholicism, to Charles I married to Henrietta Maria of France, Charles II married, as mentioned above, to Catherine of Braganza, and James II, whose second wife was Maria d'Este (Mary of Modena). That these Catholic brides would influence their spouses to convert to Catholicism and that they would produce Catholic children was one of the factors in the execution of Charles I in 1649 and was the reason that Catherine of Braganza was accused of attempting to poison her husband Charles II in the trumped-up Popish Plot of 1679. Because of his Roman Catholicism James II, the legitimate heir to Charles II, was deposed in 1685 and his Catholic sons by his second wife were excluded from the succession. Marriage to a Catholic was his nemesis. Instead, he was succeeded in turn by his two daughters by his first wife Anne Hyde, who had been raised as Protestants: Mary II (1662–94), who ruled together with her husband William of Orange (1650–1702), and Anne (1665–1714), whose consort was George, prince of Denmark (1653–1708). Since neither of these marriages produced living children, the succession was regulated in the Act of Settlement of 1701, an Act of Parliament which, with some modifications, is still in force in Britain today. It declared that the lawful heir to the throne was Sophia, electress of Hanover (1630–1714), and that she would be succeeded by her Protestant heirs. Her claim came through her mother Elizabeth Stuart, electress Palatine and queen of Bohemia (1596–1662). Queen Anne and Sophia of Hanover both died in 1714 and Sophia's son, Georg Ludwig, elector of Hanover, succeeded to the throne as George I, king of Great Britain and Ireland. This is an egregious example of how confessional considerations trump patrilineal succession.

The French Revolution in 1789 threw a grenade into the calm assumption that a dynasty such as the Bourbons that had reigned for almost two centuries would continue to do so forever. France became a republic until Napoleon declared himself emperor in 1804, whereupon he divorced his first wife Joséphine de Beauharnais in order to marry a Habsburg, Marie Louise, princess of Austria (1791–1847). Napoleon made his son by Marie Louise Napoleon II, king of Rome (1811–32), planning that Napoleon II would succeed him as emperor of France and that the blood of the Holy Roman emperors flowing in his veins would legitimate the succession. Here, at the beginning of a new social order, we see the power of dynastic marriage and of royal bloodlines. However, Napoleon II died of tuberculosis as a young man and, though Napoleon I's nephew reigned from 1852 until 1870 as Napoleon III, France had ceased to be a dynastic state.

Genealogy and Dynastic Marriage

Since the purpose of dynastic marriage is to ensure the smooth transfer of power, title and property to the designated successor and so guarantee the stability of the dynastic state, it is vital to prove that the bride's bloodlines will enable the worthy continuation of the dynasty. Her origins have to be shown to be, at the very least, worthy of those of her husband. The new union, therefore, has to be embedded in a genealogy whose purpose is to demonstrate that the dynasty is everlasting. In past centuries this was the task of the court genealoger, who was often identical with the court historiographer. A work of genealogy begins by tracing the descent of the whole clan from one original ancestor, said to be the absolute beginning of the dynasty and thereby constituting a link between all its members down the centuries. Dynasties in the early modern period were particularly keen to trace their descent from the Trojans and they invented such figures as Francus, supposedly the Trojan ancestor of the French, in the same way that Aeneas was considered to be the ancestor of the Romans. By referring to these mythical ancestors, the genealogers kept the distant past alive in the present.[14] There was a great explosion of genealogical works in the sixteenth and seventeenth centuries thanks to the printing press, and they often combined depictions of family trees and coats of arms with short passages narrating the history of the family. These works continued to expand in number and in extent during the seventeenth and eighteenth centuries, with noble and royal houses bringing their family trees up to date at regular intervals in works that chronicled the succession and displayed the marriage alliances contracted by the family in question.

Genealogy is not just explained by means of family trees but also through works of heraldry, a genre with an unbroken tradition from the Middle Ages up to our own day and always employed when a new marriage alliance is proposed. Three examples out of many may serve to illustrate this continuity. In 1452 Albrecht VI of Austria (1418–63) married Mathilde, countess Palatine (1419–82). He had an illustrated manuscript armorial compiled for the occasion, the Ingeram Codex, so called after its only named author.[15] The opening pages depict the groom holding an engagement ring and the bride holding a mirror. The manuscript contains, among many other older elements bound into it, the coats of arms of the Austrian nobility.

The eighteenth century can provide a second example. When Carlo di Borbone, king of the Two Sicilies, the third son of Philip V, king of Spain, married the Saxon princess Maria Amalia there was an obvious disparity between the political and dynastic importance of bride and groom. The official publications at the time of the wedding in 1738 had to engage in a concerted attempt to show that the bride's dynasty, the Wettins, was worthy of her new Bourbon in-laws. They did this by showing that, a thousand years earlier, the two dynasties were connected. The Saxon genealoger Gottlob Christian Klügel, in his *Carl der Große und Wittekind der Große* (Charlemagne and Wittekind the Great), proceeded in three steps. He showed first that Carlo and Maria Amalia had two great-great-great-grandfathers in common in the previous century: a Habsburg in Philip III of Spain (1578–1621) and a Wettin in Johann Georg I, elector of Saxony (1585–1656).[16] The latter connection came about through Dorothea Sophia von Pfalz-Neuburg (1670–1748), Carlo's maternal grandmother, he explained. Kügel then went back another two centuries and explained that bride and bridegroom were each descended from a Friedrich – Friedrich III, Holy Roman Emperor (1415–93), in the case of Carlo, and Friedrich II, elector of Saxony (1412–64), in the case of Maria Amalia. Finally, he traced the bridal couple right back to the eighth and early ninth century in the persons of Charlemagne (747/8-814, supposedly the ancestor of the bridegroom) and his contemporary rival Wittekind (dates unknown, supposedly the ancestor of Maria Amalia). Legend had it that Charlemagne was responsible for Wittekind's conversion to Christianity, so Divine Providence, Klügel maintained, had brought this marriage about. An anonymous 60-line poem, *Vorstellung Der Hohen Anverwandschaft* (Presentation of the Noble Consanguinity), accompanied by a family tree showing Carlo and Maria Amalia's descent from Johann Georg I of Saxony, also underlined the connection to Wittekind, who was considered in the Saxon national narrative to be the ninth-century originator of the Wettins.[17] If it was an easy matter to convince the Saxons that this marriage was not an unequal one, it was a more difficult task to convince the Spanish. This is what the *Tabla Genealogica,* another genealogical work written in Spanish, though printed in Dresden, was designed to do.[18] In a beautifully engraved horizontal folio that left space for medallions of the bridal pair and coats of arms, it set out in tabular form the connection between Carlo and Maria Amalia via the Pfalz-Neuburg line. All of this effort was to ensure that the marriage would be recognized throughout Europe and that there would be no dispute about the inheritance rights of the eldest son of the marriage. This was no light matter in a century that had begun with the War of the Spanish Succession disputing the right of Carlo's father to ascend the Spanish throne in 1714.

Our third example is the marriage in 2011 of William, Duke of Cambridge, and Catherine Middleton. Not only were genealogers active in tracing the family tree of the bride, thereby proving that Ms Middleton was descended from an illegitimate daughter of the Plantagenet king Edward IV (1442–83) and so had royal blood in her veins,[19] but the Garter King of Arms and Senior Herald in England had to grant Ms Middleton a new coat of arms in advance of her wedding.[20] This indicates that, though the British monarchy has come to admit a person officially designated 'a commoner' into the dynasty, it is nonetheless thought to be important to demonstrate to British society that the monarchy is not trampling on tradition. Ms Middleton had to be made 'armigerous', that is, someone of sufficient rank to bear a coat of arms, in order to marry the future king.

The Legal Framework of Dynastic Marriage

A royal marriage is regulated by a marriage contract, which is negotiated between the representatives of the bridegroom and the bride's father and is signed and sealed before the marriage takes place.[21] In earlier centuries the principal provisions concerned the dowry that was to be paid to the groom and the financial provision for the bride during her marriage and, more importantly, during her widowhood.[22] It was in the father's interest to reduce the amount of the dowry but if he did so, he was also condemning his daughter to an impoverished widowhood, for the dowry was usually used to provide the widow with an income. The marriage contract also laid down when the dowry would have to be paid, usually in instalments. Some contracts stipulated both a dowry and a counter-dowry (*dos* and *contrados*), that is, the father of the bride and the father of the groom agreed to put in the same amount of money. The contract also usually named the dower house where the widow would reside and any property or lands over which she would have control as a widow and sometimes set out the details of her trousseau, which could amount to very valuable quantities of silver and jewellery. Karl-Heinz Spieß points out that in the late Middle Ages there were two models for the maintenance of queens at the royal courts of Europe.[23] In the first model, the queen was granted an income of her own, either the revenue of certain lands, or in England from a tax known as the 'queen's gold'. If the king retained possession of the dower lands during his lifetime, he paid his consort a fixed allowance. Under the German system the consort was far more likely to have her own needs and those of her court paid as and when they arose, without any fixed sum agreed upon in advance, but what the marriage contract did lay down was the extent of the so-called 'Morgengabe' or 'morning gift', paid to the consort the morning after the wedding night. This sum was invested for her benefit and she could dispose of the income.

Crucial too were the rights of the widow during the minority of her children and whether she was allowed to become regent for an underage son or take part in a regency council. Other important clauses concerned her renunciation of any hereditary rights in relation to her natal dynasty and, in the event that she should marry someone of lesser standing to her own, her renunciation of any superior title such as 'Royal Highness'. Clauses often set out other rights that she would have to renounce, were she as a widow to marry again, which included rights over her children from her first marriage. These contracts, together with other agreements relating to succession and inheritance, gradually built up into a body of case law regulating the alliances of any particular dynasty. This was called, in the case of the German dynasties, the 'Hausgesetz' or House Law, and each of the major dynasties had the right to establish their own.[24]

The British parliament passed several acts regulating royal marriage in Britain. The Act of Settlement (1701) has already been mentioned above, whose main purpose was to prevent a Roman Catholic from marrying the heir to the throne or from ascending the throne themselves. It is till today one of the main constitutional laws governing the succession not only to the throne of the United Kingdom of Great Britain and Northern Ireland but also to those of Commonwealth territories.[25] The Royal Marriages Act 1772 stipulates that no descendant of George II, male or female, except the offspring of princesses who have married into foreign families, may marry without the consent of the reigning monarch.[26] This Act renders void any marriage contracted without the monarch's permission and declares any children of that marriage to be illegitimate. It still applies not just to members of the British royal family but to any descendant of George II, even citizens of another country, if their marriage is to be valid in Britain. As a consequence, Ernst August, the present prince of Hanover (b.1954), and his heir the Crown Prince, also Ernst August (b.1983), both applied to Elizabeth II for permission to marry. It was agreed to amend this Act in 2011 in the so-called Perth Agreement passed by the Commonwealth Heads of Government at a meeting held in Perth, Western Australia. This limited the applicability of the Royal Marriages Act to the first six people in line to the British throne. The Act was amended thanks to the passing of the Succession to the Crown Act of 2013, enacted in 2015 and discussed below.

Dealing with Problematic Unions

The dynastic marriage was chiefly threatened by four things: a male member's morganatic marriage; a male member's bigamy; the consort's failure to produce an heir; the consort's unfaithfulness. Of these only morganatic marriage has ceased to have relevance today. If a king or indeed any male member of a dynasty married a commoner, this union was characterized up to the twentieth century as a 'morganatic marriage'. The marriage itself was legal and binding, but the wife could not take on her husband's title and no child of the marriage could inherit the title and the property. 'Morganatic' comes from the Latin *morganaticus* and refers to the 'morning gift' given to the wife by her husband after the wedding night. It was the only financial provision to which a wife of unequal birth could lay claim. This meant that, unless the king divorced his morganatic wife, he could not produce legitimate heirs and the succession was threatened. Morganatic marriages came about as a result of the mutual love and attraction of the couple, in contrast to most dynastic marriages contracted between two people who had never even seen each other and who might or might not turn out to be compatible. Morganatic marriages were often contracted when the king married a mistress, a woman with whom he perhaps already had children. This was not a problem if the husband concerned already had legitimate male heirs. An example is the second marriage of Louis XIV, king of France, to the widow Madame de Maintenon (Françoise d'Aubigné, marquise de Maintenon, 1635-1719), probably in 1683. Louis's late first wife Maria Teresa, infanta of Spain (1638-83), had given birth to a son, the Grand Dauphin (1661-1711), who himself had an heir. The succession was therefore assured and Madame de Maintenon was too old to bear children. Madame de Maintenon would have thought it quite inappropriate to be named Louis XIV's queen consort because of the disparity of their birth.

Some princes were powerful enough or sufficiently indifferent to convention and public opinion to make their mistresses not just into their morganatic wives but into their official consorts, for instance, Georg Wilhelm, duke of Braunschweig-Lüneburg (1624-1705), with Eleonore d'Olbreuse (1639-1722), Karl Eugen, duke of Württemberg (1728-93) with Franziska von Hohenheim (1774-1811) and Peter the Great of Russia (1672-1725) with Marta Helena Skowrońska, the Swedish Livonian washerwoman whom he transformed into Catherine I, empress of Russia (1684-1727). Such women were, however, often treated at court with great hauteur by ladies of higher birth and bluer blood. In contrast, George III of Great Britain considered that the marriages of his brothers the Duke of Cumberland and the Duke of Gloucester to commoners in 1771 and 1772, respectively, threatened the dynasty, which was why he proposed the Royal Marriages Act. This did not prevent his own son and heir, George, Prince of Wales (1762-1830) from marrying the twice-widowed Maria Anne Fitzherbert in contravention of the law. The Act made this marriage invalid, which meant that the union was not considered a morganatic marriage. If the marriage had been deemed valid, George's future ascent of the throne would have been threatened, as Mrs Fitzherbert was a practising Roman Catholic. Ultimately, George, the future George IV, was coerced into a disastrously unhappy marriage with his cousin Caroline of Braunschweig-Wolfenbüttel (1768-1821), which produced only one daughter.

Bigamous unions created greater problems, for instance, that of Philipp I, Landgrave of Hesse (1504-67). He married Christine of Saxony in 1523 and had seven children by her when he declared his intention of marrying Margarethe von der Saale (1522-66) in 1540. Philipp had no grounds to divorce Christine but Margarethe refused to have sex with him unless they were married. Christine bore Philipp two more children after his marriage to Margarethe, while Margarethe bore him another nine. Since Philipp was one of Martin Luther's most stalwart and prominent supporters during the Reformation, this flagrant transgression against the sacrament of marriage caused Luther severe qualms of conscience and created political problems for Philipp with his wife's relations. Henry VIII, king of England, is an even more dramatic example of what ensued when a king wished to take a new bride. Henry got divorced twice and arranged for two other wives to be executed.

Another difficult case was that of Eberhard Ludwig, duke of Württemberg (1676-1733). In 1697 he married Johanna Elisabeth of Baden-Durlach (1680-1757) and the couple seem to have become estranged after the birth of their only child Friedrich

Ludwig in 1698. Eberhard Ludwig took Christina Wilhelmina von Grävenitz (1686–1744) as his mistress and seems really to have loved her. In 1707, he announced that he had married her bigamously. Johanna Elisabeth appealed to the Holy Roman Emperor, and the mistress was banished to Switzerland. The consort was reconciled with her husband, but at a price: she, the wronged and innocent wife, had to acknowledge her 'guilt', which he graciously accepted![27] However, Christina Wilhelmina returned in triumph in 1711, so Johanna Elisabeth retreated prematurely into the life of a dowager in the Old Castle in Stuttgart, playing no part in the life of the court, which had moved to Ludwigsburg. Eberhard Ludwig did everything he could to discipline his wife, installing his people to oversee her household and opening her letters. He also withheld her allowance from 1713 to 1722 in order, presumably, to starve her into submission. Christina Wilhelmina, meanwhile, was living the life of a consort, residing in the duchess's apartments at Ludwigsburg and being showered with money and gifts. Her relationship with Eberhard Ludwig lasted thirty years and it is thought that her fall in 1731 came about because her supporters at court realized that Eberhard Ludwig was nearing the end of his life and that, after his death, she would no longer have any influence. She was banished from court by Eberhard Ludwig's son while his father was still alive, and Johanna Elisabeth resumed her role as consort for two years until her husband's death in 1733.[28]

The consort's failure to produce an heir threatened the marriage, but her unfaithfulness destroyed it. Catherine of Braganza, consort of Charles II of Britain, was unable to bear a living child and her position in Britain was for that reason precarious, with the king's advisers counselling him to divorce her and – another factor – marry a Protestant. Sophie Dorothea of Hanover (1687–1757), consort of Friedrich Wilhelm I, king of Prussia (1688–1740), had to scotch rumours that she was incapable of bearing children, when she had in fact given birth to no fewer than four, all of whom had died as toddlers. It was so important for her standing and the security of her marriage that she be known as a woman who could give birth, that she had life-size wax models made of all of her dead children and placed them in public view in the Cabinet of Curiosities to prove her fertility.[29]

Though most kings or princes had mistresses, some of whom played a prominent role at court, it was fatal if their wives were discovered to have a lover. The wife was invariably sent away from court, terrible punishment was inflicted on her lover and she lost all access to her children. Two egregious examples must suffice out of many. In order to reunite the divided territories of the various branches of the Guelph dynasty, Sophie Dorothea of Celle (1666–1726) was married against her will to her cousin Georg Ludwig, prince of Hanover (1660–1727), subsequently George I, king of Britain. She gave birth to two children, a son and a daughter, whereupon her husband returned to his mistress Countess von der Schulenburg. Sophie Dorothea wanted a divorce but her parents would not agree and sent her back to her husband in Hanover. It is thought, though not proven, that she began an affair with Count Philip Christoph von Königsmarck (1665–94) and planned to run away with him. The affair was discovered, whereupon Königsmarck vanished; it is assumed he was murdered. Georg Ludwig divorced his wife, had her name removed from all official documents and forbade her from ever seeing her children again. He divorced her in 1694 and from then until her death in 1726 she was kept as a prisoner in the Castle of Ahlden. When George I came to Britain as the new king, he was accompanied by Countess von der Schulenburg.

Just as terrible is the fate of Caroline Mathilda, princess of Great Britain, queen of Denmark (1751–75). She travelled to Denmark in 1766 at the age of fifteen to marry her cousin Christian VII, king of Denmark (1749–1808), who was mentally ill and promiscuous and prone to paranoid delusions. Nonetheless she bore him a son, the future King Frederick VI of Denmark. The king's physician was Johann Friedrich Struensee (1737–72) and he became Caroline Mathilda's lover and possibly the father of her daughter Louise Auguste. When the affair became known, Struensee was executed and Caroline Mathilde was first imprisoned in Rosenborg Castle in Denmark and then banished to her brother's territory at Celle in the Duchy of Hanover. She too was forbidden from ever seeing her children again and she died in Celle at the age of twenty-three from scarlet fever. The evolution of the concept of romantic love at the end of the eighteenth century gradually brought about the end of marriages between complete strangers, brokered to maintain or acquire political power and territory. This could not, of course, ensure the survival of a marriage, as the divorce of Charles, Prince of Wales, in 1996 illustrates, but it did prevent the tragedies and injustices just outlined.

Royal Marriage since ca. 1800

Daniel Schönpflug reminds us that, between 1800 and 1918, there were twenty-nine monarchies in Europe whose rulers came from fifteen dynasties and who ascended their thrones through patrilineal succession.[30] Dynastic marriage was, therefore, just as crucial as in the previous centuries. However, the nineteenth century brought about three changes to royal marriage: 1. European monarchs moved from being Absolutist kings, as they had been in the seventeenth century, to being constitutional monarchs, so their marriage policy had to be acceptable to the parliament and the people; 2. Royal unions were now expected increasingly to be based on love and compatibility[31] and the royal family was expected to lead a warm family life similar to that of their subjects; 3. The growth of large-circulation newspapers, of new techniques of pictorial reproduction (steel engravings, daguerrotypes, photogravure, photography and, at the end of the century, film) turned royal weddings into media events (Figure 4.2).

For a royal marriage to be based on romantic love, the parties had to meet beforehand, something that happened rarely, if at all, in earlier centuries. A striking example here is the meeting at a ball in Frankfurt in 1793 of the future King Friedrich Wilhelm III of Prussia, and Luise, duchess of Mecklenburg-Strelitz. Her sister Friederike and his brother Ludwig were also present. The Crown Prince was given first pick of the sisters and chose the elder, Luise, while his brother married Friederike. Friedrich Wilhelm and Luise began at once to exchange love letters, something unheard of in a previous century. On 10 April 1793, a few weeks after they had met and become engaged, for instance, Luise writes to Friedrich Wilhelm: 'My whole life long I will try to make you happy; my greatest care will be dedicated to discerning by every means in my power how I can give you joy; I will study your tastes in order to be directed by your wishes; in short, I swear to you that I will also *truly* be *yours*'[32] (Original emphasis).

Figure 4.2 A Memento of the Wedding of the German Crown Prince Friedrich Wilhelm of Prussia and Cecilie, Duchess of Mecklenburg-Schwerin, on 6 June 1905. Source: Deutsches Historisches Museum, Berlin /I. Desnica.

Though the marriage between Queen Victoria and Albert of Saxe-Coburg-Gotha was brokered by Albert's uncle, Leopold, king of the Belgians, who arranged a meeting when they were both seventeen, a year before Victoria came to the throne in 1837, Victoria chose Albert out of a series of possible suitors and their marriage turned into a close companionate union, ending in Albert's early death in 1861. Their daughter Victoria's marriage to the future German Emperor Friedrich III was also a love match and was publicly presented as such. They had met in London in 1851 when she was eleven and he was nineteen and corresponded thereafter. The couple became engaged at Balmoral Castle in 1855. These unions and others like them were promoted by the respective dynasties as a means of humanizing the monarchy. At a time of constitutional development when power was moving from the monarch to parliament, these marriages created an emotional link between royal family and people and were part of what historians such as Martin Kirsch have called the 'functionalization' of the monarchy, whereby the monarch becomes a figure of national integration.[33] Where seventeenth-century royal marriages took place before the members of the court behind the closed doors of the palace chapel, royal marriages from around 1800 on became events of public rejoicing. This has developed dramatically in recent decades, thanks to the advent of television and the internet.

The First World War brought many monarchies to an end: the Habsburgs ceased to rule over the Austrian Empire, the Hohenzollerns over the German Empire and the Romanovs over the Russian Empire. The kingdoms of Bavaria, Hanover, Saxony and Württemberg likewise came to an end, though many of the dynasties that ruled over them still exist today, without political power and with reduced wealth. The European monarchies that have survived are Belgium, Denmark, the Netherlands, Norway, Sweden, the UK and, after a gap of over fifty years, Spain. The old rules began only gradually to loosen. Marriage to a divorcee was still considered so impossible in Britain in 1936 that Edward VIII (1894–1972) had to abdicate in order to marry Wallace Simpson, and he and his wife had to spend the rest of their lives in exile in Paris and the United States. She was given the title Duchess of Windsor but was denied the title of Royal Highness, and the royal family refused to receive her. Edward VIII, as Supreme Governor of the Church of England, a title that the British monarch has held since the Act of Supremacy of 1558, could not, for religious reasons, marry a woman who had been divorced not once but twice.

For the heir to the British throne to marry a Catholic only became possible as recently as 2015 thanks to the Perth Declaration and the Succession to the Crown Act of 2013. This Act also allows the monarch's eldest child of either sex to succeed to the throne, not just the eldest son. This had been allowed in Sweden since 1980, in the Netherlands since 1983, in Norway since 1990, in Belgium since 1991 and in Denmark since 2009. Britain, therefore, in comparison to other monarchies, has been very slow to change. The heir to the throne is also now allowed to divorce, as Charles, Prince of Wales, did in 1996. He did not marry his second wife, however, until 2005, having been a widower since 1997, and married her only in a civil, not a church, ceremony.

The one area in which royal marriage throughout Europe has universally modernized in the last decades is that monarchs and their spouses no longer have to be equally blue-blooded. The modern royal marriage is expected to mirror the marriage of private citizens in that the couple are expected to fall in love based on shared interests and values. They are also expected to stay together in a companionate marriage and to make their harmonious union visible to their subjects. All this develops further the model that began to be established in the nineteenth century. Modern royal couples are also expected to have a close and loving relationship with their offspring and to bring them up themselves, not, as in previous centuries, handing them over to servants and tutors. That marriage to a commoner is universally accepted can be seen in every royal house in Europe. Willem-Alexander, king of the Netherlands, married the Argentinian banker Máxima Zorreguieta-Cerruti in 2002; Fredrik, crown prince of Denmark married Mary Donaldson, an Australian advertising executive, in 2004; Victoria, crown princess of Sweden, married the businessman Daniel Westling in 2010, while William, duke of Cambridge, married Catherine Middleton in 2011. Felipe VI, king of Spain, went one step further in 2004 when he married Letizia Ortiz Rocasolano. She is not only a commoner but also a divorcee, a surprising turn of events for the queen consort of a Roman Catholic country. In each case, these couples met and fell in love in an informal everyday context, unlike the marriages brokered by diplomats and senior family members that were the norm up to the Second World War. Since the abdication of Juan Carlos, the previous king of Spain, Prince Philip, duke of Edinburgh, is the only royal consort who is himself also of royal blood.

Given that the ancient system of monarchy depends on dynastic continuity based on the principle that the eldest offspring of the monarch succeeds to the throne, it is no wonder that royal marriage has been so slow to change. The choice of the royal bride or bridegroom is no longer dictated by political, confessional and territorial considerations. The marriage itself, however, is seen as a matter of public concern, which the monarch's subjects have every right to know about and be emotionally involved in, because it plays a role in the stability of the nation. For this reason, the partners in a royal marriage cannot choose to be childless, nor can they be of the same sex, no matter that such unions have become acceptable to their subjects.

Notes

1 Frank Lorenz Müller, 'Stabilizing a "Great Historic System" in the Nineteenth Century? Royal Heirs and Succession in an Age of Monarchy', in *Sons and Heirs. Succession and Political Culture in Nineteenth-Century Europe*, ed. Frank Lorenz Müller and Heidi Mehrkens (Basingstoke: Palgrave Macmillan, 2016), 1–16, 3.
2 Heinz Duchardt, 'The Dynastic Marriage'. In *European History Online (EGO)*, published by the Institute of European History (IEG), Mainz 2011. http://ieg-ego.eu/en/threads/european-networks/dynastic-networks/heinz-duchhardt-the-dynastic-marriage (accessed on 7 July 2016).
3 Daniel Schönpflug, 'Dynastic Networks', in *European History Online (EGO)*, published by the Institute of European History (IEG), Mainz 2011. http://ieg-ego.eu/en/threads/european-networks/dynastic-networks/daniel-schoenpflug-dynastic-networks (accessed on 7 July 2016).
4 Linda Maria Koldau, 'Familiennetzwerke, Machtkalkül und Kulturtransfer: Habsburgerfürstinnen im 16. und 17. Jahrhundert', in *Grenzüberschreitende Familienbeziehungen. Akteure und Medien des Kulturtransfers in der Frühen Neuzeit*, ed. Dorothea Nolde und Claudia Opitz (Cologne: Böhlau, 2008), 55–72.
5 Gonzalo Alvarez, Francisco C. Ceballos and Celsa Quinteiro, 'The Role of Inbreeding in the Extinction of a European Royal Dynasty', *PLoS ONE* 4, no. 4 (2009): e5174. doi:10.1371/journal.pone.0005174
6 Dirk van der Cruysse, *Madame sein ist ein ellendes Handwerck'. Liselotte von der Pfalz – eine deutsche Prinzessin am Hof des Sonnenkönigs* (Munich: Piper, 1995), 199.
7 Antonia Fraser, *Marie Antoinette. The Journey* (London: Weidenfeld and Nicholson, 2001).
8 Robert K. Massie, *Catherine the Great. Portrait of a Woman* (New York: Random House, 2011), 87.

9   See Helen Watanabe-O'Kelly, 'The Consort in the Theatre of Power: Maria Amalia of Saxony, Queen of the Two Sicilies, Queen of Spain', in *Queens Consort, Cultural Transfer and European Politics, 1550-1750*, ed. Adam Morton and Helen Watanabe-O'Kelly (London: Routledge, 2016), 37–63.
10 See Almut Bues, 'Art Collections as Dynastic Tools: The Jagiellonian Princesses Katarzyna, Queen of Sweden', in *Queens Consort, Cultural Transfer and European Politics*, 15–36.
11 See Thomas Biskup, 'Four Weddings and Five Funerals: Dynastic Integration and Cultural Transfer between the Houses of Braunschweig and Brandenburg in the Eighteenth Century'. In *Queens Consort, Cultural Transfer and European Politics*, 202–30.
12 Michael Kaiser, 'Anna von Preußen und der Kampf um das Jülicher Erbe'. In *Frauensache. Wie Brandenburg Preußen wurde*, ed. Generaldirektion der Stiftung Preußische Schlösser und Gärten Berlin-Brandenburg (Dresden: Sandstein, 2015), 230–8.
13 Jutta Kappel and Claudia Brink, *Mit Fortuna übers Meer. Sachsen und Dänemark – Ehe und Allianzen im Spiegel der Kunst (1548-1709)* (Dresden: Deutscher Kunstverlag, 2009).
14 Helen Watanabe-O'Kelly, 'Literature and the Court, 1450-1720', in *Early Modern German Literature 1350-1700*, ed. Max Reinhart (Rochester, NY: Camden House, 2007), 621–51.
15 The Ingeram Codex is preserved in the Kunsthistorisches Museum, Vienna, A2302.
16 Gottlob Christian Klügel, *Carl der Große und Wittekind der Große, als Hohe Ahnen des Allerdurchlauchtigsten und Großmächtigsten CARLS, Königes beyder Sicilien, wie auc Dessen Allerdurchlauchtigsten Prinzeßin Braut MARIÆ AMALIÆ Königlichen Hoheit, nebst noch einigen Genealogischen Merkwürdigkeiten, die by diesen Allerhöchsten Verlobten vorkommen, kürzlich in Tabellen dargestellet* (Leipzig: Bernhard Christoph Breitkopf, 1738).
17 *Vorstellung der Hohen Anverwandschafft Des Königl. Spanischen und Churfürstl. Sächsischen Hauses, Bey höchst= glücklich getroffener Vermählung Ihro Majestät CAROLI, Königs von Neapolis und Sicilien, etc etc. Mit Ihro Königl. Hoheit, Der Durchlauchtigsten Printzeßin Maria Amalia, Königl. Printzeßin von Pohlen, und Printzeßin zu Sachsen, etc* (Dresden: Johann Christoph Krause, 1738).
18 *Tabla genealogica en la qual se vee que no solamente La Sacra Magestad de Don Carlos Rey de las dos Sicilias y La Serenissima Princessa Real de Polonia y Electoral de Saxonia, Dona Maria Amalia, su dignissima Esposa, sino tambien La Sacra Real magestad de Dona Maria Josepha, Reyna de Polonia y Electriz de Saxonia, nacida ArchiDuquessa de Austria Madre de la Real Esposa, descienden en grado ygual del Serenissimo Principe don Juan Gorge I. Elector de Saxonia Siendo juntas Las armas de las Familias Imperiales, Reales,Electorales, Archi=Ducales y Ducales petenecientes a esta Real Genealogia* (Dresden: n.pub., 1738).
19 William Addams Reitwiesner, *The Ancestry of Catherine Middleton* (Boston: New England Historic Genealogical Society, 2011).
20 www.dukeandduchessofcambridge org/the-duchess-of-cambridge/titles-and-heraldry/the-middleton-coat-of-arms (accessed on 18 July 2016).
21 Karl-Heinz Spieß, 'European Royal Marriages in the Late Middle Ages. Marriage Treaties, Questions of Income, Cultural Transfer', *Majestas* 13 (2005), ed. János Bak, Heinz Duchhardt and Richard A. Jackson, 7–21.
22 Uta Essegern, 'Kursächsische Eheverträge in der ersten Hälfte des 17. Jahrhunderts', in *Witwenschaft in der Frühen Neuzeit Fürstliche und adlige Witwen zwischen Frend-*

und Selbstbestimmung, ed. Martina Schattkowsky (Leipzig: Universitätsverlag, 2003), 115–61.
23 Spieß, 'European Royal Marriages', 18.
24 See for instance the excellent article by François van de Velde. 'The House Laws of the German Habsburgs', in http://www.heraldica.org/topics/royalty/ps1713.htm (accessed on 15 August 2016).
25 Vernon Bogdanor, *The Monarchy and the Constitution* (Oxford: Oxford University Press, 1997), 7.
26 The text of the statute as originally enacted can be seen at http://en.wikisource.org/wiki/Royal_Marriages_Act_1772.
27 Peter H. Wilson, 'Women and Imperial Politics: The Württemberg Consorts 1674-1757'. In *Queenship in Europe 1660-1815,* ed. Clarissa Campbell Orr (Cambridge: Cambridge University Press, 2004), 234.
28 Helen Watanabe-O'Kelly, 'Consort and mistress: a successful job-share?', in *Der Hof: Ort kulturellen Handelns von Frauen in der Frühen Neuzeit*, ed. Susanne Rode-Breymann and Antje Tumat (Cologne: Böhlau 2013 (= *Musik - Kultur - Gender*), 90–9.
29 *Frauensache: Wie Brandenburg Preußen wurde*, 122–31.
30 Daniel Schönpflug, *Die Heiraten der Hohenzollern: Verwandtschaft, Politik und Ritual in Europa 1640-1918* (Göttingen: Vandenhoeck & Ruprecht, 2013), 267.
31 Barbara Beck, *Glanz, Pomp und Tränen. Von der dynastischen Ehe zur Liebesheirat in Europas Herrscherhäusern* (Regensburg: Verlag Friedrich Pustet, 2012).
32 *Briefe und Aufzeichnungen 1786-1810. Königin Luise von Preußen,* ed. Malve Gräfin Rothkirch with an Introduction by Hartmut Boockmann (Berlin: Deutscher Kunstverlag, 2010), 19.
33 Martin Kirsch, 'Die Funktionalisierung des Monarchen im 19. Jahrhundert im europäischen Vergleich', in *Machtstrukturen im Staat in Deutschland und Frankreich,* ed. Stefan Fisch, Florence Gauzy and Chantal Metzger (Stuttgart:Steiner, 2007), 82–98.

Part Two

Marriage, Religion and the State

5

'Till Death Do You Part': Catholicism, Marriage and Culture War in Austria(-Hungary)*

Ulrike Harmat

On 30 March 1868, Cardinal Joseph Othmar von Rauscher sent a letter, signed by fourteen bishops, to the Austrian prime minister Prince Karl Auersperg to protest 'against the flouting of the borders of state authority'. In the letter, the bishops spoke out against what they saw as new infringements on the rights of the church.[1] A bill to re-introduce the marriage law of the Austrian Civil Code (Allgemeines Bürgerliches Gesetzbuch [ABGB]) of 1811 had just been introduced in the Upper House of the Assembly that would rescind the policy outlined just a decade earlier, in the Concordat of 1855. In the Concordat, Pope Pius IX and Emperor Franz Joseph agreed that the state would be ousted by the church when it came to marriage law. As a result, after more than seventy years of governing marriage through Austria's civil code, matrimony had again become a matter of the church alone.[2] It seemed that the new minister of justice, Eduard Herbst, had concocted a novel interpretation of the Constitutional Act on Judicial Power in order to re-introduce secular jurisdiction and state legislation in marital affairs.[3]

The gradual separation of state marriage law from canon law in Austria had begun with Joseph II's marriage patent of 16 January 1783. For the first time, marriage law was comprehensively regulated by the state. Some contemporaries and scholars have spoken about the introduction of civil marriage in this context, but this idea might be construed erroneously. The expression 'civil marriage' is frequently associated with what is understood by a 'civil wedding': a marriage ceremony conducted by civic officials. However, a civil wedding in terms of a ceremony performed before a state authority was still far away.[4] Instead, the fundamental idea behind the marriage patent was separating the Catholic sacrament of marriage from the secular idea of marriage as a contract. Under the patent, the state was to be responsible for the latter.[5] This shift in marriage law was part of a broader reformulation in Austria of the relationship between church and state during Emperor Joseph II's sole rule (1780–90). For the reformer Joseph II, the state was the 'supreme aim, and everything was to be subordinated to it'. He promoted religious tolerance and initiated a 'secularization of the political system'.[6]

As regards marriage legislation, this implied that priests and other clerics were not primarily servants of religion, but civil servants. Following this line of thinking, the transfer of marriage legislation from the diocesan courts to state courts was only a 'logical consequence'.[7] Nevertheless, Joseph II's marriage patent closely followed religious notions of the nature of marriage. And, the religion that informed marriage in this context was Catholicism.[8] In Austria, religion and the state were intertwined when it came to governing the family – even if, as the marriage patent indicated, marriage had been nominally secularized. In this sense, the governance of marriage in Austria was not dissimilar to that in Egypt at the turn of the twentieth century, as Kenneth M. Cuno shows in Chapter 6 in this book.

The separation of sacrament and contract in the case of marriage that was realized through Joseph II's patent was unacceptable for the Catholic Church and resulted in enduring conflict. Thus, almost a century later, Cardinal Rauscher spoke of a 'mutilation of marriage at which Christian, indeed even human, conscience has to baulk'.[9] And, after several regime changes, including the collapse of the empire in 1918, and two world wars, a question remained at the centre of Austrian politics: To what extent was marriage a matter for the state? The question pointed not only to the relative authority of the state over the church when it came to governing the family, but also to broader and shifting understandings of constitutionalism, liberalism and individual rights within Austria.

From Sacrament to Contract

The provisions of the Marriage Patent of 1783 were essentially adopted in the ABGB. The wedding continued to take place before the priest of one of the betrothed, who exercised the function of a civil servant when carrying out the ceremony. This way, the church still exerted a certain amount of influence on marriage in terms of personnel and organization.[10] The Austrian Civil Code took confessional differences into account, which found expression in separation and divorce law. Separation in terms of the complete dissolution of the marriage was not provided for Catholics, for whom merely a 'separation from bed and board' was possible. According to §111 ABGB, this was also the case when only one partner was a member of the Catholic Church at the time the marriage was concluded. The complete separation of a marriage (the dissolution of wedlock) was only permitted to non-Catholics – for 'substantial reasons' (§115 ABGB).[11] If a marriage was concluded by two non-Catholics and one of them converted to Catholicism, only the non-Catholic partner was entitled to seek separation (§116 ABGB).

In the pre-March era between the coming into effect of the Austrian Civil Code and the outbreak of the revolution in 1848, the Catholic Church attempted to make marriage law more restrictive. As early as 1814, a court decree introduced a new impediment to marriage, 'testifying to the preferential treatment of Catholics over non-Catholic Christians': the *impedimentum catholicismi* (impediment of Catholicism).[12] This impediment was based on the assumption of the indissoluble and sacramental nature of marriage among Christians. This led to the Catholic view that even a marriage between Protestants was not separable and that a Protestant separated by a state court could not enter into a second marriage with a Catholic. In the event that one of the two partners converted to Catholicism while married, this person could not seek a divorce and embark on a second marriage. The absurd outcome was that a binding divorce verdict by an Austrian court had no effect on the partner who had converted to Catholicism, while the ex-partner (if he or she was not a Catholic) could enter into a new marriage (albeit only to a non-Catholic). Critics repeatedly pointed out that this legislation on divorce and separation was equivalent to subordinating the state to church jurisdiction.[13]

But favourable political conditions were necessary to bring about change. The revolution of 1848 caused a shock among the ruling classes and made them look for an ally to stabilize the situation.[14] This was the opportunity for the Catholic Church to assert its demands. The outcome of this solidarity between the crown and the altar was the Concordat of 1855, in John Boyer's view 'an imprudent decision precisely because it alienated *both* the Josephinist state and incipient *bürgerlich* (middle-class) society'.[15] As a result of the Concordat,[16] the marital provisions of the Austrian Civil Code were repealed, as far as Catholics were concerned, and state jurisdiction was once more replaced by the sole jurisdiction of the church.

The church leadership celebrated the conclusion of the Concordat as a major success. The consequence of the close cooperation between the state and the church led to both partners beginning to identify with the respective aims of the other. And the crown and government even began to conceive of Austria as 'the Catholic great power'. For the church, 'the state became an auxiliary in the assertion of its claims'.[17] In pastoral letters, the Concordat was fêted as 'the constitutional climax of Catholic restoration efforts against the absolutist state and liberal currents'.[18] Cardinal Rauscher declared euphorically: 'His Majesty the Emperor has taken a higher stance, not only as a son of the Catholic Church, but also as a legislator.'[19] But criticism was not slow in coming. The poet Franz Grillparzer called the Concordat 'a bloody slap in the face to us veteran Josephinists'.[20] Ernst Viktor Zenker, a parliamentarian and the president of the Austrian Marriage Law Reform Society spoke in hindsight of a 'handing over of marriage law to the church'.[21] The Liberal Carl von Stremayr, minister of culture and education in the 1870s, put the relationship between neo-Absolutism and the Concordat in a nutshell by remarking that the 'church had been appointed by the state as an equal power in the joint subjugation of the intellect'. Joseph II's work 'had been destroyed with a scratch of the pen, and the brand of the most sinister reaction pressed on the brow of the Austrian monarchy in the face of the whole of Europe'.[22]

For the Austrian Liberals, the announcement of the Concordat was a 'major blow'.[23] For them, the introduction of a parliamentary constitutional system had top priority in the early 1860s, and any attempt by the church to reassert its authority seemed to undermine this. In Austria, the breakthrough of liberalism, which caused a rethinking of the relationship between the state and the church and found expression in the constitutional acts of December 1867, had been enabled above all by recent events in foreign policy. Austria's defeat by Prussia at Sadowa in 1866 initiated a departure from the 'Concordat State'. The transition to constitutionalism and the granting of the fundamental right to freedom of belief and conscience finally led to the removal of the Concordat system.[24] The December Constitution of 1867 was followed by the May Acts of 1868, taking marital legislation and jurisdiction away from the Catholic Church again and returning them to the state authorities.[25] Catholic marriages were again subject to state jurisdiction. The church form of wedding was retained, but a civil wedding (a wedding before a state body) was authorized as a sort of emergency form of marriage in cases where the church refused its cooperation. For instance, the provision was used when the chaplain responsible for a wedding declined to carry out the ceremony on the grounds of an impediment to marriage that was not recognized by the state. This 'emergency civil marriage' (*Notzivilehe*) became the usual form of matrimony for individuals without a religious affiliation.[26]

The three confessional laws were signed by Emperor Franz Joseph on 25 May 1868, despite strong opposition from Austrian bishops. When the bishops' conference convened in September 1867 and lobbied the monarch against the proposed laws, the emperor replied by referring to his duties as a constitutional ruler.[27] As a result, due to the May legislation the provisions of the Concordat were repealed in certain areas (marriage, school), but the Concordat itself was not rescinded in terms of international law. And, significantly, the Holy See refused to concede that the Concordat had been weakened. In his allocution of 22 June 1868, Pope Pius IX declared that the 'repulsive laws violating the sacred rights of the church [are] null and forever invalid'.[28] And, the clergy took note of this stance. For example, the bishop of Linz, Franz Joseph Rudigier, used the Papal allocution to call on the clergy to present open resistance. He was sentenced to fourteen days in prison, but was promptly pardoned by the emperor.

The showdown between liberal reforms and the episcopate ended in a semi-victory for the former, and the result was modest as far as marriage law was concerned. In reality, the laws of May 1868 were implemented in a piecemeal fashion. The secularization of marital law that might be expected of a constitutional state was still a long way off. The only noteworthy success was the introduction of the emergency civil marriage in cases where a priest refused to conduct a wedding. The indissolubility of Catholic marriages remained intact. In this respect, the almost hysterical anxiety and protests on the part of Catholic conservatives had little cause. Moreover, the actions of the state authorities not only did *not* harm the church, but actually benefitted it: 'The words *ecclesia oppressa, ecclesia triumphans* materialized to the detriment of the state … ; in this context, the Catholic mass movement appeared on the streets in Austria for the first time', resulting most prominently in the Christian Social movement.[29]

In the case of marriage reform, as elsewhere, the binary concept of a state/church culture war requires nuancing. As Christopher Clark has shown, we need to move beyond seeing the mobilization of Catholics against secularizing legislation as an essentially regressive move that obstructed the development of a modern political culture.[30] Not least, the liberal claim to be a progressive, inclusive and democratic movement lost credibility with the emergence of the new mass movements, including Christian Socialism.[31] Nevertheless, it cannot be denied that the Catholic Church rejected some of those principles most closely associated with liberal and, later, social-democratic reforms of the late nineteenth and twentieth centuries. Simultaneously, in public it endeavoured to create the impression of a church that was being persecuted, even if the emperor was on its side. The church claimed to present the (Catholic) majority of the population and painted the spectre of Austria's de-Christianization on the wall.[32] As feared by the Catholic hierarchy, the May laws did not yet constitute the headstone in church legislation, and the liberals continued to advocate the complete eradication of the Concordat. The infallibility dogma at the First Vatican Council in 1870 seemed to provide the final nail in the coffin by leading Emperor Franz Joseph to declare the Concordat void.[33] The new regulation of the relations between the Catholic Church and the state finally took place in the form of three further laws of May 1874, and the so-called Catholics' Act completely suspended the Concordat.[34] In the view of the emperor and the government, the legislation of 1874 had put an end to the Austrian cultural struggle, which, however, by no means implied the conclusion of ideological conflicts within civil society.[35] As Cole shows, the experiences of the 1860s and 1870s created 'two polarized socio-political milieux'.[36]

Culture Wars and Marriage in Austria–Hungary

In the mid-1870s, the liberal movement lost momentum, in part due to its lack of coherence, and conservative Clericals and Nationalists began to offer a viable opposition to the Liberal government.[37] The Conservatives ultimately emerged from the conflict as 'victorious losers'.[38] Political interests turned more and more away from cultural policy and towards nationalist and social concerns. An analysis of the Liberal legislation of these years shows a paradox appositely characterized by Boyer:

> Liberal proponents hoped in 1868–74 that these laws would create a new age of Liberal reason, while Catholic opponents predicted they would be disastrous for religious belief. All were agreed, however, on the significant nature of the changes. Yet, paradoxically, other 'facts' in Austrian political and social life changed so powerfully between 1874 and 1918 that what originally looked like an intrusive program by the Austrian state directed against the church had become by 1918 a minimally tenable ground for the prosperity of Catholicism.[39]

For those Catholics affected by the marriage law, the controversial settlement of 1868 only seemed to create further conflict. The legislation created a paradox in which marriage was both a legal instrument of the state and a transcendental entity that could not be undone by the state. As a result, separation from bed and board rather than divorce became official policy for Catholics, and remarriage after a failed relationship continued to remain impossible and was seen as equivalent to bigamy. The few initiatives of the 1870s aiming at bringing about a change in this respect failed,[40] and it was only around the turn of the century that the issue once more took up speed. The consequences of this political bind had to be borne by the courts, which found various ways to bypass the law.

One outcome of this situation was jurisdiction shopping for those who sought to take on a new spouse, and Austrians soon found that they could turn 'abroad', to the Hungarian half of the empire, which was governed by other laws on marriage.[41]

The situation came to be seen as an 'emergency'. As the parliamentarian Josef Kopp explained when introducing a reform bill in 1875,

> It is the surest sign of an urgent need when resort is taken to bypassing a law. But, gentlemen, that is what is happening here. ... To have their marriages divorced, people are not merely going abroad in the true sense of the word, but to a restricted foreign country – if I may say so – and in a small town on the eastern border of the Monarchy [Klausenburg, Cluj] we are experiencing something that has an enormous similarity to Rome's indulgences stuff, I mean the divorce haggling that is being pursued there.[42]

Kopp was referring to 'Transylvanian marriages', also called 'Klausenburg marriages'. The marital courts of the Protestant Reformed and the Unitarian Churches, with the aid of which most such weddings were performed, were located in Klausenburg, in an area of the empire that later became part of Romania. That the settlement of marital matters in particular came under the jurisdiction of the ecclesiastical courts was laid down in Law XXXIV/1791, which returned to the ecclesiastical courts this right that had been transferred to the civil authorities by a decree of Emperor Joseph II. The right of the Transylvanian church courts to decide on marital matters was expressly recognized by the Austrian government and later by the Hungarian government. The imperial patents with which the ABGB was published in Hungary and in Transylvania suspended the validity of their matrimonial provisions and maintained the previously existing church courts and the church regulations of the various denominations. Following the Austro-Hungarian settlement of 1867, the church matrimonial courts of the religious denominations were left unchanged.[43] On the basis of these legal provisions and section 8 of Hungarian Law LIII/1868, which declared the principles of a denomination to be no longer binding on those leaving it, it was possible for married Catholics who turned to a non-Catholic denomination to have their originally Catholic but now mixed marriage dissolved.

Until mandatory civil marriage was introduced in Hungary (1894), the situation offered an opportunity to evade Austrian marriage law. The prerequisites were considerable: separation from bed and board by an Austrian court; conversion to the Protestant or Unitarian faith; assumption of Hungarian citizenship by both marriage applicants; and, divorce by the denominational marital court in Transylvania of the marriage that had already been separated in Austria. Only then could the second wedding take place.[44] From 1879, the Supreme Court (Oberster Gerichtshof [OGH]) had held the view that these marriages were invalid in Austria.[45] Moreover, as Wilhelm Fuchs pointed out, the prerequisite of assuming Hungarian citizenship created a kind of 'new class law'. The dissolution of a Catholic marriage was only possible for 'certain privileged classes whose material status is sound and independent of Austrian citizenship'; for the poor and all those for whom Austrian citizenship was the precondition for their livelihood, this option was out of the question. Accordingly, Fuchs predicted a 'peaceful annexation' of Hungary by the wealthy population of Austria.[46]

The popularity of these marriages, which developed into a veritable line of business, is evidenced by the many advertisements in the dailies, promising Catholics separated from bed and board the realization of their hearts' desires.[47] The risk of a marriage being contested was given in those cases in which not both partners had acquired Hungarian citizenship. However, as Fuchs shows, it was more or less a question of luck as to whether the authorities intervened or not; even in cases that were well known in society, no contestation took place, unless there was some kind of 'Stückel' (document).[48]

In a petition, the Lower Austrian Bar Association pilloried these 'untenable conditions' as creating inequality.[49] This issue even later captured attention on stage in the play *Paragraph 111* that was performed by the working men's club in Favoriten (Vienna).[50] In the 1890s, the case of the married actors Alexander Girardi and Helene Odilon created a furore. Their wedding in 1893 was followed by a marital drama leading to a separation from bed and board after four years, in January 1897. The (Hungarian) second and third marriages of Girardi und Odilon were to occupy the courts until 1910.[51]

In the meantime, the legal situation had changed in Hungary. After 1879, Hungarian citizenship could only be acquired by someone who, among other things, had been living in the country without interruption for five years.[52] Initially, this seemed to be an insurmountable obstacle, but here, too, a solution could be found, as the law stipulated that this condition could be dropped, if, on adopting a foreigner, the adopter possessed sufficient funds to support his family and had been entered on the list of tax payers for five years. In 1894, the Hungarian Liberals finally achieved what the Austrian Liberals had failed to do. Reluctantly but surely, besides other church laws, on 9 December 1894 Emperor Franz Joseph signed Statute Article XXXI, initiating mandatory civil marriage in Hungary.[53] As in the lead-up to the reforms of 1868, the new civil marriage law in Hungary had been preceded by violent conflict between the state and the church. In his first government declaration, Prime Minister Sándor Wekerle had linked the political destiny of his administration to the success of church reforms,[54] and Emperor Franz Joseph ultimately had to take note that it was completely pointless to battle 'the most powerful political party in the country without causing grave domestic tremors, probably affecting the whole of the Dual Monarchy'.[55] Wekerle clung to the controversial marriage law, and on 21 June 1894 mandatory civil marriage was accepted by a sparse majority of only four votes in the House of Magnates. The new Hungarian law enabled Catholics to obtain a divorce without a prior separation from bed and board. It made life significantly easier for Austrian Catholics seeking divorce, as they could simply go to Hungary to do so and no longer needed to convert to a different denomination, as was the case in Hungary before the reform.

However, the new law still applied to *Hungarian* citizens only, meaning that those Austrians who could not shed their citizenship had to look for other options. And, a clause of the Austrian Civil Code (§83) provided a suitable alternative: it allowed individuals to apply for clemency (*Dispens*) from marriage impediments 'for important reasons', and one of those 'impediments' was existing wedlock (§62). By the interwar era, the debate about overcoming this 'impediment' to marriage reached a climax. Prior to 1918, the Austrian Ministry of the Interior held a strict line against remarriage following separation, interpreting a second union as bigamy.[56] For example, as late as 1915, the Lower Austrian governorship rejected an application for dispensation to remarry by stating that it would offend 'the sense of law and morality' on the part of the populace. However, the governorship took a completely different stance soon afterwards, in light of the perceived importance of the applicant. When the chief of staff of the Austro-Hungarian Army, Franz Conrad von Hötzendorf, approached the Lower Austrian governorship with an appeal for dispensation in the middle of the First World War (October 1915), his petition not only occupied Austrian and Hungarian lawyers but also the Ministries of the Interior and Justice and even the emperor.[57] By assenting to the marriage, the emperor put the Lower Austrian governorship on the spot, essentially making it revoke its earlier stance against second marriages after a divorce. As Conrad's wife remarked in her memoirs, the emperor 'was not amused that not everything was correct according to the strict Catholic standpoint to which he always remained faithful'.[58]

After the turn of the century, a reform movement was launched anew and on a broader front, championing above all mandatory civil marriage, in part, as a means to address these questions about second marriages. The discussion was put on the political agenda by the *Cultural Policy Association*, which had been founded in 1902 by the left-wing liberal, bourgeois reformer Robert Scheu.[59] The association announced it would hold a large-scale survey on the issue. In May 1904, the Association of Catholic Separated Married Persons was established, which sought to represent the interests of Catholics separated from bed and board.[60] In the Ministry of Justice, too, a whole series of applications and initiatives arrived concerned with the forthcoming revision of the Austrian Civil Code.[61] The stance of the Ministry of Justice towards the removal of the ban on remarriage was unambiguously negative: 'Even were this issue somehow debatable for political reasons, we would have to think long about breaking with a centuries-old tradition that has become such a part of popular life and customs'.[62]

The debate on civil marriage was complicated by the conflation of diverse feminist arguments about mistresses' rights, divorce and access to remarriage. When the *General Austrian Women's Association* demanded the 'legal recognition of concubinage' and the 'concubine's' right to upkeep and inheritance in addition to the introduction of mandatory civil marriage in 1904,[63] the Ministry of Justice rebutted that the group was only interested in pensions, social benefits and inheritance. The equation of concubinage and marriage seemed apt 'to shake the foundations of society and the state'.[64] In May 1905, the more conservative *Federation of Austrian Women's Societies* pointed out that it was 'pointless cruelty' to continue to fetter two individuals to marriages that had failed. Most 'civilized nations', they argued, even Catholic countries, had recognized this. Moreover, the group argued that the option of divorce was especially important for women: 'More deeply rooted in the family and more intimately tied to it than a man, she feels the breakdown of the domestic circle more than he does. A permanent rift with her husband weighs much more heavily on her, as she has to do without all the encouragement and rejection professional work and lively dealings with the outside world can afford him.'[65] This reasoning clearly mirrored the bourgeois discourse on the role of the sexes, with its ideal-typical notions of masculinity and femininity.[66] So, the opponents of the reform appealed above all to women by presenting its ostensible consequences and stretching the image of the 'desolate and deserted woman': 'The aged woman will then no longer be able to count on the legal protection of her marriage and thus often be thrust into the direst penury.'[67]

Ludwig Wahrmund, a lawyer and professor of canon law and one of the staunchest champions of marriage law reform, called these attempts to play off women against the reform 'a pointless and futile comedy'. It was pointless because even the canonic marriage law had allowed the separation from bed and board; futile because divorce merely constituted the 'natural consequence of an unhappy marriage'; and, a comedy 'because the lot of the divorced woman, because she is forbidden to enter into a second marriage, forced to remain alone and socially ostracized, so to speak, is made into a deplorable one'.[68] This instrumentalization of women in favour of and against the reform was also shown in the marriage law survey held between January and February 1905,[69] when the reformer Robert Scheu claimed that the 'Catholic standpoint' was the 'women's standpoint', so that there was in this issue a 'greater antithesis between man and woman than between Catholicism and an open opinion'.[70] Scheu's view fell flat with many feminists, such as Grete Meisel-Hess, a member of the radical women's movement, who claimed that most people in Austria happened to be Catholics and did not think about the consequences before they got married.[71] It was also argued that more divorce suits were filed by women than men. Indeed, from 1898 to 1905, 68 per cent of the non-mutual petitions for separation from bed and board were filed by women. Most of these women were, at least in part, financially independent. As Waltraud Heindl points out, 56.3 per cent of the women filing for divorce pursued a profession 'outside the house'.[72]

The argument that a 'civilized nation' should not leave marriage law to the church ran through the debate. It seemed that modern marriage, in which women were free to work and both spouses sought the freedom to divorce and remarry, was a secular matter of contract that should be left to the state, and not be subordinated to the church.[73]

Thus, at the International Libertine Congress in Prague in 1907, Ernst Viktor Zenker claimed that the state had to free itself from the church and make its own marriage law, in this case mandatory and exclusively civil marriage: 'The canonic marriage law such as it is practised in Austria does not fit in with and does not belong to modern civilization, and a state that wants to be a cultural nation must not subordinate itself to it.'[74] The social politician Julius Ofner, who regularly put forward motions to reform marriage law between 1906 and 1918, stated that the 'idea of the modern state' demanded a socialization of the institution of marriage, without any consideration being paid to confessional distinctions. Marriage was to be viewed by the state merely as a 'social institution',[75] as a 'regulation of sexual relations', with the aim of making the latter serve the purposes of society. So, the church had to be 'dethroned' for the benefit of the modern state.[76] Ofner's demand to adapt marriage law 'to the social and economic conditions of our age'[77] in the course of a reform of the Austrian Civil Code fell on deaf ears. When the draft of the amendment to the Austrian Civil Code was passed by the Upper House on 19 December 1912, there was no mention in it of marriage law. Karl von Grabmayr, the vice president of the Imperial Court, who had advocated the reform in the Upper House and hence received a letter of gratitude from the Association for Marriage Law Reform (in which it had been stated that the reform was now 'on the way'), replied by saying: 'Sadly, you overestimate my influence. The circles opposing marriage law reform are invincible at the moment and will probably remain so for quite some time.'[78] Grabmayr's pessimistic attitude was to turn out to be realistic. It took another twenty-five years, until 1938, for mandatory civil marriage to be introduced.

Marriage and Social Democracy

When it came to secularizing marriage law, the heirs of the Austrian Liberals after the collapse of the Habsburg Monarchy in 1918 were the Social Democrats. Like their predecessors, however, they failed to reform marriage law. The Viennese Programme of the Social Democrats had demanded the introduction of mandatory civil marriage as early as 1901, and the *Arbeiter-Zeitung*, which criticized the 'bourgeois freedom heroes' for their half-heartedness in the cause of marriage law, declared: 'People can be found, who, when they do something, do it properly'.[79] The Social Democrats were to remain short on keeping this promise. The arguments for and against the reform of marriage law had not changed since the Liberal era. The representatives of the Catholic Church and its extension, the Christian Social Party, argued on principle, viewing even the slightest reform project as an attack on religion, while the Social Democrats referred to the needs of people, accusing the opponents of reform of heartlessness and ignorance.

However, the political system had fundamentally altered in 1918/19, with the result that the Christian Social movement had lost clout. The Social Democrats assumed responsibility of government, hoping that the collapse of the monarchy had also brought about 'emancipation from the bishops and archbishops'.[80] The church clung to the principle of the indissolubility of marriage and endeavoured to assert its dogma via the state with the aid of the Christian Social Party. There may have been no more bishops in parliament, 'but the Christian Social Party was ideologically firmly tied to the hierarchy', and Prelate Ignaz Seipel[81] was a reliable representative of Catholic interests. When, in January 1919, the Undersecretary of State for Justice, the Pan-German Julius Roller, submitted a moderate bill on marriage law to the Justice Committee, the Christian Socials were alarmed, seeing it as a first step towards the separation of church and state.[82] The Catholic Imperial Women's Organization protested the proposal on apparently feminist grounds, claiming that in a matter concerning 'women's honour and women's rights', it seemed that women were to be subjected to the mercy of the 'dictatorship' of a National Assembly that had only been nominated for a transitional period (Provisional National Assembly). The group argued: 'We protest that three weeks before the coming into effect of women's suffrage, a law has been passed that interferes with the heart of family life and that is rejected by the entire devout Catholic population'.[83] The elections to the constituent National Assembly were to take place on 16 February 1919. On 18 December 1918, all Austrian women who had reached the age of twenty at the beginning of 1919 had been given the right to vote for the first time. The report by the Justice Committee to the Provisional National Assembly had pointed out that the reform was so urgent – also by dint of the countless 'wartime marriages' – that 'although women are also interested in it', it should not be left to the constituent National Assembly; apart from that, the reform was called for most pressingly by women.[84]

The fact that the Christian Social Party and the Episcopal Office now also invoked women's suffrage or canvassed for their votes induced the feminist Olly [Olga] Schwarz to make a 'reckoning', stating that 'those parties in particular that have hitherto been the strongest opponents of equality for women ... now seek to beguile women with sweet allurements into moving into the camp of regression. Woe betide the women that follow these enticements'.[85]

The Social Democratic women's weekly *Die Wählerin* supported the reform. It argued that the indissolubility of marriage means that couples who were merely separated but not divorced were forced to dispense with the idea of finding a new and happier relationship or were compelled to live in an undesirable 'common law marriage'. The paper reasoned: 'However decent a woman may be, however impeccable a man, some blemish was attached to them in the eyes of petty people. A divorced woman! For many people, that is still something that is a bit fishy'.[86] For Social Democratic women, it seemed that the existing marriage law did not reflect the realities of modern, urban life. For example, Helene Bauer referred to an urban–rural divide, stating that in the countryside 'marriage is deeply rooted in the ground and is permanent and inseparable due to its economic basis. ... the inseparability of the rural marriage is not the result of external control by the state and church, but of the rural way of life, from whose innermost core political and social revolutions have bounced off almost without a trace up to today'.[87]

Christian Socialists, too, played up a presumed divide in urban and rural values when it came to marriage, but it was sometimes tinged by an anti-Semitic subtext. Christian Social propaganda chiefly targeted rural female voters, who were, for instance, given leaflets depicting a 'farmer's wife leaving one side of the house with a little bundle, while a young lady in a plume hat strides in through the other door'. It seemed that easy access to divorce and remarriage could result in hardship and embarrassment for loyal, hardworking rural wives as modish urbanites took on new roles as lovers and second wives.[88] The topoi of the 'whore cult' and 'free love' played major roles in this controversy. Outrage against the Social Democratic proposals for marriage law reform was further aggravated by the Viennese Cardinal Piffl, who bemoaned that, 'Marriage and school are to be completely deprived of church influence ... marriage uprooted from the holy ground of sacramental grace and re-planted in the quagmire of carnality, finally to degenerate into polygamy and the whore cult.'[89] And for the bishop of Linz, Gföllner, anyone who interfered with marriage was 'a criminal', seriously jeopardizing not only families and the church, but also the state.[90] At the same time, the 'spirit of the age' and the Social Democrats were demonized, the latter being equated to the Bolshevists who had just overturned political and social life in Russia, in part, by reforming marriage and family law. The priest and later Bishop Alois Hudal, a pronounced anti-Semite, decried 'the complete heathenization of the family' and public life. He described the main antagonist of Austria's 'religious rebirth' as socialism 'permeated with Jewish elements'.[91] The Social Democratic proposal on civil marriage that had been put forward in January 1919 ultimately failed.[92] The bill had been rejected by the Christian Socials and the Pan-Germans. The following day, the *Reichspost* noted with gratification that the 'Jewish reform' had been scuttled, and the 'destruction of marriage' thwarted.[93]

These fault lines on the marriage debate remained set into the early 1930s. After their defeat, the Social Democrats once more announced that they would untiringly push for the reform.[94] Following the elections to the constituent National Assembly of 16 February 1919, from which they emerged as the strongest party, they behaved nonetheless with noticeable restraint in deference to their coalition with the Christian Socials. The Social Democratic chancellor Karl Renner stated that the party would not introduce any bills for the time being and declined a motion to this effect by Albert Sever that spring.[95] In the coalition agreement with the Christian Socials, it was finally arranged that the relationship between the church and the state, including marriage legislation, should in principle be settled within the framework of the constitution.[96] The demand for the separation of church and state had been a major component of the Social Democratic Party programme since the party congress at Hainfeld (1889). Among other things, the action programme of the Federation of Social Democratic Deputies of 1919 called for: complete freedom of belief and conscience; the abolition of all state compulsion to confessional upbringing; and, the adoption of German marriage law.[97] The Christian Socials feared that in a new constitution the Social Democrats and Pan-Germans would attempt to enforce the principle of the separation of church and state, and therefore lobbied to keep in place the constitution of 1867.[98] Ultimately, the Social Democrats acquiesced. In June 1920, the coalition with the Christian Socials broke up, and after the elections that autumn, the Social Democrats withdrew into opposition. As a result, the movement to reform marriage law fell to the wayside. Once reform of marriage law was off the table, an attempt was made to offer Austrian Catholics a way out of the marriage dilemma, now on a broader basis through regular administrative channels, and not merely as a privilege of the few.

With regard to Hungarian/Transylvanian marriages, the Supreme Court had declared in 1924 and 1934 that a marriage dissolved abroad was to be respected by Austrian courts, as the marital partner concerned had become a foreigner, but new was the finding by the court that – because marriage was a two-sided legal relationship – this also applied to the person's former spouse who had not acquired Hungarian citizenship. But these two verdicts from the period of the Republic 'no longer had any relevance for the practice of bypassing the provisions of the General Civil Code on the ban on remarriage'.[99] To this end, a different and more convenient tool had been found in 1919: dispensation marriages. These marriages, which came to be associated with the name of the short-term Social Democratic governor of Lower Austria, Albert Sever, were initially intended as a stopgap or makeshift arrangement until the reform of marriage law. The Austrian Civil Code (§83) allowed regional governments the right to grant clemency for marriages with impediments, and the State Office of the Interior under the Social Democrat Karl Renner began issuing Catholics separated from bed and board dispensation from the 'impediment of existing wedlock' (§62). As a result, Catholics (after separation) were now able to enter into a second marriage without having to run across the border to Hungary and take on a new citizenship. The ruling by the State Office of the Interior was based on a case in which a wife – after separation – had acquired Hungarian citizenship and then entered into a second marriage in 1916, before the collapse of the Habsburg Monarchy and, with it, the possibility to jurisdiction shop for remarriage in Hungary. Her husband from the first marriage then appealed to the Lower Austrian provincial government with a request for dispensation from the impediment of 'existing wedlock' (§62) to remarry. He argued that his marriage was considered as dissolved for his ex-wife and should therefore also be considered as separated for him. The fact that he was technically still considered married to his ex-wife, while she could go on and marry a new husband, was a 'situation … deriding any sense of justice'.[100] After his plea had been rejected, he appealed to the State Office of the Interior, which issued a path-breaking new ruling in 1919 allowing remarriage for spouses who had been separated from bed and board. Under the Lower Austrian provincial governor Albert Sever, these kinds of dispensations to remarry became a mass phenomenon. Indeed, the so-called 'Sever marriages' survived their eponym by many years, and issuing of dispensations was continued by the Social Democratic provincial governor of Vienna, Karl Seitz, until 1934. Of course, the practice was not without its opponents. The Christian Socials accused Sever of encouraging bigamy, but had to concede that many of their partisans also appealed for such dispensations.[101] Subsequently, dispensations were not only issued by Social Democratic provincial governors, but later also by the Office of the Federal Chancellor. This resulted in various agreements, so as not to cause the Christian Social Chancellor and Prelate Ignaz Seipel the embarrassment of having to sign dispensations. In his absence, they were handled by the Pan-German vice chancellor. Continuing to issue dispensations formed a fixed point in the coalition agreement between the Christian Socials and the Pan-German Party. In 1929, the task of granting dispensations was moved to the Department of Trade, which earned the Pan-German Hans Schürff the sobriquet of 'Minister of Trade and *Marital Intercourse*'![102] Nonetheless, the policy continued to cause outcry, including a lawsuit about whether anyone could challenge a dispensation marriage and have it declared null and void. The ensuing and sometimes absurdly different assessments of these dispensation marriages are evidenced by the case of an employee of the Austrian Railway who ended up as a 'bigamist against his will' as a result of the confused legal situation.[103] In 1930, the number of such marriages was estimated at about 50,000, but their validity remained questionable.

Marriage in the Christian Corporate State

On 1 May 1934, the date of the publication of the authoritarian corporate constitution, which was enacted 'in the name of God', the Concordat agreed upon with the Holy See by Federal Chancellor Engelbert Dollfuß and Minister Kurt Schuschnigg on 5 July 1933 was also ratified.[104] At the time the Concordat was signed (1933), the Christian Socials still had to make allowances for opposition by the Social Democrats and Pan-Germans, so the plan was originally aired to use the Concordat to pass on to introducing optional civil marriage and, at best, to separating state marriages between Catholics. Following the gradual coup d'état by Dollfuß' government in 1933/34, the ban on the Social Democratic Party and the destruction of its organizations, 'the political balance of power had shifted in favour of the Christian Socials and the Catholic faction to the extent that political concessions were no longer necessary'.[105] So, the state marriage law reform had receded into the distance, and the Catholic Church had achieved its goal. By exploiting the new political situation, the government no longer contemplated tackling a state marriage law reform. The Christian Corporate State 'established the old union of state and church under the banner of the Austrian Counter-Reformation'.[106] The outcome was a further dissipation of marriage law.[107] As regards the controversial inseparability of Catholic marriages, things stayed as they were. Nor was the uncertain situation of the tens of thousands of dispensation marriages concluded prior to 1934 resolved, apart from the fact that dispensations were only issued in cases of emergency civil marriage. Church marriages remained indissoluble, meaning that separated spouses could not remarry.[108]

The only way to ensure that a marriage could later be separated legally was by quitting the Catholic Church *before* getting married. Perhaps not surprisingly, there was a wave of defection from the Church in the First Republic. At its peak in 1927, those who stepped out of the Church numbered 28,837, which contrasted sharply with the 552 new entrants to Catholicism in Austria.[109] To counter the secessions, the provisions for seceding from a church or religious community were amended during the period of Austrofascism.

Ultimately, it was through the annexation of Austria by Nazi Germany in March 1938 that marriage law in Austria was conclusively reformed. On 1 August, the 'Act on Standardizing Law on Marriage and Divorce in the Province of Austria and Remaining German Territory' took effect. The law introduced mandatory civil marriage in Austria for the first time; removed the ban on divorce and remarriage for Catholics that had been so vehemently contested over the earlier decades; abolished the contested institution of separation from bed and board; and, legalized the existing dispensation marriages.[110] The new marriage law was an outgrowth of long-standing debates about the relationship between church and state in Austria, but it was above all a reflection of National Socialist ideology.[111] The policy laid out numerous restrictions on marriage based mainly on racial, demographic and health-related criteria. So, the Marriage Act of 1938 cannot be considered in isolation from the previous legislation,[112] which was significant for 'the process of permeating and interlocking the law with racial theory'.[113]

The 1938 marriage law was both liberalizing and restrictive. On the one hand, the secularization of marriage law had long been the demand of completely different political groups which sought to replace church marriage with civil marriage and divorce.[114] On the other hand, however, the new bans on marriage that the law put in place served to bring about Nazi racial ideology, leading to a massive curtailment of marital liberty. Similarly, divorce law was put in the service of National Socialist ideology, which was shown above all by the example of 'mixed marriages', a term that had previously applied to confessionally mixed marriages and now referred to so-called 'racially mixed' marriages between Jews and non-Jews. The new divorce law was now intended to make it easier for the 'Aryan' partner to separate from an 'undesirable' spouse. The main objective of the Nazi onslaught was 'to expropriate "non-Aryan" property and drive the Jews into exile' and the social and political pressure on intermarried couples 'became both vicious and intense'.[115] On the whole, marriage was regarded not simply as a matter of individual choice, with civil marriage and divorce available to that end. Rather, under the 1938 law, marriage became a responsibility that one carried out for the greater community, the ethnic community of the *Volksgemeinschaft*. As a result, there was greater interference in and de-privatization of marriage. From the outset, the aim was to return women to their allegedly 'natural' intended purpose in the household and family, defined by their 'ability to bear offspring'.

The tragedy of the conflict concerning the introduction of mandatory civil marriage in Austria remains that it was left to the National Socialist dictatorship to implement it. As a result, the Marriage Act of 1938 became discredited by its permeation with racist and biological elements. That the secularization of marriage law and a strict separation between state and church were long overdue is beyond doubt. The issue proved a central point of conflict in the eighteenth century under Emperor Joseph II; it emerged again in the heated response to the Concordat between Austria and Pius IX in 1855; and, it continued to frame debate about the nature of the relationship between church, family and state in the new democratic Republic of Austria between 1918 and 1934. And, in the aftermath of the Second World War, the Catholic Church promptly endeavoured to return to the status quo in Austria prior to the introduction of the National Socialist Marriage Law of 1938.[116]

The Catholic Church and its new partner, the Austrian People's Party (*Österreichische Volkspartei* / ÖVP), argued that the Concordat of 1933 was still in existence and that mandatory civil marriage was against Austria's 'legal tradition'.[117] They claimed that the civil marriage was National Socialist legislation, thus disavowing the policy by referring to the time of its introduction (1938). However, civil marriage was not an invention of the National Socialists. It had been introduced in Germany already in 1875, so this criticism was misrepresentative. This critique of civil marriage was, nonetheless, on the decline in Austria. After 1945, the Socialists were in a more favourable position; unlike in 1918, they were now the defenders of the status quo. Moreover, even within the ÖVP, the proponents of the old marriage law lost ground. After decades of fiercely defending confessional marriage law, initially in an alliance between the crown and the altar, then in union with the Christian Social Party, the Catholic Church's attempts 'to win back conservative cornerstones of the Austrian legal system'[118] were doomed to failure.

Notes

* For Darim († 2017).
1 Cölestin Wolfsgruber, *Joseph Othmar Cardinal Rauscher, Fürsterzbischof von Wien. Sein Leben und sein Wirken* (Freiburg im Breisgau: Herder'sche Verlagshandlung, 1888), 257.
2 *Staatsgrundgesetz vom 21. December 1867 über die richterliche Gewalt*. Reichs-Gesetz-Blatt (RGBl.) für das Kaiserthum Österreich 144, Artikel I: all jurisdiction in the state is exercised in the name of the emperor.
3 Stenographic minutes of the Upper House of the Imperial Parliament 1861–1918: 30. Meeting of the 4th session on 21 March 1868, 590.
4 Stefan Schima, 'Das Eherecht des ABGB 1811', *Beiträge zur Rechtsgeschichte Österreichs* 2, no. 1 (2012): 13–26, here 15.

5 Bruno Primetshofer, *Ehe und Konkordat. Die Grundlinien des österreichischen Konkordats-Eherechts 1934 und das geltende österreichische Eherecht* (Vienna: Herder, 1960), 5.
6 Marita Gilli, 'Fortsetzung und Radikalisierung des Josephinismus in den revolutionären Bewegungen bis 1848', in *Was blieb vom Josephinismus? Zum 65. Geburtstag von Helmut Reinalter*, ed. Christian Ehalt and Jean Mondot (Innsbruck: Innsbruck University Press, 2010), 121–34, here 121.
7 Primetshofer, *Ehe und Konkordat*, 5.
8 The multinational Habsburg Monarchy was multi-confessional too, particularly in the Hungarian half of the empire (Transleithania); however, according to the census of 1910, 79 per cent of the population of Austria (Cisleithania) belonged to the Roman Catholic faith. Cf. Die Gesellschaft der Habsburgermonarchie im Kartenbild. Verwaltungs-, Sozial- und Infrastruktur nach dem Zensus von 1910. *Die Habsburgermonarchie 1848–1918* 9, no. 2: *Kartenband*, ed. Helmut Rumpler and Martin Seger (Vienna ÖAW, 2010), 72: map 4.1.
9 Joseph Othmar Kardinal Rauscher, *Die Ehe und das zweite Hauptstück des bürgerlichen Gesetzbuches* (Vienna: Wilhelm Braumüller, 1868), 42.
10 Oskar Lehner, *Familie – Recht – Politik. Die Entwicklung des österreichischen Familienrechts im 19. und 20. Jahrhundert* (Vienna: Springer, 1987), 29.
11 The marriage impediment of different religious affiliations (§64 ABGB) stipulated that marriage contracts between Christians and 'persons not professing the Christian faith' could not be concluded validly. There were special provisions for the marriages of Jews (§§133–5 ABGB).
12 Schima, *Eherecht* 22.
13 Cf. Friedrich Maassen, *Unser Eherecht und das Staatsgrundgesetz* (Vienna: Leuschner & Lubensky, 1878), 25.
14 Karl Vocelka, *Verfassung oder Konkordat? Der publizistische und politische Kampf der Liberalen um die Religionsgesetze des Jahres 1868* (Vienna: ÖAW, 1978), 27.
15 John W. Boyer, 'Religion and Political Development in Central Europe around 1900: A View from Vienna', *Austrian History Yearbook* 25 (1994): 13–57, here 14.
16 Patent of 5 November 1855, Reichsgesetzblatt (RGBl.) 195 and Patent of 8 October 1856, RGBl. 185.
17 Gottfried Mayer, *Österreich als katholische Großmacht. Ein Traum zwischen Revolution und liberaler Ära* (Vienna: ÖAW, 1989), 207.
18 Georg Franz, *Kulturkampf. Staat und Kirche in Mitteleuropa von der Säkularisierung bis zum Abschluß des preußischen Kulturkampfs* (München: Callwey, 1954), 56.
19 Pastoral letter of 25 February 1857, quoted in Albert Ettmayer, *Die Hirtenbriefe des Wiener Fürst-Erzbischofs Joseph Othmar Kardinal Rauscher. Ein Beitrag zur österreichischen Kirchenpublizistik in der zweiten Hälfte des 19. Jahrhunderts* (PhD thesis, University of Vienna, 1982), 69.
20 Quoted in Vocelka, *Verfassung oder Konkordat?* 33.
21 Ernst Viktor Zenker, *Kirche und Staat unter besonderer Berücksichtigung der Verhältnisse in Österreich* (Vienna: Hartleben, 1909), 70.
22 Quoted in Vocelka, *Verfassung oder Konkordat*, 34.
23 Laurence Cole, 'The Counter-Reformation's Last Stand: Austria', in *Culture Wars: Secular-Catholic Conflict in Nineteenth-Century Europe*, ed. Christopher Clark and Wolfram Kaiser (Cambridge: Cambridge University Press, 2003), 285–312, here 289.

24 Cf. *Staatsgrundgesetz vom 21. Dezember 1867 über die allgemeinen Rechte der Staatsbürger*, RGBl. 142. Article 14: 'Full freedom of belief and conscience is granted to everyone ... .'
25 In an Act of 25 May 1868, RGBl. 47, Article I, the provisions of the Austrian Civil Code were re-instated for Catholics.
26 Article II.
27 Boyer, *Religion and Political Development*, 19; Fritz Fellner, 'Kaiser Franz Joseph und das Parlament. Materialien zur Geschichte der Innenpolitik Österreichs in den Jahren 1867–1873', *Mitteilungen des Österreichischen Staatsarchivs* 9 (1956): 287–347, here 314.
28 Quoted in Vocelka, *Verfassung oder Konkordat?*, 163.
29 Franz, *Kulturkampf*, 127.
30 Christopher Clark, 'The New Catholicism and the European culture wars', *Culture Wars*, ed. Clark and Kaiser, 11–46, here 45.
31 Clark, 'Catholicism', 46.
32 Ernst Hanisch, 'Bis daß der Tod euch scheidet. Katholische Kirche und Ehegesetzgebung in Österreich', *Justiz und Zeitgeschichte. Symposiumsbeiträge 1976-1993 I*, ed. Erika Weinzierl et al. (Wien: Jugend & Volk, 1995) 189–203, here 196.
33 Handwritten letter of 30 July 1870. Quoted in Peter Leisching, 'Die Römisch-Katholische Kirche in Cisleithanien', in *Die Habsburgermonarchie 1848-1918*, IV: *Die Konfessionen*, ed. Adam Wandruszka and Peter Urbanitsch (Vienna: ÖAW, 1985), 1–247, here 55.
34 Law on the external legal relations of the Catholic Church, RGBl. 50/1874.
35 Cf. Franz Joseph's statement or 'justification' to the Bohemian episcopate in Franz, *Kulturkampf*, 153.
36 Cole, *Counter-Reformation*, 291.
37 Leisching, *Die Römisch-Katholische Kirche*, 63.
38 Lothar Höbelt, 'Die Konservativen Alt-Österreichs 1848 bis 1918: Parteien und Politik', in *Konservativismus in Österreich. Strömungen, Ideen, Personen und Vereinigungen von den Anfängen bis heute*, ed. Robert Rill and Ulrich E. Zellenberg (Graz: Stocker, 1999), 109–52, here 116.
39 Boyer, *Religion*, 14.
40 Cf. Ulrike Harmat, *Ehe auf Widerruf? Der Konflikt um das Eherecht in Österreich 1918-1938*. Special issue of *Ius Commune* 121 (Frankfurt am Main: Vittorio Klostermann, 1999), 24-30.
41 Ludwig Wahrmund, *Dokumente zur Geschichte der Eherechtsreform in Österreich* (Innsbruck: Wagner, 1906), 892.
42 Wahrmund, *Dokumente*, 905.
43 Section 14 of Law XLIII/1868 and section 14 of Law XLIII/1868. Cf. Wilhelm Fuchs, *Die sogenannten Siebenbürgischen Ehen und andere Arten der Wiederverehelichung geschiedener österreichischer Katholiken* (Wien: Manz, 1889), 27–32.
44 Cf. Wilhelm Fuchs, *Siebenbürgische Ehen*, Juristische Blätter 8, no. 48 (1879): 589–92, here 589.
45 See Harmat, *Ehe auf Wiederruf*, 53–5.
46 Fuchs, *Siebenbürgische Ehen*, Juristische Blätter 8, no. 48 (1879): 592.
47 Wilhelm Fuchs, *Siebenbürgische Ehen*, Juristische Blätter 7, no. 13 (1883): 145–46, here 146.
48 E.g. an application for the legitimization of children, etc. For instance, it was common knowledge that a senior civil servant in the Ministry of Culture and Education,

who could not change his citizenship for professional reasons, had entered into a Transylvanian marriage. Nevertheless, the marriage remained uncontested. Cf. Fuchs, *Die sogenannten Siebenbürgischen Ehen*, 62.

49 Petition by the Committee of the Lower Austrian Bar Association to the House of Representatives, cf. Österreichisches Staatsarchiv (ÖStA), Allgemeines Verwaltungsarchiv (AVA) Zl. 1994/05 zu Zl. 16651/1907.

50 Valery Grey, *§111. Österreichisches Original-Volksstück in drei Akten* (München, Stuttgart and Vienna: Lenau, 1911).

51 For the case Girardi/Odilon cf. Margarete Grandner and Ulrike Harmat, 'Begrenzt verliebt. Gesetzliche Ehehindernisse und die Grenze zwischen Österreich und Ungarn', in *Liebe und Widerstand. Ambivalenzen historischer Geschlechterbeziehungen*, ed. Ingrid Bauer, et al., special issue of *L'Homme* 10 (2005), 287–304.

52 Law article L/1879, passed on 20 December 1879, announced on 24 December 1879. Cf. Dezső Markus, *Magyar Közjog* (Budapest: Grill, 1905), 176.

53 See Back Fritz, *Das ungarische Ehegesetz nebst der Rechtsprechung des ungarischen Obersten Gerichtshofes und ausführliche Erläuterungen* (Vienna: Manz, 1906).

54 Besides mandatory civil marriage, these included 'state acceptance of the Israelite religion', free practice of religion and the introduction of a civil marital status register. Géza von Geyr, *Sándor Wekerle 1848–1921. Die politische Biographie eines ungarischen Staatsmannes der Donaumonarchie*. Südosteuropäische Arbeiten 91 (München: Oldenburg, 1993), 134.

55 Moritz Csáky, *Der Kulturkampf in Ungarn. Die kirchenpolitische Gesetzgebung der Jahre 1894/95* (Vienna et al: Böhlau, 1967), 101.

56 Harmat, *Ehe auf Widerruf*, 147.

57 See Ulrike Harmat, 'Divorce and Remarriage in Austria-Hungary: The Second Marriage of Franz Conrad von Hötzendorf', *Austrian History Yearbook* 32 (2001): 69–103.

58 Gina Conrad von Hötzendorf, *Mein Leben mit Conrad von Hötzendorf. Sein geistiges Vermächtnis* (Leipzig: Grethlein 1935), 35.

59 John W. Boyer, 'Freud, Marriage and Late Viennese Liberalism', *Journal of Modern History* 50/1 (1978): 72–102, here 81.

60 Cf. Submission to the Austrian Ministry of the Interior: ÖStA, AVA, k.k. Ministerium des Innern, Praes. 13. Mai 1904, no. 21920/1904.

61 Cf. Joseph Unger, *Zur Revision des Allgemeinen bürgerlichen Gesetzbuches. Eine legislativgeschichtliche Studie* (Vienna: Alfred Hölder, 1904).

62 AVA k.k. Justiz-Ministerium no. 24360/354/1904 (Post 1/12).

63 AVA k.k. Justiz-Ministerium no. 28503/422/1904 (Post-No. 1/10).

64 Ibid.

65 Cf. Petition by the Federation of Austrian Women's Societies of 6 May 1905, in Wahrmund, *Dokumente*, 1247.

66 Waltraud Heindl, 'Geschlechterbilder und Geschlechterrollen. Ideologie und Realitäten', in *Die Habsburgermonarchie 1848-1918*, vol. 9, no. 1, part 1: *Soziale Strukturen. Von der feudal-agrarischen zur bürgerlich-industriellen Gesellschaft*, ed. Helmut Rumpler, et al. (Vienna: ÖAW, 2010), 701–41.

67 Appeal by the Catholic Central Committee of February 1906, in Wahrmund, *Dokumente*, 1300.

68 Ludwig Wahrmund, *Die Eherechtsreform in Österreich. Vortrag gehalten am 17. November 1906 zu Innsbruck* (Innsbruck: Wagner, 1907), 38.

69 Cf. *Protokolle der Enquete betreffend die Reform des österreichischen Eherechts* (vom 27. Jänner bis 24. Februar 1905 (Vienna: Kulturpolitische Gesellschaft, 1905).

70　*Protokolle*, 3.
71　Ibid., 15.
72　Waltraud Heindl, 'Aspekte der Ehescheidung in Vienna um 1900. Grenzen und Möglichkeiten der Erforschung des Problems', *Mitteilungen des Österreichischen Staatsarchivs* 33 (1980): 218–46, here 231.
73　In a way, these debates echoed those a century later in post colonial Gabon, where similar questions about modernity coursed through discussions about the role of the state in regulating the family, as Rachel Jean-Baptiste shows in Chapter 11 in this book.
74　Zenker, *Kirche und Staat*, 180.
75　Ofner's motion in Wahrmund, *Dokumente*, 1303.
76　*Protokolle*, 230.
77　AVA k.k. Justiz-Ministerium No. 21544/444/1901 (Post-No.1): 997 Appendices to the stenographic minutes of the House of Representatives (XVII session): Ofner's motion of 18 October 1901.
78　Cf. *Die Fessel. Zentralorgan für Eherechtsreform* 1 (1913), 5.
79　*Arbeiter-Zeitung* (11 November 1901), 1.
80　*Arbeiter-Zeitung* (25 January 1919), 1.
81　Hanisch, *Katholische Kirche*, 197. Seipel became chairman of the Christian Social Party in 1921 and was Austrian Federal Chancellor from 1922 to 1924 and from 1926 to 1929.
82　For the debate in the Justice Committee, cf. Harmat, *Ehe auf Widerruf*, 74–6.
83　Parlamentsarchiv Vienna, Akten des Justizausschusses der konstituierenden Nationalversammlung, Zuweisungen an den Justizausschuss: petition from 22 January 1919. This was entirely in the interests of the Episcopal Office, in whose name Cardinal Friedrich G. Piffl had protested that 'violence was being done to Catholic religious sentiments' in the name of liberty without pious Catholics being given the opportunity to take a stance on their own account. Cf. Wiener Diözesanblatt vom 23. Jänner 1919, 8.
84　Beilage 145 zu den Stenographischen Protokollen der Provisorischen Nationalversammlung für Deutschösterreich 1918 und 1919, I. Bd. Wien 1919, 1. The bill had desisted from introducing mandatory civil marriage and merely demanded the separability of marriage also for Catholics.
85　Cf. *Der Morgen. Wiener Montagsblatt* of 27 January 1919, no. 4, 12.
86　*Die Wählerin. Sozialdemokratisches Frauen-Wochenblatt* of 16 January 1919, no. 7, 1.
87　Bauer Helene, 'Ehe und soziale Schichtung', *Der Kampf. Sozialdemokratische Monatsschrift* 20 (July 1927): 319–24, here 320.
88　This was the reproach by the Social Democrat Sever to the Christian Socials in the National Assembly. Cf. stenographic minutes of the 73rd session of the National Assembly on 10 December 1921, 2498. Catholic Congresses were termed by Sever as 'election rallies' for the Christian Socials. Ibid. 2499.
89　Ibid. 2499.
90　Kutschera Richard, *Johannes Maria Gföllner. Bischof dreier Zeitenwenden* (Linz: OÖ Landesverlag, 1972), 57.
91　Alois Hudal, 'Der Katholizismus in Österreich. Sein Wirken, Kämpfen und Hoffen', in *Der Katholizismus in Österreich. Sein Wirken, Kämpfen und Hoffen*, ed. Alois Hudal (Innsbruck: Tyrolia 1931), 11–26, here 22.
92　Ibid.
93　*Reichspost* (25 January 1919), 1–3.
94　*Arbeiter-Zeitung* (25 January 1919), 1.

95 Harmat, *Ehe auf Widerruf*, 93.
96 Cf. Coalition agreement of 17 October 1919, in Felix Ermacora, *Materialien zur Österreichischen Bundesverfassung*, I: *Die Länderkonferenzen 1919/1920 und die Verfassungsfrage* (Vienna: Braumüller, 1989) Appendix G.
97 Cf. Klaus Berchtold, *Österreichische Parteiprogramme 1868-1966* (Vienna: Verlag für Geschichte und Politik, 1967), 234.
98 RGBl. 142/1867.
99 Christian Neschwara, 'Eherecht und "Scheinmigration" im 19. Jahrhundert: Siebenbürgische und ungarische, deutsche und Coburger Ehen', *Beiträge zur Rechtsgeschichte Österreichs* 2, no. 1 (2012): 101–17, here 115.
100 Lower Austrian provincial archives (NÖLA) Zl. IIIa-346, V-48-b, 1919. This happened before the Supreme Court changed his view in 1924.
101 Harmat, *Ehe auf Widerruf*, 191.
102 *Die Fessel* (1929), no. 8/9, 2. Harmat, *Ehe auf Widerruf*, 342.
103 For the case of Gustav Heider, see Harmat, *Ehe auf Widerruf*, 515–28.
104 Ernst Hanisch, *Der lange Schatten des Staates. Österreichische Gesellschaftsgeschichte im 20. Jahrhundert* (Vienna: Ueberreuter, 1994), 310.
105 Lehner, *Familie*, 115.
106 Hanisch, *Schatten*, 310.
107 Cf. Lehner, *Familie*, 117.
108 See Harmat, *Ehe auf Widerruf*, 481–515.
109 Cf. Ernst Hanisch, *Die Ideologie des politischen Katholizismus in Österreich 1918-1935* (Vienna, Salzburg: Geyer, 1977), 3.
110 Harmat, *Ehe auf Widerruf*, 533–5.
111 Cf. Mariken Lenaerts, *National Socialist Family Law. The Influence of National Socialism on Marriage and Divorce Law in Germany and the Netherlands* (Leiden: Brill, 2015).
112 'German Citizens' Act' and 'Act for the Protection of German Blood and German Honour' of 15 September 1935, 'Act for the Prevention of Hereditary Defective Children' of 14 July 1933, 'Hereditary Health Act' of 18 October 1935.
113 Claus Mühlfeld and Friedrich Schönweiss, *Nationalsozialistische Familienpolitik. Familiensoziologische Analyse der nationalsozialistischen Familienpolitik* (Stuttgart: Enke, 1989), 45.
114 Lehner, *Familie*, 156.
115 See Evan Burr Bukey, *Jews and Intermarriage in Nazi Austria* (Cambridge: University Press, 2011), 88. In addition to other discriminatory measures there were house searches, arrests, and frequent denunciations by neighbours that included letters slandering Gentile wives as 'married whores'.
116 For the marriage law debate after 1945, see: Ulrike Harmat, '"eine gottesräuberische Usurpation?" Die Debatte um die obligatorische Zivilehe in Österreich nach 1945 bis zur Anerkennung des Konkordats 1957', *Beiträge zur Rechtsgeschichte Österreichs* 4, no. 1 (2014): 84–120.
117 As the Archbishops-Coadjutor, Franz Jachym, stated in 1955; see Franz Jachym, *Kirche und Staat in Österreich* (Wien: Österreichische Bischofskonferenz, 1955), 35.
118 Lehner, *Familie*, 218.

6

Modernizing Marriage in Egypt

Kenneth M. Cuno

In late 1999, Egypt's lower house of parliament began discussion of a revision of the personal status law, which governs most aspects of family life, including marriage, divorce, child custody and inheritance. Two provisions in the draft legislation were especially contentious. One enabled married women to travel abroad without the consent of their husband, and the other enhanced their ability to obtain a divorce without their husband's agreement. Western reportage represented these provisions as expanding women's autonomy, but Egyptians debated them mainly in terms of what was good for the family. Proponents as well as opponents voiced a conviction that the family is the basic unit in society, with the important role of child-rearing. In their view, the fate of the family is the fate of the nation. A harmonious and stable family life is a social good, and the law should promote, in the words of one commentator, 'an increase in the coherence and stability of the family, and not the opposite'.[1]

In its final form, Law No. 1 of 2000 omitted mention of travel, though it enabled women to seek a judicial divorce unilaterally on the ground of incompatibility, while sacrificing their financial settlement (the bridal gift and temporary maintenance), in what is known as a *khulʿ* divorce.[2] Men, on the other hand, continue to be able to divorce their wives unilaterally by repudiation (*talaq*) and without cause (though with financial consequences), and there is no restriction on the ability of married men to travel. These inequalities reflect the persistence of what Nadia Sonneveld has called the maintenance–obedience relationship in marriage: the wife owes the husband obedience, including sexual submission, and he owes her and their children maintenance.[3] It also reflects a notion of domesticity in which a woman's primary role is to care for a home and children. In the debate over reform of the personal status law, the social importance of the family unit and the maintenance–obedience relationship were taken for granted. The question was whether the proposed changes would strengthen families, as proponents argued, or lead to their breakup, as opponents insisted.

This construction of the conjugal family as the basis of society, its stability as a social good, and women's dependency and domesticity is an artefact of colonial modernity, although it is widely understood by Egyptians to come from their own traditions and Islam. In other semi-colonized societies like Siam and China, as discussed by Tamara Loos and Lisa Tran in this book, local reforming intellectuals and government officials similarly adopted a version of the European model of the conjugal family as 'modern'. Following European social science, they associated this couple-and-child-centred family with social advancement and rejected multi-generational households and polygyny as symptomatic of backwardness. In Egypt as well as in Siam, China and colonized India, discussed in this book by Leigh Denault, at about the same time that the new family ideology was taking hold, the modernizing state increased its regulation of marriage through civil registration and court arbitration, imposing uniform standards and leaving relatively little space for informality.

In Egypt, from the mid-nineteenth to the early twentieth century, reforming, 'modernist' intellectuals constructed a family ideology that valorizes monogamous and companionate marriage, women's education and domesticity, and the maintenance–obedience relationship as a hybrid of European ideas and precolonial Islamic norms regarding marriage and marital relations. The new family ideology became well established between the two world wars, as evidenced by publicly voiced concerns over supposed threats to marriage and the family,[4] and new usage of the term *usra*, which previously denoted lineage, to refer to the conjugal family.[5] Egypt's original constitution of 1923 did not mention the family, but constitutions since 1956 have declared the family to be 'the basis of society' and 'founded on religion, morality and patriotism'.[6]

While modernist intellectuals promoted a new vision of marriage and the family, other, contingent developments contributed to changes in the marriage system. The ruling khedival (viceregal) family abandoned slave concubinage and polygyny in favour of royal endogamy and monogamy during the last quarter of the nineteenth century. The khedives were trendsetters and the public example of monogamy they set was a standard for the upper class to emulate. After the turn of the century, also, a new style of conjugality emerged among the middle class, which was characterized by a relatively higher age of marriage, enhanced involvement of the bride and groom in spousal choice, and neolocality. This chapter follows these developments up to the beginning of codification of Muslim family law in Egypt in the 1920s.[7]

Muslim Jurisprudence and the Family

During the nineteenth century, the Ottoman Empire and its Egyptian province adopted a civil law system based on the French model, preserving an enclave of Muslim family law (personal status law) administered by the Sharia courts until the judicial system was unified in 1955. Separate religious courts administered Christian and Jewish personal law.[8] The idea of 'the centrality of the family in Islam'[9] is an artefact of colonial scholarship, as well as an effect of the restriction of the jurisdiction of the Sharia courts to family matters during the nineteenth-century reorganization of the judicial system.[10] It also begs the question of the meaning of 'family'. Historically, Muslim jurisprudence privileged the extended patrilineal family over the conjugal family[11] by providing for separate as opposed to joint marital property, and partible inheritance in which agnates shared when there were no sons as heirs. Moreover, it permitted polygyny and easy divorce, at least on the part of men, which were sources of marital instability.[12] The family idealized in modern discourse is, however, the conjugal family.

Precolonial Muslim writings recommended marriage for licit sexual relations and procreation, but there was no particular emphasis on parent–child relations. Nor did it contain a domestic ideology. Women had no special obligation when it came to raising children, and were not required to do housework.[13] The modern family ideology, on the other hand, valorizes the family as the site where children are raised and where their character is formed, and women, as mothers, are construed as primarily responsible for their care.

Handbooks composed by jurists expressing the historic (and, one must add, male) view of marriage and marital relations circulated in Ottoman Egypt and their readership undoubtedly expanded with the introduction of print technology in the mid-nineteenth century. A late example of that genre was Muhammad b. Umar al-Nawawi's *Sharh* or explication of *The Silver Necklace on an Explanation of What the Two Spouses Are Due*, the original text probably dating from the late sixteenth or seventeenth century.[14] The title reflects the way that marriage was construed as a contractual relationship (albeit an asymmetrical one) in which the wife and husband were due certain things from each other. The wife was due maintenance (*nafaqa*) from her husband, which the jurists explained consisted of food, clothing and lodging. In court cases and fatwas, food and clothing were accounted in monetary terms according to the social status of the couple, and likewise lodging, which also had to meet certain criteria such as privacy, quality of neighbourhood and accoutrements to be legal. For his part, the husband was due obedience (*ta'a*) from his wife, which involved her staying in the marital home and not leaving without his permission, submitting to him sexually, guarding his home and possessions in his absence and guarding her chastity. Wifely disobedience (*nushuz*) appears in the juridical literature and in legal cases nearly exclusively in the form of the wife leaving her husband – leaving the marital home – and usually taking refuge with her parents or other relatives. However, the jurists regarded a woman who went out of her husband's home even temporarily without his permission – say to work during the day, returning in the evening – as disobedient. Spousal obligations were not theoretical. Women added stipulations to the marriage contract guaranteeing their ability to visit relatives and friends and receive guests, to go out to the public bath or to go out to a job. A woman could sue her husband for arrears of maintenance and even have him imprisoned for the debt, and in some juridical interpretations, she could obtain a divorce on the ground of non-support. A man could obtain an order of obedience against a runaway wife, requiring her to return to him, and if she remained obstinate, he was not obliged to pay her maintenance.[15]

These handbooks are remarkable for their frank comparison of a woman's position in marriage to that of a slave or a captive. Writers invoked that point, along with a frequently cited *hadith*, or statement attributed to the Prophet, describing women as deficient in intellect and faith as reasons for men to treat their wives with patience and forbearance.[16] Although marriages were usually arranged by a woman's guardian, spousal compatibility was preferred, and so some jurists recommended that she not be married off to a much older man, and that she be allowed to meet her prospective husband with her face uncovered in advance of the wedding. A married woman was entitled to companionship from her husband, with or without sexual relations. Some women stipulated in the marriage contract that their husband not be absent for a lengthy time. Women disliked polygyny, and its deterrence was by far the most common contractual stipulation in Ottoman Egypt. A woman who could not avoid a plural marriage was entitled to treatment equitable with her co-wives, not only in maintenance but also in companionship, which took the form of the husband spending alternate nights with them.[17]

In Egypt, handbooks such as these were in circulation into the early twentieth century. Al-Nawawi's *Sharh* had four printings between 1878 and 1919, which illustrates the persistence of conservative family norms in an era that witnessed the onset of the British occupation (1882) and, partly in response, the rise of a multifaceted nationalist movement. This era also saw the expansion of periodical publishing, and the first public expressions of feminist sentiment.[18] However, even before those events, modernist intellectuals had begun to formulate a family ideology that drew on post-Enlightenment European social science and ideas of progress, but which also was in dialogue with precolonial Muslim writings on marriage like al-Nawawi's.

Modernist Intellectuals and the New Family Ideology

The idea that the conjugal family is the basis of society and that marriage should be companionate and lasting, with the aim of forming a family and raising children, was not historically Islamic but originated in Enlightenment thought. A corollary of that was domestic ideology, or domesticity, the notion that women's vocation is to manage the family household and raise children. In the second half of the nineteenth century, modernist intellectuals in Egypt and other Ottoman provinces joined those ideas with the maintenance–obedience relationship in producing their own, hybrid family ideology, and advocated reform of the family for the sake of social improvement. The modernists followed recent trends in European thought in holding that women should be educated to be able to fulfil their domestic roles properly as well as to be good companions for their husbands.

This cluster of ideas about the reform of family life owed its power to the association of the conjugal family with 'civilization' – that is, with development and advancement. The earliest exponents of the connection between women's education and child-rearing that I have found in the Ottoman Empire were the Lebanese educator Butrus al-Bustani (1819–83), in a speech on the education of women in 1849, and the Turkish writer Namık Kemal (1840–88), in an essay on the education of women published in 1867.[19] In Egypt Rifa'a al-Tahtawi (1801–73) and Ali Mubarak (1823–93), state servants involved in the development of education on the European model, drew a similar connection between the education of women and proper child-rearing. In his book, *The Faithful Guide for Girls and Boys* (1872), al-Tahtawi proposed universal education for girls as well as boys at the elementary level, arguing that it was the norm in modern civilized countries and reassuring conservatives by citing examples of literate Muslim women in history who were virtuous. Much of the *Murshid* was concerned with promoting harmonious marriages. Al-Tahtawi drew on the marriage handbooks in recommending against child marriage and in favour of prenuptial meetings to allow prospective spouses to get to know each other.[20] Both he and Mubarak opined that educating women not only made them better mothers but also better companions for their husbands, ensuring the harmony and stability of the family. In Mubarak's novel-like *Alam al-Din* (a fictional travel account, 1882), Taqiyya, the wife of the eponymous Azhari, Shaykh Alam al-Din, seemed to embody al-Tahtawi's ideal. Under the shaykh's tutelage, she proved capable of learning to read, memorized the Qur'an, and mastered advanced books, all while not neglecting her marital duties. Education enhanced her role as a mother and helpmate.[21]

Al-Tahtawi and Mubarak also discouraged polygyny and easy divorce in the interest of family stability. They were the most distinguished products of the first two student 'missions' sent to France by the reforming Ottoman governor Muhammad Ali Pasha (r. 1805–48), who founded the dynasty that reigned until 1952. The Pasha and all but one of his successors before the British occupation turned to France for instructors in the new government schools they established, and began sending students to France for advanced training in the 1820s. Consequently, generations of Egyptian intellectuals and officials were exposed to European ideas mainly through the French language if not through study in France. Al-Tahtawi and Mubarak deployed arguments drawn from European social science as well as Muslim jurisprudence and history. In recommending against polygyny, al-Tahtawi noted that the Qur'an required men to treat plural wives equitably (Q 4:3), and that those who failed to do so would be punished on the day of judgement. Polygyny was also a source of family discord.[22] Mubarak expressed similar views, adding a comment on the virtue of self-restraint, and comparing polygyny to the behaviour of animals. The fictional Shaykh Alam al-Din opined that polygyny was not unique to Muslim societies (and implicitly not intrinsic to them). Less accurately he claimed that the Turks had introduced the practice, and only the ruling class had large harems. If the rulers set a virtuous example, the condition of the country would improve.[23]

The views of these men were reformist, not feminist, as some have argued.[24] Al-Tahtawi's plan limited girls to an elementary education, sufficient for them to take on the duties of household management and child-rearing. Neither he nor Mubarak suggested that women should have any role other than a domestic one, and both approved of the prevailing custom of veiling and seclusion. Nevertheless, the implications of the family ideology they articulated were important for women. They asserted that women had the ability to acquire an education, as opposed to lacking intellect and faith, and that their vocation was to manage households, not to be imprisoned in them. Women were responsible for child-rearing, which was key to social advancement.

In the following generation, female as well as male modernists developed these ideas further. The writer Aisha al-Taymur (1840–1902), the journalist Zaynab Fawwaz (ca. 1850–1914) and Malak Hifni Nasif (1886–1918), a teacher and essayist who wrote under the pen name Bahithat al-Badiya ('Searcher in the Wilderness/Desert'), are known as early feminists. However, they embraced the new family ideology and its corollaries, the conjugal family ideal and domesticity. They too linked the education of women with domesticity. In an 1889 essay, al-Taymur endorsed the education of girls, saying it would enhance their ability to manage a household and to rear children. Writing in 1896, Fawwaz declared, 'women are the basis of civilization, as the first school for every one of the human race', and that individuals acquired their good or bad characters from their mothers as children. She also agreed that educated women made better helpmates for their husbands and were more able to share in family life with them. Nasif wrote often about girls' education, disdaining the accomplishments taught by foreign governesses and in foreign schools, and arguing that the government schools prepared girls better for the roles of household management and child-rearing.[25]

The commitment of Fawwaz and Nasif to the conjugal family ideal and companionate marriage was most evident in their criticism of polygyny. For Fawwaz, who was briefly in a plural marriage, it was 'a curse' on the entire family. It condemned women to jealousy and extreme hardship, men to a lifetime of misfortune and children to enmity towards their half-siblings. Nasif invoked her own experience as a second wife, calling polygyny 'the fiercest enemy of women, their unique devil'. It broke women's hearts and led men to dissemble and be subjected to spiteful accusations.[26] While not going beyond their male counterparts' view of polygyny as destructive of family life, they conveyed the special anguish it caused women, unlike most male writers.

Fawwaz and Nasif also had in common professional work experience, and differed from most male modernists in arguing that women should be free to pursue an education beyond the elementary level and to engage in work activity outside the home. Religion did not forbid it, they argued, and family life would not suffer as a result.[27] Fawwaz insisted that neither religion nor nature limited women to the home and domestic duties. In Europe, with its advanced civilization, women worked. Egyptian women also worked in trades, crafts, construction and agriculture. It was but a custom for urban middle- and upper-class women to remain at home.[28] Nasif noted that many women needed to work: those who were unmarried, barren, widowed, divorced or whose husbands needed assistance in supporting a household. They should have the opportunity to become teachers or doctors, and not be expected to take lowly jobs. In Nasif's ideal, respectable women would work as professionals in a homosocial environment, unlike working-class women, whom she disdained as having bad morals because of their contact with unrelated men in the workplace.[29]

Muhammad Abduh (1849–1905) and Qasim Amin (1863–1908), contemporaries of the women mentioned above, shared many of their views as well as al-Tahtawi's and Mubarak's views on family and marriage, including the importance of the conjugal family and companionate marriage, and the valorization of women's education and domesticity. Like the women writers discussed, Amin is associated more with the cause of women's emancipation. His book *The Emancipation of Women* (1899) unleashed a storm of controversy for advocating that women uncover their faces in public, although most of it was devoted to women's role in the family.[30] Unlike the other writers discussed, Abduh and Amin had legal training and served as judges in the National Court system, and Abduh also served as Grand Mufti, the chief Islamic jurist of Egypt, during 1899–1905. Their professional background and experiences made them especially concerned about strengthening family life through the reform of Muslim family law.[31] The abuses they addressed were: first, the failure of married men to support their wives and children; second, divorces pronounced irresponsibly by men; third, the inability of women to escape marriages in which they suffered from non-support, desertion or abuse; and, finally, men's abuse of polygyny.

The first three of these problems were exacerbated by the nineteenth-century reorganization of the legal system. This process was similar but not identical to Ottoman legal reorganization in the same era, due to the status of Egypt as an autonomous province since the rule of Muhammad Ali. In both Istanbul and Cairo, the object was to end the regime of foreign extraterritoriality imposed by the European powers.[32] Officials drafted new codes of criminal, commercial and property law following the French models. Codes of family law came later, in the twentieth century, but new regulations and procedures were introduced in the Sharia courts, which adjudicated Muslim family law.[33] In a step towards a uniform law, the Egyptian Sharia courts were instructed to apply only the predominant opinions of the Hanafi school of jurisprudence, instead of allowing rulings in accord with the four Sunni schools, which had been the practice since medieval times.[34] Under the old system, contractual parties and litigants could forum shop among the schools to their best advantage, but the new procedural rules forbade that.[35] The Hanafi school put married women at a disadvantage in a number of common situations. Unlike the other schools, it did not account arrears of maintenance automatically as a debt against the husband; rather, the amount had first to be set formally by a judge or in an agreement between the spouses. There was, of course, an additional problem in enforcing judicial orders to pay maintenance. When it came to divorce, the Hanafi school doubly disadvantaged women. First, it validated a triple (and hence irrevocable) divorce pronounced by a man on a whim, in anger, while intoxicated, or conditionally – that is, depending on an event, or on something proving true or false. Second, and unlike the other schools, it did not allow women to seek a divorce for non-support, desertion or abuse; the only ground accepted was impotence. The other schools allowed a judge to declare a man missing for four years deceased, but the Hanafi school presumed him to be alive, and his marriage intact, until he would be in his nineties.[36] Forum shopping was also eliminated in the Ottoman provinces under direct imperial rule, but the government softened the harshness of Hanafism by permitting women to petition for annulments according to Shafi'i and Maliki jurisprudence in cases of non-support and desertion.[37] It is not clear why Egyptian officials did not do the same.

When discussion of the composition of a code of family law began in the 1890s, Abduh proposed selectively to (re-)introduce elements of Maliki law to address some of the problems resulting from Hanafization. Applying Maliki opinions would make arrears of maintenance accumulate as a debt from the time of non-payment, and enable women to petition a judge for a divorce on the ground of non-support, desertion or abuse, or to declare a missing husband deceased after four years.[38] Amin proposed in addition to make general use of a device recognized in Hanafi law, known as the delegated divorce. In it, a man agreed to delegate the right of unilateral divorce to his wife, which she could exercise at any time, as a deterrent against his misbehaviour. These reforms were necessary to enable women to free themselves from marriages in which men failed to fulfil their responsibilities, or disappeared. However, it was also necessary to restrain frequent and irresponsible divorce by men. To that end, Amin proposed mandatory arbitration before any repudiation became final.[39]

Both men opposed polygyny, and Abduh in particular linked plural marriage with divorce and the breakup of families. Towards the end of his life, he offered a radical reinterpretation of the Qur'anic verses regarding polygyny. Initially, he and other modernists had argued that the well-known verse (Q 4:3) allowing men to marry up to four wives but cautioning them, 'If you fear you will not be just, then one,' set a nearly impossible standard. Since so few men could live up to it, it was better to limit themselves to one wife.[40] The historical interpretation of a later verse (Q 4:129), 'You will not be able to be equitable between your wives, be you ever so eager,' was that a man could not be expected to have equal affection for his wives, nor maintain equal sexual activity with them. However, in his later interpretation, Abduh argued that the latter verse referred to 'the inclination of the heart', and implied the abolition of polygyny. He recommended that polygyny be allowable only in the case of a barren wife, and that a man should establish that and his ability to support an additional wife before a judge.[41] Amin, who was close to Abduh, opined that the two verses contained 'a permission and an interdiction' of polygyny, and that it was justifiable only when the wife had an illness that prevented her from fulfilling her marital duties or was barren.[42]

The hardening of Abduh's and Amin's attitudes towards polygyny reflected their concern for the stability of the conjugal family. Amin made this clear in stating that polygyny was contrary to the ideal of 'a united family in which children live in the embrace of their parents, a sincere love holding them together'.[43] The first Egyptian codes concerning marriage and divorce, issued in the 1920s, made use of Abduh's suggestion that Maliki opinions be adopted to improve the situation of married women. However, polygyny was left unrestricted until 1979, when it was made a ground for divorce. Abduh's and Amin's ideas in particular influenced Muslim family law reform from North Africa to Southeast Asia.

Monogamy in the Khedival House

The new family ideology, including the conjugal family ideal and domesticity, spread in educated, middle- and upper-class circles in the early decades of the twentieth century, but it was not a force for change before that time. However, in the last quarter of the nineteenth century, Europeans and Egyptians alike remarked a turn away from polygyny in the upper and ruling classes.[44] The ruling khedival (viceregal) family pioneered that turn and were influential in publicly displaying their monogamy.

The first five rulers in the khedival dynasty had practised polygyny and slave concubinage in emulation of their suzerains, the Ottoman sultans, but political considerations led Khedive Ismail (r. 1863–79) to abandon that system in favour of royal endogamy, which necessarily entailed monogamy. Ismail himself had fourteen recognized consorts, all of slave origin, four of whom were contractual wives. In February 1873, he married off a daughter and three sons, including the Crown Prince, Tawfiq, in a series of lavish public weddings (Figure 6.1). Marriage to a (recently manumitted) slave woman was not celebrated; however, each of the princes was married to a princess from the extended khedival family. The future Khedive Tawfiq

Figure 6.1 Khedive Tawfiq and Khediva Amina Ilhami, mid-1880s. Professional photography in Egypt dates from the mid-nineteenth century, and portraits of married couples appear to have become popular in the upper class along with the spread of the conjugal family ideal. This one was taken perhaps a decade after the Tawfiq and Amina's wedding (another family portrait using the same backdrop includes four children). These photos were not for public display; feminist activists allowed their unveiled portraits to be published only in the 1920s. Nevertheless, the khedival family's trendsetting domestic style was not hidden from readers of the press nor Amina's many lady visitors. Courtesy the Bibliotheca Alexandrina Memory of Modern Egypt Digital Archive.

(r. 1879–92) was married to Amina Ilhami, his second cousin once removed and herself the granddaughter of a khedive.[45]

Subsequently, nearly every member of the khedival family married a prince or princess. The major exception was Tawfiq and Amina's son, Khedive Abbas II (1892–1914), who married Iqbal Hanim, his personal slave, in 1895, shortly after she bore him a daughter. In a departure from custom, the birth of their child as well as their marriage were publicly announced and celebrated. Fifteen years later, however, the khedive discreetly married a second woman, Javidan (Djavidan) Hanim, a Hungarian countess, with no public acknowledgement. Polygyny was (and is) still legal, and the official silence surrounding Abbas's polygyny contrasted strongly with the open display of it by his grandfather Ismail. The difference suggests that it had fallen into general disfavour among the educated middle and upper classes on the eve of the First World War.[46]

Why did Khedive Ismail, who bridled at criticisms of plural marriage, engineer a change in the ruling family's style of conjugality? Earlier, he had secured from the Sultan a decree changing the mode of succession in the khedivate from the Ottoman system of succession of the oldest male to primogeniture. In an instant, Tawfiq became the heir apparent, displacing two cousins. For a time, those princes sought to rally support against Ismail and Tawfiq, and so Ismail seems to have decided upon a strategy of marriage within the extended khedival family as a means of enlisting the support of the collateral lines of the family for his descendants' rule. Marriage to an Ottoman or Egyptian princess necessarily entailed monogamy, due to the status of the bride and her family. Monogamy was therefore not Ismail's aim, but it was an effect of his strategy of royal endogamy. The official gazette (in Arabic) justified the adoption of primogeniture as giving the khedivate greater stability and as something favoured by European states, while making no mention of monogamy at all in the detailed articles describing the four princely marriages of 1873. However, Ismail was alert to European opinion and let it be understood that he 'in mature age wished to adopt the European law of one wife', in addition to primogeniture. Similarly, his monogamous son Tawfiq opposed harems and slavery, and mentioned the benefits of women's education for companionate marriage and child-rearing, at least when speaking to Europeans.[47]

Tawfiq's voicing of the conjugal family ideal was a sign of the circulation of the family ideology that was promoted by the modernist reformers, as well as of his concern to cultivate European opinion, even before the expansion of the periodical press, which further popularized the ideas of companionate (and monogamous) marriage and domesticity around the turn of the century and later. However, there were additional contingent factors that inclined the khedival family and the upper class in general towards monogamous marriage. Four years after the four princely weddings, the Anglo-Egyptian Convention for the Abolition of Slavery prohibited the traffic in African slaves. After seven years (1884) the ban was extended to the trade in 'white' slaves, who were mainly Circassian women. Iqbal, Khedive Abbas's wife, was one of four slave women gifted to him by his mother Amina, who evidently had procured them surreptitiously.[48]

Slave concubinage was part of the old system of ruling- and upper-class polygyny, and an integral part of the political system. Polygyny enabled ruling- and upper-class men to make a show of their wealth and virility, and to ensure they had sons. Normally a slave woman would not object to becoming a concubine or to being elevated to the status of contractual wife (a man had to free his slave to marry her), since in either case her status improved. However, the majority of women in the harems in the ruling class were celibate, and trained to become the consorts of other elite men. In Siam, subordinates showed their allegiance to the king by sending their daughters to his harem,[49] while in Ottoman ruling-class culture, harem women were married out to subordinate men or gifted to superiors, in order to cement bonds between households. The khedives practised this on a grand scale, choosing harem women to be the wives of officers and officials and providing them with trousseaus that included property, in order to bind them to themselves.

This system of 'household government' worked as long as there was a suitable supply of slave women and the khedives had complete control of state finances. But in 1876, one year before the anti-slavery convention was agreed upon, Egypt went bankrupt. Over the next several years, as the traffic in slaves ended, European creditors imposed a stringent financial settlement, and the khedives lost personal control of state revenues. Tawfiq was the first khedive subjected to a civil list. Heavy-handed foreign control provoked a nationalist movement, the Urabi Revolution (1881–2), which was suppressed by a British invasion that inaugurated a long-term occupation. In the new colonial political order, family and politics were separated, and ruling-class harems quickly became obsolete.

Emergence of a Middle-class Style of Conjugality

Independent of the spread of the reformers' family ideology and the impetus given to it by the example of the khedival family, the age at marriage rose markedly in the early twentieth century, and the trend may have begun as early as the late nineteenth century. This demographic development occurred society-wide and prior to the embrace of the new family ideology by the educated. Incomplete census data from the middle of the nineteenth century suggest that nearly half of all girls in Cairo married between the age of ten and fourteen, while village women married at higher ages. There was a correlation between wealth and child marriage, due to the concern of those families to arrange matches that would preserve their property and status. Aisha al-Taymur and the feminist leader Huda al-Sha'rawi (1879–1947), both from upper-class families, were married off at the ages of fourteen and thirteen, respectively.[50] A campaign against child marriage led the government to set a minimum age of sixteen for women and eighteen for men in 1923, but by then the percentage of child brides was in the low single digits in nationwide censuses. The trend in the age of marriage has been steadily upward since then.[51] Although this development cannot be attributed to the spread of education and new ideas, the effect of education among middle- and upper-class men is detectable after the turn of the century.

Marriages were normally 'arranged', not only in the process of choosing a spouse, but also through negotiations preceding the writing of the contract. In addition to the dower and the portion of it paid promptly, the bride and groom or their guardians could negotiate a number of other issues, including a trousseau provided to the bride by her parents. The bride's family might seek a commitment to monogamy by the groom, or other guarantees concerning her freedom to visit relatives and friends, the place of the marital residence and so on. The higher the status of the bride's family, the more likely they were to impose such stipulations.[52]

Marriage at a relatively young age necessitated dependence on family to pay the costs. Women as well as men of the age of discretion were entitled legally to marry on their own, but the dower, trousseau and ceremonial costs were important reasons for the involvement of elder family members in marriage decisions, especially for those marrying for the first time. Widowed and divorced men and women had more autonomy in marriage decisions.[53]

Personal memoirs, most of them by men, offer a vivid if retrospective view of a changing marriage system around the turn of the century. Those who married before the First World War tended to do so within a system of family patriarchy that limited their autonomy in the choice of a bride just as it limited the choices of women. Muhammad Ali Allouba (1875/1878–1956), a lawyer, politician and diplomat, married in 1904, a year after becoming a lawyer in the appeals court. His family searched for a suitable bride for him in his home town of Asyut, in Upper Egypt, and then in Cairo, where his father rented a house for six months as a base of operations. They eventually pursued a match suggested by a friend and relative: there were reciprocal visits by members of each family, and the two fathers agreed on the terms of an engagement. Nefisa Amin Hanafi wished to have a look at her future husband from behind a *mashrabiyya* lattice, which was the custom in Cairo, but Allouba objected to that because he was not able to see her, and so she agreed to have her father travel to Asyut to inspect him. The two fathers drew up the marriage contract on the day of the wedding, and the bride and groom met for the first time. Looking back from the mid-twentieth century, Allouba wrote that the custom of not meeting before marriage persisted, especially in Upper Egypt, though he thought it was better for couples to meet and get to know one another beforehand. However, he did not object to arranged marriages and expressed scepticism towards love matches. Love can cloud one's judgement; it should come after marriage, but not before.[54]

Allouba and his bride's inability to meet before their wedding day was typical of their social class. Until around the time of the First World War, the middle- and upper-class marriage system discouraged prospective brides and grooms from meeting before their wedding day, effectively foreclosing the possibility of mutual attraction playing a role in spousal selection. Yet by the early twentieth century the question of whether attraction and even love ought to be a factor in choosing a spouse had become a subject of discussion. Malak Hifni Nasif opposed 'blind' marriages in which the couple met for the first time at their wedding, arguing that prenuptial meetings were necessary to permit a man to arrive at an estimate of the learning and character of his fiancée and her family. Nevertheless, she opposed 'the European practice of allowing the engaged pair to get together for a period of time so that they can come to know each other'. That might indeed result in love, which was undesirable, because it could blind one to the other's faults.[55]

The idea that love might precede marriage was more common by the middle of the twentieth century, at least in novels and films if not always in practice, but as Allouba made clear, it was still suspect. Thus, 'modern', 'enlightened' opinion in the early twentieth century accepted the desirability of prenuptial meetings, evidently not realizing that precolonial religious scholars had endorsed it. But there was too much at stake in marriage to allow the young to follow their hearts and freely choose their spouses. Literate Egyptians were familiar with the ideal of marriage for love, since it was a trope in novels, including the many translated from European languages,[56] and, increasingly, in journalism. But in the writings of that era and later, there was no desire expressed for complete autonomy in selecting a mate. The spread of the new family ideology did not lead to the abandonment of arranged and negotiated marriages, though the system of spousal selection and prenuptial negotiation has changed considerably since the early twentieth century. Unlike then, young men and women today have the opportunity to meet and get to know potential spouses at school and in university, and they are much more involved in prenuptial negotiations. But in the late twentieth century, arranged marriages remained the norm.[57]

Another feature of the old system that continued into the early twentieth century was, for men from the middle and upper classes like Allouba, the bringing of brides into the household of the husband's father. Although Allouba was a lawyer and capable of supporting himself and his wife, his father negotiated his marriage contract, paid his dower, and added a wing to the family home in Asyut for the young couple.[58] Patrilocal marriage and joint households were the ideal. This changed rapidly after the First World War, as couples increasingly established separate, neolocal households. To some extent, the trend was favoured by the delay of marriage by men pursuing an advanced education – to form a joint household one necessarily had to marry while one's father was alive. However, since the end of the nineteenth century the periodical press had promoted the new family ideology, with its emphasis on a companionate relationship between husband and wife.[59] This conjugal family ideal encouraged young couples to establish independent households to enable them to develop their relationship and to nurture their children. The joint family household was inconsistent with that ideal, in which 'the family' was defined as the conjugal couple and their children rather than the extended lineage (Figure 6.2).

The transition to conjugal family households diminished the power of family patriarchs who had exercised authority over the younger men as well as the women in the joint household system. With an independent income and a separate household budget, young men in the middle and upper classes enjoyed more autonomy, as did their wives. However, it remains commonplace for urban extended families to reside in adjacent or nearby apartments, often within the same building, which they may own, like the building in Istanbul described by the novelist Orhan Pamuk.[60] In the census data these next-door related families appear as separate conjugal family households. Familial and other social relations extend beyond the formal boundaries of households in all societies, but the preference for close proximity of related conjugal families illustrates how an originally north-western European ideal, the neolocal conjugal family household, was adapted and indigenized not only in Egypt, but also across the Middle East. There was a comparable development in Turkey, as Pamuk outlines, where joint family households became obsolete at about the same time. Nonetheless, 'functional connections' between households persist 'even today in Istanbul or other major Turkish cities, where intergenerational, interhousehold, extended family ties are particularly strong, even in a situation where nuclear family households overwhelmingly predominate as the statistical norm. These vital ties still provide, and appear to have then provided, services, often for child care, that the demographically

Figure 6.2 Family portrait, probably 1920s. Family portraiture spread to the middle class in the early twentieth century. This couple and their children may have lived in either a joint or a conjugal family household. However, posing for an intimate photo such as this one was a performative act of self-representation as a conjugal family. Courtesy of the Rare Books and Special Collections Library, The American University in Cairo.

modest circumstances of most households could not otherwise afford.'[61] I have a similar impression from years spent in Cairo, where this practice affords a young couple autonomy while enabling them to rely on the extended family for assistance, especially child care, and to look after aged parents.

Conclusion

Discussions in Egypt and the Ottoman Empire, Siam, China and India in the nineteenth and twentieth centuries about reforming family life and law reflected the conviction, acquired from Europeans, that the conjugal family was the basis of society and that stable and healthy families were a key to social advancement. In Egypt this discourse produced a hybrid family ideology that, along with the reorganization of the judicial system, associated religion closely with the sphere of domestic relations. The religious basis of the personal status law obliges reformers, including the activists who promoted the *khulʿ* law of 2000, to ground their proposals in religious sources: Qur'an, Sunna and historic jurisprudence. In doing so they, like Abduh a century earlier, are recovering the flexibility of premodern interpretations.

The new family ideology became hegemonic after the First World War, but before that it did not drive changes in the marriage system that were already underway due to political and material factors. The harem system became obsolete once family ceased to do political work, and in any event it would not have survived the abolition of the slave trade. These events occurred soon after Khedive Ismail's decision to marry his sons to princesses from the extended khedival family, which in effect imposed monogamy upon them. His grandson Abbas's cover-up of a polygynous marriage offers a gauge of the extent to which public opinion had turned against polygyny in the interval. The khedival family's monogamy set an example at the top of society for others to follow.

The educated middle class also developed a new style of conjugality, the gist of which was greater involvement in spousal choice and neolocality. This occurred against the background of a society-wide rise in the age at marriage for both sexes, something that has gone unexplained so far. Education was a factor for the middle class, especially men who acquired an advanced education and started a career, like Allouba, before marrying. Involvement in spousal choice is not the same thing as complete autonomy, due to the importance of family in negotiating what amounts to a prenuptial agreement. The emphasis is on getting the arrangements right, so as to put the marriage on a sound basis, in the hope that it will be enduring.

In the mid-twentieth century, some social scientists believed that industrialization and urbanization would result in a common marriage and family formation system resembling the modern Western model.[62] Subsequently, however, historians discovered that the conjugal family pattern in north-western Europe was not modern but had existed centuries earlier. By the end of the century, moreover, the conjugal family pattern was not predominant in all newly industrializing and urbanizing societies, and it was losing its pre-eminence in Europe and North America.[63] This raises the question of whether any particular marriage and family pattern may be deemed 'modern'.

Notes

1. Muntasar Ismail, 'Al-Khulʿ Bayn al-Shaʿb wa Majlis al-Shaʿb,' *Uktubur* magazine, 23 January 2000, 17.
2. Subsequently, the courts recognized the right of women to travel abroad without the permission of a guardian (father or husband), although husbands still may sue in a Family Court to prevent their wife from travelling. For a discussion of Law No. 1 of 2000 see Kenneth M. Cuno, 'Divorce and the Fate of the Family in Modern Egypt,' in *Family in the Middle East: Ideational Change in Egypt, Iran, and Tunisia*, ed. Kathryn Yount and Hoda Rashad (New York: Routledge, 2008), 196–216; and Nadia Sonneveld, *Khulʿ Divorce in Egypt: Public Debates, Judicial Practices, and Everyday*

Life (Cairo: American University in Cairo Press, 2012). On the right to travel, see Sonneveld, *Khul' Divorce*, 52–4; and The Egyptian Association for Community Participation Enhancement, *Second Shadow Report for the CEDAW Coalition: Egypt 2009*, http://www2.ohchr.org/english/bodies/cedaw/docs/EACPE_E.pdf , 57.

3 Sonneveld, *Khul' Divorce in Egypt*, 17–34.
4 See, e.g., Hanan Kholoussy, *For Better, For Worse: The Marriage Crisis That Made Modern Egypt* (Stanford: Stanford University Press, 2010).
5 Amira El Azhary Sonbol, 'A History of Marriage Contracts in Egypt,' in *The Islamic Marriage Contract: Case Studies in Islamic Family Law*, ed. Asifa Quraishi and Frank E. Vogel (Cambridge, MA: Harvard University Press, 2008), 113, 117n3.
6 The constitutions of 1923 and 1956 can be found in Yusuf Qazmakhuri, *Al-Dasatir fi al-Alam al-Arabi* (Beirut: Dar al-Hamra, 1989). See also The Constitution of the Arab Republic of Egypt, 1971 (as amended to 2007), www.constitutionnet.org/files/Egypt%20Constitution.pdf; the 2012 constitution in https://archive.org/details/dostor-misr-2012.pdf; and the 2014 constitution in Dustur Misr, http://dostour.eg/.
7 This chapter draws on my previous work, in particular *Modernizing Marriage: Family, Ideology, and Law in Nineteenth- and Early Twentieth-Century Egypt* (Syracuse: Syracuse University Press, 2015).
8 On legal systems containing such religious 'enclaves' see Ran Hirschl, 'Comparative Constitutional Law and Religion', in *Comparative Constitutional Law*, ed. Tom Ginsburg and Rosland Dixon (Cheltenham: Edward Elgar, 2011), 422–40.
9 John Esposito and Natana Delong Bas, *Women in Muslim Family Law*, xiv; see also Brinkley Messick, *The Calligraphic State: Textual Domination and History in a Muslim Society* (Berkeley: University of California Press), 61–2.
10 See, for example, Messick, *The Calligraphic State*, 61–2. Similar processes underlay the construction of other indigenous legal systems as essentially applying to the family, for example: Narendra Subramanian, *Nation and Family: Personal Law, Cultural Pluralism, and Gendered Citizenship in India* (Stanford: Stanford University Press, 2014), 8–16, 59–62; Tamara Loos, *Subject Siam: Family, Law, and Colonial Modernity in Thailand* (Ithaca: Cornell University Press, 2006), 5; M. B. Hooker, *Legal Pluralism: An Introduction to Colonial and Neo-Colonial Laws* (Oxford: Oxford University Press, 1976), 94–100, 119–89; and Martin Chanock, *Law, Custom and Social Order: The Colonial Experience in Malawi and Zambia* (Cambridge: Cambridge University Press, 1985), 3–6.
11 Defined as the conjugal couple with or without children; also called the simple or nuclear family.
12 Mounira Charrad, *States and Women's Rights: The Making of Postcolonial Tunisia, Algeria, and Morocco* (Berkeley and Los Angeles: University of California Press, 2001), 28–50.
13 Kecia Ali, *Marriage and Slavery in Early Islam* (Cambridge, MA: Harvard University Press, 2010), 6; Abd al-Majid Ali al-Hanafi b. Shaykh Ali Ismail al-Idwi, *Matla' al-Badrayn fi ma Yata'allaq bi-l-Zawjayn* (Cairo: n.p., 1278/1862), 14.
14 Muhammad b. Umar al-Nawawi, *Sharh Uqud al-Lujayn fi Bayan Huquq al-Zawjayn* (Cairo: al-Matba'at al-Wahbiyya, 1879). On this book and others in the genre see Cuno, *Modernizing Marriage*, 80–1. Since the norms of Islamic jurisprudence varied across time and space, my discussion makes use of sources in circulation in late Ottoman Egypt. 'Islamic' norms and practices elsewhere may have differed.
15 On stipulations see Nelly Hanna, 'Marriage among Merchant Families in Seventeenth-Century Cairo,' in *Women, the Family, and Divorce Laws in Islamic History*, ed. Amira

El Azhary Sonbol (Syracuse: Syracuse University Press, 1996), 150. On maintenance and obedience see Kenneth Cuno, 'Disobedient Wives and Neglectful Husbands: Marital Relations and the First Phase of Reform of Family Law in Egypt,' in *Family, Gender, and Law in a Globalizing Middle East and South Asia*, ed. Kenneth M. Cuno and Manisha Desai (Syracuse: Syracuse University Press, 2009), 3–18.

16 Al-Nawawi, *Uqud al-Lujayn*, 7; Abd al-Majid Ali, *Matlaʿ al-Badrayn*, 11.
17 Al-Nawawi, *Uqud al-Lujayn*, 4–5.
18 Margot Badran, *Feminists, Islam, and Nation: Gender and the Making of Modern Egypt* (Princeton: Rrinceton University Press, 1995), 61–88; Beth Baron, *The Women's Awakening in Egypt: Culture, Society, and the Press* (New Haven: Yale University Press, 1994), passim.
19 Butrus al-Bustani, speech on 'The Education of Women' (1849), in Fu'ad Afram al-Bustani, *Al-Muʿallim Butrus al-Bustani: Taʿlim al-Nisa' wa Adab al-Arab, Dars wa Muntakabat*, 2nd edn (Beirut: al-Matbaʿat al-Kathulikiyya, 1966), 97; Namık Kemal's essay 'On the Education of Women: a Draft' (1867) is discussed in Emel Sönmez, 'Turkish Women in Turkish Literature of the 19th Century,' *Die Welt des Islams* 12, nos. 1–3 (1969): 8–11.
20 Rifaʿa Rafiʿ al-Tahtawi, *Al-Murshid al-Amin li-l-Banat wa al-Banin* (Cairo: Supreme Council of Culture, 2002), 62–4, 66–8, 138–9.
21 Ali Mubarak, *Ali Mubarak al-Aʿmal al-Kamila*, ed. Muhammad Imara (3 vols.; Beirut: al-Mu'assasa al-Arabiyya li-l-Dirasat wa al-Nashr, 1979), 1: 341–2.
22 Al-Tahtawi, *Al-Murshid al-Amin*, 138, 148.
23 Mubarak, *Al-Aʿmal al-Kamila*, 1: 463–70.
24 Muhamad Imara, *Rifaʿa al-Tahtawi Ra'id al-Tanwir fi al-Asr al-Hadith* (Cairo: Dar al-Shuruq, 1988), 333–68; Leila Ahmed, *Woman and Gender in Islam: Historical Roots of a Modern Debate* (New Haven: Yale University Press, 1992), 137, 267n23.
25 Aisha al-Taymur, 'Family Reform Comes Only through the Education of Girls,' in *Opening the Gates: An Anthology of Arab Feminist Writing*, ed. Margot Badran and miriam cooke (2nd edn, Bloomington: Indiana University Press, 2004), 130–2; Zaynab Fawwaz, untitled essay No. 69 in *al-Rasa'il al-Zaynabiyya* (Cairo: al-Matbaʿa al-Mutawassita, 1905), 214–16; Bahithat al-Badiya, 'Madarisuna wa Fatayatuna,' in *al-Nisa'iyyat: Majmuʿa Maqalat Nushirat fi al-Jarida fi Mawduʿ al-Mar'a al-Misriyya* (Cairo: Matbaʿat al-Jarida, 1910), 15–17. The individual essays in this collection are undated but all appeared during 1908–9.
26 Fawwaz, Essay No. 59, 'Mujmal Hayat al-Nisa'," (1898), in *al-Rasa'il al-Zaynabiyya*, 122–3; Bahithat al-Badiya, 'Taʿaddud al-Zawjat, aw al-Dara'ir,' in *al-Nisa'iyyat*, 27–31. See also Mervat Hatem, *Literature, Gender, and Nation-Building in Nineteenth-Century Egypt: The Life and Works of ʿA'isha al-Taymur* (New York: Palgrave Macmillan, 2011), 100–11, for a discussion of al-Taymur's portrayal of two plural marriages in *Nata'ij al-Ahwal*.
27 Zaynab Fawwaz, 'Fair and Equal Treatment,' in Badran and cooke, *Opening the Gates*, 223–5; Bahithat al-Badiya, 'A Lecture in the Club of the Umma Party,' in Badran and cooke, *Opening the Gates*, 228–31.
28 Fawwaz, 'Fair and Equal Treatment,' 223–5; and essay no. 51 in *al-Rasa'il al-Zaynabiyya*, 170.
29 Bahithat al-Badiya, 'A Lecture in the Club of the Umma Party,' 228–30; and 'Al-Hijab wa al-Sufur,' in *al-Nisa'iyyat*, 8–9.
30 Qasim Amin, *Tahrir al-Mar'a*, in *Qasim Amin al-Aʿmal al-Kamila*, ed. Muhammad Imara (Cairo: Dar al-Shuruq, 1989). Hereafter cited as *Tahrir al-Mar'a*. There is an

English translation of this book in Qasim Amin, *The Liberation of Women and The New Woman: Two documents in the History of Egyptian Feminism*, trans. Samiha Sidhom Peterson (Cairo: The American University in Cairo Press, 2000), but it is of poor quality and useful for only a rough idea of the original text.

31 Most family issues were heard in the Sharia courts, but judges in the National Courts heard suits involving the enforcement of family law in such areas as maintenance and child custody. Moreover, Abduh conducted a study of the Sharia Court system in 1899, and as Grand Mufti he regularly dealt with Muslim family law.

32 Siam faced a similar situation: see Chapter 3 in this book and Richard S. Horowitz, 'International Law and State Transformation in China, Siam, and the Ottoman Empire during the Nineteenth Century,' *Journal of World History* 15, no. 4 (2005): 445–86.

33 Reorganization of the Ottoman Sharia courts is discussed by Iris Agmon, *Family and Court: Legal Culture and Modernity in Late Ottoman Palestine* (Syracuse: Syracuse University Press, 2006), especially chapters 3 and 4; and Jun Akiba, 'A New School for Qadis: Education of the Sharia Judges in the Later Ottoman Empire,' *Turcica* 35 (2003): 125–63.

34 'Islamic law' or Sharia has been a scholarly endeavour resulting in multiple, changing opinions over time. See Haifaa Khalafallah, 'The elusive 'Islamic law': rethinking the focus of modern scholarship', *Islam and Christian-Muslim Relations* 12, no. 2 (2001): 143–52.'

35 On the old system of legal pluralism, see James E. Baldwin, *Islamic Law and Empire in Ottoman Cairo* (Edinburgh: Edinburgh University Press, 2016), 85–88. The requirement that judges rely on Hanafi jurisprudence was enshrined in three laws, *La'ihat al-Qudat*, 28 Rabi' II 1273/26 December 1856 and *La'ihat al-Mahakim al-Shar'iyya*, 9 Rajab 1297/17 June 1880, in Filib Jallad, *Qamus al-Idara wa al-Qada'*, 4 vols. (Alexandria: al-Matba'a al-Bukhariyah, Yani Lagudakis, 1890–92), 4: 129–32 and 4: 145–56, and *La'ihat Tartib al-Mahakim al-Shar'iya wa al-Ijra'at al-Muta'alliqa bi-ha*, 27 May 1897, in *Majmu'a al-Awamir al-Ulya wa al-Dikritat al-Sadira fi Sanat 1897* (Bulaq: al-Matba'a al-Amiriyya, 1898), 155–75.

36 The best summary of these disadvantages is in Muhammad Abduh, *Al-A'mal al-Kamila li-l-Imam Muhammad Abduh*, ed. Muhammad Imara (6 vols.; Beirut: al-Mu'assasa al-Arabiyya li-l-Dirasat wa al-Nashr, 1972), 2: 657–8.

37 J.N.D. Anderson, 'Recent Developments in Shar'ia Law II', *The Muslim World* 41, no. 1 (1951): 37.

38 Abduh, *Al-A'mal al-Kamila*, 2: 657–8.

39 Amin, *Tahrir al-Mar'a*, 400–6, 408–10.

40 Abduh, *Al-A'mal al-Kamila*, 2: 71, 77, 78, 80, 83.

41 Ibid., 2: 88–92, 5 : 170.

42 Amin, *Tahrir al-Mar'a*, 395–6.

43 Ibid., 394–5.

44 For example, Earl of Cromer, *Modern Egypt* (2 vols; New York: Macmillan Co., 1908), 2:158; and Amin, *Tahrir al-Mar'a*, 393.

45 The four princely weddings were covered in the official gazette, *al-Waqa'i' al-Misriyya*, 491–3 (21 January, 28 January and 4 February 1873).

46 The abrupt transition to monogamy can be seen in Aziz Khanki's history of the 'wives' of Egypt's rulers, 'Zawjat Hukkam Misr min Muhammad Ali Basha al-Kabir ila Jalalat al-Malik Faruq al-Awwal,' special issue of *al-Musawwar* on the occasion of the wedding of King Faruq and Queen Farida, 1938. Reprinted in Khanki, *Nafahat*

Tarikhiyya (Cairo: al-Matbaʿa al-Asriyya, n.d.), 43–55. On Abbas's clandestine polygyny, see Samir Raafat, 'Queen for a Day,' *Ahram Weekly*, 6 October 1994. http://www.egy.com/historica.

47 *Al-Waqaʾiʿ al-Misriyya*, 27, no. 4 (June 1866); Ellen Chennells, *Recollections of an Egyptian Princess by Her English Governess, Being a Record of Five Years' Residence at the Court of Ismael Pasha, Khédive* (2 vols.; London: William Blackwood & Sons, 1893), 1: 222.

48 A. D. Comanos Pacha, *Mémoires du Dr. Comanos Pacha publiés à l'occasion de son jubilé de 40 ans d'exercise médical* (Cairo: Imprimerie de la Societe Orientale de Publicite, 1920), 48–52.

49 See Chapter 3.

50 Badran and cooke, *Opening the Gate*, 125; and Huda Shaarawi, *Harem Years: The Memoirs of an Egyptian Feminist* (New York: Feminist Press, 1986), 18.

51 In 1907, 5.5 per cent of women were married below the age of fifteen, and 48 per cent of fifteen- to nineteen-year-olds were married. By 1927, these percentages had fallen to 1.5 and 34.8, respectively. See William Wendell Cleland, *The Population Problem in Egypt: A Study of Population Trends and Conditions in Modern Egypt* (Lancaster, PA: Science Press, 1936), 42, Table VI.

52 Ahmad b. Umar al-Dayrabi, *Kitab Ghayat al-Maqsud li-Man Yataʿati al-Uqud* (Cairo: Matbaʿ al-Wahbiyya, 1880), 51; Hanna, 'Marriage among Merchant Families,' 150–3.

53 On the ability of adult women to self-marry see Cuno, *Modernizing Marriage*, 148. Young adults were normally considered to have reached the age of discretion, and adulthood was reached with the first signs of puberty or, at the latest, the age of fifteen.

54 Muhammad Ali Allouba, *Dhikriyyat Ijtimaʿiyya wa Siyasiyya* (Cairo: General Egyptian Book Organization, 1988), 54–6. Allouba discreetly avoided using his wife's name. I found it in photos posted by his family: http://www.flickr.com/photos/kelisli/8607991460/in/photostream.

55 Bahithat al-Badiya, 'Ya li-l-Nisa' min al-Rijal wa Ya li-l-Rijal minhinna,' *al-Nisaʾiyyat*, 24; and 'A Lecture in the Club of the Umma Party,' 234–5.

56 Marilyn Booth, 'Women and the Emergence of the Arabic Novel,' in *The Oxford Handbook of the Arabic Novel*, ed. Waʾil Hassan (Oxford: Oxford University Press), 2017.

57 In the late 1980s, 80 per cent of women surveyed said that their marriages had been arranged. In rural and lower-income urban communities, the bride's or groom's family searched for a suitable match on the basis of 'certain ascribed characteristics ... [that took] precedence over personality and individual choice.' Then the two families negotiated the terms of marriage, including financial arrangements: Diane Singerman and Barbara Ibrahim, 'The Costs of Marriage in Egypt: A Hidden Dimension in the New Arab Demography,' in *The New Arab Family*, ed. Nicholas S. Hopkins, *Cairo Papers in Social Science* 24, nos. 1–2 (2001): 88–9. Also Homa Hoodfar, *Between Marriage and the Market: Intimate Politics and Survival in Cairo* (Berkeley: University of California Press, 1997), 51.

58 Allouba, *Dhikriyyat*, 56.

59 Beth Baron, 'Making and Breaking of Marital Bonds in Modern Egypt,' in *Women in Middle Eastern History: Shifting Boundaries in Sex and Gender*, ed. Nikki Keddie and Beth Baron (New Haven: Yale University Press, 1991), 278; Marilyn Booth, *May Her Likes be Multiplied: Biography and Gender Politics in Egypt* (Berkeley: University of California Press, 2001), 172–3, 191, 207.

60 Orhan Pamuk, *Istanbul: Memories of the City* (New York: Knopf, 2005).
61 Alan Duben and Cem Behar, *Istanbul Households: Marriage, Family and Fertility, 1880-1940* (Cambridge: Cambridge University Press, 1991), 55.
62 See, for example, William Goode, *World Revolution and Family Patterns* (New York: Free Pres, 1963).
63 Michael Anderson, *Approaches to the History of the Western Family, 1500-1914* (2nd edn; Cambridge: Cambridge University Press, 1995), 10–13; John Bongaarts, 'Household Size and Composition in the Developing World in the 1990s,' *Population Studies* 55 (2001): 263–79; 'The Changing American Family,' a report issued by the Pew Research Center, 18 November 2010, http://www.pewsocialtrends.org/2010/11/18/five-decades-of-marriage-trends/.

7

'A Babel of Law': Hindu Marriage, Global Spaces and Intimate Subjects in Late-Nineteenth-Century India

Leigh Denault

In 1884, Bombay writer, editor and social reformer Behramji Malabari published *Notes on Infant Marriage and Enforced Widowhood*.[1] This pamphlet turned an 1884 suit for the restitution of conjugal rights, brought by Dadaji Bhikaji against his wife, Rukhmabai, into a cause célèbre in his battle against the practice of child marriage.[2] Rukhmabai's stepfather, and Dadaji's uncle, Dr Sakharam Arjun, had arranged their marriage when Rukhmabai was 11 and Dadaji 19, and although they had conducted the first stage of the marriage ceremony they had never cohabited. Dr Arjun had previously continued to agree to postpone cohabitation as Dadaji was suspected of having tuberculosis and was also engaged in full-time study. Later, Rukhmabai refused to cohabit with her husband and his family. Dadaji brought suit for restitution of conjugal rights in a colonial court, which, his counsel argued, had the jurisdiction to award Dadaji both the 'person and property' of his wife. Rukhmabai refused, on the grounds of her husband's 'immoral' behaviour, lack of education and inability to provide for her, as well as his ill health and the fact that their marriage had been arranged before her age of majority. Rukhmabai won the first case in the District Court, but lost on appeal to the Bombay High Court in 1887. Her case was discussed in the British House of Lords, and her marriage ultimately dissolved by royal decree. With support from social reformist friends and doctors in India, and suffragists in England, Rukhmabai went on to study medicine in London and returned to India in 1895, where she began what would be a 35-year career in medicine as India's first practising female doctor. She never remarried.

Alongside the case of Phulmoni in Bengal in 1890,[3] Rukhmabai's trial and Malabari's publication of her story and letters created a movement in support of the Age of Consent Act in 1891, raising it from 10 to 12. The nature of Hindu marriage, and the issues of widow remarriage, age of consent and child marriage were among the first social reform issues to be taken up by Indian nationalist leaders interested in using print and the public sphere to reach a broader audience.[4] Women's rights activist Ramabai Ranade helped Malabari to found the Rukhmabai Defence Committee, organizing public meetings, press coverage and debates. Rukhmabai herself explained her position, initially anonymously, in letters to the *Times of India*, drawing national and international attention. Malabari deliberately courted British public opinion, travelling to Britain in the late 1880s. Pandita Ramabai Sarasvati, among the first female nationalists and public intellectuals, worked alongside Rukhmabai to organize an international feminist campaign against the sexualization of children, a campaign that brought radical arguments for female autonomy, and female voices, to a global public.[5] Social-purity campaigns in Britain embraced Malabari's quest for legislative reform of the age of consent, while Indian public opinion was divided.[6] By 1886, the movement and the debates that it generated were so well known that the Indian popular press both reported on and caricatured reformist efforts regularly. The *Oudh Punch*, a satirical magazine published in Lucknow, featured a cartoon in which a number of young Hindu widows were begging an elderly widower to marry one of them instead of a child bride.[7]

Debates on Hindu marriage provide a reminder that legal historians must decentre the colonial state to understand the course of social reform.[8] From the onset of British colonialism in India, every major movement was driven by Indian reformers: long before the Rukhmabai case, Rammohan Roy's efforts against *sati* or widow immolation stirred a newly empowered utilitarian-liberal colonial state to enact legislation,[9] while Ishwar Chandra Vidyasagar provided a motive force for campaigns to allow widow remarriage.[10] The colonial legislative apparatus became a tool for Indian reformers, who were also in conversation with multinational reform movements, but these debates were not directed by colonial administrators, centring instead around competing Indian visions of law, marriage and social order. In fact, Lord Dufferin's response to a deputation led by Sir T. Madhao Rao to demand intervention, as reported in a Hindi newspaper in 1886, was that 'the Government sympathized with the movement, but could not interfere, and that the reform should be carried out by the people themselves'.[11] To a certain extent, this tension between reform efforts on the ground and the actions of the colonial state resembled developments decades later in Gabon amidst decolonization, as Rachel Jean-Baptiste shows in Chapter 11 in this book. The Rukhmabai case unfolded during the first years of the Indian National Congress, India's first self-proclaimed 'All-India' political organization. Issues of social and legal reform were central to constructing the public spheres that sustained the early Congress. Lawyers as well as publicists played a leading role in early anti-colonial nationalism, and, like their global contemporaries, Indian jurists stressed the importance of intimate and gendered social roles and institutions in ordering civil society, and in defining 'tradition' or 'modernity'.

The debates that I will explore in this chapter grew out of responses to Malabari and Rukhmabai. I will draw primarily on publications by Indian jurists and legal scholars, some of them preserved in Tagore Law Lectures and published pamphlets and debates, and others curated by Dayaram Gidumal, Malabari's biographer as well as a lawyer and reformer.[12] His *Handbook for Social Reformers* included a broad range of opinion, from rural district officials and religious scholars to lawyers and radical Bombay newspaper editors, and demonstrated both discontent with a tangled colonial legal system and the importance of a comparative legal frame in evaluations of Indian jurisdictional and regional debates.

The Rukhmabai case was ostensibly about the government of female bodies and sexuality, and the protection of Hindu tradition from colonial 'interference'. But it became a platform to debate Hindu conceptions of marriage, law and society, and whether and how the normative Hindu heterosexual family should be restructured. In the course of these debates, a conservative or orthodox Hindu position was more fully articulated, and ideas of Hindu law and tradition more sharply defined. Revivalist nationalist editor and politician Bal Gangadar Tilak protested the first District Court ruling in the Rukhmabai case, while eminent jurist Vishvanath Narayan Mandlik participated in the public debates as a defender of Hindu tradition. The Rukhmabai case helped to define positions within emerging public and political orders which would in turn define Indian politics and law for decades to come. Concern about Hindu law, marriage and orthodoxy would delineate boundaries between upper and lower castes, between Hindus and Muslims, between conservatives and reformers, and between differing national legal traditions. A particular kind of female body was being constructed and policed, but also an Indian body politic.

Constructing Conservatism and Defining a Hindu Public

The historiography on colonial Indian social reform debates for many years broadly accepted the two positions that contemporaries identified: on the one hand, radical 'reformers' wishing to modernize Hindu law, through legislative intervention, to bring it into consonance with international standards, versus conservative 'revivalists', or conservative defenders of Hindu orthodoxy opposed to state 'interference' in Indian custom.[13] The revivalists were often cast as parochial and reactive, and the reformers as globally aware and forward-looking, or, less positively, as 'Westernized', 'hypocritical' and out of touch with 'Indian opinion'. But when we look more closely, the reformers and conservatives are not so clearly or so diametrically opposed. Most public Indian intellectuals and jurists in the late nineteenth century were self-consciously looking for a middle way between tradition and reform, or were 'quietist', looking inward rather than seeking to confront 'the West' or other Indian publics.[14] Indian religious traditions were not set in stone: both Hinduism and Islam had undergone fundamental changes in the precolonial and colonial periods.[15] In this sense, debates in India about reforms to family law reflected those in Siam and Egypt in the same period, as discussed in Chapters 3 and 6 in this book. Both those wishing to change Indian religions and those purporting to adhere to an orthodox tradition made use of the same new associational forms, print cultures, and traditional and modern venues for debate and discussion. S. N. Mukherjee has argued that both radical and conservative groups represented, not necessarily a religious schism within Hinduism or Islam, but the emergence of a new kind of 'bourgeoisie' within colonial society.[16] But, as C. A. Bayly notes, the recognition that the line between reform and revival was sometimes blurred does not mean that there were no ideological differences between radical 'reformers' and neoconservative 'revivalists'. He argues that the need to 'protect Hindu knowledge from oppression' and to 'guard the purity and livelihoods of Indians from colonization' would define Indian neoconservatism for decades to come.[17]

Debates on marriage reveal how Indian jurists, neoconservatives and social reformers both attempted to reform a 'multi-centric' colonial legal system. Rather than simply wield colonial law as a weapon to combat social evils, most reformers sought to reshape legal subjects and jurisdictions, while conservatives agreed generally that the colonial legal system as it stood enforced and upheld a version of Hindu orthodoxy that was neither Hindu nor orthodox. One lawyer, Trimulrao Venkatesh, stated at a public debate in the 1880s in Bombay: 'Suppose the dates and numbers of all Regulations and Acts passed up to date by the Government of India and the Local Governments, together with those sections which repeal former enactments or define the territorial extent over which an Act is to operate, were effaced altogether, and the bare enactments placed in the hands of the public – what a beautiful Babel of Law would we all have ... ? Well this is the real state of what we call our Hindu Law.'[18] Controversial cases on Hindu marriage highlighted jurisdictional conflict, confusion over the nature of marital custom and how it should be legally determined, and the arbitrary and autocratic nature of colonial law in its changing treatment of Hindu marriage.

Conservatives may have represented reformers as exponents of 'state interference', but many nationalists as well as orthodox Hindus saw Malabari's emphasis on colonial legislative intervention as hostile to their struggle for greater political representation and autonomy for Indian colonial subjects. The debates led to the creation of the National Social Conference in 1887, a separate organization which could debate controversial social reform issues outside of the Indian National Congress. In 1889, the National Social Conference passed a resolution stating that marriage to a girl under the age of twelve should be treated as a criminal act, and called for a mass education programme to educate people about the dangers of sexual intercourse before the age of fourteen. Nationalists such as Tilak argued passionately against the Conference, seeing it as an agent of the colonial state set to destroy Indian culture. The colonial government, however, itself refused to act until a clear consensus had emerged.[19] In 1890, after Malabari had gained the support of the British press, the Government of India finally launched an inquiry which gathered 'opinions' from a cross-section of colonial society, from Indian princes to orthodox clerics, conservative and liberal nationalists and reformers, and district-level officials and professionals.[20]

V. N. Mandlik, conservative champion of orthodox Hindu values by the 1880s, had in his youth been seen as a radical voice for female education.[21] In 1887, he published a short piece on the proposal to abolish imprisonment in cases in which Hindu women refused to comply with court decrees for the restitution of conjugal rights. His explanation of the problem from both a legal and social angle demonstrated the range of responses within conservative Hindu circles. Mandlik was, like many of his opponents, among the first Indians to receive a Western education, and among the first to qualify as lawyers. He agreed with his reformist colleagues that individuals were likely to suffer under a system of arranged child marriages, but argued that 'congregation in society is inconsistent with freedom from restrains of some kind or other on the individual units composing it.'[22] Rukhmabai's proposal that mutual dislike and lack of sympathy should be grounds for dissolving a marriage – alongside proposed legislation that would make non-compliance with a decree for the restitution of conjugal rights grounds for marital dissolution – would, according to Mandlik, 'have the effect of making marriage dissoluble at the mere will and caprice of a party'. This would be, he noted, revolutionary, a legislative act that undermined the 'particular sanctity' of Hindu marriage, which justified the restraint on 'individual liberty in view of the good of society'.[23] Further, Mandlik pointed out that the proposed legislation was inherently unequal, as the alimony amount stipulated was set too low, and that further, it would only be available in any event to propertied women, perpetuating existing inequalities. In earlier pamphlets against reformist use of legislation, Mandlik stated pointedly that the reformers should let women speak for themselves, and formulate their own remedies. He represented India's female rulers and widows as being 'in excellent company and need no lecture from the present writer'.[24] Such an act of legislation, moreover, was antithetical not only to Hindu law, but to English, Scottish and Irish law as well, and Mandlik compared degrees of coercion permitted in enforcing marital obligations, noting that no one seemed to call England 'uncivilized' for a failure to offer easy access to divorce and annulment.[25]

In short, the leader of the conservative Hindu response was in some ways anything but 'orthodox'. He pointed out how Rukhmabai's case brought to national, and international, attention the question of divorce or annulment as well as of child marriage. Muslim law in colonial India represented marriage as a contractual relationship, one that could be dissolved through divorce, but Hindu marriage was held to be a sacrament that made two beings into one, and was thus indissoluble. This was a defence of Hindu marriage, based on its fundamental legal distinctiveness, which was widely understood and deployed by the 1880s. An Aligarh newspaper argued in 1887 that 'Hindus should strongly protest against the proposed change in the law' on the basis that 'A Hindu marriage is a religious sacrament and not a civil contract.'[26]

However, the annulment or dissolution of marriages by caste *panchayats* or councils of arbitration was relatively common, and accepted as custom that had the force of law, particularly among non-Brahmin groups.[27] Rukhmabai and Dadaji were both from a lower caste, and their case was therefore also an example of a growing trend towards encouraging Brahminical customs among groups that had formerly not practised them.[28] Lower-caste groups had a very different conception of debates on law and society. In 1885, Jotirao Phule, revolutionary low-caste reformer from Maharashtra, devotee of Thomas Paine and admirer of American abolitionism, wrote to the famous Brahmin social reformer M. G. Ranade refusing to participate in his social reform conference. Phule declined on the grounds that

> the conferences and books of those who refuse to think of human rights generally, who do not concede them to others and going by their behavior are unlikely to concede them in future, cannot make sense to us. ... [Ancient Hindus] included in their pseudo religious texts an account of how they turned us into slaves and thus gave our enslavement religious authority. ... These upper-caste authors ... who can only make ceremonial and meaningless speeches in big meetings can never understand what we shudras [lower castes] ... suffer.[29]

Nor was Phule's radical global vision, which linked caste oppression in India with slavery in the United States, singular. Phule became first in a long line of lower-caste reformers to argue that elite Hindu marriage practices were linked to gendered social and caste-based oppression more widely.[30] Similarly, recent scholarship has emphasized the radical nature of the demands made by both upper- and lower-caste Hindu women in the course of the debates.[31]

Hindu marriage did not represent a static tradition preserved from an ancient past, but an inherently modern concatenation of new economic pressures, legal conceptions and social capital on the part of different culture brokers within colonial society.[32] Indeed, the practice of child marriage seems to have increased among aspiring groups in Hindu society during the colonial period, as middle-class respectability and social capital became more closely linked to visible orthopraxy, embodied in the 'correct' performance of scriptural rituals surrounding marriage.[33] In the course of debating the meaning of custom, Indian jurists, writers, religious organizations, satirists and reformers also began to rethink the role that law might play in shaping Indian society. Far from preserving the home as a source of authentic custom, both reformers and revivalists wished to refashion society by renovating domestic spaces and roles.[34] Indian marriage practices were actively reimagined and renovated during the late colonial period within a comparative legal frame.[35] Central to framing social and biological reproduction, marriage practices became intimately entangled with the project of creating a new legal and social imaginary, an India without the 'interference' of colonial governance.

Hindu Law, National 'Well-being' and Social Orders

By 1887, R. Raghunath Rao,[36] an outspoken advocate of the internal reform of Hindu law and marriage, would write, 'For the well-being of any nation, its religion, its sociology and its politics must be sound … look at my country; when my forefathers were in the highest esteem of the nations of this planet … when, however, their descendants neglected their religion, their society became degenerated.'[37] Hindu and Muslim religion in India, he believed, had been the 'direct and nearly exclusive source of law'.[38] He undertook, like many other legal scholars after him, to translate carefully from texts that were regarded as unimpeachable sources of Hindu doctrine to prove that 'Hindu law' was not what some Hindu publicists claimed, and was not in fact in any way incompatible with reformist conceptions of marriage: 'wherever marriage affairs are talked of in our Vedas, the bride is described as a female wishing to have a husband and being competent then to lead a married life. … They declare that she should be married after her development into a full blown woman. They bear evidence to the existence of female ascetics. … In the teeth of these authorities if some of my brethren choose to hold that Infant marriage is sanctioned by law, all I can do is pray to our Heavenly Father for their being set right'.[39]

In the 1878 Tagore Law Lectures on *The Hindu Law of Marriage and Stridhan*, Gooroodass Banerjee opened by asking 'What is Hindu law? What are the sources of that law? Who is governed by it?'[40] Banerjee drew a distinction between *dharmaśāstra*,[41] the body of rules regulating civil conduct and religious ceremony, and 'law in the sense which the term is used by English jurists'.[42] For ancient Hindu jurists such as Manu, he suggested, there was no distinction between law or religion. And while later works of Hindu law did make a distinction between moral and legal directives, elsewhere in the text penalties for violation of rules included 'consignment to a region of torments in the next world'.[43] Law was not the purview of the sovereign, Banerjee suggests, but part of a divine cosmology to which sovereigns were also subject. Following Henry S. Maine, Banerjee noted that the Mughals, like other 'Asiatic governments', were 'tax-taking and not … law-making', leaving a Hindu conception of law as constructing primarily a moral order 'untouched'.[44]

Yet Banerjee did not argue that Hindu law was itself unchanged from an ancient past: 'what was excused as necessary or desirable innovation in one generation, came to be revered as custom in the next'. Different interpretations of Hindu law further gave rise to multiple 'schools',[45] itself a disputed term introduced by colonial jurist H. T. Colebrooke. Further, different bodies of law and customary codes were limited geographically, and administered by private tribunals, making for a 'highly elastic' system which accommodated new usages and interpretations, until 'its spontaneous growth was suddenly arrested by the administration of the country passing into the hands of the English, and a degree of rigidity was given to it which it had never before possessed'.[46] By making changes to existing law a matter that must be determined by action of the courts, judicial decisions became the sole means of effecting changes to Hindu law in the late colonial period. Lawyers would then insist on following legal decisions, which conflicted with traditions of Hindu legal scholarship that emphasized 'correctness' of interpretation above precedent.[47]

Similar shifts were underway in Islamic law in British India, although in some places, like the Muslim-majority province of Punjab, an insistence on the colonial administration of religious law and its 'indispensability' challenged colonial conceptions of the region as governed by 'custom' as well as British distinctions between public and private spaces.[48] More generally, it has been argued that British administration of Islamic law delegitimized mosaic and non-hierarchical pre-colonial institutions of learning and authority, a Muslim 'middle ground', leaving anxious laypersons and new generations of clerics and intellectuals to rush to the defence of religious tradition, reconstructing authority from the margins.[49] Yet these defences and reconstructions of law remained entangled with imperial and global jurisprudence. Gauri Viswanathan has stressed the necessity of reading British and Indian legal, religious and social histories alongside each other, instrumentalizing Edward Said's suggestion that we need to see 'cross-currents' by reading histories 'contrapuntally'.[50] Viswanathan argued that in both India and Britain, treatment of religious law and religious minorities was part of the same process, and project, of constructing secular nationhood. Indeed, Banerjee's definition of law as the secular exercise of sovereignty to define civic life owed much to Maine as well as Mayne,[51] as did his historicist belief that social institutions must be understood in reference to their evolution, and could then be used to understand the 'stage of social progress' that a civilization has achieved.[52] He further suggested that there was a similar progression from 'practice' to 'custom' to 'law' as societies moved from 'savagery' towards civilization.[53] Custom was for Banerjee by nature 'inconsistent with the general rule of law'.

The construction of custom as oppositional to law, however, elided the intimate connection between the maintenance of particular forms of Indian personal or customary law, and the creation of new categories of legal subjecthood, which further reframed and constrained claim-making on the colonial state. Personal law in colonial India defined religious 'communities'. Hindus were legally constructed as those subject to Hindu law, a definition that extended even to those who had converted, thus marking 'Hindu' as an ethnic and territorial (as different schools governed different regions) as well as religious category.[54]

Banerjee's conception of custom as a stage on the way to the formation of law obscures the extent to which custom and law coexisted and contested jurisdictional spaces in the colonial Indian courts. Sripati Roy, while acknowledging that 'Custom is of far earlier origin than Law' at the outset of his 1908 Tagore Law Lectures, and conceptualizing 'custom' as reflecting the fractured exercise of 'family' authority, rather than sovereign authority, insisted on circumstances in which custom and law were in jurisdictional dispute.[55] The Anglo-Indian judicial system continued, despite itself, a precolonial mosaic legal tradition,[56] blending bodies of customary and personal law relating to India's various religious communities with Mughal and English-derived civil and, by 1860, criminal codes. Judicial reforms after 1857 had reduced jurist discretion and insisted on recourse to statute, which forced greater attention to legislation as a source of rulings.[57] Similarly, a rising tide of social reform legislation, including the 1872 Native Marriage Act III, which ultimately applied only to members of the small but influential Brahmo Samaj religion after significant public outcry, crystallized concern over the domain of state authority and the jurisdictional authority of Indian custom and 'Hindu law'.[58] The 'fixing' of legal traditions formerly defined by judicial discretion in interpreting precedent and textual authority provided the context for the politicization of marriage in the 1880s and 1890s. Multiple codification programmes and attempts to establish canonical texts across a hugely diverse subcontinent had resulted in numerous partially applied judicial reforms, and frequent recourse to authorities who could determine the nature of 'custom' in particular cases.[59] Indian jurists heavily criticized the gap between arbitration of 'custom' in the *panchayat* and the colonial court, arguing that these supposedly 'traditional' bodies were in fact often more permissive or 'liberal' in their decisions.[60]

Reformists conceived of a new kind of 'All-India' legal space, which seemed to be required given both the multiplicity of local variation and the need to take regional difference into consideration. This was a space in which both colonial law and custom could be critically assessed, and a more scientific survey of Hindu law attempted. For some, it was a space in which multiple traditions should be reconciled; for others, preserved. Ranade, a famous jurist and social reformer, carefully traced textual authorities on widow remarriage and age of marriage in order to establish the beginnings of such a re-working of 'Hindu law' surrounding marriage, thereby reintegrating an authoritative and renovated conception of Hindu Law into the Anglo-Indian system.[61] This project would feed into the formalization of a Hindu Code in 1919, and, ultimately, the redefinition of systems of personal law in the independent Indian state. Through debates on Hindu marriage, Ranade, and other reformist jurists, came to advocate a reintegration of Indian law into the colonial judicial system as a basis for a national approach to social reform, not a straightforward adoption of colonial law.

Plural Law and Colonial Tangles

The British administration introduced legal tangles that would not only haunt Indian efforts to break free from colonial identity politics, but also provide opportunities for jurists imagining different forms of governance. The colonial system laid claim to coherent suzerainty and sovereignty over diverse subjects, yet its unevenness was starkly apparent to litigants and jurists alike. Indian Christians existed in a form of 'legal limbo' until the later nineteenth century. Although codifying Christian personal laws was a stated desire of a colonial state in the quest of a uniform legal order, ambiguities abounded. Efforts to construct Christian personal law alongside Hindu and Muslim law by delving into imperial gazetteers, colonial ethnographies and case law eventually gave way to Indian Christian laws of marriage, divorce and inheritance based on English law, enshrining Christianity as 'European' rather than Indian.[62] Hindu and Muslim jurists complained that a similar process of 'confusion' was underway within other legal codes, and that what was needed was not an end to 'state intervention', but the beginning of a rationalization, along more sympathetic lines, of Hindu legal systems. High court government pleader Shantaram Narayan argued passionately that it was not just the role but the duty of the state to 'fix a reasonable standard of age for marriage. The question is as much political as it is social. All civilized governments have so regarded it'.[63] He noted that,

> I do not see why the Government in India should not make laws on the subject of marriage. ... Some people argue as if the State ... has not yet interfered with our social customs. What do we witness every day in our Courts of Justice? We have a Hindu Law, it is true, but is not that law involved in confusion, and is it not a fact that our courts are expounding it as best they can, and bringing into vogue, in effect, new adaptations which Hindu lawyers of a bygone age would have probably stared at? The whole administration of the Hindu law is, in fact, based upon a legal fiction, and it affords a signal example of the fact that our customs are already being regulated by judiciary interference of a sort.[64]

Jurisdictional confusion was a growing concern for Indian jurists engaged in trying to define 'custom' and 'law', apart from problems of interpretation in the courtroom and the messy social life of colonial legislation. The civil courts were charged with defining, interpreting and adjudicating custom on a case-by-case basis. This resulted, Bernard Cohn argued, in a distorting process of distilling 'universal' definitions and legal precedents from highly specific and contextualized disputes.[65] Narayan spoke passionately in favour of law as an engine for social reform, and explicitly framed marriage as a political as well as a social issue. But he was not just calling for the colonial state to intervene in specific cases, but to rethink its entire approach to the administration of Hindu law. Another reformer responded to Narayan, suggesting that 'What is urgently needed is, if I may say so, State interference with its own interference. The State should, at least, redress the grievances caused by its own tribunals and its own laws'.[66] Narayan's speech draws attention to how reformers and orthodox religious authorities alike felt that Hindu law had been fundamentally misunderstood and misapplied in British courts. Rather than setting up a contrast between custom and law, they framed the distinction between Hindu and colonial legal systems as a matter of structure and precedence: the colonial system provided a basic structure for jurisprudence, with certain Hindu legal authorities relied upon for precedence in case law, rather than a fundamental difference in the conception of law itself. It was not merely legislation, but attention to what constituted authority in Hindu law that was seen as necessary to formulate a solution.

The 'legal imaginary' being debated was inherently comparative, and both radicals and conservatives argued with reference to legal and social precedent from outside of India. On 5 September 1886, in Bombay, a large public meeting of some 3,000 was held at Madhav Bagh, 'against legislative interference in the matter of child marriage by the government', chaired by V. N. Mandlik. Mandlik noted that in 'such an advanced country as the United States of America, the age of consent is the same, viz., 12 for females and 14 for males. In New York an attempt was made to raise these periods to 14 and 17 respectively, but they were so disrelished by the people that a law was passed in 1830, restoring the old periods of 12 and 14 as before'.[67] Another lawyer added that while there was a low age of consent in England as well, there 'the people are always in advance of their laws', pointing out that married women between the ages of fifteen and twenty in England made up 3.1 per cent of the population, while in the North-Western Provinces of British India that figure was 87.7 per cent.[68] In response, Shantaram Narayan, who presented himself as 'humbly an advocate of legislative interference in the matter of infant marriage', stated that,

> All civilised Governments have dealt with the question of marriage, of the mutual relations between men and women, as one of which the State has a right and is bound to take cognizance. For instance, in Germany, the marriageable age fixed by law for men is 18, and for women 14; in Belgium 18 and 15; in Spain 14 and 12; in France 18 and 15; in Greece 14 and 12; in Hungary (for Protestants) 18 and 16 and (for Catholics) 14 and 12; in Portugal 14 and 12; in Russia 18 and 16; in Saxony 18 and 16; in Switzerland 14 and 12; in Austria 14 and 14 respectively.[69]

Hindu reformers argued about custom according to the terms which Roy maps out in his Tagore Law Lecture of 1908: custom could be overruled on the grounds that a given custom was 'unreasonable' (here reformers marshalled scientific arguments against early marriage) or immoral (and here reformers deployed arguments about equality, human dignity and the kind of society that unjust 'customs' produce). One 'Hindu social reform missionary' quoted from controversial feminist writer Alice Mona Caird to the effect that 'modern' marriage should be based on the 'frank recognition of the equality of all subjects, male and female, before the law, and also the recognition that every member of the community ought to be free to enter into what contracts he pleases, provided he injures no other individual and does not interfere with the welfare of the community'.[70] Self-described 'defenders' of Hindu orthodoxy rebutted these arguments by suggesting that the reformist alternatives had, far from producing more equal or just societies, led to social disintegration and subjugation. The *Nyaya Sudha* newspaper responded to Malabari's campaign in 1886: 'He desires to suppress the evil customs which have been in vogue for hundreds of years, with the aid of Government, at once; but he ought to know that in Europe social reform was achieved with much bloodshed in many generations'.[71]

Even Gooroodas Banerjee had connected marriage to 'the struggle for existence between societies', suggesting that 'regular sexual relations' gave a military as well as social advantage to societies that had forsaken 'promiscuity' for marriage and organized child rearing practices.[72] One Hindu reformer quoted from Darwin's *Descent of Man*: 'Darwin tell us: "a nation which produced, during a lengthened period, the greatest number of highly intellectual, energetic, brave, patriotic, and benevolent men, would generally prevail over less favoured nations."'[73] Yet to claims that early marriage would lead to the 'degeneracy and decay of the whole race',[74] a 'pernicious custom' rendering Hindus without 'strength to become soldiers … unfit as colonizers',[75] an 'anti-reformer' replied by comparing marriage customs both across India and globally:

> One gentleman says it is women that bring about infant marriages. Another says women have no status in society. … A third talks of sundry diseases, and concludes that because they exist in certain castes they exist throughout India. A fourth talks of disparity between the age of the bride and the bridegroom, as if such disparity is unknown in England or France or Germany or Russia or America, as if that old story of January and May is not typical of certain marriages. … All such vapid and vaporous talk proves nothing.[76]

Some jurists used the idea of a connected Aryan 'Golden Age' to challenge the claim that social practices such as child marriage or female seclusion were of ancient origin, using Vedic texts to refute the antiquity as well as the morality and social utility of such customs.[77] In 1805, Colebrooke had put forward the idea of an 'Aryan' 'Golden Age' of ancient Sanskritic civilization in India, a concept that would be important for both Indian intellectuals such as Rammohan Roy and Indological scholars like Max Müller.[78] This approach, which was deployed in early-nineteenth-century campaigns against *sati*, was by the 1880s a common argumentative tactic: the *Hindustan* newspaper, in a report on the number of widows in India, noted that 'there are passages in the Hindu shastras … which recommend widow marriage, but the Hindus have allowed custom to over-rule their sacred books'.[79]

But there was also a strategic realignment of Hindu law, suggesting its original connection to a wider 'Aryan' legal 'family', which enabled cross-cultural comparison in legislative reform movements. Gidumal quoted Max Müller to the effect that 'the Hindu' was among the last to leave the 'Aryan family'. But he added: 'The Hindu not only found a new world, but, in the fulness [sic] of time, his brethren also. My dear friends, let us eschew all jealousy of the Englishman, for the Celt, the German, the Greek, the Italian, the Slavonian, and the Parsi are all our Aryan brethren, having more or less the habits and customs which characterized our ancient fathers'.[80] This legal 'brotherhood' legitimated comparison by undermining claims of Hindu exceptionalism.

Comparison was therefore a strategy which could be deployed in a multitude of ways. Orthodox groups defended the particularities of 'Hindu civilization' and the potential of Sanskrit texts to spark a purely Indian 'renaissance':

> Our world, as geology teaches us, is not merely as old as the English civilization. … Now I say that history repeats itself, that probably there was as good a civilization before in India as the English, that is, a civilization perfectly consistent with the existence of extremes of riches and poverty, with the existence of sweaters and millionaires, miserable workmen and bloated capitalists, fashionable ladies and dying street-walkers. … The English may one day have to adopt – what we have adopted – a caste system to prevent competition – a joint family system to preserve union and domestic happiness. … The European renaissance was due to the study of Greek and Latin classics. But there will be a greater renaissance when Sanskrit classics are as much studied.[81]

The above quote was used by Gidumal to represent what he called the 'Hindu fatalist' perspective: the idea that over time, societies self-regulate, and that Hindu law and sacred texts provided a more-than-adequate wellspring for social renewal. In a book on Hinduism published in 1893, Guru Prosad Sen took Malabari to task for not appreciating that the mean age of marriage was rising in Bengal without legislative intervention, not due to the impact of what he termed 'sentimental reform', but the 'crude effect' of economic forces. Finding eligible matches, Sen argued, was becoming more difficult, as was securing the funding to entice a son-in-law who had even attempted his entrance exams, let alone graduated. 'Every University *honour* has its corresponding value,' Sen wrote, and rules on marriage had always varied across regions. While 'thirty years ago a Hindu of the *Bhadralog* class in Bengal would have lost caste if he had kept his daughter unmarried up to the age of puberty – the caste rules were never so strict in other parts of India'.[82]

Gidumal's 'Hindu fatalists' and 'anti-reformers' were both operating within a comparative legal and social frame. One anti-reformer, arguing against the proposition that ancient Aryans had marriage customs more like the present-day English, asked whether they should then move to adopt 'corsets and waist laces and late marriages and hysterics'. He added, 'Our fathers and mothers may have had their courtships and their love-meetings. But they found out, in the course of time, as the English too will one day find out, that love is a distracting feeling which sane men ought to be free from as much as anger or hatred. This was the conclusion to which the Greeks and the Romans also eventually came.'[83] An editor of a Hindi newspaper echoed this sentiment in commenting on an Allahabad High Court divorce case, *Wingrove v. Wingrove and McPherson*, of 1886, observing that 'cases of this kind occur so frequently' in England that the British government was obliged to introduce separate courts to settle disputes relating to matrimonial rights. Indians should, the writer cautioned, 'take a warning from the unfortunate results of what are called love-marriages, and adhere to their own forms of marriage, which may be modified, if necessary, to suit the altered state of things'.[84]

Conclusion

Late-nineteenth-century anxieties about the irrationality and eclecticism of the colonial regulation of marriage provoked new kinds of engagement with comparative legal and social theory by Indian jurists. Jurisdictional confusion prompted fundamental questions about the nature of law itself, drawing on earlier arguments from Colebrooke and Müller about the connectedness of 'Aryan' law and a historicist approach to law past and present. Ultimately, however, this comparative legal turn had divergent results. For some, state regulation of marriage came to be seen as a defining characteristic of a modern or civilized country. Jurists such as Gidumal and Ranade argued that the state regulation of marriage had been debated and discussed around the world, and that all 'modern' states saw marriage as a just realm for their intervention, bringing Hindu law into a realm of comparative world legal cultures, which provided an alternative body of knowledge on the appropriate spheres for state intervention and the nature of civil society. It was colonialism, they argued, and not Indian social practices, which kept India from being 'modern'.

For others, comparison led to a reaffirmation of Indian exceptionalism and of a particular evolutionary social path. A revaluation of the nature of custom, and its relationship with law, became a shared tenet that could unite different strands of Indian nationalism. Those representing the forces of orthodoxy and reform both insisted that Hindu law be seen as commensurate with Anglo-Indian Law, not that Anglo-Indian Law enforce particular versions of Hindu practice. The difference came in whether or not Hindu law should be reformed to become more consonant with global legal practice. Debates over marriage ultimately defined a new Hindu conservative position, with far-reaching consequences: the marginalization of lower-caste and non-Brahmin perspectives, the use of Islamic law as foil, and the establishment of the protection and policing of rituals concerning female sexuality and autonomy as critical to maintaining the integrity of Hindu law and Hindu identity.

Marriage had become politicized globally during the nineteenth century.[85] The process that Étienne Balibar called 'the nationalization of the family'[86] saw states taking an increasing interest in promoting particular forms of heteronormative family life, and the regulation of marriage became a constituent of governance. Mrinalini Sinha has argued for the use of the 'imperial social formation' as a means of recognizing that colonialism entailed 'combined but uneven development', which linked Britain with its empire on social, economic and ideological levels, constructing 'national' as well as 'global' frames for conceptions of self and other, identity and culture, discourse and public spheres.[87] Competing conceptions of marriage and custom fed into the construction of an 'All-India' Hindu legal space which both expanded and contracted those governed by, and potentially subject to, Hindu law. Mandlik wrote: 'Although the Hindu system is so catholic that some of the oldest works thereon receive the tribes like the Shabara within its folds, and although it is so tolerant that it leave people of all races and creeds free to worship God according to their own beliefs, yet no one but a Hindu can possess that intimate knowledge of the Hindu Shastras, and the daily observances enjoined therein.'[88] This was an argument specifically intended to discredit Malabari, a Parsi and thus a 'stranger'[89] with no grounds to propose legislation for Hindus. While arguing for a 'broad church' of Hinduism, this position also reinforced a view of Indian society as composed of multiple parallel but non-overlapping legal systems which clearly defined and demarcated communities.

Debates on marriage offer a window into how India's jurists and activists interacted with critical publics, both in India and abroad, drawing on historical and international comparison to build arguments about the nature of law, of custom and of Indian culture. For colonial British observers, the world outside of Europe was often seen to be 'singularly empty of law', mired in 'primitive' and kinship-bound forms of hierarchy, in the (in)famous formulation by Henry Sumner Maine.[90] Maine saw the development of systems recognizing 'contract' as central to sociopolitical and economic development, and traced Europe's legal precocity to Roman precedent. More recently, Maine's legal historicism has been seen as emblematic of a new phase of Eurocentrism, which shifted from encouraging Indian legal 'progress' towards managing and maintaining India's essential legal 'difference'.[91] This entailed a closer analysis of what colonial officials deemed customary law, focused on kinship and ancient proprietary rights, and which would become a baseline for indirect rule across the British colonial world. Yet just as the colonial government was constructing its 'ethnographic state',[92] encounters between world religions and global legal systems more clearly defined both those religions and emerging conceptions of religious freedom, secularism and civil society.

Debates about marriage involved fundamental questions about the nature of law itself, a process which not only foreshadowed but also guided decolonization. The sometimes hostile but frequently intellectually fertile interaction between missionaries, jurists and Islamic and Hindu clerics and priests in the nineteenth century resulted in the more careful iteration of orthodoxy and orthopraxy, which was in turn drawn into the formation of new public identities for particular groups. As Rachel Sturman argues, the independent Indian state maintained a particular kind of legal pluralism in independent India, perpetuating debates about legal personhood and citizenship and coexisting uneasily with more universalist national legal frameworks, such as the Hindu Law Acts.[93] The Indian constitution would maintain colonial forms of personal law: The continuing inconsistencies and tensions between personal, customary and civil law are reverberations of earlier Indian debates on social reform and the role of law in shaping civil society, tensions which were never fully resolved.[94] Through these social reform and legislative campaigns and debates, colonial officials, nationalist reformers and orthodox Hindus alike legitimated their authority by claiming guardianship of Hindu women's bodies, and through them, a body politic.

Notes

1 *Notes on Infant Marriage and Enforced Widowhood* (1884) and later *An Appeal from the Daughters of India* (1890).
2 For details on the case and its significance for a nationalist interpretation of the 'woman question', see: Sudhir Chandra, *Enslaved Daughters: Colonialism, Law and Women's Rights* (Delhi: Oxford University Press, 1998).

3 See Ishita Pande, 'Phulmoni's body: the autopsy, the inquest and the humanitarian narrative on child rape in India,' *South Asian History and Culture* 4, no. 1 (2013): 9–30.
4 Tanika Sarkar, 'Rhetoric against Age of Consent: Resisting Colonial Reason and the Death of a Child-Wife,' *Economic and Political Weekly* 28, no. 36 (4 September 1993): 1869–78, and 'A Pre-History of Rights: The Age of Consent Debate in Colonial Bengal,' *Feminist Studies* 26, no. 3 (2000): 601–22; Uma Chakravarti, 'Whatever Happened to the Vedic Dasi? Orientalism, Nationalism, and a Script for the Past,' in *Recasting Women: Essays in Indian Colonial History*, ed. K. Sangari and S. Vaid (New Brunswick, NJ: Rutgers University Press, 1990), 27–87.
5 Padma Anagol-McGinn, 'The Age of Consent Act (1891) Reconsidered: Women's Perspectives and Participation in the Child-Marriage Controversy in India,' *South-Asia Research* 12 (1992): 100–18.
6 See Antoinette Burton, 'A "Pilgrim Reformer" at the Heart of the Empire: Behramji Malabari in Late Victorian London,' *Gender and History* 8, no. 2 (1996): 175–96.
7 *Oudh Punch*, Lucknow, 11 March 1886, Punjab, North-Western Provinces, Oudh, Central Provinces, Central India and Rajputana Newspaper Reports 1886 [Hereafter NR] IOR/L/R/5/63 [India Office Records, British Library].
8 See Tanika Sarkar, 'Conjugality and Hindu Nationalism: Resisting Colonial Reason in the Death of a Child-Wife,' in *Women and Social Reform in Modern India*, ed. Sumit Sarkar and Tanika Sarkar (Bloomington: Indiana University Press, 2008), 259–81, at 262.
9 See Lata Mani, *Contentious Traditions: The Debate on Sati in Colonial India* (Berkeley: University of California Press, 1998).
10 Subal Chandra Mitra, *Isvar Chandra Vidyasagar* (Calcutta: New Bengal Press, 1902). See also Lucy Carroll on the extent to which relatives used the new legal distinctions on widow's property rights introduced by the Bill to dispossess them (whereas customary law would allow both widow remarriage and property retention): 'Law, Custom and Statutory Social Reform: The Hindu Widow's Remarriage Act of 1856,' *Indian Economic and Social History Review* 20 (1983): 363–88.
11 *Nyaya Sudha*, Harda, 10 March, 1886 NR 1886 IOR/L/R/5/63.
12 Dayaram Gidumal Shahani, *The Status of Women in India: or a Handbook for Hindu Social Reformers* (Bombay: Fort Printing Press, 1889).
13 See Deepa Das Acvedo, 'Developments in Hindu Law from the Colonial to the Present,' *Religion Compass* 7, no. 7 (2013), 252–62.
14 See Barbara Metcalf, 'Imagining Muslim futures: debates over state and society at the end of the Raj,' *Historical Research* 80, no. 208 (2007), 286–98.
15 See Vasudha Dalmia and Heinrich Von Steitencron (eds), *The Oxford Hinduism Reader* (Oxford: Oxford University Press, 2007).
16 SN Mukherjee, 'Class, Caste and Politics in Calcutta, 1815-1838,' in *Elites in South Asia*, ed. Edmund Leach and SN Mukherjee (Cambridge: Cambridge University Press, 1970), 33–78.
17 C. A. Bayly, *Recovering Liberties: Indian Thought in the Age of Liberalism and Empire* (Cambridge: Cambridge University Press, 2011), 91–2.
18 Gidumal, *The Status of Women in India*, xiv.
19 The Indian Penal Code of 1860 prohibited sexual intercourse with a girl below the age of 10, but the colonial state was cautious about further legislative intervention. The extension of the minimum age to 12 by Act X of 1891, also known as the Age of Consent Act, provoked widespread public objections. After this, the colonial government remained removed from further reform effort. Indian reformers

managed to persuade the Government of India to pass the Child Marriage Restraint Act, popularly known as the Sarda Act, only in 1929. See Mrinalini Sinha, *Specters of Mother India: The Global Restructuring of an Empire* (Durham, NC: Duke University Press, 2006) and Sumita Mukherjee, 'Using the Legislative Assembly for Social Reform: The Sarda Act 1929,' *South Asia Research* 26 (2006): 219–33.

20. 'Papers Relating to Infant Marriage and Enforced Widowhood in India,' *Selections from the Records of the Government of India*, CCXXIII, Home Dept. Serial No. 3. Calcutta: Superintendent of Government Printing, 1886.
21. Narayan Vishvanath Mandlik (ed.), *Writings and Speeches of the Late Honourable Rao Saheb Vishvanath Narayan Mandlik, CSI ... with a sketch of his life by Damodar Ganesh Padhye* (Bombay: Native Opinion Press, 1896), 22–3.
22. Ibid., 193.
23. Ibid.
24. Ibid, 175.
25. Ibid, 193.
26. *Bharat Bandhu*, 1 July 1887. NR 1887 IOR/L/R/5/64. Werner Menski notes that 'there are many repetitive comments in the literature about whether Hindu marriages are contractual or sacramental'. See Werner F. Menski, *Hindu Law: Beyond Tradition and Modernity* (Oxford: Oxford University Press, 2009), 281–2. See also Gooroodas Banerjee, *The Hindu Law of Marriage and Stridhan* (Calcutta: Thacker, Spink & Co., 1879), 30–1.
27. Sripati Roy, *Custom and Customary Law in British India. Tagore Law Lectures, 1908* (Calcutta: Hare Press, 1911), 291–5. For more recent discussion, see: J. D. M. Derrett, 'Divorce by Caste Custom,' in *Essays in Classical and Modern Hindu Law*, Vol. 4: *Current Problems and the Legacy of the Past* (Leiden: E. J. Brill, 1978), 95–104; Flavia Agnes, *Law and Gender Inequality: The Politics of Women's Rights in India* (Oxford: Oxford University Press, 2001), 18–26.
28. A process which anthropologist M. N. Srinivas described as 'Sansrkitization'. MN Srinivas, 'A Note on Sanskritization and Westernization', *The Journal of Asian Studies* 15, no. 4 (1956): 481–96.
29. Jotirao Phule, 'Letter to the Conference of Marathi Authors,' in *Selected Writings of Jotirao Phule*, trans. GP Deshpande (New Delhi: Leftword Books, 2002), 200–1.
30. On non-Brahman movements that centred 'family' and 'caste', using 'conjugality' as a lever for claiming new rights for women in colonial Tamil Nadu, see: Mytheli Sreenivas, *Wives, Widows, and Concubines: The Conjugal Family Ideal in Colonial India* (Bloomington: Indiana University Press, 2008).
31. See Anagol-McGinn, 'The Age of Consent Act (1891) Reconsidered'.
32. Rochona Majumdar, *Marriage and Modernity: Family Values in Colonial Bengal* (Durham, NC: Duke University Press, 2009), 1–19.
33. See Malavika Kasturi, *Embattled Identities: Rajput Lineages and the Colonial State in nineteenth-century North India* (Delhi: Oxford University Press, 2002).
34. See Judith Walsh, *Domesticity in Colonial India: What Women Learned When Men Gave Them Advice* (Oxford: Oxford University Press, 2004).
35. Majumdar, *Marriage and Modernity*.
36. R. Raghunath Rao was minister to the Maharaja of Holkar, a former civil servant in the Madras Presidency, and founding member of the Indian National Congress.
37. Dewan Bahadur R. Raghunath Rao, *A Lecture on the Marriage Laws of the Hindoos. Delivered at Indore, reproduced from the Central Indian Times* (Indore: Canadian Mission Press, 1887), 4.

'A Babel of Law' 165

38. Ibid., 15.
39. Ibid., 25–6.
40. Banerjee, *The Hindu Law of Marriage and Stridhan*, 1.
41. *Dharmaśāstra* refers to a treatise on *dharma*. European orientalist scholars and translators tended to equate dharmaśāstra with a legal code, translating '*dharma*' as 'law'. But dharma was also translated as 'religion'. See Ludo Rocher, 'Hindu Conceptions of Law', in *Studies in Hindu Law and Dharmaśāstra*, ed. Donald R. Davis, Jr. (London: Anthem Press, 2012), 39–41; for a postmodern analysis of classical Hindu law, see Menski, *Hindu Law*.
42. Banerjee, *Hindu Law of Marriage*, 2.
43. Ibid., 3.
44. Ibid., 4.
45. Banerjee names these as 'Benares, Mithila, Bengal, Dravida, and Maharashtra'. Ibid, 5–7.
46. Banerjee, *Hindu Law of Marriage*, 8.
47. Ibid., 15–16.
48. R. Ivermee, 'Shari'at and Muslim community in colonial Punjab, 1865-1885', *Modern Asian Studies* 48, no. 4 (2014): 1068–95.
49. Iza Hossin, *The Politics of Islamic Law: Local Elites, Colonial Authority and the Making of the Muslim State* (Chicago: University of Chicago Press, 2016).
50. Gauri Viswanathan, *Outside the Fold: Conversion, Modernity and Belief* (Princeton: Princeton University Press, 1998), 4.
51. John Dawson Mayne, *A Treatise on Hindu Law and Usage* (Madras: Higginbotham & Co., 1878). See Rachel Sturman, *The Government of Social Life in Colonial India*, ch. 4.
52. Banerjee, *Hindu Law of Marriage*, 21–2.
53. Ibid., 25–6.
54. Established by the Privy Council case of *Abraham v. Abraham*; see Chandra Mallampalli, *Race, Religion, and Law in Colonial India: Trials of an Interracial Family* (Cambridge: Cambridge University Press, 2011).
55. Sripati Roy, *Custom and Customary Law*. Tagore Law Lecture, 1909, 1.
56. Mitra Sharafi, 'The Marital Patchwork of Colonial South Asia: Forum Shopping from Britain to Baroda,' *Law and History Review* 28, no. 4 (2010): 979–1009.
57. See Nandini Chatterjee, 'English Law, Brahmo Marriage, and the Problem of Religious Difference: Civil Marriage Laws in Britain and India,' *Comparative Studies in Society and History* 52, no. 3 (2010): 524–52.
58. See Tanika Sarkar, 'Conjugality and Hindu Nationalism', 261.
59. Derrett considers the search for a definitive 'code' as a basis for rationalizing Hindu law: J. Duncan M. Derrett, *Religion, Law and the State in India* (Delhi: Oxford University Press, 1999), 225–74. See also Praveena Kodoth, 'Courting Legitimacy or Delegitimising Custom? Sexuality, Sambandham and Marriage Reform in Late Nineteenth Century Malabar', *Modern Asian Studies* 35, no. 2 (2001): 349–84.
60. Bayly, *Recovering Liberties*, 118–19.
61. Gidumal, *Status of Women in India*, Appendix VI: 'Shastric texts on the subject of Infant Marriage by Rao Bahadur MG Ranade.'
62. Chandra Mallampalli, *Christians and Public Life in Colonial India: Contending with Marginality* (London: RoutledgeCurzon, 2004).
63. Behramji Malabari, 'Papers on Infant Marriage and Enforced Widowhood,' 196.
64. Gidumal, *The Status of Women in India*, 107. See also Sturman *Government of Social Life*, 148–95.

65 See Bernard Cohn, 'Some Notes on Law and Change in North India', in *An Anthropologist among Historians and Other Essays* (New Delhi: Oxford University Press, 1987), 568–74.
66 Gidumal, *Status of Women in India*, lxxi.
67 Ibid., xv.
68 Ibid.
69 Ibid, 106.
70 Ibid, ilix.
71 *Nyaya Sudha*, Harda, 10 March 1886. NR 1886 IOR/L/R/5/63.
72 *Hindu Law of Marriage and Stridhan*, 25–6.
73 Gidumal, *Status of Women in India*, l.
74 Ibid., Mr. SN Tagore, lxxii.
75 Ibid., Sirdar Gopalrao Hari Deshmukh, lxxii.
76 Ibid.
77 See Thomas R. Trautmann, *Lewis Henry Morgan and the Invention of Kinship* (Berkeley: University of California Press, 1987).
78 See Colebrooke's essay 'On the Vedas, the Sacred Writings of the Hindus,' originally published in *Asiatic Researchers* 8 (1805): 369–476, republished in *Essays on the Religion and Philosophy of the Hindus*, ed. H. T. Colebrooke (London: Williams & Norgate, 1858).
79 *Hindustan*, Kalakankar, 3 August 1886. NR 1886 IOR/L/R/5/63. The *Hindustan* editor noted on 26 September that their paper 'strongly disapproves of the custom of child-marriage, but is opposed to State interference in social matters'. The paper throughout the 1880s reported favourably on widow remarriage and families who had pledged to avoid child marriage.
80 Gidumal, *The Status of Women in India*, LIX.
81 Ibid, li–lii.
82 Arvind Sharma, *The Study of Hinduism* (Columbia, SC: University of South Carolina Press, 2003), 58.
83 Gidumal, *Status of Women in India*, xlviii–xlix.
84 *Nyaya Sudha*, Harda, 5 May 1886. NR 1886 IOR/L/R/5/63.
85 See the work of Rosalind Coward, *Patriarchal Precedents: Sexuality and Social Relations* (London: Routledge, 1983); Mary Lyndon Shanley, *Feminism, Marriage and the Law in Victorian England, 1850–1890* (Princeton: Princeton University Press, 1989); Ann Laura Stoler and Frederick Cooper (eds), *Tensions of Empire: Colonial Cultures in a Bourgeois World* (Berkeley: University of California Press, 1987).
86 Étienne Balibar, 'The Nation Form: History and Ideology,' in *Race, Nation, Class: Ambiguous Identities*, ed. Immanuel Wallerstein (London: Verso, 1991), 101–2.
87 Mrinalini Sinha, 'Teaching Imperialism as a Social Formation,' *Radical History Review* 67 (1997): 176–80.
88 V. N. Mandlik, 'Government Interference in Matters of Social Reform Amongst the Hindus,' *Bombay: The Hermitage* (3 April 1885), in *Writings and Speeches of the Late Honourable Rao Saheb Vishvanath Narayan Mandlik*, 170.
89 Damodar Ganeshi Padhye, 'A short sketch of the life of the late Rao Sahib V.N. Mandlik, CSI,' in *Writings and Speeches of the Late Honourable Rao Saheb Vishvanath Narayan Mandlik*, 23.

90 Henry Sumner Maine, 'Minutes on Codification in India,' 17 July 1879, cited in Elizabeth Kolsky, 'Codification and the Rule of Colonial Difference: Criminal Procedure in British India,' *Law and History Review* 23, no. 3 (2005): 631–86.
91 See Karuna Mantena, *Alibis of Empire* (Cambridge: Cambridge University Press, 2011).
92 A phrase coined by historical anthropologist Nicholas Dirks in his *Castes of Mind: Colonialism and the Making of Modern India* (Princeton: Princeton University Press, 2001), 43–60.
93 Rachel Sturman, *Government of Social Life in British India.*
94 For a consideration of personal law and the postcolonial state, and debates on the Hindu Code Bill, see Eleanor Newbigin, *The Hindu Family and the Emergence of Modern India: Law, Citizenship and Community* (Cambridge: Cambridge University Press, 2013).

8

English Exports: Invoking the Common Law of Marriage across the Empire in the Nineteenth Century

Rebecca Probert

As David Cannadine has argued, Britain and its empire were, or at least were perceived to be, part of one interconnected whole, and the history of Britain cannot be understood without the empire any more than the empire can be understood without Britain.[1] This interconnectedness is particularly clear in the context of one particular English[2] export: what became known as a 'common law' marriage.[3] At a time when virtually the only route to a valid marriage in England and Wales was via an Anglican ceremony, the English courts upheld Anglican marriages celebrated overseas as being celebrated in accordance with the 'common law' of marriage. Then, as nineteenth-century religious toleration led to other denominations being able to celebrate their own marriages in England and Wales, and the empire began to be identified as a broad Christian domain rather than a specifically Protestant enterprise,[4] the rationale for recognizing marriages celebrated overseas changed so as to enable a wider range of ceremonies to create a binding union overseas as well. Yet all this was done without any explicit acknowledgement of change; instead, judges reinterpreted history so that it could be claimed that the new approach was grounded in past precedents.

While only a small number of cases ever reached the English courts, there was clearly a perception that these were not isolated instances and that there might be many more couples whose marriages would be open to challenge were a different approach to be taken. Judges on occasion resorted to passionate rhetoric about the dire consequences of not recognizing particular marriages in the context of the expanding empire. This was, after all, an era in which marriage held a central place: few couples lived together unmarried, and illegitimacy carried a considerable stigma.[5] There was a general presumption in favour of the validity of marriages; there was also a sense of pride in, and affinity with, the men and women of 'Greater Britain'[6] that meant that domestic judges would try to uphold their marriages wherever possible. There were, however, very clear limits to this flexibility. It was specifically the marriages of British men and women that were being upheld: the courts were noticeably more reluctant to recognize marriages involving a British man marrying a member of the indigenous population. The emphasis on the empire as Christian in identity and mission continued to exclude those of other faiths and traditions. In this sense, experiences with marriage in the British Empire resembled those outlined by Lisa Tran, Tamara Loos, Kenneth M. Cuno and Leigh Denault in their chapters in this book, as international exchanges and contact seldom led to the homogenization of marital law and practices across the globe – at least, not in the short term. In order to show these interconnections, I will first set out the law as it stood in England and Wales and then trace how domestic law was applied to an increasing range of overseas marriages. I will then analyse how nineteenth-century judges (re)interpreted the law within an imperial context so that a 'common law' of marriage could be exported across the empire.

Marriage Law at Home: The Growth of Religious Toleration

There was, of course, no 'British' law of marriage in this period. Scotland and Ireland each had their own distinctive laws.[7] Within England and Wales, marriages were governed by the canon law, the law of the church, until 1754. The terminology invoked the common framework that had applied before the Reformation, but the English courts had very much developed their own approach in the centuries that had elapsed.[8] While in theological terms all that was necessary for a binding union was the free consent of both parties, in the eyes of the law a marriage did not come into being unless it was solemnized by an episcopally ordained clergyman – that is, a clergyman of the established church, the Church of England.[9] The canon law laid down a number of additional formalities that were deemed desirable, but failing to comply with these did not affect the validity of the marriage, although it did potentially expose the parties to punishment for marrying 'clandestinely'.

In 1753, legislation was passed to stamp out clandestine marriages and ensure that couples only entered into binding unions after giving due notice of their intentions and in a public forum.[10] The Clandestine Marriages Act required all marriages to be preceded by the calling of banns or the obtaining of a licence. All marriages other than the tiny number authorized by the Archbishop of Canterbury's special licence then had to be celebrated in the Anglican Church, even if the parties were Catholics or Dissenters. A failure to comply with these basic requirements rendered the marriage void. In practice, however, the changes were not as significant as this might suggest: the vast majority of couples had married in church before the Act, and continued to do so afterwards.[11] There were, however, a number of crucial exemptions set out in the Act. These formal requirements only applied in cases where the marriage was taking place in England and Wales, and did not apply to Jews (who, as legal aliens, were governed by Jewish law), Quakers (who were in any case unlikely to comply, given that they had developed their own distinctive marriage practices) or members of the royal family (whose marriages could not be seen as being subject to the permission of the authorities).[12]

While reform in 1823 mitigated the consequences of failing to comply with the law, it was not until 1836 that a broader range of routes into marriage was created. The Marriage Act introduced the possibility of marrying in a purely civil ceremony, preceded by giving notice to civil authorities and accompanied by a new centralized system of registration. Anglican marriages were left virtually untouched by the new legislation, save that couples could choose to give notice to the civil authorities rather than having the banns called or obtaining a licence. Jews and Quakers were brought within the system insofar as they were required to give notice to the civil authorities and ensure that their marriages were registered. Adherents of other religious groups also had to give notice to the civil authorities and were not entrusted with the registration of their marriages – instead, a civil registrar had to be present to carry this out. In addition, they were only able to marry in a registered place of worship that had been licensed for marriage.

Despite the additional hurdles that those marrying in a religious ceremony – other than an Anglican, Jewish or Quaker one – faced, the Act was clearly significant in signalling greater religious toleration. In this it reflected broader changes that were taking place both politically and socially. There had been a considerable growth in non-conformism since the 1753 Act was passed, and the repeal of the Test and Corporation Acts in 1828 meant that adherence to the Anglican Church was no longer a prerequisite for participation in public life. Attitudes towards Catholicism had also shifted. The creation of the United Kingdom of Great Britain and Ireland in 1801, bringing together the existing union of England, Wales and Scotland with the Kingdom of Ireland, required a change of approach: as Peter van der Veer has commented, 'the creation of the British nation-state required the inclusion of the Catholic minority',[13] and from 1829 Catholics too were able to sit in Parliament. In the meantime, however, the changes occurring overseas were no less dramatic, as the next section will show.

Marriages Overseas: The Expansion of the Empire and the Reach of English law

As a general rule, a marriage's validity depended on the law of the place where it was celebrated, or the *lex loci*.[14] This was justified on the basis that each different jurisdiction was entitled to set its own laws and expect them to be respected. It was a simple way of managing potential conflict between different jurisdictions with different views as to how a marriage should be formed, but it was premised on a basic assumption of equality between those different jurisdictions, as well as a certain degree of familiarity in the rules to be applied.[15] It was not an approach that could accommodate too much difference. From an early period, though, the need to comply with local regulations was lessened by the fact that domestic law applied in factories – that is, the foreign trading stations of merchant companies[16] – and in concessions. On one level this was not an exception to the general rule, as these trading stations and concessions were seen as belonging to the country of origin of the merchant company rather than the country where they were located. In practical terms, it meant that where the subjects of a particular country were abroad in significant numbers, exceptions to the local regulations were created.

As the British spread across the globe as conquerors, rather than visitors, more exceptions began to be carved out. The transformation of the empire from one based on trade to one based on conquest[17] led to greater numbers of British troops fighting overseas and the consequent need for the courts to decide what approach should be taken to any marriages entered into by such persons. The brides, it should be noted, were often the widows of fellow comrades: This was a period in which a significant number of women accompanied their spouses to war, 'following the drum' and undertaking washing and cooking for the regiment.[18] In 1808, Lord Ellenborough CJ rather tentatively put forward the suggestion that it could be implied that the king's troops took the law with them but hedged his bets by holding that if this was not the case, it should be presumed that the marriage had complied with the local law.[19] A decade or so later, Sir William Scott doubted whether the husband, 'an officer of the army of occupation', was subject to French law when his marriage was conducted in France by the chaplain of the British forces, but the point was not resolved.[20]

It was clearly not an unusual question, since Scott noted that he had received a number of letters from clergymen on the issue, and three years later he gave a definitive answer in *Ruding v. Smith*.[21] The context is important to understand why he chose to break with the general rule that the *lex loci* would apply in this particular case. The marriage in question had been celebrated at the Cape of Good Hope in 1796 by the chaplain of the British forces. The Cape had surrendered in 1795 but the terms of that surrender preserved the prerogatives of the inhabitants, and the Cape Colony did not come under British rule until 1807.[22] Under Dutch law as it then stood, marriages according to the established church – in this context the Calvinist Dutch Reformed Church – had to take place in the parish church of the parties, after banns or licence; marriages between those who were dissenters from the established religion had to take place before a magistrate. In addition, parental consent was required for the marriages of women under the age of 25, and for men under the age of 30. The marriage of the 21-year-old husband and 19-year-old wife in a private house by an Anglican chaplain clearly failed to comply with the local law and would therefore have been void if that was the law to be applied.

Of course, the Cape's requirements were not that dissimilar to those that applied in England and Wales: such a marriage would also have been void under the 1753 Act. The difference was that at home the couple would have had the option of marrying in church whereas in the different religious background of the Cape they would have been treated as dissenters and required to go through a civil ceremony. Scott, now Lord Stowell, clearly viewed that as unacceptable. Referring to the anomaly that Jewish marriages in England and Wales were governed by Jewish law, and resorting to hypothetical examples that he clearly regarded as unarguable ('nobody can suppose that whilst the Mogul Empire existed, an Englishman was bound to consult the Qu'ran for the celebration of his marriage'[23]), he invoked a higher law to argue for the recognition of Anglican marriages between English men and women 'settled in countries professing a religion essentially different'.[24]

If taken to its logical conclusion, this reasoning would have had profound implications for the recognition of marriages both overseas and at home. So Lord Stowell identified a specific reason for displacing the *lex loci* and applying English common law. The justification, he thought, lay in the very reason for the British presence in the Cape:

> It would be a most bitter fruit of the victories of [England's] subjects, if they were bound to adopt the jealous and oppressive systems of all the countries which they subdued.[25]

As he noted, the husband was there as a soldier rather than as a settler and had in no way submitted to Dutch law. The strength of Stowell's rhetoric may have been inspired more by the broader context than any specific deficiencies of Dutch law; in 1796 the colony had been occupied by the French and memories of Napoleon's domination of Europe were still fresh at the time the case was heard. It also reflects the growing confidence in the role the British were to play overseas. Britain was now the major world power and did indeed have the capacity to 'subdue' other countries; crucial to its sense of mission, however, was this perception of the territories it was entering as both alien and inferior.

Stowell sought to limit the potential consequences of his decision by spelling out the particular circumstances of the case that justified the departure from the usual rule in this case:

> In my opinion, this marriage (*for I desire to be understood as not extending this decision beyond cases including nearly the same circumstances*) rests upon solid foundations. On the distinct British character of the parties – on their independence of the Dutch law, in their own British transactions – on the insuperable difficulties of obtaining any marriage conformable to the Dutch law – on the countenance given by British authority, and British ministration to this British transaction – upon the whole country being under British dominion – and upon the other grounds to which I have adverted.[26]

Had this been interpreted as Scott clearly intended – as a narrow exception to a general rule where all of these particular factors were replicated – then its scope would have been relatively limited. The danger, of course, in adding justifications for a particular approach is that each is taken separately, rather than cumulatively. Scott's comment that there were 'insuperable difficulties in obtaining any marriage conformable to the Dutch law'[27] in time gave rise to a second, and potentially broader, exception whereby a marriage that complied with English law would be recognized if it was impossible for the parties to comply with the *lex loci*. In *Kent v. Burgess*[28] Sir Lancelot Shadwell airily stated that,

> Every one who reads the judgment of Lord Stowell in the case of *Ruding* v. *Smith* must perceive that that learned Judge came to the conclusion that the marriage in that case was good, because difficulties, which he denominates insuperable, existed in effecting a marriage according to the Dutch law.[29]

The more unfamiliar the location, the more likely the court was to hold that 'insuperable obstacles' existed to compliance with the local law. In *Kent v. Burgess* the parties had gone through a ceremony of marriage in Antwerp without complying with the necessary formalities, and the counsel's argument that it was valid at common law was rejected on the basis that no insuperable obstacles to a valid marriage existed. Later, however, the obstacles came to be regarded as being as much cultural as practical or physical: the fact that a couple could have married according to the local form did not mean that they should be expected to do so.[30]

From the mid-nineteenth century *Ruding* was also cited to justify a further extension of the common law, this time to the increasing number of overseas territories under British rule. From one perspective the rule that the law of England and Wales supplanted that of the conquered territory simply reflected the fact that this was now British territory. As the judge pointed out in *The Countess of Limerick v. the Earl of Limerick*, which involved the question of the validity of a marriage that had been celebrated on Norfolk Island in 1842, 'Norfolk Island is a Colony planted by this country and the common law, therefore, is in force in it.'[31] But the need to rely on the common law rather than local regulation was itself due in part to the scale and range of the burgeoning empire. As Ferguson has noted, by the early nineteenth century 'Great Britain had acquired the largest empire the world had ever seen, encompassing forty-three colonies in five continents',[32] and it was to grow far larger over the course of the nineteenth century. It was also an increasingly varied empire. Earlier colonies in North America had involved a higher degree of settlement. By contrast, the territories acquired from the late eighteenth century onwards were more varied in terms of their indigenous population, modes of governance and degree of British settlement. Australia and New Zealand were claimed for the Crown in the late eighteenth century, and various Caribbean islands, together with the Cape Colony and Malta, were ceded to Britain in the wake of the Napoleonic Wars. Trading agreements with bodies such as the East India Company evolved into direct rule by Britain in India and the acquisition of Singapore, while further east Hong Kong was acquired in the course of the First Opium War with China. Later in the nineteenth century came the 'scramble for Africa' and British occupation of or power over countries such as Egypt, the Gambia, Natal, Rhodesia, Sierra Leone and Uganda.

As one commentator has noted, the colonies were 'governed through a bewildering array of administrative systems, which were due more to local improvisation than any coherent philosophy of imperial rule'.[33] This meant that the common law was not of universal application throughout the empire, even on the specific issue of marriage. The American colonies that had been founded in the seventeenth century had largely passed their own legislation on marriage and been self-governing in such matters[34]; the Australian colonies were subsequently to do so, and, legislation was passed by the British Parliament to validate marriages in certain countries. Other territories were acquired from other European nations and the local law was explicitly retained. In the case of *Ward v. Dey*,[35] it was noted that the parties had married in St Lucia, where for the purposes of marriage French law was recognized by the British as the law of the island. In other areas, such as India, the British had gradually extended their influence from trading enclaves within which English law applied, and there was a long-standing tradition of leaving the marriages of the indigenous population to the personal laws of the parties.[36]

Other lands, by contrast, were perceived as empty and devoid of law – or at least of any law that it was thought could be applied to British settlers[37] – and treated differently as a result:

> Where Englishmen establish themselves in an uninhabited, or barbarous country, they carry with them not only the laws, but the Sovereignty of their own State; and those who live amongst them and become members of their community, become partakers of and become subject to the same laws.[38]

In such places the common law of marriage applied, at least until it was supplanted by local regulation. The slippage between 'uninhabited' and 'barbarous' was a significant one: after all, very few areas of habitable land were entirely uninhabited, even if the native populations did not establish settlements in the same way, but categorizing the local population as 'barbarous' provided nineteenth-century empire builders with justification both for their occupation and the imposition of their own laws. It also provided a measure of internal unity: 'The internal rivalries, animosities, and political conflicts between British Christianity faded into the background of what came to be seen as the difference between British Christian civilization and the barbarity of the colonized peoples'.[39]

It is no coincidence that the common law of marriage was being held to apply to British possessions at the same time that there was a hardening of opinion towards interracial relationships: both trends were rooted in the same attitudes. Bayly has commented on how eighteenth-century ideas about the unity of mankind were 'slowly being replaced by the vision of a ladder or hierarchy of development'.[40] In eighteenth-century India, for example, interracial relationships had initially been encouraged.[41] It was not uncommon for an Englishman to marry an Indian woman: between 1780 and 1785 one-third of the wills of Englishmen in Bengal contained a bequest to Indian wives or companions or their children.[42] But by 1830, it was only one in six, and by mid-century, the practice had disappeared.[43] The decline has been attributed to a combination of factors: the growing perception that the British should function as 'a small, aloof, elite',[44] which required social distance to be maintained between the rulers and the ruled; the presence of missionaries who 'provided witnesses able and willing to denounce lapses from propriety'[45]; and the increasing number of Englishwomen in India (and indeed in other parts of the empire).[46] Specific prohibitions were generated by and reinforced these general trends. From 1791 provisions restricted the options open to the children of British men by Indian wives, and from 1835 intermarriage was barred.[47] By the mid-nineteenth century, as Gill has noted, a combination of Evangelism and 'scientific' racism in the wake of colonial rebellion in the 1850s 'gave authority to increasing proscriptions on matrimonial practices between colonizer and colonized, and fortified imperial hierarchies based on differences in race and gender relations'.[48]

To sum up, over the course of the nineteenth century the displacement of the rule that the validity of a marriage would be tested by the law of the place where it was celebrated occurred in stages – first with specific enclaves applying their own laws, next with the more mobile army not being subject to the law of the conquered territory, and then with the common law applying to individual Britons in any part of the empire that was not subject to specific regulation. But all this begs one crucial question: What did the common law actually require for a valid marriage?

Marrying Domestic and Imperial Developments: Common Law for the New Imperial Context

One crucial factor that facilitated the expansion of the 'common law' concept of marriage in the early nineteenth century was that there had been a key change in what the law was thought to require. In the decade or so that had elapsed between the decisions in *R v. Brampton* and *Ruding v. Smith*, it had been held in *Dalrymple v. Dalrymple* that the common law of marriage required only the bare exchange of consent, without there being any need for an ordained minister to be present.[49] The marriage in question in that case had taken place in Scotland: the presiding judge (who had no training in Scots law) took the view that since there had been no legislation governing marriage in Scotland, the relevant law must be the canon law, and that it would be necessary to look to the canon law that had been applied across Europe before the Council of Trent in the mid-sixteenth century to determine the applicable rules.[50] His perception of the canon law as a seamless whole that would be applied in the same way across different jurisdictions meant that he also assumed that the same rules applied in England and Wales before the 1753 Act – in other words, that a bare exchange of consent had been sufficient to create a marriage before legislative intervention.

In light of the developing empire, it was convenient that English and Scots law were perceived as sharing a history that could be projected into a joint future. After all, Scottish soldiers and settlers were a major component of the empire. Five years later, in *Latour v. Teesdale*,[51] the global reach of the decision in *Dalrymple* became clear. A Roman Catholic marriage ceremony involving British subjects in Madras was upheld by the English courts on the simple basis that there had been an exchange of consent between the parties. In other words, the credentials of the person conducting the ceremony were now irrelevant and his very presence unnecessary.

Reading the case, it at first sight seems odd that the court should have been willing to recognize a ceremony that deliberately flouted the custom of the colony. Objection having been made to the grant of licence for the pair to be married by the officiating clergyman of the settlement, the pair 'went to the Black town of Madras' where the ceremony of marriage was performed by a Portuguese Roman Catholic priest. He, however, explicitly told the couple that unless they were both Roman Catholics the marriage would not be valid and that it would be necessary for them to be married according to the rites of their own religion. The couple did not claim to be husband and wife during the remainder of their time in Madras (admittedly only a week), but declared themselves to be married during the course of the voyage home 'and cohabited together as such'. On their arrival in England they went through another ceremony of marriage, this time with the consent of the wife's trustees. The recognition of the Madras marriage might therefore seem both unnecessary and undeserved. But the question for the court was in fact whether the wife was entitled to her full share under her father's will, which had stipulated that any of his children who married without the consent of the trustees would forfeit a moiety of their share. By recognizing the Madras marriage, the judges were actually ensuring that the wife did not benefit from it, thus signalling their disapproval of a couple who tried to force trustees to give their consent by presenting them with a fait accompli.

It should however be noted that the potential impact of the decisions in *Dalrymple* and *Latour* that a simple exchange of consent could constitute a marriage was soon constrained by legislation. The following years saw a number of acts being passed to clarify the validity of marriages celebrated in various British territories. Those in India, for example, were dealt with by legislation in 1818 which provided that marriages conducted by ordained ministers of the Church of Scotland[52] should have the same force as those solemnized by clergymen of the Church of England.[53] In Newfoundland, by contrast, local conditions meant that the desirability of marriages being celebrated with a religious ceremony had to be tempered with practicality: The legislation stated that marriages would be void unless solemnized by a person in Holy Orders but immediately added the proviso that 'nothing contained in this Act shall extend or be construed to extend to any Marriages that may be had under Circumstances of peculiar and extreme Difficulty in procuring a Person in Holy Orders to perform the Ceremony'.[54]

Legislation was subsequently passed in 1823 to confirm the validity of marriages solemnized by the Anglican chaplain at St Petersburg,[55] and later that year more general legislation – billed as 'An Act to relieve His Majesty's subjects from all Doubt concerning the Validity of certain Marriages solemnized abroad' – confirmed the validity of marriages 'solemnized by a Minister of the Church of England in the Chapel or House of any British Embassador or Minister residing within the Country to the Court of which he is accredited, or in the House of any British subject residing at such Factory'.[56] It also – effectively giving statutory weight to the recently decided *Ruding v. Smith*[57] – confirmed the validity of marriages 'solemnized within the British Lines by any Chaplain or Officer, or other Person officiating under the orders of a Commanding Officer of a British Army serving abroad'.[58] Further legislation passed two years later conferred authority on consuls to solemnize marriages where no chaplain was resident.[59] What all these disparate pieces of legislation had in common was that they assumed that the solemnization of marriage by an Anglican clergyman was the norm, but that carefully limited exceptions could be made for the ceremony to be performed by another official. The intention was to ensure that marriages continued to be performed with a degree of formality and were properly recorded, rather than potentially permitting any exchange of consent to suffice.

Before long, however, the assumption that marriages should and would be celebrated by an Anglican clergyman began to be challenged. At home, the Marriage Act 1836 permitted marriages according to the rites of other denominations. Following Catholic emancipation and the abolition of the legal disabilities previously attaching to nonconformity, the chaplains appointed by consuls to officiate in foreign parts could be nonconformist or Catholic.[60] The missionaries who provided spiritual succour to settlers were drawn from a wide range of denominations,[61] the Baptist Missionary Society having been founded as early as 1793 and the Wesleyan Methodist Missionary Society in 1813.[62]

Against this changing background, the controversial (if correct) decision of the House of Lords in *R v. Millis*[63] in 1843 came as something of a shock. The case itself involved two marriages rather close to home: George Millis had gone through a marriage in Ireland celebrated by a Presbyterian minister and had then left his first wife and married a second in an Anglican ceremony in England. The question to be decided – initially by the Irish courts and then, on account of its importance, by the House of Lords – was whether he was guilty of bigamy. The rhetoric used by those arguing that he was had little to do with the criminal law or the law of Ireland; instead, dire warnings were issued about the dangers of not recognizing the ceremony conducted by the Presbyterian minister as a marriage. Lord Campbell, for example, claimed that,

> Vast numbers of marriages have been celebrated in the East Indies and elsewhere by Presbyterian and Missionary ministers of various persuasions, under circumstances in which no validating statute would apply to them: and where the attendance of a minister of religion could not be procured, many marriages have taken place without any scruple of the parties, or their parents or relatives, before consuls, military officers, magistrates and captains of ships.[64]

And, Lord Brougham put the adverse consequences of departing from the interpretation laid down in *Dalrymple* still more forcefully:

> Marriages innumerable have been contracted both by sectarians in this country and by persons of all descriptions in our vast possessions beyond the seas, possessions on which the sun never sets, all of which are now found out to be void, all these parties fornicators and concubines, all their issue bastards.[65]

It is clear that the security of marriage was an important consideration. After all, status, rights and the legitimacy of children all turned on the validity or otherwise of the union.

Nobody wanted to overturn whole swathes of marriages unnecessarily, at least not where the match was otherwise suitable, and the growing number of British women travelling overseas as missionaries, teachers and nurses in the nineteenth century meant that there were potentially more marriages at risk.[66]

Despite this emotive rhetoric, these considerations did not ultimately prevail over the analysis of what the law actually was. Millis was acquitted of bigamy on account of the fact that his first marriage was not legally recognized, and the case was regarded as establishing that a contract *per verba de praesenti* was not a valid marriage.

Any potential consequences for domestic marriages were swiftly addressed by legislation with both prospective and retrospective effect.[67] The implications for marriages overseas, by contrast, were left to be resolved by the courts and it was only a few months before the status of a ceremony conducted by a missionary fell to be decided.[68] Parke B applied *Millis* and refused to recognize the ceremony as a marriage.[69] The very next year, however, the literal application of *Millis* was challenged by Dr Lushington in a case on the validity of a marriage celebrated in New South Wales by a Presbyterian minister.[70] The question did not, in fact, depend on the common law at all, since legislation had been passed in the colony 'to remove doubts as to the validity of certain marriages had and solemnized within the Colony of New South

Wales' and explicitly provided that Presbyterians and Catholics could be married 'by an ordained minister of the Presbyterian Church of Scotland, or by a priest or minister of the Roman Catholic Church, duly empowered by his proper superior respectively' and that such marriages 'shall be ... of the same force and effect as ... if such marriage were had and solemnized by clergymen of the Church of England'. The difficulty was that the couple whose marriage was in question were not, in fact, members of the Presbyterian Church at all. Much of Dr Lushington's judgement focused on the distinction between directory and mandatory requirements, and the general reluctance to invalidate a marriage unless an act explicitly stated that it should be void. But he also made much of the apparent paradox that since the Act did not apply to ordained ministers of the Church of Scotland who were *not* 'duly empowered', any marriages they had conducted would be governed by the common law and therefore 'in a preferable position to a marriage where a part only of the prescribed forms was omitted'.

It seems scarcely credible that he should not have been aware of the House of Lords decision in *Millis*, but he made no mention of it, and his argument only makes sense if he assumed that episcopal ordination was not a requirement. Since ministers of the Presbyterian Church of Scotland were not episcopally ordained, they would have fallen foul of this requirement and their marriages, far from being valid under English common law, would not have been recognized. Two years later, when the issue of the marriage's validity came before him again,[71] he was more forthright in holding that consent to become man and wife 'is a sufficient marriage to enable me to pronounce, when necessary, a degree of separation'.[72] His justification was one both of precedent – casting doubt on whether *Millis* truly deserved to be regarded as such[73] – and the pragmatism of upholding marriages[74] entered into under circumstances where an episcopally ordained clergyman might not have been readily available.[75]

So within a very short period of time the decision of the House of Lords that the presence of an episcopally ordained minister was necessary to create a valid marriage had been quietly set aside and in its place was the assertion that consent was all that was needed, returning to the mistaken interpretation propounded in *Dalrymple*. Yet although the case for allowing consent alone to suffice was supported by arguments about the need to uphold marriage across the empire, judges do rather seem to have downplayed the religious infrastructure that did exist. This can be illustrated by the arguments made in a case heard in the Supreme Court of Bombay, *Maclean v. Cristall*, which was regularly cited as authority within the English courts. It involved a ceremony conducted by a Congregationalist missionary at Surat in the East Indies. The judge repeated the rule that 'although colonists take the law of England with them to their new home, they only take so much of it as is applicable to their situation and condition' and held that the requirement of an episcopally ordained priest was not applicable to India since 'the law in its terms was never capable of being applied' to countries where there was 'no church establishment, or parochial divisions'.

However, the requirement that a marriage be celebrated by an episcopally ordained priest was independent of the rules stipulating where the marriage should be celebrated. The latter requirement could reasonably be held to be inapplicable to the colonies as 'a mere municipal regulation', as could the specific requirements of the Clandestine Marriages Act of 1753. Under the canon law the presence of an episcopally ordained priest was sufficient to create a marriage *wherever* the ceremony took place.[76] To say that English law was not capable of being applied in the colonies is therefore to imply the impossibility of marriages being celebrated by Anglican priests in that context, which was clearly not the case. Many colonies had their own Anglican establishment.[77] Surat had a Protestant church, and had the parties in *Maclean v. Cristall* been content to wait a day or two longer, they could have married there, the new chaplain having been appointed the very day after the marriage took place.

But while the requirement of an episcopally ordained minister was *capable* of being applied in the colonies, it would have been inconvenient to have insisted upon it. Whatever the legal reality of what had been required for a valid marriage in England and Wales before 1754, the practical reality of the British Empire in the mid-nineteenth century was that the Anglican Church no longer enjoyed a dominant position.[78] It was, therefore, the acceptance of a broader range of Christian denominations as having the authority to conduct marriages – both at home and abroad – that underpinned the new 'common law' of marriage, rather than any purist, pre-Tridentine concept of a marriage as based solely on an exchange of consent. In many cases the disputed marriage had actually taken place according to the rites of the Church of England, but there was some question as to whether all of the formalities had been observed.[79] In other cases the celebrant belonged to another, usually Protestant, denomination.[80] Indeed, in none of the cases in which English courts were asked to consider the validity of a marriage celebrated overseas was the marriage based on a simple exchange of consent.

Tellingly, the common law was never applied to uphold an interracial marriage. In a case involving a union between a British man and an aboriginal New Zealand woman, counsel attempted to argue that in a 'barbarous' country any contract expressed in words of the present tense would be upheld as a marriage but Page Wood V-C nonetheless held that there was insufficient evidence to presume a marriage.[81] By contrast, when a British couple married in China, the case proceeded on the basis that they could rely on their 'common law right' to be married according to the rites of the Church of England.[82] Emphasis was placed on the fact that the parties were in a remote part of China (although Shanhaikwan was to become a popular beach resort not long after). So the application of the common law of marriage to colonial possessions depended very much on *who* was getting married, as well as where the marriage was taking place.

Conclusion

The nineteenth-century idea that British men and women took the 'common law' of marriage with them and could rely on it in situations where they could not be expected to comply with the local law reflected broader ideas about the place of the British in the world, in particular the idea of a 'Greater Britain' united by a common Christianity. The 'common law' that governed their marriages was shaped both by nineteenth-century perceptions of what the law had been, relying on the supposed uniformity of the canon law, and by a pragmatic view as to what the law needed to be in order to fit with the varied situations in which it might need to be applied. It was an approach that enabled the English courts to uphold marriages celebrated according to Christian rites between British men and women overseas. The irony of course was that it was possible to be far more radical in reshaping legal doctrine when it was believed to be of ancient pedigree, as in the case of 'common law marriage', than it would have been had the novelty of that doctrine been recognized. And once the idea of common law marriage had been established as legal doctrine, the courts continued to apply it to disputed overseas marriages even beyond the bounds – both temporal and geographical – of the British Empire.

Notes

1 David Cannadine, *Ornamentalism: How the British saw their Empire* (London: Penguin, 2002).
2 The complications as to what was 'British' and what was 'English' were particularly acute in the context of marriage law overseas. The focus in this chapter is on the English courts, but the law being applied was something of an amalgam, as is explained further below.
3 On the evolution of the terminology see Rebecca Probert, 'Common Law Marriage: Myths and Misunderstandings', *Child and Family Law Quarterly* 20, no. 1 (2008): 1–22. The marriages described in this chapter were all preceded by some ceremony and should not be confused with the US concept of a common law marriage arising as the result of cohabitation.
4 See Linda Colley, *Forging the Nation, 1707-1837*, 2nd edn (London: Pimlico, 2003), on the Protestant identity of the eighteenth-century empire and Hilary M. Carey, *God's Empire: Religion and Colonialism in the British World, c. 1801-1908* (Cambridge: Cambridge University Press, 2011) on how this changed over the course of the nineteenth century, in particular with the absorption of Catholic populations into the empire.
5 See Rebecca Probert, *The Legal Regulation of Cohabitation: From Fornicators to Family, 1600-2010* (Cambridge: Cambridge University Press, 2012).
6 On the concept of 'Greater' Britain see for example Duncan Bell, *The Idea of Greater Britain: Empire and the Future of World Order, 1860-1900* (Cambridge: Cambridge University Press, 2009).
7 This is not the place for a detailed discussion of those laws, but perceptions of Scots law do play a part in the story: see further text at n 50 below. On Irish marriage law, see Maebh Harding, 'The Comeback of the Medieval Marriage per verba de praesenti in 19th Century Bigamy Cases', in *Law and the Family in Ireland 1800-1950*, ed. Niamh Howlin and Kevin Costello (Basingstoke: Palgrave MacMillan, 2017).
8 On the regulation of marriage across Europe, see John Witte, *From Sacrament to Contract: Marriage, Religion and Law in the Western Tradition*, 2nd edn (Louisville: Westminster John Knox Press, 2012).
9 R. Probert, *Marriage Law and Practice in the Long Eighteenth Century: A Reassessment* (Cambridge: Cambridge University Press, 2009).
10 For the motivations behind the passage of the Act see Probert, *Marriage Law and Practice*, chs 5 and 6.
11 Probert, *Marriage Law and Practice*, chs 3 and 7 on practices before and after the Act.

12 See further Probert, *Marriage Law and Practice*, ch. 6. The Act said nothing about how the validity of exempted marriages was to be determined, although on the basis of the existing case law it was inferred that Jewish marriages were to be assessed according to the requirements of Jewish law and that the marriages of Quakers and members of the royal family were to be governed by the law as it stood in 1753, prior to the passing of the legislation.
13 Peter van der Veer, *Imperial Encounters: Religion and Modernity in India and Britain* (Princeton: Princeton University Press, 2001), 38.
14 *Scrimshire v. Scrimshire* (1752) 2 Hag Con 395; 161 ER 782; see also *Harford v. Morris* (1776) 2 Hag Con 422; 161 ER 792; *Middleton v Janverin* (1802) 161 ER 797.
15 Perhaps unsurprisingly, all the early cases on this point involved marriages either just north of the Scottish border or just across the channel in Europe.
16 For discussion of their role see for example Niall Ferguson, *Empire: How Britain Made the Modern World* (London: Penguin, 2004), 24.
17 See generally Colley, *Forging the Nation*, ch 3.
18 See generally Annabel Venning, *Following the Drum: The Lives of Army Wives and Daughters* (London: Headline Review, 2006); Rebecca Probert (ed.), *Catherine Exley's Diary: The Life and Times of an Army Wife in the Peninular War* (Kenilworth: Brandram, 2014). Unions between soldiers and women native to the country being conquered were less likely to appear in the reported case law, perhaps because the latter had little chance of litigating in the English courts if abandoned. The few cases that did involve such unions tended to be brought by those whose rights would be affected by the validity or otherwise of the marriage.
19 *R v. Brampton* (1808) 10 East 282; 103 ER 782. The case involved a marriage between the widow of one soldier and a sergeant in St Domingo.
20 *Burn v. Farrar* (1819) 2 Hag Con 369; 161 ER 773, 370.
21 (1821) 2 Hag Con 371; 161 ER 774.
22 See Brian Stanley, *The Bible and the Flag: Protestant Missions and British Imperialism in the Nineteenth and Twentieth Centuries* (Leicester: Apollos, 1990), ch 4.
23 (1821) 2 Hag Con 371; 161 ER 774, 385.
24 Ibid.
25 Ibid, 381.
26 Ibid, 394, emphasis added.
27 Ibid.
28 (1840) 11 Sim 361; 59 ER 913.
29 Ibid., 376. See also *Ward and Codd v. Dey* (1849) 1 Rob Ecc 759; 163 ER 1204, 761.
30 See, for example, *Phillips v. Phillips* (1921) 38 TLR 150, discussed below.
31 (1863) 4 Sw & Tr 252; 164 ER 1512, 253.
32 Ferguson, *Empire*, 51.
33 Timothy H. Parsons, *The British Imperial Century, 1815-1914: A World History Perspective* (Lanham: Rowman & Littlefield Publishers Inc, 1999), 29.
34 See, for example, John Adair, *Puritans: Religion and Politics in Seventeenth Century England and America* (Stroud: Sutton Publishing, [1982] 1998), 18; Alan Taylor, *American Colonies: The Settling of North America* (London: Penguin, 2001).
35 (1849) 7 *Notes of Cases* 96.
36 J. Duncan M. Derrett, *Religion, Law and the State in India* (London: Faber and Faber, 1968).
37 See, for example, the rather cursory discussion of the precolonial position in New Zealand in *Armitage v. Armitage* (1866) LR 3 Eq 343.

38 *The Advocate-General of Bengal on behalf of Her Majesty v. Ranee Surnomoye Dossee* (1863) IX Moore, Indian Appeals 391; 19 ER 786, 398, 428.
39 van der Veer, *Imperial Encounters*, 40.
40 C. A. Bayly, 'The British and Indigenous Peoples, 1760-1860: Power, Perception and Identity', in *Empire and Others: British Encounters with Indigenous Peoples, 1600-1850*, ed. Martin Daunton and Rick Halpern (Philadelphia: University of Pennsylvania Press, 1999), 20.
41 Ronald Hyam, *Empire and Sexuality: The British Experience* (Manchester: Manchester University Press, 1990), 116.
42 William Dalrymple, *White Mughals: Love and Betrayal in Eighteenth-Century India* (London: Flamingo, 2003), 34.
43 Ibid., 52.
44 Kenneth Ballhatchet, *Race, Sex and Class under the Raj: Imperial Attitudes and Policies and Their Critics, 1793-1905* (London: Weidenfeld & Nicolson, 1980), 96.
45 Ibid., 144.
46 Ibid., 5. See also Patricia Grimshaw and Peter Sherlock, 'Women and Cultural Exchanges', in *Missions and Empire*, ed. Norman Etherington (Oxford: Oxford University Press, 2005), 181 on the position in Southern Africa; Emily J. Manktelow, 'The Rise and Demise of Missionary Wives', *Journal of Women's History* 26, no. 1 (2014): 135–59.
47 Hyam, *Empire and Sexuality*, 116.
48 Rebecca Gill, 'The Imperial Anxieties of a Nineteenth-Century Bigamy Case', *History Workshop* 57, no. 1 (2004): 58–78, at 59 and 65.
49 *Dalrymple v. Dalrymple* (1811) 2 Hag Con 54; 161 ER 665: see further Rebecca Probert, 'Sir William Scott and the Law of Marriage', in *Judges and Judging in the History of the Common Law and Civil Law: From Antiquity to Modern Times*, ed. Paul Brand and Joshua Getzler (Cambridge: Cambridge University Press, 2012).
50 On the complexities of Scottish marriage law see for example Eleanor Gordon, 'Irregular Marriage: Myth and Reality', *Social History* 47, no. 2 (2013): 507–25, at 1.
51 (1816) 8 Taunt 830; 129 ER 606.
52 Under certain conditions, including that the ministers had been 'appointed by the United Company of Merchants of England trading to the East Indies to officiate as Chaplains within the said Territories'.
53 An Act to remove Doubts as to the Validity of certain Marriages had and solemnized within the British Territories in India, 1818, 58 Geo. III, c. 84, s. 1. See further the *Report from the Select Committee of the House of Lords appointed to inquire into the present state of the East India Company, and into the trade between Great Britain, the East Indies, and China* (1830) PP 646, Vol VI, 494.
54 An Act to regulate the Celebration of Marriages in Newfoundland, 1817, 57 Geo III, c. 51, s. 1. Given the vagueness of this provision, it is unsurprising that further and more specific legislation was passed a few years later: see An Act to ... make further Provision for the Celebration of Marriages in the said Colony, 1824, 5 Geo IV, c. 68.
55 4 Geo IV, c. 67.
56 4 Geo IV, c. 91.
57 (1821) 2 Hagg CR 371.
58 Section 1.
59 6 Geo IV, c. 87, s. 10.
60 Carey, *God's Empire*, 46.

61 On the role of nonconformist missionaries in the empire more generally, see Stanley, *The Bible and the Flag*; Andrew Porter, *Religion versus Empire? British Protestant Missionaries and Overseas Expansion, 1700-1914* (Manchester: Manchester University Press, 2004).
62 Carey, *God's Empire*, 54.
63 (1843-4) 10 Cl & F 534; 8 ER 844. See Rebecca Probert, '*R v Millis* reconsidered: binding contracts and bigamous marriages' (2008) 28 *Legal Studies* 337.
64 *Millis*, 800.
65 Ibid., 737-8.
66 Grimshaw and Sherlock, 'Women and Cultural Exchanges', 174.
67 See Probert, '*R v Millis*'.
68 *Catherwood v. Caslon* (1844) 13 Mee & W 261; 153 ER 108. The ceremony was conducted by an American missionary at the consulate office in Beirut.
69 It should be noted that this was an action for 'criminal conversation' whereby a husband sued his wife's lover for damages. The courts had traditionally insisted on strict proof of a legal marriage in such cases and the judge reasoned that the alleged 'wife' may have gone to live with her lover precisely because she had discovered that she was not in fact bound to her supposed husband.
70 *Catterall v. Sweetman, falsely calling herself Catterall* (1845) 1 Rob Ecc 304; 163 ER 1047.
71 The issue in the second case was whether the court had jurisdiction to pronounce a sentence of separation between the couple on the basis of the wife's admitted adultery.
72 (1847) 1 Rob Ecc 580; 163 ER 1142, 583.
73 Ibid., 582-3.
74 Or rather, in this context, allowing them to obtain a divorce.
75 Ibid., 583.
76 See further Probert, *Marriage Law and Practice*, ch. 5.
77 See, for example, Stanley, *The Bible and the Flag*, ch 4; Carey, *God's Empire*, 51.
78 Carey, *God's Empire*, 70.
79 *Culling v. Culling and Nicholson* [1896] P 116; *Phillips v. Phillips* (1921) 38 TLR 150; *Pawson v. Pawson; Matthews v. Matthews* (1930) 99 LJ (P) 142.
80 *James v. James and Smyth* (1881) 51 LJ (P) 24 (marriage celebrated by a Roman Catholic priest according to the rites of the Roman Catholic Church, there being no established church in British Burma); *Lightbody v West* (1902) 87 LT 138 (marriage solemnized by a Methodist Episcopalian minister); *Wolfendon v. Wolfendon* [1946] P 61 (marriage celebrated at Scottish mission church).
81 *Armitage v. Armitage* (1866) LR 3 Eq 343. In a similar vein, it was held in *Re Sheran* (1899) 4 Terr LR 83, that the Northwest territories of Canada were not so barbarous that marriage *per verba de praesenti* between a white man and an Indian woman could be found.
82 *Phillips v. Phillips* (1921) 38 TLR 150.

Part Three

Marriage, Kinship and Community

9

Finding the Ordinary in the Extraordinary: Marriage Norms and Bigamy in Canada

Mélanie Méthot

In 1858, eighteen-year-old Philomène Déry became the lawful wife of Charles Verreault. At her 1870 bigamy trial, she confessed she left Verreault after five months of conjugal life as he 'abused her, threatening to kill her and once set fire to the house to get rid of her by that means'. She gained the support of the *Montreal Star* court reporter who referred to her as a 'respectably dressed, middle aged woman'. The reporter vilified the first husband writing: 'Verreau [*sic*] is one of the ugliest specimens of humanity in this city', and he reviled the 'Romish Clergyman [who] lodged the information' about her bigamous second marriage.[1] At her trial, Déry mentioned she thought her husband was dead. Eight years had passed since she had last seen Verreault when she married Edmond Labrecque in Montreal Notre-Dame Basilica, which was far from her previous home. Déry did not lie about her identity, correctly identifying her parents on the marriage licence, but she was less than honest in portraying herself as a spinster. In the end, the judge sentenced her to five months of hard labour for her offence.[2] In the eyes of the Catholic priest who denounced her, even though her legitimate husband was a scallywag, there was no excuse for marrying bigamously. The court agreed. Nonetheless, the bigamous marriage between Déry and Labrecque could not have disturbed public morals very much: they lived together for four years before anyone informed the authorities.

As an unconquered frontier, group of colonies and independent state, Canada has witnessed enormous transformation since the eighteenth century. In this context, monogamous marriage has stood consistently as a pillar of society for colonial settlers and, later, citizens of the new country. Legal scholar Constance Backhouse argues that, in Canada, marriage was probably 'the most important social institution in nineteenth-century society. It was believed to provide the bedrock upon which all other social relationships were constructed and it was universally touted as natural and essential to the smooth functioning of civilization'.[3] Studying turn-of-the-twentieth-century reform movements, James Snell explains how social reformers associated marriage with social morality. Snell contends that reformers responded by calling on the Canadian state to defend marriage through strict enforcement of rigid standards of sexual morality.[4] Other scholars establish a direct link between marriage and Canadian nation-building.[5]

Researchers have been trying to understand how marriage operated as this societal foundation. In her acclaimed book, *The Importance of Being Monogamous*, Sarah Carter illustrates how there has been no single definition of marriage in Canada; definitions changed over time and varied across communities. This was certainly the case across Canada's various provinces and, earlier, colonies. Taking into account the matrimonial story of Philomène Déry, one may add, individuals, families, society, legal entities and religious bodies all articulated their own conceptions and expectations of marriage.

'Event history' encourages scholars to explore the extraordinary to extract the ordinary.[6] By analysing bigamy cases (the extraordinary), one grasps legal, religious, social and individual attitudes and expectations towards marriage (the ordinary). In contrast to other contexts in which authorities accepted forms of plural marriages (concubines, polygamy) – as Kenneth M. Cuno and Lisa Tran have shown in this book – in British North America, the act of marrying another person during the life of a former spouse without having first dissolved legally the bond that unites them as husband and wife constituted a serious crime. An examination of bigamy cases before criminal courts in Nova Scotia and Quebec, the two oldest colonies in British North America, allows one to highlight local factors that influenced marriage practices. Quebec is unique among the Canadian provinces with its predominantly Roman Catholic population. In his study on nineteenth-century marriage and the family in Quebec, the historian Serge Gagnon argues that the Catholic Church had an almost absolute monopoly on the institution of marriage.[7] Until the late 1900s, church registers in Quebec served as the only civil and vital records, although by the 1960s it was possible for couples to register their marriage solely with the government.[8] In contrast, although overwhelmingly Christian, Nova Scotia's population encompassed several creeds. In 1871, the largest religious denominations were Presbyterian (27%), Roman Catholic (26%), Baptist (19%), Episcopal (14%), Methodist (10%) and Lutheran (1.3%). As a result of diversity no one religious denomination became the sole agent when it came to marriages. Civil registration of marriages began in 1758 with the introduction of procedures for obtaining a marriage licence. Initially the licence was optional. Mandatory civil registration began in 1864 and has continued since, although compliance was not universal throughout the province until the early twentieth century.

In addition to their distinct religious complexions, the two provinces had different civil laws on marriage and its potential dissolution. Nova Scotia established its divorce court in 1750. By contrast, Canada as a whole remained without an analogous court even after National Confederation in 1867. Section 91 of the Canadian constitution gave the federal government power over divorce and marriage and as such the Federal Parliament legislated on marriage and divorce; however, the provinces retained the power over the solemnization of marriage. Furthermore, although marriage and divorce fell under federal jurisdiction, colonies with divorce courts continued to hear divorce cases. In Quebec, deprived of any means to obtain a judicial divorce, those who wanted to legally separate from their spouse and start a new life with a different partner had to appeal to parliament for a statutory divorce. It made the procedure not only long and expensive but also almost inaccessible to most Quebecers. Between 1867 and 1900, the Canadian Parliament granted only two legislative divorces per year.[9] In Quebec, the 1866 Civil Code reaffirmed the long Catholic tradition that marriage could only be dissolved by the natural death of a spouse.[10] Residents could petition the

Catholic Church to annul a union or to grant a separation of beds. They could also apply to the civil courts for a separation of property.[11] However, as Christine Hudon has shown, in the nineteenth century, church officials granted few annulments.[12] Although it had its own divorce court, only a small number of Nova Scotia couples went through divorce proceedings throughout the nineteenth and early twentieth century.[13] Could this limited number of divorces and annulments indicate how committed church, state, society and individuals were to the institution of marriage? The sociologist Robert Pike demonstrates that Canadian divorce rates prior to the liberalization of divorce laws in 1968, when the federal government introduced the 'no fault' divorce, provide a very poor indication of the actual rate of marriage breakdowns, arguing one has to consider judicial separations, migratory divorces and desertions.[14]

Exploring the prosecuted cases of bigamy in Quebec and Nova Scotia, this chapter reveals the tensions that existed between confessional, legal, communal and individual assumptions about marriage. Examining in detail the stories told by men and women as accusers, witnesses and defendants, it is possible to gain a clearer understanding of these diverse views on marriage. Expectations and understanding of matrimony varied greatly. Sometimes they espoused the predominant social discourse; on other occasions, they showed a rather different view. Men and women married for various reasons, although both genders married because it was what was socially expected. Some bigamy prosecutions illustrate how marriage was a family affair. Newspaper coverage of bigamy cases shows how Canadians believed in two fundamental tenets of marriage: that promoted family stability and that it ensured public morality.

The only noticeable distinction between the two provinces in terms of beliefs about marriage emerges from a closer look at how religious authorities dealt with bigamy. In Quebec, priests turned to the criminal courts only when their own internal mechanisms failed to restore public morality. They were convinced that they had absolute moral authority on marriage. Also, when priests were involved in bigamy trials, they commented on the moral character of their parishioners. In Nova Scotia, ministers were routinely called as witnesses, mostly to testify that a marriage had taken place. They often specified that the couple had a licence or that banns were published. Under Nova Scotia law clergymen could pay a penalty for solemnizing a marriage without publication of banns or if the couple did not have a proper marriage licence.[15] Criminal courts in both provinces dealt harshly with male bigamists who renounced their duty of caring for their family and/or endangered the transfer of family wealth. Although jurists did not make it explicit in bigamy cases that marriage served to protect women and children, the courts did not hesitate to assign that function when passing judgement. As we have seen in Chapter 8, courts in other contexts also sought to endow marriage with a protective quality for the families of British soldiers fighting overseas and in cases involving children's legitimacy and women's status. While there were many understandings of marriage, in Canada, monogamy remained the only socially accepted form of union throughout the nineteenth and twentieth centuries. The sudden drop in the number of prosecuted cases after the Second World War does not reveal a sudden shift in attitudes towards bigamous relationships. It instead coincides with the rise of the welfare state, women entering the labour market in greater numbers and parliamentary debates on reforming divorce laws.[16] The idea of everlasting marriage, in part, for the protection of women and children, slowly gave way to a less stringent form of union. Nevertheless, the Canadian government continues to ascribe a central function to marriage: marriage provides family stability, and as a 2011 Canadian government 'well-being' website states, 'The family is an essential building block in Canadian society and serves fundamental social and economic roles (earning, caring, parenting, reproduction, and participating in community.)'[17]

Prosecuting Bigamy

Bigamy has always been considered a serious offence in Canadian law. The two provinces showed their commitment to monogamous marriage by making bigamy illegal and subject to punishment. Jean-François Perrault, notary to the Court of King's Bench for the District of Quebec, explained that, 'If a person, being married, remarry while the first spouse is alive, it will be felony, and the guilty party will suffer death as in the case of felony.' He identified a few exceptions such as 'seven years absence', 'annulment granted by an ecclesiastical court' or 'minors who contracted a marriage'.[18] De facto, no bigamist ever received the death penalty since the crime was a felony with 'benefit of the clergy'.[19] The *Nova Scotia Revised Statutes* of 1859 defined bigamy in similar terms: 'Whoever being married, shall marry any other person during the life of the former husband or wife, whether the second marriage shall have taken place in the province or elsewhere, shall be guilty of felony, and shall be imprisoned for a term not exceeding two years, and fined at the discretion of the court.' The second section of the statute stated exceptions:

> Provided that nothing in the last preceding section shall extend to any second marriage contracted out of this province by any other than the subject of her majesty, or to any person marrying a second time whose husband or wife shall have been continually absent from such person for the space of seven years, and shall not have been known by such person to be living within that time, or shall extend to any person who at the time of such second marriage, shall have been divorced from the bond of the first marriage, or to any person whose former marriage shall have been declared void by the sentence of any court of competent jurisdiction.[20]

Quebec's criminal laws revealed the striking influence of religious authorities. Nova Scotia legal text refers to 'any court of competent jurisdiction' while Quebec specifies 'annulment granted by an *ecclesiastical* court'. Bigamy was considered serious in both colonies yet very few individuals were prosecuted before Canada became a country (see Figure 9.1). After Confederation, the House of Commons passed an initial set of nine statutes including *Offences Against the Person*. Section 58 reaffirmed the Canadian government's stance on bigamy: 'Whosoever, being married, marries any other person during the life of the former husband or wife, whether the second marriage has taken place in Canada, or elsewhere, is guilty of felony, and shall be liable to be imprisoned in the Penitentiary for any term not exceeding seven years and not less than two years, or to be imprisoned in say other gaol or place of confinement for any term less than two years with or without hard labour.'[21] Like its Nova Scotia predecessor, the Canadian statute was completely stripped of religious connotation. In 1892 the first Canadian Criminal Code defined bigamy as: (i) 'The act of a person who, being married, goes through the formalities of a marriage with another person in any part of the world whatsoever'; or (ii) 'The act of a person who goes through the formalities of a marriage in any part of the world whatsoever with someone she knows to be married'; (iii) 'The act of a person who goes through the formalities of a marriage or simultaneously on the same day.'[22] In (i) there is deception on the part of one spouse to the other; in (ii) the spouses together deceive the state; for (iii), one must see the government's refusal to legitimize polygamous unions.[23]

From the late nineteenth century Canadian jurists conceived of bigamy as an attack on the state, as an assault on its ability to regulate unions between men and women. The state saw marriage as much more than a way to regulate sexual morality, it was also a means to ensure that estates were passed to the next legitimate generation. Marriage also gave some protection to wives and children because husbands had the responsibility of providing for their family.[24] The illegitimate wives of bigamists would end up with nothing since the state did not recognize the union.[25] Bigamist men were thus putting these women and their children in a precarious situation. They were committing a double crime: They not only jeopardized the future of the illegitimate family but they also forfeited their responsibility to provide for the legitimate one. Sentencing practices capture the gender aspect of the crime. Among men, 21 per cent received sentences of two years or more, while judges sentenced only 6 per cent of women to the penitentiary.[26] In the eyes of the court, women bigamists were not committing as serious an offence as men. Still, when found guilty, male and female bigamists often received prison terms varying from a few days at the county jail to five years at the penitentiary.

Beyond sentencing practices, judges revealed through their commentary that they considered marriage an institution meant to protect women and children. Crown Attorney Corley unambiguously stated: 'Bigamy is a serious offence against the state, and against the children of a bigamous marriage.'[27] When Quebec judge Leet gave a sentence of three years to bigamist John Davis, he admonished the defendant: 'You are the father of nine children and a grandfather, yet you have passed yourself off as a single man, entered the home of a lovely young woman and have committed a crime against a home and morality. The law allows me to give you a sentence of seven years, and I had seriously thought of giving you five years. I have no respect for you and little mercy, and your sentence shall be three in the penitentiary at St-Vincent-de-Paul.'[28] Judges had to balance between their desire to make an example by punishing the guilty party and the harm done to the victims, as the breadwinner could no longer provide for the family while in prison.

Nova Scotia courts displayed the same attitude. In 1894 Judge Johnston of Halifax applied a light sentence to bigamist Eliza Gross: three days at the city jail. He explained how 'William Joseph, the husband of the accused, had undoubtedly acted like a brute to his wife. He had deserted her and ordered the family effects to be sold, causing the wife to sleep on the bare floor or go out on the street.' He specified: 'The evidence, however, showed that the woman had committed bigamy, but under the circumstances the lightest penalty would be imposed.'[29] For the judge the defendant was the real victim here since her husband had failed to take care of her. He deemed Gross to be of good character and as such he believed she was a victim of circumstances. A Sherbrook magistrate encapsulated the courts' take on bigamists who abdicated their responsibility to provide for their family:

> The damage he has caused the young woman he had married at Richmond was irreparable: it was especially useless to plead that the crime had been committed in ignorance. To the contrary, he had violated a law most universally known in the world, and had done so in the most deliberate and cold-blooded manner. As to the abandoned wife in Ireland, the Court would not refer to her nor the injury done to her beyond noting the fact that the prisoner had not shown any repentance of his crime, nor any desire to return to his rightful wife.[30]

According to the magistrate, both spouses, the new wife and the legitimate one, were victims. The gravity of James Hunt's crime earned him a two-year sentence at the penitentiary. Nearly fifty years later, Quebec judge Gustave Marin issued a similar statement when he sentenced Paul Allard: 'You left your wife with a child and you have brought nothing but misery to the woman with whom you went through the bigamous marriage ceremony. I am going to give you a lesson.' Judge Marin took into consideration the harm done to the victims when he sentenced Allard to two-year imprisonment. He added: 'I learned that you have disowned the name of your mother with false documents.'[31] The last part of Judge Marin's declaration alludes to the responsibility of the state to manage the transfer of family wealth. False identification blurred parental lineages. Judge Marin's comment also explains how some individuals were able to thwart the authorities by lying about their age, name or origins.[32]

The business of heritage and lineage came to the forefront when in 1943 Senator John Wallace de Beque proposed a bill to protect illegitimate children of bigamous marriages:

> The whole difficulty is that men or women disappear and if the one who is left remarries on a reasonable assumption that the other party to the marriage is dead after seven years, everything is all right unless the other party turns up. The one who remarries is protected from criminal prosecution, and from bigamy, but the second marriage is declared void and children by it, if any, are illegitimate. The bill would have the effect of sustaining the second marriage and protecting the rights of children.[33]

The Attorneys General of British Columbia, Saskatchewan, Ontario and Prince Edward Island supported the bill, but it was defeated 27 to 19 and nothing more was done to protect the rights of illegitimate children. During the debate, Senator Marcotte reaffirmed Quebec's view that the family was 'the essence of society'. He declared: 'Marriages make the family stable and permanent. It is its formula, its conception, its binding tie. If you break that tie, you disunite the family, you disperse its members, you weaken and destroy the foundation of society.'[34] Something was nevertheless changing. In one of the most recent cases found in the Quebec judicial archives, Judge Gagnon showed mercy to a confirmed bigamist. The record does not reveal who laid the complaint. The legitimate wife acknowledged that she had been receiving money from her husband every month for the past ten years. Although the union was over, the man continued to take care of his first wife and their children. In this case Judge Gagnon sentenced him to only one day already served.[35] It seems the Catholic Church did not have that much influence on the bench. Bigamy laws existed to protect women and children, but in this case, sending the accused to prison would have caused harm to the legitimate wife. Deprived of his salary, he may not have been able to provide for both his families. Perhaps Judge Gagnon took into consideration that in 1951, Quebec residents were still forced to seek the passage of a private act of parliament to divorce, a process that remained cumbersome until the federal government passed no-fault divorce legislation in 1968 and eased the procedures.

On the one hand, the qualitative analysis of state discourse through laws and judgements reflects the important functions the courts ascribed to marriage throughout the period under study; on the other hand, the quantitative analysis reveals how each province prosecuted relatively few bigamists. At the time of Confederation, the population of Nova Scotia was less than 400,000, while Quebec boasted nearly 1.2 million. In 1901, Nova Scotia's population had not yet reached half a million and Quebec's stood at 1.6 million. Ten years later, Quebec counted 2 million inhabitants; Montreal, its metropolis centre, was the home of one out of four residents. Nova Scotia nearly hit the half a million mark in 1911, Halifax being the most urban centre with a population of 47,000.

Figure 9.1 illustrates the provinces followed the same prosecution pattern. The number of cases peaked between 1911 and 1920 and again between 1941 and 1950. It dropped significantly after the Second World War, a drop compounded by the rapid population increase the provinces experienced during those years. It seems that particularly in times of crisis, authorities have had less tolerance towards those who seemed to make a mockery of marriage. Newspapers certainly argued that in times of war citizens were more susceptible to enter into one or two marriages. The *Halifax*

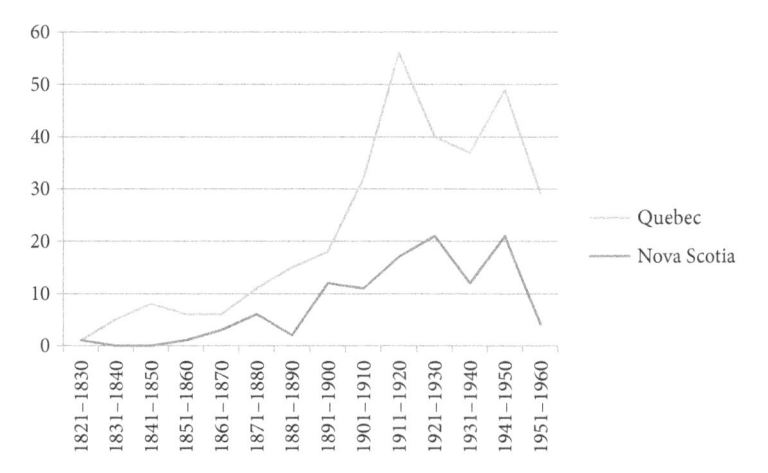

Figure 9.1 Number of Prosecuted Cases of Bigamy in Quebec and Nova Scotia.[36]

Chronicle commented on the increased number of bigamy convictions during the Great War.[37] *The Times* reported: 'There was a disposition among Judges earlier in the war to treat bigamy by men serving in the army as an offence for which a light sentence might be imposed. It has followed that there has been more bigamy, and it is now a matter of frequent observation by Judges that the offence is seriously on the increase.'[38] Strangers in a new land, it was easier to contract a second marriage than if one remained in one's own community. As settler colonies and later as immigration destinations, it makes sense that one would find in Nova Scotia and Quebec men who had left wives in the former home country and took new ones in British North America, or abandoned wives who felt they had no choice but to contract a new union to have a better chance at raising their children. The judicial archives in both provinces contain several of these cases. At the same time, transnational bigamy was harder to prove if the spouse was still in the old country. For a guilty verdict, prosecutors needed evidence of both marriages and concrete proof the defendant knew that the first spouse was still alive.

Despite the difficulty in prosecuting bigamous marriages, it seems that there was less tolerance of bigamy during wartime and an attempt to crack down on the issue. In 1940, the *Globe and Mail*, praising the good work of the Morality Department of the Toronto Police,[39] noted that 'There has been an increase in bigamy prosecutions of about 300 per cent in the last year.'[40] Between 1942 and 1947, Charles Forget, Montreal liaison officer and member of the Montreal Morality Department, pursued seventeen suspected bigamists.[41] It was the desire to ensure stability through monogamous marriage that prompted their investigation into the lives of married couples. Not only did people have more opportunities to commit bigamy, but also governments gave more tools to its agencies to track potential bigamists. The higher number of prosecutions in the time of war is the result of three combined factors: a commitment from the provinces to the family which is seen as an agent of stability, quick marriages and greater surveillance from the state. Legal treatises, comments from judges and the work of morality squads all testify to the state's vested interest in regulating marriages. Bigamy was so reprehensible because it confused who belonged with whom and how property would be transmitted, let alone how children would be raised.

Bigamy and Marital Norms

The cases reviewed in the previous section indicate that throughout the period judges understood marriage as an institution that protected women and children, and also as a legal mechanism to transfer family wealth. From newspaper coverage, one can tease out broader understandings of marriage in society. For instance, the *Globe* criticized the courts when it stated: 'The Judge or Magistrate who, by imposing light sentences [on bigamists], teaches the public to think lightly of what is never less than a grave menace to society, may be promoting perilous social demoralization.'[42] The warm reception of the 1929 ruling of Quebec judge Lacroix, who ruled American divorces illegal when he found Canadian Assad Eddy guilty of bigamy, also equated stability with long-lasting marriages.[43] Eddy sent his legitimate wife to Reno so she could secure a divorce. He then proceeded to marry a young woman in New York before returning to Montreal to live with her. Unsatisfied with her new husband, the 'new' wife asked the court to annul her marriage to Eddy. Finding Eddy guilty of bigamy, Judge Lacroix confirmed that American divorces would not be recognized in Canada. Reporting on the verdict, a journalist at the *Globe* noted that thousands of married couples would be subject to jail sentences. He nonetheless praised the decision: 'Judge Lacroix has done a service in delivering a jar[ring] to the complacence with which the United States divorces are regarded in the Dominion. The laws of the Republic have no jurisdiction over people living here, the easy divorce laws which invite moral laxity least of all.'[44] For him, marriage ensured public morality.

As early as 1874 newspapers warned their readers about these illegal divorces when commenting on bigamy cases or providing legal advice.[45] The day of the Lacroix judgement, in a front page column, a contributor raised an important issue about all the Canadians who obtained a divorce in the United States when he subtly dropped: 'These people, apparently, are unmolested by the law officers unless action is demanded by some interested party.'[46] His statement reminds one that the number of prosecuted cases does not reflect the real incidence of bigamy. How many cases remained undetected or were accepted by family and community?[47] As we saw in the 1870 case of Philomène Déry, the press seemed indignant that a priest denounced her bigamous marriage. Divorces obtained in an American jurisdiction had no legal force in Canada, but despite the Lacroix judgement, they continued to satisfy public opinion. Like Austrians who shopped around for easy divorce jurisdictions, as Ulrike Harmat has shown in this book, residents from Quebec (and Ontario) continued crossing the 49th parallel to end their binding union, even if their divorces were not technically legal in Canada.

Given widespread acceptance of bigamous marriages, it seemed unclear who would denounce bigamists. The question of what motivated those who initiated proceedings for bigamy has received little historical attention, but an appreciation of the circumstances in which cases were brought to trial is essential for understanding popular attitudes towards the law and gauging the extent to which bigamy was an accepted social practice. First husbands who had abandoned their partners had little interest in informing authorities unless they wanted a divorce. What better way for a first spouse to prove adultery than to show proof of marriage? And if someone was unhappy with his or her present marital state, they could accuse their spouse of bigamy. However, second wives who discovered after the fact that their union was illegitimate feared for their security. The charges coming from the Society for the Protection of Women and Children suggest that when bigamy cases came to light, the onus was primarily on men to own up to their responsibilities and take care of their first wife. For all the cases in which we have been able to identify informants, we have found that most were directly affected by the offence, including first or second spouses (180) or extended family members (28). Twelve members of the clergy informed authorities about their parishioners, including eight in Quebec and four in Nova Scotia.

The numbers seem very low considering priests and ministers were in charge of the records. Nova Scotia allowed civil marriage, but most couples, even those who obtained a licence, chose to marry in a church ceremony. Responsible to verify potential barriers to the union, clergymen would not perform the ceremony unless they knew there were no impediments. For example, two weeks after Alex Strachan married Hanna Louisa

Margenson, the Presbyterian minister who had united them denounced him to the Halifax authorities. The record does not divulge what prompted the minister to inform the police. Perhaps a parishioner told the minister the groom had been married in England. Strachan spent a month in Halifax county jail before a magistrate found him not guilty. Lack of material witnesses led to the verdict.[48]

In Quebec, the testimonies of the few priests who denounced bigamists reveal they turned to the criminal courts only when their own institutional mechanisms failed to put an end to what they considered scandalous unions. For instance, Vicar Cyrille Samson wrote to the attorney general complaining that Exilda Dumais and Cléophas Carrier, both Catholics, brought scandal to his parish when an Anglican minister married them, despite the fact Mrs Dumais remained married to Edouard Boutin.[49] Since the Catholic Church did not recognize the authority of an Anglican minister to marry Catholics he could not accuse the couple of bigamy, but he felt that the secular court should do something about the illegal union. He wrote: 'From a religious point of view, there is no doubt that there is no marriage and that the couple incurred the excommunication by communication "in divinis" with the heretic. But is bigamy one of those cases, which are liable to the rigors of the law? If yes, I count that you will arrest as soon as possible the said woman. The scandal is terrible for the population of a good parish.'[50] The other cases involving priests as informants confirmed that they resorted to secular justice only when they were unable to resolve the scandal themselves.[51]

Priests in Quebec seem to have played another important role at bigamy trials, vouching for the moral fibre of their parishioners. When Julie Morin was accused of bigamy in 1880, the local priest testified that 'he did not put any questions to the prisoner before marrying her because she was recognized by the people of St Roch as widow of Robitaille who had been prayed for some years previously as dead in St Roch's Church.'[52] Young Joseph Honoré Leblanc returned from the United States married to his cousin Lucie Tardif; the bishop found out and ordered them to separate. The couple obeyed. Thinking he was entitled to remarry, Leblanc married Eliza Petit Gabin. The court record does not indicate who denounced Leblanc, but the priest who had celebrated the second marriage wrote to the court to explain: 'I knew he had been married, but he was related to the 4th degree, the bishop would have allowed him to contract a second marriage. He never hid the existence of his first wife. According to the Catholic Church, the first marriage was worthless.'[53] These two examples illustrate how members of the Catholic clergy in Quebec never doubted they had the moral authority on the sacrament of marriage. Being responsible for publication of banns, sole keepers of civil records, they felt completely in charge of the institution of marriage. The Nova Scotia bigamy files suggest members of the clergy were routinely called upon to testify whether or not a wedding had taken place; their role seems to be limited as keepers of the record. Family members, however, played a more important role. The involvement of relatives and in-laws in denunciations and testimonies offers evidence of how marriages were the concern of the extended family. In twenty-eight instances it was a family member that denounced the bigamist. Not happy with the choice of his daughter, the father of Octavie Viau accused Alphonse Landa of bigamy only one year after their wedding.[54] Other family members acted more promptly and denounced their new in-laws within a matter of days. In 1883, Nelson Gray did not hesitate to accuse his daughter-in-law of bigamy a mere two weeks after she married his son Adam.[55] Anna Johnson had apparently wed Robert William Rhames in Dublin in 1877 under the name Anna Maria Tottenham. Unfortunately, if there was a case file, it has not survived. An entry in the Montreal prison ledger, census records, newspaper articles and marriage certificates constitutes the only existing documents to shed some light on this peculiar case: on 5 October 1883, Nelson Gray accused his new daughter-in-law of bigamy. The next day, she found herself in a prison cell. The *Montreal Star* wrote about her guilt, while *La Patrie* (Montreal French newspaper) questioned her culpability. A mere four days after her arrest, she decided to change her plea from not guilty to guilty. The judge sentenced her instantly to eighteen months of hard labour. It took less than a week to deal with Anna Maria Johnson's suspected transcontinental bigamy. At the very least, the facts of the case show Johnson did not have a very competent defence attorney; and yet, the most puzzling aspect of the case remains that as soon as Johnson got out of prison, she married Adam Nelson Gray again and under the same name she had in 1883. Data from 1901 indicate that the wealthy lumber merchant, Nelson Gray Sr. perhaps enjoyed considerable authority as patriarch of the family. Living in his household, we find his 67-year-old wife Marjory, 42-year-old son Adam Gray, a widower, two middle-aged daughters, a younger son and a fourteen-year-old granddaughter.[56] The romantic might imagine that the patriarch disapproved of the union of his son Adam with Anna Maria Johnson and used his connections to frame her. In this telling, true love won as the couple married again after she served her eighteen-month sentence. In reality, the records will never allow us to know with certainty if this was the case.

   In Nova Scotia too, informants lost no time in sharing their objections to newly minted unions. Only a few months after her daughter married Frederick Webb, Annabel Wilneff accused her new son-in-law of bigamy.[57] In March 1897, Judge Johnston sentenced the 27-year-old Webb to four years at Dorchester Penitentiary. Wilneff succeeded in separating the couple. Webb did not serve his full sentence, receiving a pardon in January 1898. The prison sentence appears to have served as an informal divorce since, not yet discouraged from matrimony, Webb married Katie Mackenzie in 1901. No one informed the authorities of the oft-married man; perhaps in his new home in Cape Breton nobody knew of his past. On the marriage licence, he simply identified as a bachelor. In these instances, as in the other cases when family members lodged a complaint, there also seemed to be some underlying disapproval of the chosen spouse. Sometimes they succeeded in breaking the union, but other times the will of the couple was stronger. In at least one instance, the motive for denunciation was undoubtedly inheritance.[58] These denunciations by family members indicate how, in Canada during this period, marriage went beyond the union of two individuals – it was also a family affair.

Upholding Marriage

Ginger Frost has argued that bigamists felt they had to go through a marriage ceremony despite the fears of prosecution. Ironically, it was out of respect for the institution of marriage that individuals illegally went through wedding rituals. Analysing the motives of individuals, one sees that marriage could offer social security, emotional well-being or a sense of respectability. Minnie Higgins's statement exposes one of the reasons why some women would commit bigamy. She declared that she had married again 'for the upkeep of my house and children'. She found herself in Halifax jail for only one day. The record does not indicate who laid the complaint, who paid her bail or what happened next.[59] The story of young Mildred McDonald who married Horace Alexander sheds some light on the motive Higgins identified. Two years after they married, Alexander enlisted in the Canadian Expeditionary Forces. A few days after the 1918 armistice, Mildred posed as a spinster and married bachelor Peter S. Smith.[60] At her 1921 bigamy trial, her legitimate husband, who had lodged the complaint, testified that while he was overseas he received a letter informing him she had given birth to a child that he could not have fathered. Alexander confessed that, although he had not informed his wife, from that moment on, he had intended to get a divorce. When she announced the birth of the child, it is very likely that McDonald realized her indiscretions would result in the breakdown of their marriage. The difficulties of raising a child alone and maybe love led her to marry Smith. Alexander's motivation in denouncing his wife was clear; he had to prove bigamy to obtain a divorce. In Nova Scotia in a time when divorces were difficult to obtain, bigamy indictments could prove a useful tool to receive a divorce. Even in Quebec, proving bigamy could get one out of an unhappy union. In 1924, Justice Bruneau annulled a 21-year-old union. Laura Couture discovered her 'husband's' American divorce had not invalidated his first marriage and asked for an annulment.[61]

When Laura Rosenberg married Hiram Davidson in 1902, she thought it was more important to save her honour than to secure a legitimate union. While she was aware that Davidson had a wife and three children in Romania, the case file indicates that it was due to the influence of the family of his pregnant girlfriend that Davidson wed Laura. Laura's family insisted on the marriage even though they were aware of Hiram Davidson's Romanian family. Against this context, it is puzzling that only Laura, his illegitimate wife, was charged with bigamy.[62] The case has parallels with that of Louis Bloom. Bloom (alias Schwartz) sailed for America in 1905, allegedly leaving behind his wife and two children. Shortly after his arrival in Rochester, New York, he married Ethel Lewick. He left her after a few months of conjugal life to settle in Montreal. Lewick discovered that he had a legitimate wife and two children in Russia a few weeks after he left her. When she did, she travelled to Montreal to lodge an allegation of bigamy against him. Upon arrival, she discovered that Bloom had married yet again, this time Ethel Schneider, a mere week earlier. In a society that praised sexual morality, marriage constituted the only sanctioned way to have carnal relations. As newspapers at the time suggested, the 28-year-old blacksmith seems to have promised marriage only to get women into bed.[63]

Marriage as a means to enable sexual relations also emerged at the trial of Clarence de Bellefeuille. De Bellefeuille married Valentine Archambault in 1926 and the four years they lived together produced two children. At his 1934 bigamy trial Mrs De Bellefeuille declared that her husband had thrown her out because he had met a new woman. Eva Goyette lived conjugally with de Bellefeuille for three years before they married. In the trial, the judge reasoned that De Bellefeuille had not intended to commit bigamy. His family had cleverly manipulated him, presenting a death certificate of his legitimate wife to clear the path for his marriage to his lover. The judge reflected: 'Since the accused had cohabited for a long time with Miss Goyette, I do not see why it was necessary or useful for the accused to commit a crime to get the favours of the lady.'[64] Although the three cases are not identical, each offers evidence of couples who appear to have entered matrimony to legitimize sexual relations.

Men and women seemed to hold differing motivations to enter or re-enter matrimony via bigamy. And, questions of morality surfaced, albeit in different ways, for both men and women in discussions about and verdicts on bigamy cases. The marked need for women to find a husband to secure their financial security matched the views implicit in marriage policy and court verdicts. Husbands were expected to provide for their families. That men and women were ready to engage in such a serious offence attests to the pressure they felt to be married. As Marta Danylewycz explains, women had few socially acceptable alternatives in nineteenth- and early-twentieth-century Canada but to get married.[65] On balance, there was a consensus that marriage was morally correct and socially beneficial, even if it meant, for some, taking up a bigamous marriage. Few cases involved bigamy simply for sex or money. Instead, bigamy generally offered a means to enter a supportive marriage when it proved impossible to divorce legally. From this perspective, it becomes difficult to ascertain how many bigamous marriages went undetected or unreported simply because they fulfilled a vital social function.

In sum, the study of bigamy prosecutions in Nova Scotia and Quebec shows that each province – and later unified Canada – conceived of the crime as an attack on the state and its capacity to regulate the family. The state was even more vigilant in times of war as it believed monogamous marriage provided needed stability. The courts saw in marriage a means to protect women and children. In this context, judges showed lenience towards female bigamists who remarried to escape the economic hardships following abandonment by a first husband. Men who reneged their responsibility to provide for their family received harsh punishments. In Quebec, the Catholic clergy felt it had the moral authority on marriage, but the bench did not always side with the clergy. Denunciations by a member of the extended family confirm that marriage was often a family affair. Testimonies attest that women felt a need to marry to secure their future, while others entered bigamous relationships because marriage was the only way to live as a couple. Individuals who committed bigamy showed they felt pressured to live in a marital state. In very few instances were bigamists trying to defraud a spouse or the state, or to get around the rulings of the Church.[66]

Following a 1943 failed bill which aimed to protect illegitimate children of bigamous marriages, the issue of bigamy seemed to recede into the shadows. Members of parliament discussed it in 1954 when reviewing amendments to the criminal code, and the issue emerged again in debates between 1951 and 1967 about reforming divorce law. In 1985, the Law Reform Commission of Canada reiterated the federal government's commitment to monogamous marriage as a fundamental institution of society, deeming bigamy a serious crime.[67] Nonetheless, the limited number of bigamy cases prosecuted in the post-war era combined with the fact that, when prosecuted, bigamists received lighter sentences if any, suggests that already at that time, the functions the state attributed to marriage were changing. As the welfare state assured a minimum of comfort to citizens, as women entered the labour force in greater numbers and became less dependent on male breadwinners and as discussions on reforming divorce laws became more frequent, the idea of everlasting marriage and men providing for their families lost ground.

In every Canadian province but Quebec (the province has had its own civil code since 1774), common law unions (couples that live together in an arrangement akin to marriage, but without an actual ceremony or legal documents) are recognized and as such couples receive the same rights as married people (since marriage is under provincial jurisdiction, the number of years the couple have to live together to qualify for common law status varies between two to three years). Quebec does not grant the same rights to individuals who choose 'de facto unions'.[68] In concrete terms, it means that although partners in 'de facto unions' (called 'common law unions' in the rest of Canada) enjoy some government benefits, they do not have the same 'protections' that married couples enjoy. For one, if they separate, they do not have a right to the division of their property; also, a de facto partner will not inherit from his or her companion unless the will names the said partner. Only in Quebec, because the province has its own civil law, has marriage preserved its exclusive historical functions in ensuring the transmission of wealth and a guarantee of protection. The analysis of prosecuted cases of bigamy in Canada has highlighted how individuals, families, society, religious elites and the courts have ascribed different meanings to marriage. Moreover, it shows that the institution of marriage has not remained static. It changes to adapt to new realities.

Notes

1 'Case of Bigamy. A Woman Has Two Husband', *Montreal Star*, 23 February 1870.
2 Bibliothèque et Archives nationales du Québec (BAnQ) à Montréal, E17, S1, SS1, 1870, #478.
3 Constance Backhouse, '"Pure Patriarchy": Nineteenth Century Canadian Marriage,' *McGill Law Journal* 31 (1986): 312.
4 James Snell, '"The White Life for Two": The Defence of Marriage and Sexual Morality in Canada, 1890-1914,' *Social History* 16, no. 3 (1983): 112.
5 Joanna Sweet, 'Equality, Democracy, Monogamy: Discourses of Canadian Nation Building in the 2010-2011 British Columbia Polygamy Reference', *Canadian Journal of Law and Society* 28, no. 1 (2013): 1–19; Sarah Carter, *The Importance of Being Monogamous. Marriage and Nation Building in Western Canada to 1915* (Edmonton: University of Alberta Press, 2011); Pílar Cuder-Dominguez, 'Negotiations of Gender and Nationhood in Early Canadian Literature,' *International Journal of Canadian Studies* 18 (1998): 115–31; Carolyn Strange and Tina Loo, *Making Good: Law and Moral Regulation in Canada, 1867-1939* (Toronto: University of Toronto Press, 1997), 104–5.
6 Nathalie Zemon Davis, *Le retour de Martin Guerre* (Paris : R. Laffront, 1982).
7 Serge Gagnon, *Mariage et famille au temps de Papineau* (Québec: Presses de L'Université Laval, 1993), 266.
8 http://www.familyhistoryalive.com/Quebec-Vital-Records–Births-Marriages-and-Deaths.html (accessed on 21 September 2014).

9 James Snell, *In the Shadow of the Law. Divorce in Canada* (Toronto: University of Toronto Press,1982), 10–11.
10 Edouard Lefebvre de Bellefeuille, *Code Civil du bas Canada annoté* (Montréal: Beauchemin et Valois,1879).
11 Sylvie Savoie, 'Women's Marital Difficulties: Requests of Separation in New France', *History of the Family* 3, no. 4 (1998): 473–86; Marie-Aimée Cliche, 'Les procès en séparation de corps dans la région de Montréal, 1795-1879', *Revue d'histoire de l'Amérique française*, 49, no. 1 (1995): 71.
12 Christine Hudon, *Prêtres et Fidèles dans le Diocèse de Saint-Hyacinthe* (Québec: Septentrion, 1996), 378.
13 Philip Girard, 'The Supreme Court of Nova Scotia: Confederation to the Twenty First Century', in *The Supreme Court of Nova Scotia, 1754-2004: From Imperial Bastion to Provincial Oracle*, ed. Philip Girard, Jim Phillips and Barry Cahill (Toronto: University of Toronto Press, 2004), 74.
14 Robert Pike, 'Legal Access and the Incidence of Divorce in Canada: A Sociohistorical Analysis', *Canadian Review of Sociology & Anthropology* 12, no. 2 (1975): 114.
15 Martin I. Wilkins, W. A. Henry and James R. Smith, *The Revised Statutes of Nova Scotia*, 2nd Series (Halifax: J. &W. Compton, 1859), 404. None of the officiating ministers in bigamy cases were fined.
16 It is also possible that since many of these cases of bigamy were discovered via prison registries (judicial archives do not have indexes according to crime), cases were not found as frequently for the recent past because the accused never set foot in a prison. This would nevertheless illustrate a change of practice, perhaps even a change of mentality.
17 http://well-being.esdc.gc.ca/misme-iowb/.3ndic.1t.4r@-eng.jsp?iid=78 (accessed 26 July 2013).
18 Jean-François Perrault, *Questions et réponses sur le droit criminel au Bas Canada* (Quebec: C. Lefrançois, 1814), 44–6.
19 The beneficiaries of this privilege have evolved over time: initially only available to clerics, it has come to be applied to anyone who was able to pass a reading test from the Bible.
20 Wilkins, et al., *The Revised Statutes of Nova Scotia*, 446.
21 http://eco.canadiana.ca/view/oocihm.9_08050_2/200?r=0&s=1 (accessed 17 June 2016).
22 https://archive.org/stream/criminalcodevic00canagoog/criminalcodevic00canagoog_djvu.txt (accessed 17 June 2016).
23 Canadian criminal law distinguished between bigamy, the act of marrying again without dissolving the legal ties that bound one spouse to the other, and polygamy (section 293), the act of living conjugally with more than one spouse.
24 John Witte Jr. retraces the origins of this view in his comprehensive study of bigamy and polygamy. See his *The Western Case for Monogamy over Polygamy* (Cambridge: Cambridge University Press, 2015), 369.
25 As Canada opened the definition of marriage at the beginning of the twenty-first century to include same-sex unions, some scholars argued it was an opportunity to legalize polygamy as it would give legitimacy to all the women caught in polygamous unions and desirous to escape their situation. Researchers were particularly thinking about the polygamous Mormon sect living in Bountyful, British Canada. Angela Campbell et al., *Polygamy in Canada: Legal and Social Implications for Women and Children. A Collection of Policy Research Reports* (2015), http://www.crilf.ca/Documents/Polygamy%20in%20Canada%20-%20Nov%202005.pdf (accessed on

21 September 2016). More recently, Lisa M. Kelly proposed that at the very least, the women in existing polygamous unions should have access to relief when the relationship breaks down: 'Bringing International Human Rights Law Home: An Evaluation of Canada's Family Law Treatment of Polygamy', *University of Toronto Faculty of Law Review*, 65, no. 1 (2007): 2.

26 One finds the same pattern in Alberta: Mélanie Méthot, 'Bigamy in the Northern Alberta Judicial District, 1886-1969: A Socially Constructed Crime That Failed to Impose Gender Barriers', *Journal of Family History* 31, no. 3 (2006): 260.
27 'No Excuses for Bigamy', *Globe*, 22 July 1910.
28 'Three Years for Davis, Bigamist', *Montreal Star*, 14 November 1913.
29 'Convicted of Bigamy', *Halifax Chronicle*, 9 July 1894.
30 'Richmond Bigamy Case', *Sherbrook Record*, 12 December 1898. Witte notes: 'Defendants who compounded their crime by stealing marital property, abandoning their minor children or pregnant wife, or leaving massive debts for the abandoned spouse and family to cover generally faced harsher punishments.' 309.
31 '2 ans pour bigamie', *La Patrie*, 10 April 1942.
32 As a measure to limit contested unions, the public nature of banns worked better than licences. Indeed, banns allowed the public to inform the church if the proposed marriage should be prohibited. If no one objected, it meant the community accepted the new union, even if it did not conform to the tenant of the church.
33 'Would Protect 'Enoch Arden' Marital Cases', *Globe and Mail*, 31 March 1943.
34 Senate Debates, 19th Parliament, 4th session, http://parl.canadiana.ca/view/oop.debates_SOC1904_01/169?r=0&s=1 (accessed on 8 September 2015).
35 BAnQOutaouais, TP9, S2, SS1, SSS1 #740, 1951.
36 Data collected at provincial archives in Quebec and Nova Scotia through prison records, judicial court books and proceedings for the period 1800-1960. BAnQ, Prison registries (E17), Court cases and Plumitifs (TP9, TP12 and TL). Nova Scotia Archives and Record Management (NSARM) Record Center Halifax Regional Municipality (RCHRM): Supreme Court cases 1750-1969 (RG39C), Halifax County Court Cases 1895-1933 (RG38C), Divorce cases (RG39D), police magistrate (RG38J), Court of General Sessions of the Peace (RG34 series 312 J1).
37 *Halifax Chronicle*, 23 December 1918.
38 'Court of Criminal Appeal. An Increase in Bigamy', *The Times*, 21 December 1917.
39 The Toronto morality squad was first established in 1887 in order to deal with Sabbath observance, drunks and wife-beaters. Strange and Loo, *Making Good*, 61.
40 The article did not specify where. 'Provincial Police Advised for Military Camp Areas', *Globe and Mail*, 16 October 1940.
41 BAnQMontreal, TP12, SS2, SS29, SSS7.
42 'The Crime of Bigamy', *Globe*, 8 February 1912.
43 'Coupable de bigamie', *Le Canada*, 5 April 1929.
44 'A Jar for Divorce', *Globe*, 6 April 1929. 'Foreign Divorce for Canadian Is Ruled Invalid', *Winnipeg Tribune*, 5 April 1929.
45 See for instance 'Council of Public Instruction', *Globe*, 6 May 1874. 'Judgement Deferred in Windsor Bigamy Case. Question of Validity of Ohio Divorce for the Courts of Canada', *Globe*, 21 March 1916. 'Divorce Followed by Bigamy Charge. Important Legal Question Raised by Montreal Case', *Globe*, 24 September 1930. 'Remarriage Risk Following Divorce', *Globe and Mail*, 16 January 1943. 'Bench's View on Bigamy Supported by Lawyers', *Globe and Mail*, 22 June 1945.
46 'Decision on Divorce is Unexpected Jolt to Ontario Couples', *Globe*, 5 April 1929.

47 We do not know how she arrives at that number, but Ginger S. Frost argues that in nineteenth-century England, 'possibly only 1 in 5 bigamy cases made it to court'. *Living in Sin. Cohabiting as Husband and Wife in Nineteenth-Century England* (Manchester: Manchester University Press, 2008): 73.
48 'Married Too Much', *Halifax Citizen*, 5 and 14 May 5 1870.
49 'Les Époux Carrier accusés de bigamie', *Le Soleil*, 26 August 1915. 'La femme Carrier avait trois maris', *Le Soleil*, 29 September 1915.
50 BAnQQuebec, TP12, S1, SS1, SSS1, Box 189, 1915, 204728-204731, 205348-205355.
51 Mélanie Méthot, 'Le mariage, c'est l'affaire de l'Église: pouvoir d'État et bigamie', *Revue Canadienne de droit et société* 31, no. 2 (2016): 1–21.
52 *Morning Chronicle and Commercial and Shipping Gazette*, 29 April 1880.
53 BAnQMontreal, E17, S1, SS1, 1860 #162 and 1861 #42 et TP9, S2, SS1, SSS1, 1860, s.n.
54 BAnQMontreal, E17, S1, SS1, 1878 #350, Centre de Pré-archivage, 'Landa,' #873.
55 BAnQMontreal, E17, S1, SS1, 1883, #82.
56 BAnQ online, Mariages non-catholiques de la région de Montréal, 1766-1899.
57 NSARM, RG 38, vol.242, A8884, 'Queen vs Webb'.
58 The niece of William Russell first accused his wife, Julie Morin, of bigamy so she could inherit her uncle's fortune instead of his legal wife. When the court found Morin not guilty, the niece contested her uncle's will. LCW Dorion, Queen's Bench Reports (Montreal: Eusebe Senecal & fils, 1882).
59 Library and Archives Canada, RG13, vol.231, file 86-105, 1919.
60 NSARM, Halifax County Court, 1998-019/153, Cause Book 1921-1968. Halifax Supreme Court, RG39 'c' criminal, Box 705, #30 King vs. Alexander'. Https://www.novascotiagenealogy.com (accessed on 24 September 2014).
61 'Court Grants Decree', *Globe*, 31 October 1924.
62 BAnQMontreal, Centre de Pré-archivage, 'Laura Rosenberg,' 1902.
63 'Louis Bloom alias Louis Swartz, Arrested on Vagrancy Charge said to have Three Wives', *Montreal Gazette*, 6 November 1906; 'When I See a Nice Woman I Want to Marry Her', *Montreal Star*, 7 November 1906. BAnQMontreal, E17, S1, SS1, 1906. Centre de Pré-Archivage, 'Louis Bloom', #2714.
64 BAnQMontreal, TP9, S2, SS1, SSS1, 1934, #298, 'Notes et Jugement du Juge Lacroix', 7 November 1934.
65 Marta Danylewycz, *Taking the Veil: An Alternative to Marriage, Motherhood and Spinsterhood in Quebec 1840-1920* (Toronto: McLelland and Stewart, 1987).
66 In 1943, Irene Hornby received a four-year sentence because she married soldiers for their military pensions. BAnQMontreal, TP12, S2, SS29, SSS7, 1943, #3337.
67 Law Reform Commission of Canada (1985), http://www.lareau-law.ca/LRCWP42.pdf (accessed 22 September 2015).
68 http://www.justice.gouv.qc.ca/english/publications/generale/union-a.htm (accessed 18 June 2016).

10

Equality before the Law? The Intermarriage Debate in Post-Nazi Germany

Julia Woesthoff

In 1960, the prominent Catholic journal *Herder Korrespondenz* echoed the concerns of authorities and the broader media when it worriedly reported that marriages between German women and foreign Muslim men 'exceeded one hundred a year'. The Muslim men discussed here – and in the long first decade of the intermarriage discourse that followed – were by and large students and interns from the Middle East (rather than Turkish guestworkers), who had most likely met their German brides-to-be at university or their place of work. These international romantic liaisons were not the only cause for worry about the state of matrimony in Germany, however; the journal also expressed apprehension about the institution of marriage in the Federal Republic more generally.[1] It is hard to find the cause for concern. During the same year, well over 500,000 couples married in Germany; 96 per cent of those marriages occurred between German partners. Indeed, Germany saw a veritable post-war marriage boom in the early 1960s while the divorce rate had dropped almost by half since 1950.[2] The number of marriages between German women and Muslims was negligible, yet it generated major concern.

In raising the alarm about the unions between German Christian women and foreign Muslim men, *Herder Korrespondenz* was in good company, joined by newspapers, popular magazines, bulletins by religious agencies and internal correspondence between a number of state agencies and Christian lay organizations. These sources saw cause for concern that in retrospect seems premature (given the strains on marriage in later years) and exaggerated, given marriage rates in general and intermarriage in particular. Nonetheless, the rhetoric of alarm that circulated among lawmakers, religious leaders and mass media in the 1960s signals the seriousness with which they viewed any changes to marriage because of its presumed centrality for national stability. Rather than dismissing their concerns as misguided, this chapter considers why marriage – and concerns about changes to it – remained so important to Germans during the 1960s and how a variety of groups saw in marriage a way to discipline gender and race at a moment that was paradoxically characterized by new demands for equality. To do so, this chapter will outline the laws that have affected marriage and intermarriage, will detail the strange frenzy over marriage between German Christian women and Muslim men from abroad in the press and then will discuss institutions for assisting women in these relationships. These concerns about instability and intermarriage revealed an unwillingness towards gender equality coupled with racism that was justified in cultural rather than biological terms. Ultimately, an analysis of the discourse around intermarriage expands our understanding of the institution's centrality to post-war German debates about equality, family, citizenship and national community.[3] As Chapter 5 on nineteenth-century debates over marriage, church and the state in Austria also demonstrates, the idea that marriage (and family) were central to national(ist) concerns was neither limited to Germany nor to the twentieth century.

As the intermarriage debate in post-war Germany unfolded, the marital unions between German women and Muslim men were most often labelled as 'marriage to foreigners', 'foreigner marriage' or 'marriage with Muslims'. Early on, the term 'mixed marriage' (*Mischehe*) was also applied – if rarely – and always with clarifying additions, such as 'mixed marriages between Christians and Muslims' or 'the Christian–Muslim mixed marriage'.[4] The term has historically been used in Germany to indicate an inter-confessional or interfaith marriage, also between Catholics and Protestants. However, its explicitly racialized definition during the Third Reich that focused on preventing Christian–Jewish marriages meant that the term has seldom been employed since 1945, unless one is talking about the historically specific circumstances during the Nazi period. By and large, by the mid-1960s, references to 'mixed marriage' in the context of Christian–Muslim unions disappeared. By the early 1970s, women who themselves were married to foreigners, regardless of their confession, and who had started a grass-roots movement to champion their own cause, preferred the term 'binational marriage' (*binationale Ehe*), a term still widely used in Germany in discussions about marriages between Germans and foreigners. No one phrase perfectly represents the unions on which this chapter focuses to indicate that the issue of marital relationships between Muslim men and German Christian women was not exclusively about nationality nor just about religion, however, I am generally using the English term, 'intermarriage'.

The early intermarriage discourse has to be understood in the context of German recovery after the war. In the wake of fascism's defeat, 'family was … important in defining Germanness', as family historian Robert Moeller argued. As the book *Domestic Tensions, National Anxieties: Global Perspectives on Marriage, Crisis and Nation* so incisively shows, the centrality of the institutions of marriage and family to the national project, and the moral panics about 'the nation' that any changes to those institutions could engender, have not been particular to Germany.[5] However, as Moeller maintains, 'Particularly in the Federal Republic, at a moment when a political language of "nation" and "nationalism" was highly problematic, an idealized conception of the family took on enormous significance as a repository of quintessentially German values that had survived the Third Reich'.[6] As such, marriage was at the heart of what Hanna Schissler has called the 'normalization project of the 1950s'.[7] It encompassed 'physical rebuilding, economic recovery and the associated construction of what was perceived as "normal life" in the "private sphere" … accompanied in many quarters by a degree of silence about the recent past'.[8] Officials in the Federal Republic astutely worked to avoid any association with Nazi-era racialized social policy and in the context of the intermarriage debate were quick to assure constituents and each other that racial ideology (understood in biological terms) played no part in the dire warnings they broadcast about the marital unions between German women and their Muslim foreign partners.[9] As Rita Chin and Heide Fehrenbach have noted, however, post-war concepts of cultural difference, while avoiding arguments based on genetic notions of incompatibility, nevertheless justified discrimination on political, legal and economic grounds.[10] This was true for the intermarriage debate as well.

Overall, the years between the late 1950s and the early 1970s, when the issue of intermarriage also became ever more prominent in popular discourse, ushered in profound changes in Germany, variously described in the literature as a period of modernization, liberalization, individualization or democratization.[11] 'In the context of marriage and family planning', however, 'at least the first half of the 1960s was a continuity of the 1950s', as Ute Frevert has argued, so that those years had 'the character of an incubation period'.[12] The simultaneously traditional and liberalizing character of the period is reflected in the legal code's treatment of women. To shore up major support for traditional family values and to ward off any potentially corroding influences, by 1953 the conservative Christian Democratic government under Chancellor Konrad Adenauer established the Federal Ministry of Family Affairs, and its inaugural head, Franz-Josef Wuermeling, became synonymous with conservative family politics. The years-long debate about the implementation of Article 3 ('Equality before the Law') of the constitution is indicative of the conservative climate that prevailed at the time that was certainly also influenced by the intensifying Cold War and the Federal Republic's role in providing a bulwark of stability for the West, not least by reasserting traditional gender norms that seemed to be under threat in the communist east. Those arguing against the tenets of Article 3 believed it to be fundamentally at odds with another tenet of the constitution – the special protection of marriage and family – and its implementation could only spell the demise of the bedrock of society, the nuclear family.[13] Developments towards equality spurred by the experiences of the Second World War were not limited to Western nations at the time, but were part of broader global developments across Asia and Africa as the chapters by Rachel Jean-Baptiste and Lisa Tran in this book reflect as well. Revisions to bring the Civil Code in line with the Basic Law were finally passed in 1957, mostly providing improvements related to the wives' economic standing. For example, joint ownership of property became the norm, and partners were granted the right to administer their own individual wealth. The concept of the 'housewife marriage', however, continued to reflect 'the idea of a "natural functional division" between the sexes': the wife running the household and the husband seeking paid employment outside the home to support his family.[14] This official understanding of marriage remained largely intact until further legal reforms were enacted in the late 1970s.[15] As Christine von Oertzen has argued, however, the institutionalization of part-time work, which began in the early 1960s, needs to be considered a 'specific [form of] modernization of the gender roles' at the time, even if the changes worked within prevalent gender norms rather than challenging them.[16] What has so far not received sufficient attention is how ideas about as well as resistance to race and gender equality intersected in the post-war context, most acutely visible in debates about marriages between German Christian women and foreign Muslim men.

Although women had achieved a modicum of equality in the context of marriages between Germans, the German legal landscape continued to limit women's rights when marrying a foreigner. It is true that by 1957, women had finally officially gained the right to retain their citizenship upon marriage to a foreigner, and similar citizenship law reforms occurred across Europe between the late 1940s and 1960s; naturalization, however, was not a gender-neutral process.[17] While granting German citizenship to foreign women marrying German men became a mere formality the same year the equality statute was passed, the same was not true for foreign men marrying German women.[18] Denied access to German citizenship, it was also exceedingly difficult for foreign husbands to qualify for a residency permit, which meant that the couple had to emigrate to the husband's home country to live together as soon as his studies in Germany were completed. In 1969, the naturalization and citizenship law was revised, so that neither foreign men nor foreign women were able to gain German citizenship automatically upon marriage, though the general process of naturalization was made easier for foreign spouses of either gender, as long as the prospective immigrants met certain conditions, among them assimilation into German culture, including language acquisition and renunciation of their original citizenship.[19]

Yet, gendered differences remained. Until 1975, the children of binational couples only received the father's citizenship, creating major problems for German women in cases of divorce and child custody battles and for the children's future in Germany.[20] And finally, until the early 1970s it was not considered unconstitutional to expel foreign husbands from Germany, even for minor infractions, simply expecting German women to follow their partners abroad. Here as well the foreigner law that governed the husband's life in Germany overrode the precepts of the German constitution supposedly protecting his German wife's rights; the special protection of marriage and the family trumped women's rights because women were meant to follow their husbands in order to maintain the integrity of the family as a unit.[21] What was preserved was a particular understanding of national character, embodied in the institution of family, that apparently neither included foreign non-Christian husbands (who in other legal circumstances could have been considered future German citizens) nor the German women they married.

Marriage and Family in Germany Imperilled?

The debate about marriages between German women and Muslim men happened against the backdrop of debates about the state of marriage in Germany more generally. Despite the outwardly encouraging numbers of marriages and births in the early 1960s, apparent signs of the institution's demise – at least in its idealized version – were discussed at length in the press. One of the concerns was the staggering numbers of so-called *Frühehen* (literally 'early marriages') between teenagers. As Dagmar Herzog has shown, despite official championing of conservative mores, 'between 80 and 90 percent of young people were practicing premarital coitus' and many of these couples experienced unplanned pregnancies. Rather than face the spectre of illegitimacy, many couples married.[22] Moreover, while becoming a wife was still a desirable goal for the vast majority of women, not least because of expanding educational and professional opportunities for married women, they increasingly eschewed becoming a *house*wife. For example, in 1960, the German tabloid *Bild* ran an article with the headline 'Marriage – YES, Housewife – NO,' about a survey conducted by the German Association for Home Economics (Deutsche Gesellschaft für Hauswirtschaft, DGH for short) that showed that 81 per cent of housewives were fed up with housework.[23] According to the paper, housewives portrayed their lives as 'undignified "drudgery"' and considered it a 'slave existence'. Three years after the introduction of the equality statute that seemed to promise parity between the sexes, traditional family structure prevailed, and women were increasingly chafing at the constraints it imposed on them, a fact that was increasingly more difficult to overlook.

Even if people had not themselves felt something amiss with the institution of marriage, they could hardly ignore a flurry of articles on the topic, which seemed to find its crescendo in the summer and fall of 1962. At the time, some of the most popular magazines in Germany reported in a breathlessly urgent fashion on the results of a US- and Europe-wide survey whose authorship was widely attributed to UNESCO, inquiring 'How Happy Are People in Marriage?'[24] While the level of women's dissatisfaction was disheartening across the two continents, the results for Germany were particularly alarming. As *Spiegel* magazine succinctly reported (and bluntly judged) the study's findings: 'While 92 percent of German husbands – in apparent self-delusion [*Selbstverblendung*] – deem their domestic life as "happy," only 19 percent of their wives share their assessment.'[25] *Bunte* reporter Heinrich Kern and his colleague at *Quick* Gerhard Jaeckel respectively characterized the findings as 'shattering' and 'the most devastating statistics I have ever held in my hands'.[26] The results far exceeded the 60 per cent of married women in Europe and the United States who felt 'disappointed, discouraged, discontented and unhappy', as the survey apparently reflected. Moreover, *Spiegel* reported that Germany also occupied the top spot when it came to crimes committed out of jealousy, 'leaving in the dust the classic countries of wild Othellos, Italy and Spain'. Given the reports that frequently circulated in the press about hot-blooded, skirt-chasing Mediterranean guestworkers who tended to temper their sexually fuelled 'hot little rage with cool steel', this was surprising news about German men indeed.[27] The modern post-war incarnation of marriage had apparently become so thoroughly unmoored from any recognizable, time-honoured traditions that it rather resembled, as the *Spiegel* so vividly put it, 'an improvised jam session [between the partners], where it's not even clear who plays what instrument, never mind how and according to which rules'.[28] And *Bunte* lamented: 'Is marriage only a temporary living arrangement, authorized by the state through a piece of paper issued by the marriage registrar? Is nothing left of the concept of marriage but a contract that one can enter into and dissolve whenever one feels like it? Is marriage nothing but a suit to be tossed out when it's worn out?'[29] Solid marriage rates alone were not a robust indicator for the vitality of traditional marriage and family at a time when seeking divorce also lost its stigma, as the media reports suggested. Those reports also identified women's demand for greater equality and freedom as the root cause for the perceived moral upheaval.

Multi-page spreads published in a variety of magazines could not agree, however, on who was to blame for women's growing dissatisfaction and the concomitant threat to traditional family values – the women themselves or their oblivious partners. Among others, the *Spiegel* and the popular women's magazine *Brigitte* seemed to place the onus on women. The former argued that 'the emancipation of women had created more problems than it had solved'.[30] After having too few choices, women now had too many, leaving them perplexed about their 'radically changed role'.[31] On the one hand, the 'new hedonism' propounded by the media engendered an incredible 'enthusiasm for marriage [Ehefreudigkeit]'; on the other hand, it created expectations that marriage could no longer fulfil. The popular women's magazine *Brigitte* extensively discussed the changing nature of marriage and gender roles within its pages and reported that 'The Young Angry Women', as one of the articles on the topic was titled, felt 'deprived, neglected, withered' in their role as housewives.[32] The magazine, here still staunchly supporting an ideology of gender difference, dismissed complaints as simply wanting too much: 'We make demands on life that cannot be fulfilled and behave like children, who ask their mother to buy up the entire candy store.' The sooner women realized it, the sooner 'they would be able to enjoy once more what they once thought was the good fortune in marriage, and what in truth is good fortune: life with their family'.[33] Another article in the magazine pointedly stated that the marital relationship had to be nourished and that, according to the article's author, 'was the wife's responsibility'.[34]

The greatest problem was the perceived levelling of gender differences that – various observers noted at the time – were principally caused by women working outside the home. A *Brigitte* interview with a lawyer on the issue of divorce in no uncertain terms identified working women as the 'greatest danger to modern marriage'.[35] Specifically, professional women 'were as determined and self-confident at home as they were at work'. In those marriages, the lawyer argued, 'no one quite knows who wears the pants' in the family. Quoting a psychologist, the *Spiegel* also warned that gender roles might no longer be merely blurred but reversed, causing further confusion and insecurities.[36] There were, however, signs of hope. As a marriage counsellor asserted in an article, the next generation was adjusting well to the lack of a patriarchal family structure, since 'Pasha[s] practically don't exist anymore'.[37] The assessment reflected both a popular, if unselfconscious, orientalist perspective on male chauvinist behaviour and at the same time a distancing from it – a perspective that also informed the intermarriage debate discussed later in this chapter. This attitude furthermore expressed an overly optimistic assessment of the state of gender relations at the time, as some publications were quick to point out.

Reports in *Quick* and *Bunte* explicitly blamed men for the marriage crisis. *Bunte* denounced the persistent double standard, castigating men for not seeing anything wrong with maintaining affairs, which they excused with their natural sex drives that apparently did not 'allow them to be satisfied with one woman'.[38] *Quick*, whose journalist had supplemented the survey results with his own research at the office of a divorce lawyer, reported that wives complained that their husbands cheated and lied, despised and humiliated them. Husbands failed to provide a sense of security and wallowed in self-pity about the challenges they faced at work.[39] And while women's ideal image of a husband was unattainable (he should be both soft and strong, kind and stern, grown-up yet playful), the magazine maintained that women had compromised so much that they had given up on chivalry, courtesy and even manliness itself.[40]

As a result, German women were apparently losing interest in German men. As *Bunte* informed its readers: 'Marriage scandals are increasing. Adultery and marriage deception [*Ehebetrug*] are the order of the day. Therefore, hundreds of young girls are seeking their happiness in foreign lands. They marry foreigners and move to their new home [*Heimat*]. But does marriage fare better there than here? Or is somewhere else merely different?'[41] And that seemed to be the crux of the matter. The growing educational and professional opportunities for women in the post-war period also meant, in the eyes of the concerned observers, that they had greater opportunities for meeting – and marrying – foreign men. This, however, was no solution to the perceived marriage crisis in Germany. Given the tenor of the discourse surrounding it, rather than seeing it as a viable alternative, intermarriage, particularly between German women and Muslim foreigners, was presented as a rejection of marriage to a German man and by extension an abandonment of the German community and identity in favour of a new *Heimat* – an understanding actively nurtured by the state.

Pathologizing Marriage to Muslim Men

On the one hand, the German government worked hard to buttress a particular form of marriage and family while also seemingly expanding its vision of the institution. The state passed a series of policies enticing couples to have more babies while also making it more difficult to get a divorce.[42] And it was not just the conservative CDU government bolstered by clerical voices that championed traditional values. In its 1959 Godesberg programme, the left-leaning SPD 'expressed a clear commitment to protect the family and to remain vigilant in pursuing social policies that would prevent "mothers of preschool- and school-aged children from being forced to seek paid employment for economic reasons"'.[43] Furthermore, by 1957, foreign women marrying German men were able to all but automatically become German citizens. On the other hand, opening up citizenship in this way was largely informed by a particular understanding of the gendered nature of cultural difference, so that facilitating the naturalization of foreign wives reinforced rather than re-envisioned traditional understandings of the institution of marriage – in patriarchal as well as cultural terms. The incredible ease with which foreign wives were able to gain citizenship compared to the incredible difficulty foreign husbands faced when trying to qualify for a residency permit, never mind citizenship, were two sides of the same ideological coin. As Karen Schönwälder has pointed out, 'the parliamentary Committee on Internal Affairs deemed equality unnecessary' when considering the diverse rights to citizenship for foreign husbands and wives. The Federal Administrative Court upheld this view in its 1965 ruling, which did not even consider the matter in 'conflict with the equality statute of the Basic Law'.[44] As one of the department heads of the Federal Ministry of the Interior explained, 'according to life experience, there is a much greater chance that the foreign wife will adjust to the German living conditions as represented by her German husband than that the foreign husband would [adapt] if the roles were reversed'.[45] Cultural assumptions therefore affected legal strictures.

They also served to justify negative attitudes about intermarriage between German women and foreign men without acknowledging that German women's precarious position was severely aggravated by the law. Instead, those advocating against German women marrying foreign men faulted those women's character rather than state policy for problems, if not tragedies, the women might encounter abroad. The debate surrounding intermarriage, by focusing on cultural arguments rather than legal hurdles, displaced the responsibility for the problem both onto German women and their foreign partners and away from the state. Underlying these attitudes was a paradox: women were considered the anchor of the family, so making sure they stay 'German' both culturally and legally was key; yet this was only possible if their husbands were German because wives followed the culture (let alone the citizenship and place of residence) of their husbands. This also explains why marriage between German men and foreign women did not elicit any concerns.

The post-war intermarriage debate gathered steam in the years leading up to the 1960s. As a result of an educational aid programme for Third World countries, by 1958 around 4,500 Asian and African students attended West German universities.[46] That number grew in the early 1960s, though it remained tiny in comparison to the number of guestworkers arriving around the same time. For example, in 1962, 711,500 foreigners worked in West Germany, among them 18,600 Turks, accounting for around 2.6 per cent of the foreign work force.[47] In comparison, by winter semester 1961/62, approximately 7,400 students from Africa and the Middle East attended German universities.[48] It was the presence of this group of foreigners – rather than the quickly swelling ranks of guestworkers – that set the intermarriage debate in motion. To a certain extent, living arrangements and national origin can help explain state and church officials' seemingly disproportionate concern about German women marrying Muslim men and Muslim students in particular. In the early 1960s, the number of Turks in Germany was still comparatively small; most guestworkers at the time were southern Europeans. Moreover, guestworkers lived rather circumscribed lives that afforded fewer opportunities to forge relationships with German women. They worked primarily in male-dominated sectors of the economy, such as the iron and metal industry as well as construction, and the vast majority of them stayed in dormitory-style living quarters.[49] In contrast, foreign students often sought and secured private housing, and the university environment facilitated mingling with German peers. Many German commentators thus viewed Muslim students as more likely potential spouses for German women, and hence more threatening. Indeed, the very fact that male Muslim students shared campus environs and that they had respectable educational, financial and career aspirations threatened to make these Muslim men seem attractive to young German women as prospective husbands. At the time *Herder Korrespondenz* expressed its concerns about a hundred marriages between German women and Muslim men, those unions made up a very small fraction of the total of 15,600 marriages between German women and foreign men that year (and an even smaller fraction of the more than half a million German couples). By 1966, a little more than 11 per cent of all intermarriages in Germany occurred between a German woman and a man from Africa or Asia out of a total of 18,102 binational weddings between German women and foreign men that year.[50] Americans were by far the preferred wedding partners at the time, accounting for over 30 per cent of foreign grooms marrying German brides in 1966, followed by Italians, accounting for over 15 per cent of foreign grooms in intermarriages.[51] As these statistics show, the journal's concerns were already voiced *before* the number of marriages between German women and Asian and African men rose appreciably, though their numbers remained small in comparison to marriages with men of other nationalities.

Instrumental in shaping the debate about marrying foreigners were the Christian charitable organizations, the principal state-sanctioned institutions offering counselling for prospective emigrants, including women who were considering marriage to a foreigner. Especially prominent among them were the Department of Migration of the Protestant Diakonie and the Catholic association St Raphaels-Verein (later renamed Raphaels-Werk). These institutions already had a long history of aiding foreigners in Germany and Germans planning to go abroad, reaching back to the mid- to late nineteenth century. The organizations served as liaisons between state authorities and the public, including individuals seeking information and advice about marriage between Germans and non-Germans. The state was represented by the Office of Emigration within the Federal Administration Office (Bundesverwaltungsamt – Amt für Auswanderung; hereafter BVA–AfA), which provided a variety of educational materials, including bulletins that contained examples of Muslim marriage contracts and information about legal requirements for citizenship in various African and Asian countries with the express purpose to provide this information to German women – and ideally, prevent these binational unions. The BVA–AfA also distributed updates on policy and judicial decisions, newspaper articles on intermarriage, and accounts received from people who lived or had lived in the Middle East, usually with an emphasis on the problematic living conditions facing prospective German brides abroad.[52] By 1961, the Federal Administrative Office for the first time published the supplement 'Muslim Marriage Contracts' in its *Bulletin for People Working Abroad and for Emigrants: Women's Emigration*. They also disseminated didactic material that went beyond strictly legal guidance to offer advice about what German women could expect if they married Muslim men. Protestant and Catholic organizations kept each other apprised of their efforts with regard to educating the public about Christian–Muslim marriages. They exchanged their materials on intermarriage and disseminated each other's pamphlets and brochures to interested parties. They also made strenuous efforts – and often succeeded – in disseminating their information via the media, so that many articles on the topic included interviews with counsellors, printed excerpts of advice literature if not entire letters and tracts supplied by the organizations.

By 1959 the issue of unions between German Christian women and Muslim foreigners was considered increasingly pressing, as reflected in the meeting agenda of the Coordinated Working Committee on Foreigner Issues within the Office of Foreign Affairs of the Protestant Church in Germany (Koordinierter Arbeitskreis über Ausländerfragen im Kirchlichen Außenamt) in June of that year. The committee discussed a variety of problems related to intermarriages between German women and foreign students, noting in particular a lack of resources available to provide proper guidance for the women and their parents to make informed decisions.[53] Apparently, delegating the work to the confessional emigration counselling offices was not a foregone conclusion. As Bernhard Le Coutre of the Department of Emigration of the Protestant Diakonisches Werk noted, 'It stands to reason that a girl who wants to marry a foreign student in Germany does not consider herself a [potential] emigrant'.[54] Initially, it looked like the Internationaler Sozialdienst (International Social Service) might take on the task of advising German women. Within a year, however, Protestant and Catholic offices of emigration counselling became the only agencies authorized to dispense advice on intermarriage, also due to their long-standing history of providing advice to prospective emigrants.[55] The fact that the binational couples might want to stay in Germany but that it was nigh impossible for them to do so legally if the husband was a foreigner was not brought up again until the 1970s. Instead, it was the perceived deficiencies of either partner as well as their inherent incompatibility that led the experts to focus squarely on trying to dissuade women from their plans to marry foreign men.

The literature and correspondence of the 1960s (and beyond) produced by various agencies and officials who had taken up the issue of intermarriage depicted Muslim men in terms similar to those used for European Christian guestworkers from Mediterranean countries: hot-blooded, virile and gallant, with a violent streak. They acknowledged that Muslim men were (at least initially) 'exceptionally polite', 'considerate', 'generous' and exuded an 'exotic charm'.[56] In this way, they were not nearly as 'prosaic', 'matter of fact' or 'sober' as the Central European man.[57] However, they only *appeared* ideal. Experts and news reports repeatedly argued that 'Orientals' had an extraordinary ability to adjust to life in Europe, but the adjustment was only superficial. As an official in charge of women's emigration told a newspaper, 'The Orientals are very adaptable. Their different mentality usually is not noticeable when they live here.'[58] That, however, was the problem.[59] What under different circumstances could have been considered positive attributes – the ready ability to adapt to life in Germany – was viewed as highly problematic in the context of the intermarriage debate, because the law necessitated emigration to the husband's home country. In his home country, the husband would revert to his backward ways. The trope of the violent Muslim husband dominated in accounts of intermarriage in the Middle East, such that religious devotion came to be considered a predictor of violent, oppressive behaviour condoned by Muslim society at large. Some commentators conceded that life in 'Oriental' culture could vary politically and economically, yet they were nearly unanimous in their belief that two factors of Muslim culture exhibited an 'unvarying capacity to persist … : Religion and the clan, Islam and family ties'. It followed that 'the status of women and family remains fundamentally Islamic-Orientalist, even if the Oriental has studied in Europe and is trying to live a European way of life.'[60] His German wife had no choice but to surrender to these circumstances if she wanted to have any hope of making the marriage work, though experts judged even the most strenuous efforts most likely futile. This argument was repeated throughout the advice literature, asserting that cultural difference – including the violent treatment of women – could not be overcome, no matter how much Muslim men otherwise adapted to a European lifestyle while living in Germany. Rather, Muslim men were intrinsically 'Oriental' and their views on women, violence and marriage were inextricably connected and unchanging.[61]

Ultimately, however, the experts maintained that the women themselves were to blame if they ended up in an untenable position. As Gerhard Stratenwerth from the Office of Foreign Affairs of the Protestant Church in Germany argued, for example, 'The blame is not with the husband but with the girl who did not want to see what awaited her: She thought she could remain a European, and she assumed that her husband during his stay on our continent had equally become European.'[62] Not only was a woman's naiveté responsible for her own misfortune, she had also brought it upon herself through her daring behaviour, showing no 'inner restraint towards strangers'.[63] Worse, not only did they welcome foreigners' advances, but they also initiated the contact themselves.[64] Ruth Braun, head of the Wurttemberg Association of the Friends of Young Girls *(Württembergischer Landesverein der Freundinnen junger Mädchen)*, a prominent voice in the early debate, argued that foreign men 'would soon recognize how to behave, based on the attitude of the German girl. So it is due to the[ir] wrong behaviour and the girls' ideas drawn from magazines if annually a few hundred women marry and move to the Orient'.[65]

The individuals who led these organizations considered themselves German women's advocates, the would-be brides' protectors against the misery that women would surely face abroad. Walter Dambacher declared in a letter to colleagues that a woman who still chose an 'Oriental' after all the information she was provided by the confessional emigration agencies was 'afflicted with superhuman stupidity, then nothing can be done about it'. His outburst spoke of the level of frustration and concern there was for the women that these agencies attempted to assist. The possibility of directing his frustration towards lawmakers did not occur to him and his colleagues until much later. To Dambacher, the idea of Muslim husbands as heads of family in Germany was outside the realm of what could be envisioned in the country.[66] Equally preposterous was the idea of Islam as part of multireligious Germany. Instead, emigration experts tried to enlist the media to reinforce the message that unions between German women and foreign Muslim men posed a danger to German women.

As Ruth Braun's comment above indicates, those working to spread the word about these unions feared that the news media painted too rosy a picture of the phenomenon, which only motivated women further to seek out relationships with foreigners. The goal of these organizations, therefore, became informing media outlets so that they would impart the insights gathered by the various organizations. In this, they had some success. Hardly anyone drew as explicitly on the advice material as *Bunte* when it published its 10-part series 'Till Death Do You Part: Love and Marriage in Our Time'. Two entire instalments of the series represented a reader's digest of the reams of material the Christian organizations employed to deter German women from relationships with Oriental foreigners throughout the 1960s and early 1970s.[67] Even if they did not explicitly reference counselling materials, the press had a hard time resisting the tragically lurid stories of women in the Orient. The popular magazine *Stern* presented a particularly forceful example of that form of narrative, publishing a 15-part series between 9 July and 15 October 1961 titled 'The Bride has Done Her Duty'. It provided glimpses into the lives of four women who had met and married an 'Oriental'. Despite the foreign partners' varied backgrounds (both socially and geographically), the outcome of the relationship was always a version of the same theme. The Oriental husband who was rich, or had posed as being rich, was always loving and caring in the beginning and was later exposed as a selfish individual, who was either physically harming his wife or forcing her to live under untenable (i.e. uncivilized) conditions. In each instant, if the husband became violent, then his actions were explained with the fact that he was a Muslim. Each story was a vivid reminder that tragedy was the only outcome. However, each story told in the press also neglected to question the fact that women who wanted to stay with their partners had to follow them back to their home country.

By the early 1970s, the focus turned towards those intermarriage couples who lived or wanted to live in Germany but found it difficult to do so legally. Women in such relationships had started to speak up and organize themselves to address the injustices they as German citizens suffered because they were married to foreigners. They vigorously denounced the fact that they were denied the basic right of protection of marriage and family because they had chosen to marry a third-country national. Their activism effected legal changes, some of which were already underway due to the state's attempt to deal with the growing presence of guestworkers and their dependents within Germany's borders. The growing plurality of voices from the early 1970s onwards, the concomitant shift in focus towards Germany and the enactment of legal reforms initially raised hope for broader acceptance of intermarriage. However, in what other scholars have identified as growing concern about 'Re-Islamicization' from the early 1970s onwards, well-worn tropes about Muslim religion and culture continued to inform discussions that focused increasingly on Turks *qua* Muslims, whose popularity as foreign male spouses of German women slowly rose over the years.[68] By the new millennium, Turkish men led the list of most favourite husbands.

Even as the husbands from third countries gained a modicum of legal rights by the 1970s, such as a three-year residency permit upon marriage to a German spouse, those unions came increasingly under suspicion. Against the backdrop of growing numbers of guestworkers and their families settling in Germany and the rapidly rising numbers of asylum seekers, by the 1980s, binational unions were no longer merely deemed culturally questionable as they had been in the past, but they were now also considered legally suspect. State agents, political leaders and the press came to see those marriages primarily as a way for foreigners to gain residency status in Germany. What is reflected in these assumptions is a particular conception of state and family already in place at least since the post-war years.

Conclusion

Viewed in tandem, the debates about marriage and intermarriage reveal a number of important insights, not least about the limitations of equality in post-war Germany. While women's greater rights in marriage, in the workplace and in education were openly discussed in the marriage discourse – at times identified as causing more problems, at times championed as the right step forward – discussions of women's rights in the intermarriage debate were limited to pointing out that they did not exist in the husband's home country. An exploration of the legal landscape affecting women married to foreigners reveals, however, just how limited gender equality also was in Germany, last not least in the definition of national belonging. While women no longer lost their citizenship upon marriage to a foreigner, their citizenship in the 1960s was still contingent upon marriage instead of intrinsic to the relationship between self and state. The discourse on intermarriage further reflected how race and gender were mutually constitutive. Foreign wives were considered suitable citizens who followed their husbands' social and cultural cues. Foreign husbands, on the other hand, especially if they came from Muslim countries, could not be trusted to do the same. Instead, their supposedly remarkable ability to adopt European values was at best considered a transformation that could not last, despite their best intentions; at worst, it was considered a masquerade. These culturally racist assessments led observers to conclude that Muslim husbands could not be trusted to become dependable members of German society.

When considering the dual marriage debate, the timing is certainly crucial: less than two decades after the Second World War, the normalization project central to post-war recovery was barely completed and further change was on the horizon. The state at the time vigorously propagated population growth within the framework of the classic family (as long as the husband was German), making divorce more difficult while inciting couples to produce abundant offspring. The state's actions reflected very real concerns about the changes occurring in society. The media fed the sense of deep unease seconding the message that the moral fabric of society seemed to be fraying dangerously; so dangerously that it had the potential to unravel an orderly life if not civilization itself. According to *Spiegel*, couples were 'abandoned and left to their own devices', so that they had to 'construct an individual, elastic existence to persevere in the urban jungle'.[69] *Quick*, in a more hysteric pitch, reported that women in particular had the sense that they 'wasted their lives fighting a ruthless, senseless jungle war'.[70]

That a small, if growing, minority of German women wanted to create families with foreign non-Christian men, however, seemed anathema to officials, contributing to the chaos rather than providing a worthwhile alternative; intermarriage was outside the envisioned parameters for the German nation. While the concern for women emigrating to the Middle East and beyond was real, the debate also reflected the limits of how the 'bulwark of our civilization, marriage' could be envisioned in the national context, betraying gendered and racialized hierarchies of difference along the way.[71] Foreign wives were readily accepted to join the national fold, foreign husbands were not. But the limits also extended to German citizens. By 1957, the state had eliminated the most egregious law reflecting gender difference, allowing German women to keep their citizenship even if they did marry a foreigner. In reality, however, the lives of German women marrying a foreigner were governed by the foreigner law, trumping essential German rights, chief among them equality before the law as well as the special protection of marriage and family. Tellingly, rather than criticize the legal framework that made it all but impossible for German women and their husbands to stay in Germany (and that prevented German women from taking advantage of German legislation to propagate traditional family values), the discourse focused on dissuading women from entering into binational relationships, employing a form of cultural racism that inflected the intermarriage debate (and the debate about Muslim foreigners in Germany more generally) for decades to come. The discourse, in faulting women and their partners for the problems they faced, inadvertently spoke about what a normal post-war state was supposed to look like.

As other scholars have already pointed out, the state's vision of post-war normality was fundamentally based on idealized if never realized gender norms: the centrepiece of the nation – the nuclear family – included homebound wives and mothers and financially supportive husbands and fathers. That vision was challenged from the 1950s onwards, and gender roles underwent tremendous changes over the next decades. As the discussion of the intermarriage debate at the time makes clear, though, and as recent work by Friedrich Kießling, Bernhard Rieger and others has also shown, we cannot overlook the continuities that persisted as well, which were a constitutive part of the modernizing, democratizing state.[72] Particular visions of race and gender relations guided policymakers and emigration experts that reflected the inability to envision the central institution of marriage as a union between German women and foreign men, a union that was within the borders of the German state. Those notions were not challenged until the 1970s, and they remain highly contested to this day.

Notes

1 'Mischehen zwischen Christen und Muslimen', *Herder Korrespondenz* 14, no. 4 (January 1960): 150–2.
2 Barbara Müller-Dincu, 'Gemischt-nationale Ehen zwischen Frauen und Ausländern in der Bundesrepublik: Eine familiensoziologische Analyse ihrer Situation und Problematik', *Materialien zur Bevölkerungswissenschaft* no. 22 (1981): 25; Renate Künzel, 'The Federal Republic of Germany', in *Divorce in Europe*, ed. Robert Chester (Leiden: Martinus Nijhoff Social Sciences Division, 1977), 186. See also Christiane Kuller, 'Einführung: Krisendebatten um Ehe und Familie in den 1960er Jahren', in *Religion und Lebensführung im Umbruch der langen 1960er Jahre*, ed. Claudia Lepp, Harry Oelke and Detlef Pollak (Göttingen: Vandenhoeck & Ruprecht, 2016), 205–11.
3 See, for example, Robert Moeller, *Protecting Motherhood: Women and the Family in the Politics of Postwar West Germany* (Berkeley: University of California Press, 1993); Hanna Schissler (ed.), *The Miracle Years: A Cultural History of West Germany, 1949-1968* (Princeton: Princeton University Press, 2001); Eli Nathans, *The Politics of Citizenship in Germany* (New York: Berg, 2004); Geoff Eley and Jan Palmowski (eds), *Citizenship and National Identity in Twentieth-Century Germany* (Stanford: Stanford University Press, 2008); Rita Chin, Heide Fehrenbach, Geoff Eley and Atina Grossmann (eds), *After the Nazi Racial State* (Ann Arbor: University of Michigan Press, 2009).
4 See 'Mischehen zwischen Christen und Muslimen', *Herder Korrespondenz* 14, no. 4 (January 1960): 150–2; Orientdienst, *Die christlich-islamische Mischehe* [1963], n.p.
5 Kristin Celello and Janan Kholoussy (eds), *Domestic Tensions, National Anxieties: Global Perspectives on Marriage, Crisis and Nation* (Oxford: Oxford University Press, 2016).
6 Robert Moeller, 'The Elephant in the Living Room: Or Why the History of Twentieth Century Germany Should Be a Family Affair', in *Gendering Modern German History:*

Rewriting Historiography, ed. Karen Hagemann and Jean H. Quataert (New York: Berghahn, 2007), 237–8.
7   Hanna Schissler, '"Normalization" as Project: Some Thoughts on Gender Relations in West Germany during the 1950s', in *The Miracle Years*, 366.
8   Mary Fulbrook, 'The Concept of "Normalisation" and the GDR in Comparative Perspective', in *Power and Society in the GDR, 1961-1979*, ed. Mary Fulbrook (New York: Berghahn, 2013), 5.
9   See Gerhard Stratenwerth, 'Ergebnisse einer Ausländerkonferenz', in *Heirat mit Ausländern*, ed. Norbert Zimmer (Hofheim/Ts.: Verlag des Auslands-Kurier, 1968), 61.
10 Rita Chin and Heide Fehrenbach, 'Introduction', in *After the Nazi Racial State*, 29.
11 See, for example, Axel Schildt, Detlef Siegfried and Karl Christian Lammers, *Dynamische Zeiten: die 60er Jahre in den beiden deutschen Gesellschaften* (Hamburg: Hans Christians Verlag, 2000); Ulrich Herbert, *Wandlungsprozesse in Westdeutschland: Belastung, Integration, Liberalisierung, 1945-1980* (Göttingen: Wallstein Verlag, 2002); Matthias Frese, Julia Paulus and Karl Teppe (eds), *Demokratisierung und gesellschaftlicher Aufbruch: die sechziger Jahre als Wendezeit der Bundesrepublik* (Paderborn: Ferdinand Schöningh, 2003); Friedrich Kießling and Bernhard Rieger (eds), *Mit dem Wandel leben: Neuorientierung und Tradition in der Bundesrepublik der 1950er und 60er Jahre* (Cologne: Böhlau Verlag, 2011).
12 Ute Frevert, 'Umbruch der Geschlechterverhältnisse? Die 60er Jahre als geschlechterpolitischer Experimentierraum', in *Dynamische Zeiten*, 651.
13 Sabine Dreßler, 'Bedrohung oder Fundament der Ehe? Gleichberechtigung im politisch-rechtlichen Diskurs und in Eheratgebern der 1950er Jahre', in *In Liebe verbunden: Zweierbeziehunge und Elternschaft In populären Ratgebern von den 1950ern bis heute*, ed. Sylka Scholz, Karl Lenz and Sabine Dressler (Bielefeld: Transcript Verlag, 2013), 99–126.
14 Ute Frevert, *Women in German History: From Bourgeois Emancipation to Sexual Liberation* (Providence: Berg Publishers, 1989), 281, 282.
15 See, for example, Ute Frevert, *Women in German History: From Bourgeois Emancipation to Sexual Liberation* (New York: St. Martin's Press, 1989), 253–86; Eva Kolinsky, *Women in West Germany* (New York: St. Martin's Press, 1989), 41–74; Moeller, *Protecting Motherhood*; Elizabeth Heineman, *What Difference Does a Husband Make?: Women and Marital Status in Nazi and Postwar Germany* (Berkeley: University of California Press, 1999), 137–75; Dagmar Herzog, *Sex After Fascism: Memory and Morality in Twentieth-Century Germany* (Princeton: Princeton University Press, 2005), 101–40; Robert Moeller, 'The Elephant in the Living Room: Or Why the History of Twentieth Century Germany Should Be a Family Affair', in *Gendering Modern German History: Rewriting Historiography*, ed. Karen Hagemann and Jean H. Quataert (New York: Berghahn, 2007), 237–8.
16 Christine von Oertzen, 'Teilzeitartbeit für die "moderne" Ehefrau: Gesellschaftlicher Wandel und geschlechtsspezifische Arbeitsteilung in den 1960er Jahren', in *Demokratisierung und gesellschaftlicher Aufbruch: Die sechziger Jahre als Wendezeit der Bundesrepublik*, ed. Matthias Frese, Julia Paulus and Karl Teppe (Paderborn: Ferdinand Schöningh, 2003), 64.
17 See, for example, Joachim Stern and Gerd Valchars, 'EUDO Citizenship Observatory, Country Report: Austria', September 2013, 10; Ricky van Oers, Betty de Hart and Kees Groenendijk, 'EUDO Citizenship Observatory, Country Report: Netherlands', January 2013, 8f; Alberto Achermann et al., 'EUDO Citizenship Observatory, Country Report: Switzerland', June 2013, 9; Caroline Sawyer and Helena Wray,

'EUDO Citizenship Observatory, Country Report: United Kingdom', December 2014, 22; all published at www.eudo-citizenship.eu/country-profiles.
18 Nathans, *The Politics of Citizenship in Germany* 239; Karen Schönwälder, *Einwanderung und ethnische Pluralität* (Essen: Klartext, 2001), 516.
19 See Eisfeld, *Die Scheinehe*, 221f; see also, Schönwälder, *Einwanderung*, 516f; and Nathans, *The Politics of Citizenship*, 239; Helmut Broll, 'Die Einbürgerung ausländischer Ehegatten deutscher Staatsangehöriger', *Neue juristische Wochenschrift* 22 (1969): 1520f.
20 See Schönwälder, *Einwanderung*, 521.
21 Ibid., 519–21.
22 Dagmar Herzog, 'Between Coitus and Commodification: Young West German Women and the Impact of the Pill', in *Between Marx and Coca-Cola: Youth Cultures in Changing European Societies, 1960-1980*, ed. Axel Schildt and Detlef Siegfried (New York: Berghahn, 2006), 265, 268.
23 Alfred Weber, 'Heiraten – JA, Hausfrau – NEIN', *Bild*, 17 October 1960.
24 Extensive research, including inquiries to various UNESCO and UN archives, did not yield verification that the UNESCO ever actually conducted or published such a survey. However, given that some of the most popular magazines and newspapers at the time reported on its findings, the readership had no reason to question either the provenance of the study or its findings and therefore had no reason to question its authenticity, never mind its existence. Among the publications discussing the survey was 'Changing Pattern of German Marriages', *The Times*, 16 April 1959; 'Ehe: Galeere des Glücks', *Spiegel*, no. 27, 4 July 1962, 25; and Heinrich Kern, 'Bis dass der Tod euch scheidet: Liebe und Ehe in unserer Zeit (2)', *Bunte Illustrierte/Münchner Illustrierte*, no. 32, 8 August 1962, 39; Gerhard Jaeckel, 'Die deutschen Frauen sind nicht glücklich', *Quick*, no. 37, 16 September 1962, 36.
25 'Ehe', *Spiegel*, 25.
26 Jaeckel, 'Die deutschen Frauen', 36.
27 K. J. Schröder, 'Bei Luigi sitzt das Messer locker', *Weser Kurier*, 1 August 1964.
28 'Ehe', *Spiegel*, 34.
29 Kern, 'Bis dass der Tod euch scheidet (2)', 39.
30 'Ehe', *Spiegel*, 24.
31 Ibid., 27.
32 Ingrid Peters, 'Die zornigen jungen Frauen', *Brigitte*, no. 15, 1961, 75.
33 See Dora Horvath, *Bitte recht weiblich! Frauenleitbilder in der deutschen Zeitschrift Brigitte 1949-1982* (Zürich: Chronos, 2000).
34 'Zu zweit und doch allein', *Brigitte*, no. 10, 1960, 47.
35 'Verlobt, verheiratet, geschieden – warum?' *Brigitte*, no. 18, 1963, 64.
36 'Ehe', *Spiegel*, 27.
37 Ibid., 38.
38 Kern, 'Bis dass der Tod (2)', 44.
39 Jaeckel, 'Unsere Frauen', 36.
40 Ibid., 37–8.
41 Kern, 'Bis dass der Tod (1)', 43.
42 Herzog, *Sex after Fascism*, 118.
43 Moeller, *Protecting Motherhood*, 220.
44 Schönwälder, *Einwanderung*, 69 n, 516.
45 Bundesministerium des Innern (Dr. Lechner) an den Vorsitzenden des Innenausschusses des Deutschen Bundestags, 2 February 1968 (Ausschußdrucksache

Nr. 56 vom 6 February 1968), in: Archiv der sozialen Demokratie (AdsD), SPD Bundesfraktion, 5. Wahlperiode, Arbeitskreis Rechtswesen, Akte 1242, quoted in Schönwälder, *Einwanderung*, 70 n, 516.

46 See Heide-Irene Schmidt, 'Pushed to the Front: The Foreign Assistance Policy of the Federal Republic of Germany, 1958-1971', *Contemporary European History* 12, no. 4 (2003): n 104, 487; see also Karin Adelmann, '40 Jahre DSE: Von der Entkolonisierung zur Personellen Zusammenarbeit', *E+Z – Entwicklung und Zusammenarbeit*, no. 7/8 (Juli/August 1999): 206–11.

47 Ulrich Herbert, *Geschichte der Ausländerpolitik in Deutschland: Saisonarbeiter, Zwangsarbeiter, Gastarbeiter, Flüchtlinge* (München: C. H. Beck, 2001), 198.

48 See Auslandsstelle des Deutschen Bundesstudentenringes, *Das Studium der Ausländer in der Bundesrepublik* (Bonn: Auslandsstelle des Deutschen Bundesstudentenringes, 1963), Vorwort, 16.

49 Ulrich Herbert, *A History of Foreign Labor in Germany, 1880-1980.* (Ann Arbor: University of Ann Arbor Press, 1990), 230.

50 See Bundesverwaltungsamt – Amt für Auswanderung Rundschreiben Nr. 51/68, dated 10 February 1968, Archiv für Diakonie und Entwicklung (hereafter ADW), HGSt 2991.

51 Müller-Dincu, 'Gemischt-nationale Ehen', 26.

52 See *Merkblätter für Auslandstätige und Auswanderer: Frauen-Auswanderung. Beilage: Islamische Eheverträge* no. 10 (Cologne: Informationsstelle für Auswanderer und Auslandstätige, Bundesverwaltungsamt, 1961).

53 Note from Bernhard Le Coutre, 29 June 1959, ADW HGSt 2512.

54 Ibid.

55 Aktenvermerk, Betr.: Besprechung im Bundesinnenministerium am 28. August 1959 betr. Beratung für Ausländerehen, 4 September 1959, Evangelisches Zentralarchiv in Berlin (hereafter EZA) (ZA5093/11) EZA 6/9554; Letter from H. Maurer from the Innere Mission und Hilfswerk der evangelischen Kirche in Deutschland to Gerhard Stratenwerth [Vice President of the Office of Foreign Affairs of the Protestant Church in Germany], 23 June 1960, (ZA5093/11) EZA 6/9555; Letter from Stratenwerth to Maurer, 12 July 1960, (ZA5093/11) EZA 6/9555.

56 Norbert Zimmer (ed.), *Heirat mit Ausländern* (Hofheim/Ts.: Verlag des Auslands-Kurier, 1968), 16, 36; Erich Volandt, *Ausländer zum Heiraten gesucht* (Gladbeck: Schriftenmissions-Verlag, 1963), 4.

57 'Mischehen', *Herder Korrespondenz*, 151.

58 'Ein Graf Amore was in Messina nicht bekannt… Wenn Ausländer in Deutschland die 'große Liebe' entdecken. Beratungsstellen für Bräute', *Tagespiegel*, 10 May 1962. See also letter from Dambacher to R.K. (name withheld to protect the identity of the recipient), 16 July 1965, ADW HGSt 2523; Letter from Dambacher to Sister E. Engmann, 1 December 1965, ADW HGSt 2512; Hermann Haeberle, 'Ehen mit Moslems', in *Heirat mit Ausländern*, ed. Norbert Zimmer (Hofheim/Ts: Verlag des Auslands-Kurier, 1968), 3.

59 Karl-August Stuckenberg, 'Informationen über Entwicklungsländer für Fach- und Führungskräfte', Niederschrift über die 11. Arbeitstagung der Leiter der öffentlichen Auswanderer-Beratungsstellen am 2. und 3. Februar 1961 in Köln, Bundesverwaltungsamt – Amt für Auswanderung, ADW HGSt 2514.

60 Willi Höpfner, 'Die Stellung der Frau im Islam', in *Heirat mit Ausländern*, 28. See also, 'Ein Graf Amore war in Messina nicht bekannt', *Tagesspiegel*, 10 May 1962; Walter Becker, *Ehen mit Ausländern*, 1st edn (Hamm: Hoheneck Verlag, 1965), 6; Haeberle, 'Ehen mit Moslems', in *Heirat mit Ausländern*, 36.

61 Württembergischer Landerverein, *Ehe*; Becker, *Ehen mit Ausländern*; Orientdienst, *Die christlich-islamische Mischehe* [1963]; Orientdienst, ed., *Seine Frau werden?* [1965]; Volandt, *Ausländer*.
62 Gerhard Stratenwerth, 'Vom Honigmond zur Wirklichkeit', *Kirche und Mann*, January 1967.
63 Protokoll der 19. Konferenz für Ausländerfragen am 2. Juni 1966, p. 5, ADW HGSt 2513.
64 Letter from the Landesjugendamt Rheinland-Pfalz an das Außenamt der Evangelischen Kirche, Frankfurt, 21 October 1963, ADW HGSt 2991
65 Ruth Braun, *Jugend unter dem Wort*, May 1962, 9.
66 Letter from Dambacher to Mauritz, 26 October 1965; ADW, HGSt 2512.
67 'Die Braut hat ihre Schuldigkeit getan', *Stern*, 19 July to 5 October 1961.
68 See Hiltrud Stöcker-Zafari and Jörg Wegner, *Binationaler Alltag in Deutschland* (Frankfurt: Brandes und Apsel, 2004), 18, 20–1.
69 'Ehe', *Spiegel*, 34.
70 Jaeckel, 'Unsere Frauen', *Quick*, 36. In its series on marriage, *Bunte* likewise referred to the 'marriage jungle'. Kern, 'Bis dass der Tod (2)', *Bunte*, 39.
71 'Unsere Frauen' *Quick*, 37.
72 Friedrich Kießling and Bernhard Rieger (eds), *Mit dem Wandel leben: Neuorientierung und Tradition in der Bundesrepublik der 1950er und 1960er Jahre* (Köln: Böhlau Verlag, 2011).

11

Customary and Civil Marriage Law and the Question of Gender Equality in Twentieth and Twenty-First-Century Gabon and Africa*

Rachel Jean-Baptiste

As part of his inaugural actions Léon M'ba, the first prime minister of the Central African nation of Gabon, declared 1962 to be the year of the woman. The country had achieved independence from French colonial rule just two years earlier, in 1960. By 1963, in a speech delivered before the National Assembly, the vice president emphasized that the new government viewed the matters of 'feminine evolution' and 'the policy of the emancipation of women' as central to the establishment of human dignity, equality and social order in the fledgling nation.[1] The emancipation and evolution of women, he continued, would only come about by breaking with certain customs and social habits from ancient times. On M'ba's behalf the vice president elaborated, 'I want to talk about bridewealth, which in the context of the new and modern Gabon is a practice that is out-of-date, amoral, and harmful.' Bridewealth, the remittance of goods, money or varied forms of wealth or labour from the groom's kin to the bride's father or other male kin, was a customary practice across sub-Saharan Africa that legitimized a heterosexual relationship as a marriage. Bridewealth exchange could also include counter-payments from the bride's natal family to the groom's kin, representing the relationship of reciprocity and mutual aid that affinity was to provide.[2] Elder men from the groom's and bride's families facilitated a public celebration in which bridewealth goods and/or money were exchanged, thereby constituting the act of marriage. In order for couples to divorce, some ethno-language groups required the reimbursement of the bridewealth that the husband's kin had remitted to the wife's father. Thus, acts of marriage and divorce could be agreed upon, entered into and ruptured without the involvement of any state actors.

However, the custom was out of date, M'ba's government argued, because it reflected an older form of African social–political structure based on clans. Moreover, he claimed it was amoral because the practice had become a commercial operation for families to procure wealth and harmful because the considerable increase in bridewealth amounts in recent years impeded young people from marrying, thereby limiting the birth rate and threatening the robust demographic growth of the fledgling nation. In consideration of these factors, the government resolved to promulgate a law that would prohibit the custom of bridewealth exchange as the social and legal marker of marriage. This measure would mean that the only form of legal marriage would be civil marriage consecrated by specified government officials.[3] There was never any doubt that the law would pass in Gabon. It was not a democracy; elections involved a limited electorate, political opposition was often violently silenced, and the legislature merely rubber-stamped the decisions made by the increasingly autocratic executive.

The Law of May 1963 banning bridewealth declared: 'The practice known in customary law as bridewealth which consists of the remittance of sums of money or valuable objects from the future husband to the family of his future wife at the time of marriage is prohibited'.[4] Bridewealth could not be mentioned in any public or private contracts. Anyone who demanded, accepted or promised goods, money or labour as bridewealth could be subject to a prison term from three months to one year and a fine of 36,000 to 360,000 francs, a prohibitive amount of money in 1963 Gabon. No one could claim the titles of 'wife' or 'husband' and the civil benefits of marriage if the relationship had not been legitimized by an authorized civil servant and recorded in regional registries. What about marriages legalized by the customary practice of bridewealth remittance before the promulgation of the 1963 law? Those unions would still be recognized as legal marriages and the husbands and wives would enjoy all the benefits of marriage. A husband could request the reimbursement of his bridewealth if he and his wife divorced, but only up to 3,000 francs even if he had paid more than this amount. The law was meant to establish that henceforth the state would be the central arbiter of marriage, a union and process that M'ba's government defined as 'modern' in that it was entered into by individually consenting men and women and consecrated by the state rather than by kin and elders related by blood and affinity. M'ba's government made the implicit evaluation that Gabon's modernity meant mirroring processes and definitions of marriage identified with the West. The passage of this law represented a continuation of French colonial marriage and family law initiatives that had sought, but failed, to eliminate African customary practices deemed 'abhorrent' to Western principles of civilization and shifting ideas of women's rights. In this sense, independent Gabon's new marriage policy reflected broader movements in many post-colonies around to world to align marriage and family law with presumed Western norms.[5]

Bridewealth exchanges have long been a theme of contestation in twentieth-century francophone African history, and indeed across the continent. Christian missionary and colonial government representatives of varied European nationalities viewed bridewealth exchange as the 'sale' of African women from fathers to husbands. African societies in Gabon considered bridewealth as representing women's importance and facilitating relationships of mutual care between families related by marriage. However, bridewealth practices shifted as African societies became cash economies and integrated into the fluctuating global economy. Since the beginning of the twentieth century, and reaching a crescendo through booms and busts of the Depression and the Second World War, a host of African political leaders from chiefs of varied ethno-language groups to elite French-educated men, alongside French colonial officials and Catholic and Protestant missionaries, decried escalating bridewealth costs and attempted to regulate bridewealth amounts.

These varied coalitions also sought to reform areas of marriage and family law such as divorce, inheritance and the custody of children. At the heart of these contestations over how to regulate marriage and family law was the question of how to expand, restrict and define 'women's rights'. The colonial state did not succeed in implementing bridewealth regulation legislation and, moreover, the 1963 law prohibiting bridewealth also failed. Marriage by bridewealth continues to be the more prevalent form of conjugality in Gabon today. As elsewhere in Africa, legal plurality – a plethora of kin, community and neighbourhood fora, religious figures and NGOs, not just one hegemonic sector of society or the state – mediates the landscapes that define relationships of affinity and the question of gendered rights and gender roles. In their everyday lives, people related by kith and kin – lovers, husbands, wives, elders and youth, brothers and sisters – debated and articulated their own conceptions of the types of conjugal relationships they wanted to form and how the exchange of money and other forms of wealth, varied religious beliefs and customary and civil law would mediate marriage.

Utilizing oral histories of Gabonese men and women of differing generations, United Nations documents, newspaper articles and archival government documents such as legislative debates and bodies of law, this chapter analyses political contestations around the question of bridewealth and gendered rights in marriage in twentieth- and twenty-first-century Gabon. The case study of bridewealth practices and regulation in Gabon is important in that it encapsulates the changing and complex landscape of marriage and family law across postcolonial Africa in the 1960s and beyond as states and societies sought to construct the social, legal and cultural fabric of new nations. The twentieth and twenty-first centuries ushered in substantial change – the meeting of diverse ethno-language groups and religious expressions, monetization, migration to urban areas and across borders in search of livelihood, colonialism, decolonization and the reconfiguration of nations, and economic booms and busts. Marriage and family life and marriage and family law were crucial sites in which ordinary citizens and people in positions of political and social authority debated these transformations and their intersections with gendered human rights and the relationship between state and citizens.

Though African men faced constraints in marital choice, it is contestations over women's rights that have dominated national and international debates about marriage and family law in Africa. To what degree were women to have a choice of marriage partners and access to the children and wealth that women's social and biological capacities produced? Which institutions or persons – the state, jurists, individual men, individual women, chiefs, elders and religious figures such as pastors, priests and imams – would have the moral and legal sovereignty to regulate marriage and family life? How would societies negotiate the changing meanings of 'customs', 'civil law' and the legacies of colonial rule to define modern women's rights in marriage in theory and practice?

By the 1990s, various sectors of civil society called for increased democratization against the tide of autocratic rule that had marked Gabon and many governments across the continent since the 1960s. As a new wave of national and international rhetoric against gender inequality rose at the dawn of the twenty-first century, NGOs and other sectors of civil society in Gabon revived the question of how customary and civil laws were to configure how people formed their families. Gabon is typical for the ways in which states across the vast and complex African continent attempted to legislate marriage and family life, but also epitomizes how a heterogeneous citizenry variably critiqued or rejected state sovereignty over their conjugal lives even in the face of autocratic rule.

Colonial Legacies in African Marriage and Family Law

A legacy of European colonial rule that encompassed much of the continent from the late nineteenth to mid- to late twentieth century was the very idea of 'modernity'. In European discourses, Africa was the atavistic foil to European advancement and civilization.[6] From Asia to Africa in the nineteenth and twentieth centuries, European proponents of imperialism justified colonial rule as rescuing indigenous women from 'barbaric' marriage and sexual practices ranging from widow burning to child marriage to clitoredectomy.[7] As argued by Pamela Scully, European missionaries and government officials justified imperial aspirations and abolitionist movements in Africa with representations of African women as 'needing aid from the West to free them from terrible patriarchy' of husbands and fathers.[8] In what was to become French West and Equatorial Africa, abolitionists and missionaries forwarded the trope of the slave-like status of African women, 'sold' or forced into marriage as early as childhood, living in polygamous households and toiling on land controlled by husbands, as well as the possibilities of European and Christian traditions bringing freedom.[9]

Islam had not reached indigenous populations in Gabon at the dawn of the twentieth century and most Gabonese followed a mixture of traditional and Catholic religious practices.[10] In keeping with the French policy of secularism in state policies, Catholic conceptions of marriage bore some, but limited, imprint in colonial and postcolonial marriage and family law. Catholic missionaries and colonial officials had a fraught relationship. Missionaries and colonial officials agreed upon attempts to limit bridewealth amounts or to require women's consent for marriage, but government officials upheld the legality of polygamy in the face of missionaries' proselytization of monogamy. In reality, the fluidity of customary practices across Africa allowed women varied avenues to direct their marital careers. A now voluminous literature by historians of women in Africa has questioned colonial discourses, demonstrating the agency with which African women negotiated and reconfigured marital choice, divorce and control of their persons, wealth and children as well as the importance of love in male–female relationships.[11]

Colonial rhetoric and policies claiming to 'free' African women contradicted practices of colonial states seeking to conserve women's labour, sexuality and reproductive capacities within the control of fathers and husbands. In Anglophone Africa, in regions ranging from the Gold Coast in West Africa to Malawi in Central Africa, colonial states and some African chiefs and elder men enacted uneven attempts to 'invent' customary marriage law that reinforced fathers' control over whom their daughters' married, husbands' control over women's labour and limits on divorce.[12] In Gabon, a duality in colonial discourses in regard to African women was at play in the varied government-sponsored efforts to regulate bridewealth and codify customary marriage and family law in the colonial period. On the one hand, French colonial government employees and missionaries represented African women as beasts of burden needing intervention. On the other hand, colonial civil servants instituted courts presided over by African chiefs and French judges with the mandate to limit women's avenues for divorce and reduce women's mobility.[13]

The composition of bridewealth underwent vast change across sub-Saharan Africa over the course of the twentieth century. At the beginning of the twentieth century, oral sources and European observers note that the composition of bridewealth – cattle in certain regions in West, Southern and East Africa, bars of iron in Equatorial Africa, and imported and local cloth and alcohol or farm labour throughout – varied across the continent. European colonial rule and taxation policies accelerated the monetization of African economies. While cattle remained the main form of bridewealth in areas such as Kenya or South Africa, in some urban areas of West and Central Africa bridewealth came to assume a greater composition of cash and imported goods between the 1920s and 1950s.[14] Colonial officials, African political leaders such as chiefs and elite men, and young men seeking to marry decried bridewealth inflation, where men with female dependents asked for increasingly prohibitive amounts that made marriage unattainable.

The composition of bridewealth in the principal form of money took hold in Gabon by the 1920s. Though bridewealth amounts varied from ethno-language group to ethno-language group, marriage by bridewealth was the dominant rite of marriage across Gabon by the mid-twentieth century. Bridewealth amounts were particularly elevated in the capital city of Libreville in the Estuary province that bordered the Atlantic Ocean and the northern province of Woleu-N'tem among those of the Fang ethno-language group. While no single ethno-language group holds a clear majority in Gabon, the Fang are significant in that they are a large minority in a country of at least forty ethno-language groups. In the period of French colonial rule, Fang residents of these areas participated in what I call a 'bridewealth economy', in which disbursements of cash to legitimize marriage or divorce fuelled the aspirations of wealth, health and well-being of fathers, mothers and elders with control over female dependents (Figure 11.1).[15]

The monetary economy expanded and replaced a barter economy for most aspects of daily life. Bridewealth shifted, many Gabonese argued, from serving the purposes of acquiring a wife for the bride's brother and ensuring the circulation of women to funding extra-conjugal expenses such as housing, food, luxuries and health care. The need for money for quotidian life also made the Gabonese vulnerable in times of global economic fluctuations. The economy depended upon exports such as timber in the colonial period. With the drop in timber prices in the 1930s and during the Second World War, the shortage of money meant that bridewealth became an important source of cash. Alarmed by the rapidity with which Fang Gabonese adopted the use of cash into their daily lives, French researchers analysed the 'problem of bridewealth inflation' in great detail.[16]

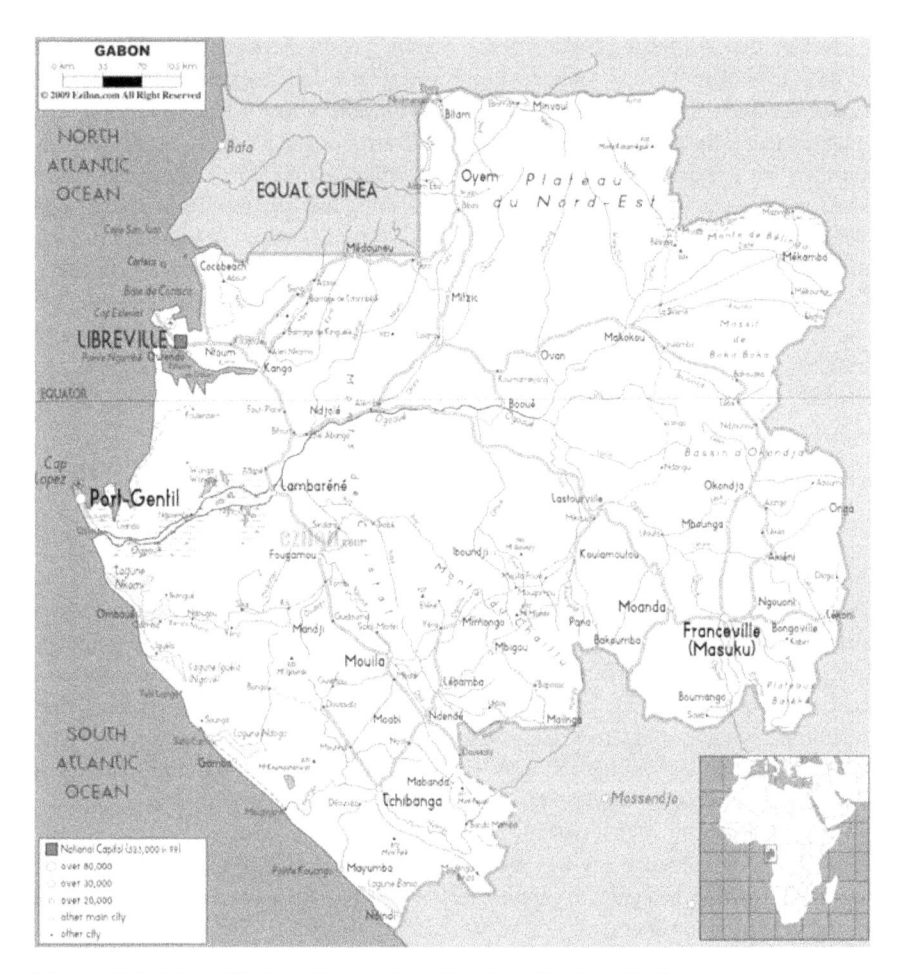

Figure 11.1 Map of Gabon. Source: Jean-Baptiste, *Conjugal Rights*.

Serving as a district chief in the French colonial service, Léon M'ba convened a 1947 meeting of Fang dignitaries who interpreted increasing bridewealth amounts as an indication of how Fang customs had become corrupted by European materialistic norms.[17] Attendees conceptualized the need to limit bridewealth inflation, not as an initiative to ensure the greater equality of women, but to prevent fathers-in-law from exacting too much control over young men who attempted to reach social adulthood through forming their own households.[18] Between the 1930s and 1950s, varied colonial officials, chiefs, missionaries and African legislators debated varied pieces of legislation aimed at placing limits on bridewealth amounts. Although they succeeded in issuing some pieces of legislation, all of them remained unenforced and ineffectual in the face of daily practice.[19] Men and women alike continued to uphold and practice bridewealth exchange.

Rather than espousing the blanket acceptance of Western mores and civil laws as indicative of modernity, Gabonese men and women articulated that customs and traditions could also be 'modern' and ensure women's rights.[20] As Gabon approached independence from French colonial rule, in courts of public opinion and in daily practice, men and women affirmed the centrality of marriage by customary laws of bridewealth exchange as foundational to establishing the very meanings of marriage. Varied constituencies argued that reform, not the abolition of bridewealth, was needed. Yet, M'ba's government insisted upon the prohibition of bridewealth and a host of other marriage and family laws not always in keeping with the sentiments of the general populace as government policy that would bring Gabon into being as a modern society.

State Attempts to Legislate Marriage and Family Law in the Early Years of Independence

In spite of increasingly autocratic rule by M'ba, a debate did ensue in May 1963 at the National Assembly over proposed bridewealth legislation. This debate provides a window into the differing opinions of elite men of varied Gabonese ethno-language groups about the significance and meaning of marriage to the nation and the role of the state in configuring the question of women's rights in marriage.[21] They unanimously viewed heterosexual marriage as the bedrock of the nation. Delegates emphasized that the young nation of Gabon was underpopulated and that efforts to facilitate marriage would increase the birth rate. Delegates also agreed that the current practices of high bridewealth payments had no place in modern Gabon. However, Assemblymen saw two problems that the passage of the law would raise and therefore they hesitated to support such a measure. One was the reality that legal plurality existed in Gabon.

While some Gabonese married according to civil marriage laws carried over from French colonial rule or Catholic marriage rights in church, most Gabonese married under customary bridewealth remittance. A delegate named M. Migolet reminded his colleagues that Gabon had two distinct court systems regulated by different bodies of law, customary courts and courts of civil law. The head of the Assembly corrected him by pointing out that according to the letter of law, meaning the government-issued document called the Civil Code that outlined marriage and family laws such as the suppression of bridewealth, only courts of civil law existed. However, he conceded, legal plurality operated in reality. State courts presided over by French, and increasingly Gabonese judges, adjudicated marriage, family and inheritance, property and economic exchanges, and criminal acts based on bodies of law adapted from French laws. Additionally, chiefs presided over neighbourhood and village courts. These courts adjudicated over the same matters as state courts, according to varied bodies of customary laws of the country's diverse ethno-language groups. The vice president promised delegates that M'ba would be laying out legislation to eliminate this duplication of procedures, courts and bodies of law.[22]

A second matter that delegates debated was whether the law could have the opposite effect and decrease marriage rates. Tempering Prime Minister M'ba's desire for the emancipation of women, delegates stated that for fathers to have control over their daughters, elder men and women to have control over youth and husbands to have control over their wives was the bedrock of social order. Young women, particularly those living in Libreville, suggested M. Biyogo, had already been rejecting marriage altogether or choosing to marry the suitors of their choice rather than those whom their parents chose for them. The government should not rush to create a situation in which young women were completely liberated. Parents' negotiation of bridewealth, he argued, ensured that daughters would marry whether they wanted to or not. M. Gondet urged that a delegation of young women should go around villages and proselytize the law since young women would be more receptive to the words of other young women.[23] The delegation would emphasize to their fellow countrywomen that even if they were married without bridewealth, they should still respect the authority of their husbands. Mr Ekke Aya'a added, 'I also fear the independence that this law would give to our children and to women.' He relayed a proverb of his ethno-language group that, 'If you listen to the cries of women and children, you risk getting hurt in the knees', implying that conceding to the demands of women and children would cripple elder men in their normalized position of power. Customary laws in Gabon, particularly for the Fang, dictated that husbands who had paid bridewealth always received child custody in the case of divorce.[24] Making bridewealth remittance illegal would not disrupt this default legal practice, M'ba's government assured delegates. This pledge that civil authorities would continue to award husbands exclusive custody of children belied the claims by M'ba's government that new civil laws that replaced customary laws would expand women's rights in marriage.

The vice president of the assembly admonished the delegates for their anxieties, emphasizing that the passage of the law would not result in women gaining their complete independence. Instead of the acceptance of bridewealth by their fathers tying them to their marriages, it would be the legitimization by state officials that would attach women to the marital contract. He also assured the delegates that the suppression of bridewealth would not diminish parental authority. Trying to calm the Assembly, M. Engouang Engone urged composure and deliberation in considering the passage of this law since, in discussing bridewealth, 'it is the very heart of Gabon that you have touched'. M. Engone characterized bridewealth as a hallmark of national identity to be preserved. But, for the good of the nation, he argued, the National Assembly should approve the law. However, he predicted that the law would never be applied. The twenty-year-old girl who wanted to marry today, he argued, has a father who is rather old, a man who would be anxious to acquire his daughter's bridewealth. Furthermore, he added, deep in the bush, the heads of administrative divisions would not even apply the law after its passage. The county would continue to have two different bodies of law in a single republic.[25] The law was adopted unanimously. Nevertheless, the prescient words would come true.

In a national speech broadcast to the country a few days later, Léon M'ba outlined the positive picture of marriage and family life that would emerge in the aftermath of the 1963 law.[26] Some countrymen and Europeans advised him against pursuing this law, M'ba revealed, cautioning that bridewealth was so imbedded in Gabonese culture that suppressing it could incite civil disorder. Instead, he emphasized the strides that the nation would make. From this moment forward, a man and a woman would be the individuals to decide to marry, to consecrate their marriage before a judge or government official. No need to call the cousin in the town of Koulamoutou in central Gabon or the uncle in Cocobeach in northwest Gabon or for a marriage to take 5–6 months to be finalized; and especially, there was no need to go before customary courts, presided over by uneducated old men. Rather, marriages would be consecrated by 'a real judge'.

Likely responding to some protests against the law by men who had paid high bridewealth prior to the passage of the law, a modification of the suppression of bridewealth law appeared in August 1963.[27] The amendment outlined how the reimbursement of bridewealth would be determined for people who had married through bridewealth before the law: the wife would have to reimburse the husband the entire bridewealth amount if a divorce was pronounced within the first five years of marriage; three-quarters of bridewealth if the divorce was between 5 and 10 years of the marriage; one-half if between 10 and 15 years; and one-quarter if between 15 and 20 years. There were three instances in which no reimbursement of bridewealth would take place: if the marriage had lasted for more than 20 years; if there were at least four living children from the marriage; or if the husband were found to be at fault in the divorce verdict.

As much as M'ba's administration touted the law as forwarding the emancipation of women, contradictory ideas about women's rights to choose a marriage partner, divorce and retain custody of children remained. This law and its amendments demonstrated the commitment to the idea that the state, not family patriarchs and matriarchs and extended kin, held the authority to determine the processes that made a relationship a legal marriage. In the modern nation, the state would be the central arbitrator and judge. Women who married after the passage of the law could now divorce without the burden of having to reimburse bridewealth. However, the amendment compelled women to stay in their marriages for longer periods of time. The longer a woman remained married, the smaller the amount of bridewealth she would have to reimburse. Another idea in the law was that a wife had already reimbursed her husband's bridewealth payment if she gave birth to many children. Finally, a man who was not a good husband by the court's standards was not entitled to reimbursement. In these ways, bridewealth reimbursement became a right tied to fecundity and the length of common marital life, a measure that compelled men and women alike to think twice before divorce. The Penal Code of 1963 further elaborated on a host of criminal infractions related to marriage.[28] A husband and his wife or wives were to maintain sexual relationships within the conjugal contract that had been legitimated by the state in 'modern' Gabon.

Bridewealth in Law and Practice since the Passage of the 1963 Law

How closely were these pieces of legislation followed, particularly the crucial law suppressing bridewealth, in everyday practice and in the system of courts? In July 1964, J. Carre, identified as the head legal adviser in the presidency of Léon M'ba, surveyed the registry of the first-degree civil courts for the new nation, which were officially charged with adjudicating cases related to marriage and family law. He wrote, 'Legal judgments are decided upon with a great amount of variability and the regulations of the 1963 law are rarely applied'.[29]

Across the continent in the late twentieth and twenty-first centuries, postcolonial governments debated the relevance of customary, Islamic and civil laws inspired by European mores and Christianity in new family codes. As was the case in South Africa with its 1988 Recognition of Customary Marriages Act, the legal codes in many African countries recognized, alongside civil marriages, unions legitimized under various bodies of customary law.[30] In countries with large Muslim populations such as Mali, Nigeria and Tanzania, governments also recognized varied interpretations of Sharia marriage and family law along with other regimes of law. Gabon is exceptional in that legal plurality existed in practice, but was not officially sanctioned by state law.

Though the 1963 law suppressing bridewealth still exists in Gabonese civil law, oral interviews I conducted with residents of Libreville confirm the continued widespread disregard of the policy. Women as well as men disavow the idea of bridewealth as representing the sale of women but rather see it as a testament to the importance of relationships between fathers and mothers and their children and extended kin. To my interviewees, bridewealth signified the strength of community and kinship ties. Contrary to M'ba's idea that the 'clan' was no longer relevant, the Gabonese have maintained kin networks to weather social and economic precariousness. Fang male and female informants who married since 1963, living in regions ranging from Libreville to Lambaréné in the southeast to the northern provinces of Woleu-N'tem, relayed that bridewealth amounts, both those paid at the time of their marriages and those that accumulated over the course of several years, exceeded the limits outlined in the law.[31]

Even the minority of couples who had married in a civil union or Catholic ceremony also married according to customary rites of bridewealth remittance (Figure 11.2). These couples divorced through first-degree courts of civil law, but made no mention of bridewealth in these proceedings, only to subsequently petition neighbourhood customary courts and family councils to regulate bridewealth reimbursement.[32] As observed by Gabonese legal expert Honorine Nzet Biteghe, there are many more customary marriages than civil marriages in Gabon. She further elaborated, 'Though the letter of the law is that customary marriage is not recognized by law, the fact is that no Gabonese family will accept that a daughter go before the mayor's office with a man [to legalize their marriage] without also going through customary marriage. If the law was applied, we would all be in prison since the law specifies that anyone who pays bridewealth, or accepts such gifts should go to prison.'[33] It did not matter to families in what order their children married, whether the customary, civil or religious ceremonies preceded or followed one another. In principle, the public did not regard a couple as 'really married' until the customary rites had been completed.

Ties of community and kin, not the state, were the principal forces that delineated how a heterosexual relationship became a marriage. In everyday practice and belief, ordinary citizens determined how the circulation of money and goods sealed or ruptured relationships of affinity. With the payment of bridewealth, a couple was

Figure 11.2 Bridewealth Payment, 2002. Source: Rachel Jean-Baptiste.

married. Without the reimbursement of bridewealth, there could be no divorce – the couple was still married.[34] As Yvonne N'dong, a woman neighbourhood chief in Libreville expressed in a 2006 interview, 'In our custom, you are married once you have been bridewealthed (*doté*). We don't recognize the right of the state to direct marital status. Without bridewealth, you're not married. But as long as your parents say OK for you to leave with the suitor who wants to marry you and your parents accept the initial payment of goods, you are married and the full bridewealth payment can be completed afterwards.'[35] University lecturer Marie France Adndeme Allogho reiterated this, expressing that, 'Even with the effort to replace bridewealth with alliances in front of the mayor, it doesn't work. It's the negotiations and gathering of the family groups that matter. Even for someone like me who is a college professor, I am not married in the eyes of society unless bridewealth has been paid.'[36] Elite, middle-class and impoverished Gabonese alike shared the view of the 'real' marriage as customary marriage, not civil or religious marriage rites. Gabonese couples who have spent significant amounts of time living in Europe or the Americas or who have the intention of living outside of Gabon – and therefore must have a civil marriage in order to get passports and visas – have *both* a civil and a customary bridewealth marriage ceremony. As one couple explained to me, many like them who consider themselves to be faithful Catholics do not get married in a church ceremony until they are elderly because the faith views divorce as a 'sin'.[37] As the wife elaborated, they were married by bridewealth customs in their youth and 'I didn't marry my husband this way [in the Catholic Church] until we are now old and close to death and I know with certainty we will not divorce'. Many people were unaware of the 1963 law prohibiting bridewealth, with some interviewees even telling me that Léon M'ba passed a law stating that one can only be married with bridewealth.[38]

Even with the nearly universal belief of marriage by bridewealth as the 'real' marriage, Gabonese individuals also protested that high bridewealth amounts were a social ill and reflected the corruption of this traditional practice. Bridewealth payments served as a crucial means for male heads of household to obtain cash to weather economic vulnerability as the oil wealth of post-independent Gabon began to dry up by the 1900s.[39] As one octogenarian resident of Libreville opined, while President M'ba may have had the intention of emancipating women with the law erasing bridewealth from the marriage contract, the initiative did not fulfil its intended consequences. On the contrary, he asserted, 'bridewealth had become more and more expensive with this time of precariousness. People don't respect anything anymore other than money'.[40]

Three Libreville neighbourhood chiefs who I interviewed in 2006 decried how 'the culture of money had laid waste to Fang culture'.[41] They criticized fellow citizens with daughters and female dependents as demanding exorbitant amounts of money and goods such as cars and foreign appliances in bridewealth payments. Chief Alphonse in particular decried, 'Before, marriage was an exchange and bridewealth facilitated that in-laws love each other. Rather than trying to make themselves "white," Fang people need to return to the simple criteria and nonmaterial values of Fang culture of the past.' Like many Gabonese, these three chiefs ascribed a mythical quality to the time and space of precolonial Gabon during which customs ensured social harmony. They articulated a sentiment of nostalgia for an era before contact with Europe. The populace needed to return to traditional ways in order to preserve the Gabonese future. This articulation of the need to return Gabonese conjugality to conceptions of customary law of the past in order to preserve the country's future would permeate the debates between the populace, legislators and NGOs, an emerging voice in the country's civil society in the twenty-first century, about how to regulate marriage and family law.

NGOs, Democratization and the Question of Gender Equality since 1990

National, continent-wide and international transformations occurring between the 1980s and 1990s led to increasing calls for political reform and democratization in Gabon. As structural adjustment policies resulted in economic instability and the Cold War thawed, many dictatorial regimes in Africa began to crumble. Economic stagnation and recession that swept much of the continent in the 1990s resulted in unrest. A wave of strikes and violent protests by students, government employees and labourers in Gabon led the government of Omar Bongo, which ruled the country since Léon M'ba's death in 1967, to come to the bargaining table pledging reform. After the National Conference of 1990, the government promised freedom of the press and of people to assemble, a basic bill of rights, that the judiciary branch would be independent from the president, and the allowance of multiparty elections. In the 'emerging Gabon' post-1990, the government promoted itself as one of Africa's most stable countries, in which social order and 'the personal development of its citizens' would provide a foundation for global economic investment.[42] Subsequent elections were marred by opposition leaders' accusations of government fraud and outbreaks of violence. Bongo was re-elected in multiple elections until his death in 2008. But lip service to democratization did result in a more vocal and active civil society that insisted that Gabonese citizens had basic rights and that the government had to protect these rights.

Gender equality and marriage and family law, several sectors of Gabonese society argued, were central to political reform. Since 1983, Gabon was one of the nearly 200 countries worldwide that ratified the United Nations treaty known as the Convention on the Elimination of all Forms of Discrimination Against Women (CEDAW). Referred to as the international women's bill of rights, the agreement sought for signatory states to eliminate 'any distinction, exclusion or restriction made on the basis of sex which has the effect or purpose of impairing or nullifying the recognition, enjoyment or exercise by women, irrespective of their marital status, on a basis of equality of men and women, of human rights and fundamental freedoms in the political, economic, social, cultural, civil or any other field'.[43] Member countries were to review and erase any forms of sex discrimination in de facto or de jure laws and practices in their countries. The reform of the 1990s in Gabon resulted in an increased number of legally recognized NGOs, many of which focused on the implementation of CEDAW.[44]

After the Conference, a new Constitutional amendment guaranteed equality in Gabon without the distinction of sex in all sectors of society. New ministries and government-appointed positions included the Secretary of State on Women's Status, the Ministry for the Advancement of Women, and the Ministry of the Family, the Protection of Children and the Advancement of Women. The state sponsored commissions, colloquia, public forums and research into the condition of women in Gabon. The state also legally recognized the existence of several NGOs that focused on women's political, economic and social advancement. In 2000, with funding from the UN and the American and Canadian embassies, Honorine Nzet Biteghe helped found the NGO *Observatoire de droits de la femme et de la parité* (ODEFPA). Biteghe had completed university studies in law, worked as a magistrate prior to becoming the president of the NGO, and in 2012 was appointed as the Minister of the Family and Social Affairs.[45]

Civil laws that defined and regulated marriage, ODEFPA argued, were the locus of gender inequality in Gabon. One of its principal missions was to examine the Gabonese Civil Code, created over the course of M'ba's administration and published in 1972 and 1989, for any areas in marriage and family law that were contrary to the Constitution's new principle of sex equality. ODEFPA criticized the very definition of marriage in the Gabonese Civil Code. The document defined marriage as a relationship in which the husband was the head of the family in matters related to the distribution of and access to wealth, custody of children and the legal status of the marriage.[46] Polygamous civil marriages were legal according to the determination of the husband.[47] ODEFPA made recommendations to the government and lobbied for modifications to the Civil Code to ensure gender equality. In addition, the organization also called for any provisions in the Civil Code that advanced the rights of women to be enforced.

Another charge of ODEFPA was to increase the dissemination of knowledge about civil marriage and family law to all levels of society through radio and television programming, roundtables and conferences, and the publishing of a series of simple and easy-to-read brochures that sought to educate husbands and wives about their rights to children, wealth and legal conjugal status. The organization criticized the current laws as unnecessarily complicated and difficult for ordinary people to understand. They urged legislators to write a separate body of law, a family code that would simplify the language of rights in and of marriage.[48] In 2002, ODEFPA began 'a fight against women's ignorance about our rights'.[49] The organization provided advocacy and support to individual women who were the victims of and seeking redress for acts of domestic violence or sexual discrimination.[50] ODEPFA's publications critiqued the authority of the state to regulate the conjugal lives of its citizens as outlined to readers of the brochures: 'You are the true legislator of your family (household). The state's role is only to help you materialize your decisions.'[51] The organization also sought to enforce the obligations of parents who were never married, divorced or estranged from their children. Two pamphlets, 'What Is Legal Recognition of a Child and How to Obtain It' and 'What Is The Food Benefit for Children' sought to inform women and men of the possibility for biological fathers to legally declare the recognition of children born outside of marriage and for mothers to petition the state to garnish these men's wages.[52] Other brochures included: 'Violence Committed on Women'; 'Concubinage, Customary Marriage, Legal Marriage, or Myth'; and 'From Monogamous to Polygamous Marriage without Having to Divorce, A Reality of Positive Law in Gabon'. The organization provided advocacy and support to individual women who were the victims of and seeking redress for acts of domestic violence or sexual discrimination.[53]

The most common critique of Gabonese marriage and family law launched by ODEFPA was the disconnect between citizens, who universally enacted marriage by bridewealth, and the state, which viewed this rite as illegal. In several publications ODEFPA called attention to the hybrid constellation of laws that existed, consisting of 'a mixture of French law and traditional law, the incorporation of ancient and modern' that resulted in contradictions between written law and practised law.[54] ODEFPA pointed out that some areas of the Civil Code did expand the rights of married women, but that the vast majority of married women could not avail themselves of these protections since these laws were only applicable to the minority of women who had married according to civil procedures. For example, the Civil Code outlined the rights of widows to inherit their deceased husbands' assets. In Gabon and across much of sub-Saharan Africa, customary law held that it was the natal kin, not the wife of a deceased man, who inherited his wealth and maintained rights to bury the body. In-laws often stripped widows and orphans of all conjugal property and chased them from living in the marital home. The question of the rights of widows has been an area of intense contestation in twentieth- and twenty-first-century marriage and family law across the continent, and many courts of public opinion as well as legal courts support the rights of husbands' kin over that of widows.[55] Gabon is one of the few countries in which state law supports the rights of widows.

ODEFPA published two pamphlets that advertised the rights afforded to widows and orphans in the Civil Code.[56] The NGO sought to provide advice for 'spouses [to] put on a legal armor to prevent conflicts that can arrive following deaths'. According to the Civil Code, a widow retained her own personal property and wealth, and she was also to inherit one-quarter of her deceased husband's wealth and his full pension, if he had one. The pamphlet advised wives to keep track of their husbands' property and wealth by maintaining documentation such as bankcards and codes, paystubs, bank account numbers, deeds to property, cars and farms in their possession over the course of the marriage. It also advised women to obtain official documents such as the certificate of civil marriage that would legitimize their claims for inheritance.[57] Armed with this information, women could then participate in the family council meetings that followed a man's death and could petition state courts to intervene if the relatives of the deceased refused to cooperate. On the question of widows' rights, ODEFPA praised the government for having mitigated gender inequality in customary law's disenfranchisement of widows. On this matter, women's rights NGOs advocated for the state as the central arbiter of equitable gender rights.[58]

Yet the most persistent area of critique by ODEFPA and courts of public opinion in matters of civil marriage and family law in post-1990 Gabon continued to be the 1963 law prohibiting bridewealth. While many ordinary Gabonese citizens were not even aware of the 1963 law, educated citizens have continued to lobby for its repeal. Some argued that the refusal of the state to recognize customary marriage as a legal marriage robbed the vast majority of Gabonese of crucial rights in marriage provided by the Civil Code, such as widows' rights to their deceased husband's wealth. Instead, families formed through customary bridewealth practices followed inheritance rites outlined by customary law with impunity. Widows of customary marriage by bridewealth could not petition civil courts for the inheritance of their deceased husband's wealth since their unions were not recognized by the state.

A critical mass of NGOs lobbied for the government to repeal the 1963 law prohibiting bridewealth. As some NGOs wrote in a 2002 UN report, 'The legislature has increased the wide gulf that exists between the legislated law and the quotidian law practiced every weekend by the Gabonese.'[59] As conceptualized by the ODEFPA president, 'We, legal experts and associations, keep saying to legislators that when a piece of law has fallen into such disuse such as this, it is necessary to revisit it as the law is supposed to be an expression of the will of the people. We have to remake laws into what is applicable.'[60] These critics argued that the promise of the post-National Conference government to adhere to the will of citizens had not been met. Coherence between the conjugal practices of ordinary citizens and the letter of state law had become a filter through which citizens measured the progression of their polity towards democratization.

Such critiques spilled out into print and online journalism. A 2014 opinion piece in the newspaper *Gabon Review* interpreted the disconnect between the letter of the law and everyday practice as the Gabonese state wishing to model itself on Western norms of marriage rather than the traditional values and cultures of Gabon's varied ethnicities. These values should be the foundation of government laws, one journalist wrote, echoing sentiments expressed by legislatures in 1963.[61] The 'social body' of the nation, its citizens, the article pointed out, had rejected the law, but it still remained the law of the land on the books. The article cited the words of Gabonese sociologist Eric N'zué who characterized the 1963 bridewealth law as aberrant, counter-intuitive, and foolish on the part of those in power: 'How can a nation base its legal structure on a type of marriage that comes externally and is not based on the traditions of the people?' For the state to recognize customary marriage as legal marriage, journalist Loic Ntoutoume advocated, would facilitate not only the valorization of the richness of Gabonese culture and traditions, but also permit customary marriages to be subject to the laws and regulations for widows' inheritance that were on the books for civil marriages. Ntoutoume underlined the hypocrisy of the government in adhering to the will of the people. Ali Ben Bongo, president since 2009 following the death of his father, had publicly pledged to effectively repeal the 1963 bridewealth law. However, as Ntoutoume has signalled, a law to legally recognize customary marriage by bridewealth, alongside civil marriage, has been sitting unsigned on the desk of the prime minister since 2012.

Marriage has been a site of contestation in various African societies over the course of the twentieth and twenty-first centuries as colonial and postcolonial states and Christian, traditional and Muslim figures of authority attempted to regulate how women and men shaped social and biological reproduction. However, as the case study of bridewealth regulation and the question of gender equality in Gabon demonstrate, the state is but one of many actors who delineate the legal codes and moral landscapes that shape how people form households. In spite of research that has demonstrated the expression of same-sex desire in many African societies dating back to many centuries or even millennia, some political leaders and heads of state have expressed the view of homosexuality as 'unAfrican'.[62] In many African countries in the first few decades of the twenty-first century, homosexuality has been decreed as illegal or otherwise stigmatized. Yet, just like state attempts to mandate marriage as heterosexual and to regulate heterosexual marriage, groups and individuals in many countries have mobilized a burgeoning gay rights movement, at times placing their lives at great peril. Marriage continues to be a contested praxis around which African individuals, societies and states strive to give meaning to the emotional, political, economic and cultural contours and hierarchies of power in modern life.

Notes

* I would like to thank Lisa Materson, Lorena Oropeza, Ellen Hartigan-O'Connor and participants in the Legislating Sexuality and Gender in Africa Symposium organized by Emily Burill and Lydia Boyd at University of North Carolina Chapel Hill for their incisive feedback on drafts of this chapter.

1. Archives Nationales de Gabon (ANG,) La Documentation Gabonaise. République Gabonaise, Assemblée Nationale du Gabon, Journal des Débats. Première Séance Ordinaire du 16 Avril 1963 au 6 Juin 1963, Séance Inaugurale, 16 April 1963.
2. Though the groom's male relatives gave bridewealth payments to the bride's father or other male relatives, women could benefit from bridewealth payments. Mothers of brides and grooms received items such as pots, cloth or household accessories in bridewealth gifts and counter-gifts. Barbara Cooper: 'Women's Worth and Wedding Gift Exchange in Maradi, Niger, 1907-89', *Journal of African History* 36, no. 1 (1995): 121–40; *Marriage in Maradi: Gender and Culture in a Hausa Society in Niger, 1900-1989* (Portsmouth: Heinemann, 1997), 90–111.
3. By removing marriage from customary and confessional practice and shifting it to the realm of the state, the new law resembled the Austrian Empire's policy on civil marriage that had been enacted a hundred years earlier. See Ulrike Harmat, 'Catholicism, Marriage and Cultural Warfare in Austria-Hungary' in this book.
4. *Journal Officiel de la République Gabonaise*, Loi #2063 du 31 Mai 1963, 1 July 1963, 510.
5. See the chapters in this book focusing on Siam, Egypt and India by Tamara Loos, Kenneth M. Cuno and Leigh Denault, respectively.
6. Signe Arnfred (ed.), *Re-thinking Sexualities in Africa* (Uppsala: The Nordic Africa Institute, 2004).
7. For more on global histories of colonialism and marriage and family life see: Julia Clancy-Smith, *Domesticating the Empire: Gender, Race, & Family Life in the Dutch and French Empires* (Charlottsville: University of Virginia Press, 1998); Lynn M. Thomas, *Politics of the Womb: Women, Reproduction, and the State in Kenya* (Berkeley: University of California Press, 2003); Mrinalini Sinha, *Specters of Mother India: The Global Restructuring of an Empire* (Durham: Duke University Press, 2006).
8. Pamela Scully, 'Gender, History, and Human Rights', in *Gender and Culture and the Limit of Rights,* ed. Dorothy L. Hodgson (Philadelphia: University of Pennsylvania Press, 2011), 25. Abosede George refers to the representation of the 'abject African woman' who is the focus of Western human rights campaigns. Abosede George, *Making Modern Girls: A History of Girlhood, Labor, and Social Development in Colonial Lagos* (Athens: Ohio University Press, 2014), 226–7.
9. Maurice Delafosse, Dr. Poutrin and Monseigneur Le Roy (eds), *Enquête coloniale dans l'Afrique française occidentale et équatoriale sur l'organisation de la famille indigène, les fiançailles, le mariage avec une esquisse générale des langues de l'Afrique* (Paris: Société d'Editions Géographiques, Maritimes, et Coloniales, 1930), 1–15.
10. For more on Islamic marriage and family law in select countries, see: Susan F. Hirsch, *Pronouncing and Preserving: Gender and the Discourses of Disputing in an African Islamic Court* (Chicago: University of Chicago Press, 1998); Codou Bop, *Islam and Women's Reproductive and Sexual Health and Rights in Senegal* (Atlanta: Religion and Human Rights Project, 2003); Elke E. Stockreiter, *Islamic Law, Gender, and Social Change in Post-Abolition* Zanzibar (Oxford: Oxford University Press, 2015).
11. Kristin Mann, *Marrying Well: Marriage, Status, and Social Change among the Educated Elite in Colonial Lagos* (Cambridge: Cambridge University Press, 1985); Jean Allman and Victoria Tashjian, *'I Will Not Eat Stone': A Women's History of Colonial Asante* (Portsmouth: Heinemann, 2000); Dorothy L. Hodgson and Sheryl McCurdy (eds), *'Wicked' Women and the Reconfiguration of Gender in Africa* (Portsmouth: Heinemann, 2000); Brett L. Shadle, *Girl Cases: Marriage and Colonialism in Gusiiland, Kenya, 1890-1970* (Portsmouth: Heinemann, 2006).

12   Martin Channock, 'Making Customary Law: Men, Women, and Courts in Colonial Northern Rhodesia', in *African Women and the Law: Historical Perspectives*, ed. Margaret Jean Hay and Marcia Wright (Boston: Boston University, African Studies Center, 1982), 53–67.
13   Rachel Jean-Baptiste, *Conjugal Rights: Marriage, Sexuality, and Urban Life in Colonial Libreville, Gabon* (Athens: Ohio University Press, 2014), 134–61.
14   Jane Guyer, 'The Value of Béti Bridewealth', in *Money Matters: Instability, Values, and Social Payments in the Modern History of West African Communities*, ed. Jane I. Guyer (Portsmouth: Heinemann, 1995), 113–22; Adam Kuper, *Wives for Cattle: Bridewealth and Marriage in Southern Africa* (Oxford: Routledge & Kegan Paul, 1982).
15   Jean-Baptiste, *Conjugal Rights*, 97–134.
16   Georges Balandier, 'Aspects de l'Evolution Sociale chez les Fangs du Gabon', *Cahiers internationaux de sociologie* 9 (1950): 76–106; Joseph Eband-Essono, 'Mariage Coutumier et Modernité: Mariage Coutumier Fang', (Rapport de Licence, Département de Sociologie. , Libreville: L'Université Omar Bongo (UOB), 1997), 8–19; 'Une Théorie de la Circulation de la Dot Chez les Fangs de l'Estuaire du Gabon'(Mémoire de Maitrise, Département d'Anthropologie,Libreville : UOB, 1999), 2–6.
17   Rachel Jean-Baptiste, '"These Laws Should Be Made by Us": Customary Marriage Law, Codification and Political Authority in Twentieth-Century Colonial Gabon', *The Journal of African History* 49, no. 2 (2008): 217–40.
18   Jean-Baptiste, *Conjugal Rights*, 148–9.
19   For a more detailed analysis of francophone Africa's colonial wide laws that attempted to regulate marriage, see: Emily S. Burrill, *States of Marriage: Gender, Justice, and Rights in Colonial Mali* (Athens: Ohio University Press, 2015), 79–107 and 153–79.
20   JC Bobeyeme, 'La jeunesse Fang du Gabon et le mariage', *Journal de l'AEF* (17 December 1947), 201; François Meye, 'La Femme Africaine', *Le Journal de l'AEF* (25 January 1948), 3; François Meye, 'La Femme Africaine', *Le Journal de l'AEF* (29 January 1948), 5.
21   ANG, La Documentation Gabonaise, République Gabonaise Assemblée Nationale du Gabon, Journal des Débats. Première Séance Ordinaire du 16 Avril 1963 au 6 Juin 1963. Séance Plénière du 31 Mai 1963.
22   ANG, Assemblée Nationale du Gabon, 31 May 1963.
23   Ibid.
24   Ibid.
25   Ibid.
26   ANG, La Documentation Gabonaise, 'Discours Prononcé à Port-Gentil par le Président de la République', *Bulletin Quotidien de l'Agence Gabonaise d'Information*, Bulletin Spécial (6 July 1963).
27   *Journal Officiel de la République Gabonaise*. Décret #227/PR déterminant es modalités de remboursement des dots versées antérieure à la date d'entrée en vigueur de la loi #2063 du 31 Mai 1963 en cas de dissolution du mariage(15 August 1963), 649.
28   *Journal Officiel de la République Gabonaise*, Numéro Spécial, Loi Numéro 21–63 du Mai 1963, Code Pénal de la République Gabonaise.
29   ANG, 2DAI8. Région de l'Estuaire, Affaires Politiques et Sociales, Correspondance Relative aux droit Coutumier et tribunal indigène. République Gabonaise, Présidence de la République, Le Conseiller Technique. Note à l'attention de Monsieur le Sous-Préfet de Libreville, 4 July 1964.
30   Victoria Bronstein, 'Confronting Custom in the New South African State: An Analysis of the Recognition of Customary Marriages Act 120 of 1998', *South African*

Journal on Human Right, 3, no. 16 (2000): 558–75; I. P. Maithufi and J. C. Bekker, 'The Recognition of the Customary Marriages Act of 1998 and Its Impact on Family Law in South Africa', *Comparative and International Law Journal of Southern Africa* 2, no. 35 (2000): 182–97; Marissa Herbst and Willemien du Plessis, 'Customary Law Versus Common Law Marriages: A Hybrid Approach in South Africa', *Journal of Comparative Law* 1, no. 3 (2008): 105–18.

31   Oral Interviews in Libreville January to June 2001: Achey Oyeng; Myriam Claire Essonghe; Renée Enombo; Christine Nzoghe; Claudine Angwé. Oral Interviews in Libreville, June 2006: Jean Obame Toung; Madeline Matina; Louise Alène; Osette Ayetebe Obame; Martine Ada N'dong; Cécile Andeme N'dong; Bernadette Angone; Jean Ebale M'ba; Emmanuel Ongone Bikegne; Véronique N'nang Mebale; Thérèse Bouanga.

32   Oral Interview, Libreville, Marie France Andene Allogo, 2 June 2006.

33   Oral Interview, Libreville, Honorine Nstame Allogo Nzet Biteghe, 15 June 2006.

34   Oral Interview, Libreville, Joséphine Engone, 20 June 2006.

35   Oral Interview, Libreville, Yvonne N'dong, 17 June 2006.

36   Oral Interview, Marie France Andeme Allogo.

37   Oral Interview, Libreville, July 2006: Jacqueline Menque Mboumba; Ntoutoume Obame.

38   Oral Interview, Libreville, Alfred Belé Belé, 15 June 2006.

39   Article entitled, 'Marriage: Le Cassse-Tete de la Dot', in *Gabon Review*, 30 August 2013. http://www.bdpmodwoam.org/articles/2013/08/30/mariage-le-casse-tete-de-la-dot/#.Vtp1Zxj1rOo.

40   Oral Interview, Libreville, Janvier N'guema M'boumba, 12 June 2006.

41   Oral Interview, Libreville, 30 June 2006: Francois Assa; Alphonse Ngui; N'toutoume Obame.

42   Official website of the government of Gabon: http://www.en.legabon.org/keys-sectors/research-social-field/presentation.

43   For a summary of the Convention see: http://www.un.org/womenwatch/daw/cedaw/

44   United Nations, CEDAW, /C/GAB/6. *Comité pour l'élimination de la discrimination à l'égard des femmes. Examen des rapports soumis par les États parties en application de l'article 18 de la Convention. Sixième rapport périodique des États parties devant être soumis en 2010 Gabon.* Signed by Honorine Nstame Allogo Nzet Biteghe, 13 January 2013.

45   Oral interview, Honorine Ntsame Allogo Nzet Biteghe. Francois N'djimbi, 'Honorine Biteghe, la dame aux mille batailles', in *Gabon Review*, 8 March 2012. http://gabonreview.com/blog/honorine-nzet-biteghe-la-dame-aux-mille-batailles/.

46   Farafina Boussougou-Bou-M'bine and Honorine Nstame Allogo Nzet Biteghe, *Ètude Sur La Deuxième Partie Du Code Civil Gabonais.* Cette étude a été réalisée dans le cadre du projet 'Promotion de l'Egalité et de l'Equité de Genre au Gabon' et financée par le Fonds des Nations Unies pour la Population (UNFPA) dans le cadre de son programme 2002–6 (Libreville : UNFPA, 2007), 10–12. http://countryoffice.unfpa.org/gabon/drive/Etudesurla2epartieducodecivilgabonais.pdf.

47   Honorine Nstame Allogo Nzet Biteghe, Ministère de la Famille, de la Promotion Féminine et de la Protection de l'Enfance, Programme des Nations United Pour le Développent, *Monogame Pouvant Devenir Polygame sans Divorcer, Une Réalité du Droit Positif Gabonais* (Libreville: SARCOGI, 2003).

48   Honorine Nstame Allogo Nzet Biteghe, Ministère de la Famille, de la Promotion Féminine et de la Protection de l'Enfance, Programme des Nations United Pour le

Développent, *Veuves et Orphelins Avez Vous des Droits #2* (Libreville: SARCOGI, 2003), 15.
49 Honorine Nstame Allogo Nzet Biteghe, Ministère de la Famille, de la Promotion Féminine et de la Protection de l'Enfance, Programme des Nations United Pour le Développent, *Qu'est-ce que la reconnaissance d'un enfant et comment l'obtenir* (Libreville: SARCOGI, 2003).
50 United Nations, CEDAW C/GAB/6, *Comité pour l'élimination de la discrimination à l'égard des femmes*, 6. For more on changes in domestic violence law, see: Emily S. Burrill, Richard Roberts and Elizabeth Thornberry (eds), *Domestic Violence and the Law in Colonial and Postcolonial Africa* (Athens: Ohio University Press, 2010).
51 Nzet Biteghe, *Monogame Pouvant Devenir Polygame sans Divorcer*, 9–10.
52 Honorine Nstame Allogo Nzet Biteghe, Ministère de la Famille, de la Promotion Féminine et de la Protection de l'Enfance, Programme des Nations United Pour le Développent, *Qu'est-ce que la pension alimentaire?* (Libreville : SARCOGI, 2003).
53 United Nations, *Comité pour l'élimination de la discrimination à l'égard des femmes*, 6.
54 Boussougou-Bou-M'bine and Nzet Biteghe, *Etude Sur La Deuxième Partie Du Code Civil Gabonais*, 10
55 For more on the status of widows in varied African countries, see: Mariama Ba, *So Long A Letter* (Portsmouth: Heinemann, 1981); David William Cohen and E. S. Atieno Odhiambo, *Burying SM: The Politics of Knowledge and the Sociology of Power in Africa* (Portsmouth: Heinemann, 1992); Kenda Mutongi, *Worries of the Heart: Widows, Family, and Community in Kenya* (Chicago: University of Chicago Press, 2007).
56 Honorine Nstame Allogo Nzet Biteghe, Ministère de la Famille, de la Promotion Féminine et de la Protection de l'Enfance, Programme des Nations United Pour le Développent, *Veuves et Orphelins Avez Vous des Droits #1* (Libreville: SARCOGI, 2002).
57 Nzet Biteghe, *Veuves et Orphelins Avez Vous des Droits #2*, 2–9.
58 Nzet Biteghe, *Qu'est-ce que la reconnaissance d'un enfant*, 3.
59 Boussougou-Bou-M'bine and Nzet Biteghe, *Etude Sur La Deuxième Partie Du Code Civil Gabonais*, 14.
60 Oral Interview, Honorine Nstame Allogo Nzet Biteghe.
61 Loic N'toutoume, 'Mariage coutumier et dualité juridique', *Société* (9 October 2014). http://gabonreview.com/blog/mariage-coutumier-dualite-juridique/.
62 For more on the history of homosexuality in Africa see: Marc Epprecht, *Hungochani: The History of a Dissident Sexuality in Southern Africa* (Montreal: McGill-Queen's University Press, 2004).

Postscript: How History Mattered in Gaining Same-Sex Marriage Rights in the United States

Nancy F. Cott

The institution of marriage is a paradoxical phenomenon in the United States. It straddles elements that are, in other contexts, on opposite sides of a dividing line. Marriage is both essentially private and essentially public. It signifies both a private, intimate relationship and a public status, validated by public witness and civil law. Marriage requires free will – consent given freely – but amounts to a fixed obligation. That is, marriage as constituted in the United States represents both 'freedom' and 'governance'. In law, marriage is both a contract and a status (though these two are ordinarily opposite categories). Marriage requires the state, but for most Americans, it invokes religion. It is a civil right but also a holy ceremony (for Catholics, a sacrament). The sentimental facets of marriage are as vast as the stars. Yet in bare fact, marriage is a state creation. Justice Steven Levinson of the Hawaii Supreme Court baldly emphasized 'the state's role as the exclusive progenitor of the marital partnership' in his 1993 opinion in *Baehr v. Lewin*. He defined marriage wholly unsentimentally as a 'state-conferred legal partnership status, the existence of which gives rise to a multiplicity of rights and benefits reserved exclusively to that particular relation'.[1]

These points begin to suggest why changes in the institution of marriage became so fraught in the movement to equalize the marital rights of gay and lesbian couples in the United States. The movement began at the grass roots in the 1980s, seeking a significant change in what most Americans saw as a static, trans-historical institution. It gathered steam in legislatures and courts. The emergence of advocacy stimulated many hostile state legislatures to pass laws in the 1990s limiting marriage to one man–one woman couples, and even to install that usually tacit principle in state constitutions. Same-sex couples who wanted to marry, supported by civil rights advocacy groups, such as Lambda Legal, Gay and Lesbian Advocates and Defenders, and the American Civil Liberties Union, proceeded to challenge prohibitions on same-sex marriage in numerous state courts. It was through court actions – most effectively in federal courts rather than at the state level – that the movement eventually achieved its aim. That method might be seen as having been necessary, because marriage in the United States is a civil creation (indeed, even a civil right) resting on legal action for its validity, and second, because the US Constitution is the ultimate resort for rights guarantees for underserved groups and the constitution is reached most effectively by appeal to federal courts.

A word is necessary here about marriage and federalism – that is, the sharing of sovereign authority between the federal government and the states – in the United States. Constitutionally, the individual states, not the federal government, have sovereign power over making and breaking marriages. The various states have controlled who is eligible to marry throughout American history and have often differed on eligibility in matters of age, race, health and affinal relation, for example. That does not mean the federal government takes no cognizance of marriage or marital status. To the contrary, federal laws often refer to or build in rights, benefits or obligations based on spousal status (and family relationships based on marriage), notably in areas relating to citizenship, immigration and social welfare. Nonetheless the states retain sole power to declare who can marry, who can perform marriages, what the conditions for divorce are and punishments for failing to conform. The US Congress does not have the same power to legislate marriage as do national legislatures in countries where federalism does not exist. The US Supreme Court, however, is the arbiter over the constitutionality of both state and federal laws if they are challenged, upholding them or striking them down. By controlling the limits of state law-making, Supreme Court opinions can, in effect, create national law even in areas where the states are nominally sovereign (including voting rights and marriage eligibility).

History mattered in these court cases. First of all, American law is a historical practice. Court decisions make history and change history. Outcomes at the Supreme Court interpret and reinterpret the US Constitution to define what is lawful for the nation as a whole. Court decisions become binding precedents, as definite as any black-letter law on the books, and these holdings build upon one another in historical procession. Reversals of precedent can occur, though they are rare. And because customary practice usually follows what is lawful, Supreme Court decisions have reoriented the nation's direction on matters as crucial as freedom of speech, the right to vote, corporate conduct and racial and gender norms and rights. But history mattered in the marriage cases in particular ways that would not have been predicted. In court, claims for equal marriage rights by same-sex couples raised questions about the purposes and characteristics of marriage and the reasons that states became involved in it at all. Legislators and judges (like the general populace) tended to abstract marriage from historical context and think of it as unchanging. It became important for better-informed historians to weigh in, to give marriage in the United States a fuller history, which proved to have more complexities than most people assumed. Historians could reveal the significant changes in marriage that had already occurred, within the short space of two hundred years, and show that the proximate source of alterations was the state apparatus – the same state legislatures and courts being called upon to open access to marriage to couples of the same sex.

Replacing judges' assumptions about the past with accurate history can be very powerful. That was shown in the outcome of a gay rights case, *Lawrence v. Texas*, decided in 2003, that underlay later successes in challenging marriage exclusion.[2] It involved a challenge to a Texas law criminalizing consensual sodomy between men, in private. The Supreme Court's decision in *Lawrence v. Texas* that the Texas law was unconstitutional overturned the court's precedent of 1986 upholding a similar Georgia law. Overturning a precedent is unusual, and usually takes place many decades later; overturning a precedent after only seventeen years is extremely rare.

The court's opinion in *Lawrence* took into account new information that had been supplied in an *amicus curiae* brief submitted by historians. (Outside parties can offer their views in such 'friend of the court' briefs, to supplement lawyers' appellate arguments, after petitioning the court for permission.) The majority struck down the Texas law with the revised historical understanding in mind. The historians' brief pointed out that the 1986 decision, by making the assumption that laws against 'homosexual sodomy' were 'the legacy of millennia', rested on a misapprehension of the historical record. To the contrary, the historians' brief showed that conceptualization of 'homosexual sodomy' was a relatively recent innovation. Yes, 'sodomy' had been criminalized in Anglo-American law for centuries – but what was sodomy? The antique term included all non-procreative sex, so-called 'unnatural acts' that might be practised between man and woman, or man and animal, as well as between man and man. Older laws applied to anyone who might engage in such acts and did not identify or deem anyone a 'homosexual'. Not until the mid-twentieth century in the United States, the historians' *amicus curiae* brief showed, were homosexuals identified thus and prosecuted for similar sexual acts, through laws meant 'to classify and penalize homosexuals as a subordinate class of citizens'. The statute at issue in *Lawrence v. Texas*, enacted in 1973, was an example of such a law.[3]

The court's holding in *Lawrence v. Texas* underpinned a breakthrough in Massachusetts later that same year, when the highest court in that state decided that same-sex couples could not be denied the right to marry.[4] *Lawrence v. Texas* did not concern marriage, but its clearing away the criminality of sodomy was critical to advancing the cause of marriage rights. When the Massachusetts case was on appeal, the Boston-based group called Gay and Lesbian Advocates and Defenders, which was arguing the case on behalf of six couples, asked historians for an *amicus curiae* brief on the history of marriage in the United States.[5] (It has become so common for lawyers on both sides to line up such briefs in constitutional cases that highly visible cases can draw a blizzard of *amicus curiae* on both sides. Judges are not obliged to read them. Only references in the court's opinion show for certain that an *amicus curiae* has been heard.)

Ascertaining the state's interest in promoting, licensing and regulating marriage became central, in order to settle whether a state's excluding same-sex couples from marriage was rational and defensible. That question is in part a historical question. Defenders of the legal status quo in marriage cases typically invoked history or tradition as obviously on their side – offering, in one later instance, 'the common-sense proposition that the institution of marriage has, virtually always and everywhere, been defined as a union of man and woman because its central animating societal purpose has always, and everywhere, been to channel potentially procreative sexual relations into enduring, stable family unions for the sake of producing and raising the next generation'.[6] To test the 'common sense' of that static and universalizing view of marriage as 'always and everywhere' the same, history informed by intelligent and fair research was called upon to offer a fuller and more accurate assessment.

The historians' *amicus curiae* brief crafted for Massachusetts in 2003 and all those afterwards emphasized the evolving character of marriage in the United States, pointing out that state legislatures and courts had enabled the institution of marriage to remain vital by responding to social change over the generations by altering marriage requirements. The emphasis on marriage as a resilient institution countered the contention that marriage had a single traditional formula that must be sustained. First, however, the briefs made plain that legislatures and courts had the authority to change the very definition of marriage. That fact should be taken for granted, but it had to be articulated because so many Americans think of marriage in religious terms. They have seen marriage ceremonies performed only by clerics, in churches, and are unaware that a cleric can solemnize a marriage only because the state has authorized him or her to do so. It is fine for Americans to think of marriage as religious; they are free to think this way, and to observe their faith's strictures about marriage, themselves. They just cannot expect to use the law to impose their religious views about marriage as the rule for all. Ever since the American Revolution, marriage in all the United States has been authorized and regulated by civil authorities and is, in fact, completely in the hands of legislatures and courts to define and alter.

In stressing that it is the state's view – not any religion's view – that should be foremost, the historians' briefs also emphasized that states have several interests or purposes in licensing and promoting marriage. The opposition to equalizing marriage rights for same-sex couples typically dwelt on reproduction as the core of marriage (as in the quotation above). Counsel for the defendants in a signal California case asserted in his closing argument, for example, 'The first purpose of matrimony by the laws of nature and society is procreation.'[7] (He did not mention the laws of the state of California, which were actually at issue.) Such arguments, which were a throwback to nineteenth-century views, naturalized the institution and intentionally minimized the positive action of the state in marriage definition. More instrumental arguments for the 'limitation of marriage to opposite-sex unions', as in the state of Washington, had similar emphasis: 'Society needs a plan for raising the children that result from heterosexual sex. Civil marriage is that plan. Gay and lesbian relationships may equal heterosexual relationships in desire for commitment, but they are not equal in their contribution to society.'[8]

In the historians' perspective, a focus on procreative purpose purposely underplayed the numerous other reasons that states would license and regulate marriage, and completely ignored the fact that ability or willingness to sire or bear children is not and has never been a requirement for marriage in any of the United States. Nor has absence of either of these been a ground for divorce. Those straightforward facts, offered in early historians' briefs, impressed some judges in early cases to note that partners with no capability of having children, such as post-menopausal women, had never been excluded from marrying. Defenders of the *status quo* then shifted their emphasis from procreation per se to rearing of children, arguing that states were interested in providing an optimal environment for child-rearing, and should reserve the imprimatur of marriage for married spouses who were a man and a woman (especially if they were the biological parents), because only they provided such an optimal environment.

In offering a more varied portrait of what the state 'gets back' from marriage, historians pointed out that core state interests in marriage were broader, and included stabilizing the social order and providing economic benefit to households. The historians' briefs saw the state's economic interest in marriage as on par with any procreative purpose, pointing out that the institution of marriage helps society and the state by establishing stable households, facilitating wealth and property inheritance, and mandating reciprocal support in the marital household, thus limiting public liability for those who are vulnerable or poor. In the longer past of Anglo-American law, marriage was a form of governance as well as economy. By marrying, a man became head of his household and governed his wife and other dependents, representing them politically, while being required to take economic and legal responsibility for them in return for his political power. Today the power of the male household head over other family members has been mostly eliminated in the law; now both in a married pair are required to support one another and their children (whether biological or not). That marital obligation continues to serve the economic stability of households and society.

On the matter of continuity and change, historians pointed out that marriage was repeatedly modified in ways significant enough to alter the very character of marital roles and requirements. Courts and legislatures responsive to economic and social change in family lives and work roles rewrote and updated legal definitions of eligibility for marriage, and the institution's obligations and rights, from the nineteenth century on. Marriage had previously undergone changes as dramatic as the demand by same-sex couples for inclusion, without toppling, the historians suggested. Rarely has major change in the structure or obligations of marriage come easily. Fierce squawks of opposition arose from voices certain that any significant change would spell the doom of marriage altogether. Yet change took place. Historians' briefs concentrated on three important areas of change:

First, beginning in the 1660s in the Chesapeake colonies, civil authorities used marriage regulations to define racial categories and to create a hierarchy of races, typically citing the 'natural' basis for this. It became a very widespread practice in the United States. Forty-one of the states and territories at some point in their histories prohibited and criminalized or voided marriages of whites to persons of colour. This feature of marriage was repeatedly defended as natural and necessary – indeed a God-given mandate. After waxing and waning in various states over many decades, it was completely eliminated, three hundred years after it began, by reinterpretation of the meaning of constitutional equal protection in the Supreme Court case of *Loving v. Virginia* (1967).

Second, marriage in Anglo-American law was lifelong. State legislatures' inauguration of liberal grounds for divorce in the nineteenth century and more in the twentieth century changed what it meant to marry, with the result of making marriage more resilient, and more appealing to many people, rather than destroying it – although naysayers had imagined that such expansion of divorce was a death knell for the institution. The shift in the 1970s and 1980s from an adversary procedure to 'no-fault' procedure made marital roles and harmony more than ever a matter for spouses' decision-making rather than state prescription.

Third, perhaps most dramatically and relevantly, legislatures and courts gradually eliminated the marital doctrine of coverture (or marital unity), which subsumed the wife and her property under her husband's legal/economic identity. The asymmetrical spousal roles in the economic and legal regime of coverture were prescribed and enforced by law. The arrangement was considered fundamental and essential to marriage. But its requirements were not suited to the restless American economy. Unravelling coverture was a long process, for husbands' economic headship and command of the household had built into custom and seeming necessity. In a vestige of coverture, a husband was legally required to support his wife, and she to obey him, in every state into the late twentieth century. But the women's rights surge in the 1970s forced the end of sex discrimination and took with it the differentiation between the legal obligations and benefits of marriage for the two spouses. The emergence of the wife to individuality and equal rights within marriage eventually produced gender-neutral requirements for both spouses. States now set reciprocal and symmetrical marital duties for the two spouses, rather than hierarchical and asymmetrical requirements. Both members of a married pair are obliged to support each other; both have equal responsibility for any children. Changes of this sort laid the groundwork to make marriage for couples of the same sex imaginable and feasible.

While the initial court battles to gain marriage rights for same-sex couples took place in state courts, where state laws prescribing marriage limits were most obviously to be challenged, in 2009 an important second strategy began in federal courts, challenging the federal Defense of Marriage Act (usually called DOMA). In passing that law in 1996 the US Congress was reacting to the first instance in which a state court decision (in Hawaii) had made the granting of marriage to a same-sex couple appear imminent.[9] Very quickly, with sweeping majorities, both houses of the US Congress discussed and passed and President Clinton signed a federal law stipulating that no state had to honour the same-sex marriage policy of another state, and also stipulating that in all uses in federal law, marriage would be defined as only that between a man and a woman.[10] Thus even if a state did enable valid marriage between two men or two women, the federal government would not recognize the couple as being married; the couple would not qualify for any right or benefit that the federal government allotted specifically to married couples. Right away the constitutionality of the DOMA appeared suspect to many observers. The congressmen who passed it were aware that only the states could make or break marriages. It was in order to comport with constitutional limitations that DOMA prescribed a definition of marriage for federal law only; its defenders pointed out that it left states free to license same-sex marriage. They said that federal action of this sort was consistent with constitutional limitations. They argued further that the federal government was acting rationally to maintain a single, uniform definition of marriage for *its* purposes, when the states might soon vary in their definitions. (At the time that DOMA became law, same-sex marriage was not legal anywhere in the United States, and would not be for eight more years.)

Once same-sex marriage had existed for a number of years in Massachusetts, challenges to DOMA arose there. Married same-sex couples felt they were treated unequally by federal law refusing to recognize their marriages. Their marital status was compromised, and they were ineligible for federal benefits that other married couples gained. The state of Massachusetts itself also challenged DOMA on the grounds that it deprived the state of certain federal funds that would have attached to those couples if they were regarded as married.

In the cases against DOMA, lawyers asked historians to offer historical perspective on federalism with regard to marriage. A new historians' *amicus curiae* brief emphasized that the 'regulation of domestic relations' had been reserved to the states since the founding of the United States. The historians did not claim that the federal government was prevented from legislating about marriage altogether, because that was not accurate. Congress has often passed perfectly valid laws that bear on discrete marital rights, privileges or conditions – in social security or immigration eligibility, for instance. Nonetheless, historians could easily point out that no previous federal law had been like the Defense of Marriage Act in setting out a single federal definition for the gender composition (or any other feature) of all marriages. The supposed justification for the law – to maintain a single federal standard in the face of possibly differing state laws – was unprecedentedly sweeping and not necessarily rational, given the history of past differentiation among states. States have always varied in their definitions of eligibility for marriage and conditions for divorce, so that a person validly married in one state might not be considered married in another. For example, some states allow first cousins to marry and others prohibit that; some states but not others credit unceremonialized marriage; states set the minimum age for marrying at differing levels; and during the centuries when most American states criminalized marriage across the colour line, some allowed it. In the past, federal agencies had not decried these variations in the resulting married pairs nor found its results hard to deal with. In dispensing benefits to or requiring taxes of married couples, federal agencies had been guided by the relevant state's definition of marriage validity. The historians' brief called the Defense of Marriage Act 'a radical departure from settled federal practice'. Historical research showed no previous example of Congress giving 'disfavoured treatment' to one particular kind of state-licensed marriages by refusing to recognize those marriages at the federal level.[11] Every federal court that heard suits against DOMA called the law unconstitutional.

By 2013 a challenge to DOMA from the state of New York reached the Supreme Court on appeal, with historians among the slew of *amicus curiae* briefs accompanying it. The court's opinion in this case, *US v. Windsor*, written by Justice Anthony Kennedy (as was *Lawrence v. Texas*), struck down the DOMA as unconstitutional. Four of the nine members of the Supreme Court disagreed and wrote forceful dissents. Historians were gratified that Justice Kennedy stated that assessing Congress's action in creating DOMA required 'discussing the historical and traditional extent of state power and authority over marriage'. The court's opinion aligned nicely with the historians' brief, in noting that the federal government had accepted various state definitions of marriage in the past. The opinion called the approach of the Defense of Marriage Act an 'unusual deviation' for excluding, wholesale, all potential married same-sex couples in whatever state, prospectively.[12]

Justice Kennedy emphasized the intention of the state of New York to 'give protection and dignity' to couples of the same sex by enabling them to marry. As he reviewed the successive steps the state had taken to authorize 'lawful marriage' for same-sex couples, he stressed that the state made 'a far-reaching legal acknowledgment of the intimate relationship between two people' and deemed it 'worthy of dignity in the community equal with other marriages'. His emphasis in those sentences accomplished several things at once. First, he underlined the importance of lawful marriage as a relationship larger than a private commitment between two people. Marriage is a larger relationship because it also involves the state honouring the couple's bond, and thereby lending superior public and social validity to it. Second, Kennedy's approach underlined that the Defense of Marriage Act affronted federalism by invading New York's constitutional authority to create a privileged marital status. Third, Kennedy held that a whole class of persons who married partners of their own sex when their home state authorized it were being denied equal liberty and due process of the laws (rights guaranteed by the 14th amendment to the constitution). Kennedy said that by rendering state-authorized marriages of same-sex couples 'unworthy of federal recognition', the Defense of Marriage Act had made those marriages not only 'unequal' but also functionally 'unstable' and 'second-tier'. In passing the law, Congress had the 'purpose and effect to disparage and to injure' these couples, although their home state meant rather 'to protect [them] in personhood and dignity'. That was the double problem in the law, its deprivation of personal liberty through its warping of federalism.[13]

The language of the *Windsor* opinion made most observers feel that equal marriage rights would soon triumph. That was right. Two years later, after many federal appeals courts had drawn on *Windsor* to strike down state bars to same-sex couples marrying, a group of such cases reached the Supreme Court on appeal, under the name *Obergefell v. Hodges*.[14] Again, historians spoke up as *amicus curiae*, emphasizing the varied state purposes of marriage through history and the resultant major changes over time. Again, Justice Anthony Kennedy wrote for the majority of the court. The opinion reasoned that excluding same-sex couples from marriage rights shut them out of a fundamental liberty guaranteed by the US Constitution, and denied them the equal protection of the laws.

Four of the nine justices dissented, and even ridiculed the majority decision. Differing understandings of history animated the two camps. The dissent by Chief Justice John Roberts called marriage an 'unvarying social institution enduring over all of recorded history', and 'a social institution that has formed the basis of human society for millennia, for the Kalahari Bushmen and the Han Chinese, the Carthaginians and the Aztecs'. 'To blind yourself to history is both prideful and unwise', he chided those who thought otherwise.[15] Justice Anthony Kennedy's opinion for the court glorified marriage as the most important association in human life, while seeing it as one that 'has not stood in isolation from developments in law and society' but has 'evolved over time'. The majority opinion focused squarely on the history of marriage as a civil institution within the constitutional order of the United States, after a brief bow to the institution's 'centrality' in 'the human condition … for millennia and across civilizations'. The opinion saw 'both continuity and change' in the history of marriage in the United States.[16]

Here, the historians could be sure that their contribution as *amicus curiae* made a difference, because Justice Kennedy cited their brief. He made the point that long before the question of same-sex marriage came up, changes in marriage had taken place that 'were not mere superficial changes. Rather, they worked deep transformations in its structure, affecting aspects of marriage long viewed by many as essential'.[17] The opinion mentioned the gradual demise of coverture, once 'society began to understand that women have their own equal dignity', as one example.[18] That historical perspective underpinned the majority's approach to the legitimacy of marriage for same-sex couples and buttressed its assertion that 'changed understandings of marriage are characteristic of a Nation where new dimensions of freedom become apparent to new generations'.[19] Judicial review had previously found the gender and race inequities in the civil institution of marriage constitutionally impermissible, and now an additional inequity could be addressed. Sounding the theme of change over time in constitutional interpretation, Kennedy wrote, 'If rights were defined by who exercised them in the past, then received practices could serve as their own continued justification and new groups could not invoke rights once denied.'[20]

Obergefell v. Hodges represents an immense landmark in the struggle for equal rights for lesbians and gay men and ready acceptance of the families they form. Beyond the victory that it marks for their dignity, the decision will likely bear further political fruit. Making same-sex marriage a constitutional right could augur a new era of creative interpretation of intimate bonds in the law. It could, however, lead in a less promising direction, by further enshrining the considerable privileges (as well as responsibilities) differentiating those who are married from those who are not. At present the adult population of the United States is divided about half and half between these two statuses. Never before has the proportion of unmarried adults been so low.

Non-marriage isn't randomly or evenly distributed. Those who do not marry, or do not stay married, are predominantly poorer and less educated Americans. The dividing line is less between straight and gay than between rich and poor. Almost two-thirds of adults who have a college degree are currently married, compared to less than 48 per cent of those without the degree. As in so many other things, education here is a proxy for stable employment, income and race: a far higher proportion of whites and Asian Americans are married than African Americans and Latinos.[21]

Americans who have the benefit of higher education and the mobility, employment options and the potential for income these imply are also those far more likely to marry and stay married. In other words, marriage – as a set of responsibilities and privileges – has become associated with the ability to achieve economic stability. Poor people themselves think so, sociological studies have shown.[22] The relation between being married and having economic and educational advantage has been clear to policymakers for decades; unfortunately they tend to see the cause and effect backwards, as if tying the knot brings the goods, where the reality is that those who have the goods feel empowered to tie the knot. The economic and legal advantages of marital status pile on to the already relatively advantaged, so that the haves gain more and the have-nots fall farther behind.

The paean to marriage that the Supreme Court delivered in June 2015 thus had a double edge. The privilege of household headship that a man gained in the past by marrying consolidated men's power over women for hundreds of years. Now, men or women who marry gain access to a framework of privileges and rights unavailable to the unmarried, whose families experience pressures and penalties from which the married are exempt. Inequalities anchored by race and class and education are mirrored in marriage statistics. Whether they are only mirrored, or exacerbated and deepened, is the next marriage question.

Notes

1. *Baehr v. Lewin* 52 P.2d 44 (Hawaii 1993).
2. *Lawrence v. Texas* 538 US 558 (2003).
3. George Chauncey, 'What Gay Studies Taught the Court: The Historians' Amicus Brief in *Lawrence v. Texas, GLQ* 10, no. 3 (2004): 509–38 explains the brief and reprints it. George Chauncey was the initiating author. I and others were additional signatories.
4. *Goodridge v. Department of Public Health* 798 N.E.2d 941 (Mass. 2003).
5. Plaintiffs' lawyers in fact asked for two differing historians' briefs: one on the history of marriage, another on the history of persecution of LGBTQ individuals. Only the history of marriage briefs is discussed here (and only a selected number of the many submitted in various state and federal cases). Michael Grossberg and I collaborated in writing the brief for *Goodridge v. Department of Public Health* and additional relevant historians participated in and signed it. I was the lead author in subsequent iterations, and also made similar arguments while serving as an expert witness in numerous cases. The lead author in historians' briefs on the persecution question, and frequently an expert witness, was George Chauncey.
6. Defendant-Intervenor's Brief as official proponents of Proposition 8 in *Perry v. Schwarzenegger* [704 F.Supp.2d 921 (2010)], 38–9.
7. Defendant-intervenor closing argument in *Perry v.Schwarzenegger* 704 F.Supp.2d 921 (2010).
8. Intervenor's reply brief, No. 75934-1 Supreme Court of the State of Washington., 10 January 2005, 2–3.
9. The court decision was *Baehr v. Lewin* 852 P.2d 44 (Hawaii 1993), quoted above, which sent the question back to a lower court for further evidence. Soon, forces mobilized in Hawaii to pass an amendment to the state constitution (superior to any court decision) stipulating that marriage was between one man and one woman.
10. H.R. 3396 (104th): Defense of Marriage Act (Pub.L. 104–199, 110 Stat. 2419, enacted September 21, 1996, 1 USC. § 7 and 28 USC. § 1738C).
11. Brief of Amicus Curiae Historians in *Commonwealth of Mass. v. Department of Health and Human Services* and in *Dean Hara and Nancy Gill v. Office of Personnel Management* in the US Court of Appeals for the First Circuit [Case 10-2204, Document: 00116286536, filed 3 November 2011].
12. Slightly different briefs were filed in the Windsor case at the circuit court level and at the Supreme Court: Brief of Amicus Curiae Historians in *Edith Schlain Windsor v. Bipartisan Legal Advisory Group of the US House of Representatives*, in the US Court of Appeals for the 2d Circ., on appeal from the US District Court S.D. N.Y. Case No 10-civ-8435; Brief on the Merits for Amici Curiae Historians, American Historical Association et al., in *USA. v. Windsor*, in the Supreme Court of the United States. No 12-307.
13. *US v. Windsor*, 133 S.Ct. 2675 (2013).
14. *Obergefell v. Hodges*, 576 US ___, 135 S Ct 2584, 192 L Ed 2d 609 (2015). The permanent page citation for the case is not yet available.

15 Dissent, 22, 42. All page numbers are from *Obergefell v. Hodges* slip opinion (2015), 14-556 3204-6, available at https://www.supremecourt.gov/opinions/opinions.aspx
16 Ibid., opinion, 6.
17 Ibid., 2.
18 Ibid., 6.
19 Ibid., 2.
20 Ibid., 18.
21 The Pew Research Center updates its survey information on these topics regularly, and is a reliable source. http://www.pewresearch.org/topics/marriage-and-divorce/
22 See Kathryn Edin and Maria J. Kefalas, *Promises I Can Keep: Why Poor Women Put Motherhood before Marriage* (Berkeley, CA: University of California Press, 2005); C. M. Gibson-Davis, et al., 'High Hopes and Even Higher Expectations: The Retreat from Marriage among Low-Income Couples', *Journal of Marriage and Family*, 67, no. 5 (2005): 1301–12; P. J. Manning et al., '"Everything's There Except Money": How Money Shapes Decisions to Marry among Cohabitors', *Journal of Marriage and Family*, 67, no. 3 (2005): 680–696.

Select Bibliography

Abbott, Elizabeth. *A History of Marriage*. London: Duckworth Overlook, 2011.
Adams, Julia. *The Familial State: Ruling Families and Merchant Capitalism in Early Modern Europe*. Ithaca: Cornell, 2005.
Albanese, Patrizia. *Mothers of the Nation: Women, Families and Nationalism in Twentieth-Century Europe*. Toronto: University of Toronto Press, 2006.
Allen, Ann Taylor. 'Feminism, Social Science, and the Meanings of Modernity: The Debate on the Origin of the Family in Europe and the United States, 1860–1914'. *The American Historical Review* 104, no. 4 (1999): 1085–1113.
Anderson, Michael. *Approaches to the History of the Western Family, 1500–1914*. 2nd edn. Cambridge: Cambridge University Press, 1995.
Bachofen, Johann Jakob, *Das Mutterrecht: eine Untersuchung über die Gynaikokratie der alten Welt nach ihrer religiösen und rechtlichen Natur*. Stuttgart: Krais & Hoffmann, 1861.
Bailey, Joanne. *Unquiet Lives: Marriage and Marriage Breakdown in England, 1660-1800*. Cambridge: Cambridge University Press, 2003.
Balibar, Etienne. 'The Nation Form: History and Ideology'. Translated by Immanuel Wallerstein and Chris Turner. *Review* 13, no. 3 (1990): 329–61.
Barclay, Katie. *Love, Intimacy and Power: Marriage and Patriarchy in Scotland, 1650-1850*. Manchester: Manchester University Press, 2011.
Beck, Ulrich, and Elisabeth Beck-Gernsheim. *The Normal Chaos of Love*. Translated by Mark Ritter and Jane Wiebel. Cambridge: Polity, 1995.
Benton, Lauren, and Richard J. Ross. *Legal Pluralism and Empires, 1500-1850*. New York: New York University Press, 2013.
Berkovitch, Nitza. *From Motherhood to Citizenship: Women's Rights and International Organizations*. Baltimore: Johns Hopkins University Press, 1999.
Bernhardt, Kathryn. *Women and Property in China, 960–1949*. Stanford: Stanford University Press, 1999.
Bock, Gisela. *Women in European History*. Oxford: Blackwell Publishers, 2002.
Bowen, John. *On British Islam: Religion, Law, and Everyday Practice in Shari'a Councils*. Princeton: Princeton University Press, 2016.
Bredbenner, Candice Lewis. *A Nationality of Her Own: Women, Marriage and the Law of Citizenship*. Berkeley: University of California Press, 1998.
Brook, Heather. *Conjugal Rites: Marriage and Marriage-like Relationships before the Law*. New York: Palgrave Macmillan, 2007.
Bunting, Annie, Benjamin N. Lawrance and Richard L. Roberts, eds. *Marriage by Force? Contestation over Consent and Coercion in Africa*. Athens, OH: Ohio University Press, 2016.
Burguière, André, Christiane Klapisch-Zuber, Martine Segalen, Francois Zonabend, eds. *A History of the Family*. 2 vols. Cambridge, MA: Belknap, 1996.
Burns, Susan L., and Barbara J. Brooks. *Gender and Law in the Japanese Imperium*. Honolulu: University of Hawaii Press, 2014.

Burrill, Emily S., Richard L. Roberts and Elizabeth Thornberry, eds. *Domestic Violence and the Law in Colonial and Postcolonial Africa*. Athens, OH: Ohio University Press, 2010.
Burton, Antoinette. 'From Child Bride to "Hindoo Lady": Rukhmabai and the Debate on Sexual Respectability in Imperial Britain'. *American History Review* 103, no. 4 (1998): 1119–46.
Bush, Barbara. 'Gender and Empire: The Twentieth Century'. In *Gender and Empire*, edited by Philippa Levine, 77–111. Oxford: Oxford University Press, 2004.
Canaday, Margot. *The Straight State: Sexuality and Citizenship in twentieth-century America*. Princeton: Princeton University Press, 2009.
Carey, Hilary M. *God's Empire: Religion and Colonialism in the British World, c. 1801-1908*. Cambridge: Cambridge University Press, 2011.
Chandra, Sudhir. *Enslaved Daughters: Colonialism, Law and Women's Rights*. Delhi: Oxford University Press, 1998.
Chatterjee, Partha. *The Nation and Its Fragments: Colonial and Postcolonial Histories*. Princeton: Princeton University Press, 1993.
Celello, Kristin. *Making Marriage Work: A History of Marriage and Divorce in the twentieth-century United States*. Chapel Hill: University of North Carolina Press, 2009.
Celello, Kristin, and Hanan Kholoussy. *Domestic Tensions, National Anxieties: Global Perspectives on Marriage, Crisis, and Nation*. Oxford: Oxford University Press, 2016.
Chakrabarty, Dipesh. *Provincializing Europe: Postcolonial Thought and Historical Difference*. Princeton: Princeton University Press, 2000.
Charsley, Katharine, ed. *Transnational Marriage: New Perspectives from Europe and Beyond*. London: Routledge, 2013.
Chatterjee, Nandini. 'English Law, Brahmo Marriage, and the Problem of Religious Difference: Civil Marriage Laws in Britain and India'. *Comparative Studies in Society and History* 52, no. 3 (2010): 524–52.
Cherlin, Andrew J. *The Marriage-Go-Round: The State of Marriage and the Family in America Today*. New York: Alfred A. Knopf, 2009.
Clancy-Smith, Julia, and Frances Gouda, eds. *Domesticating the Empire: Race, Gender, and Family Life in French and Dutch Colonialism*. Charlottesville: University of Virginia Press, 1998.
Clark, Cristopher M., and Wolfram Kaiser, eds. *Culture Wars: Secular-Catholic Conflict in Nineteenth-Century Europe*. Cambridge: Cambridge University Press, 2003.
Cong, Xiaoping. *Marriage, Law and Gender in Revolutionary China, 1940-1960*. Cambridge: Cambridge University Press, 2016.
Coontz, Stephanie. *Marriage, A History: From Obedience to Intimacy, or How Love Conquered Marriage*. New York: Viking, 2005.
Cooper, Frederick, and Ann Laura Stoler. *Tensions of Empire: Colonial Cultures in a Bourgeois World*. Berkeley: University of California Press, 1997.
Cott, Nancy F. *Public Vows: A History of Marriage and the Nation*. Cambridge, MA: Harvard University Press, 2000.
Cuno, Kenneth M. *Modernizing Marriage: Family, Ideology, and Law in nineteenth and early twentieth century Egypt*. Syracuse: Syracuse University Press, 2015.
Cuno, Kenneth M., and Desai, Manisha. *Family, Gender, and Law in a Globalizing Middle East and South Asia*. Syracuse: Syracuse University Press, 2009.
Daub, Adrian. *Uncivil Unions: The Metaphysics of Marriage in German Idealism and Romanticism*. Chicago: University of Chicago Press, 2012.
Davidoff, Leonore. *The Family Story: Blood, Contract and Intimacy, 1830-1960*. London: Longman, 1999.

Davidoff, Leonore. *Thicker than Water: Siblings and their Relations, 1780-1920*. Oxford: Oxford University Press, 2011.
Demos, John. *A Little Commonwealth: Family Life in Plymouth Colony.* Oxford: Oxford University Press, 1970.
Desan, Suzanne. *The Family on Trial in Revolutionary France*. Berkeley: University of California Press, 2004.
Desan, Suzanne, and Jeffrey Merrick. *Family, Gender, and Law in Early Modern France*. University Park, PA: Pennsylvania State University Press, 2009.
Diamant, Neil J. *Revolutionizing the Family: Politics, Love, and Divorce in urban and rural China, 1949-1968*. Berkeley: University of California Press, 2000.
Dirks, Nicholas B. *Castes of Mind: Colonialism and the Making of Modern* India. Princeton: Princeton University Press, 2001.
Dollard, Catherine. *The Surplus Woman: Unmarried in Imperial Germany, 1871-1918*. New York: Berghahn, 2009.
Donzelot, Jacques. *The Policing of Families*. Translated by Robert Hurley. New York: Pantheon Books, 1979.
Duben, Alan, and Cem Behar. *Istanbul Households: Marriage, Family and Fertility, 1880-1940.* Cambridge: Cambridge University Press, 1991.
Edin, Kathryn, and Maria J. Kefalas. *Promises I Can Keep: Why Poor Women Put Motherhood before Marriage*. Berkeley: University of California Press, 2005.
Engel, Barbara A. *Breaking the Ties that Bound: The Politics of Marital Strife in late Imperial Russia*. Ithaca: Cornell University Press, 2011.
Engels, Friedrich. *The Origins of the Family: Private Property and the State*. 1884. London: Penguin, 1972.
Epprecht, Marc. *Hungochani: The History of a Dissident Sexuality in Southern Africa*. Montreal: McGill-Queen's University Press, 2004.
Evans, Harriet. *Women and Sexuality in China: Female Sexuality* and *Gender Since 1949*. New York: Continuum, 1997.
Fisher, Kate. *Birth Control, Sex, and Marriage in Britain, 1918-1960*. Oxford: Oxford University Press, 2006.
Foucault, Michel. *The Birth of Biopolitics: Lectures at the Collège de France, 1978-1979*. Edited by Michel Senellart. Translated by Graham Burchell. Basingstoke: Palgrave Macmillan, 2008.
Fournier, Pascale. *Muslim Marriage in Western Courts: Lost in Translation*. Farnham: Ashgate, 2010.
Fuchs, Rachel G., and Victoria E. Thompson. *Women in Nineteenth-Century* Europe. Basingstoke: Palgrave Macmillan, 2005.
Gardner, Martha. *The Qualities of a Citizen: Women, Immigration, and Citizenship, 1870–1965*. Princeton: Princeton University Press, 2005.
George, Abosede. *Making Modern Girls: A History of Girlhood, Labor, and Social Development in Colonial Lagos*. Athens: Ohio University Press, 2014.
Gerhard, Ute. *Debating Women's Equality: Towards a Feminist Theory of Law from a European Perspective*. Translated by Allison Brown and Belinda Cooper. New Brunswick, NJ: Rutgers University Press, 2001.
Ghosh, Durba. *Sex and the Family in Colonial India: The Making of Empire*. New York: Cambridge University Press, 2006.
Giddens, Anthony. *The Transformation of Intimacy: Sexuality, Love and Eroticism in Modern Societies*. Cambridge, UK: Polity Press, 1992.
Ginsborg, Paul. *Family Politics: Domestic Life, Devastation and Survival, 1900-1950*. New Haven: Yale University Press, 2014.

Glendon, Mary Ann. *The Transformation of Family Law: State, Law and Family in the United States and Western Europe.* Chicago: University of Chicago Press, 1989.

Glosser, Susan L. *Chinese Visions of Family and State, 1915-1953.* Berkeley: University of California Press, 2003.

Gluck, Carol. 'The End of Elsewhere: Writing Modernity Now'. *American Historical Review* 116, no. 3 (2011): 676–87.

Goldman, Wendy Z. *Women, the State, and Revolution: Soviet Family Policy and Social Life, 1917-1936.* Cambridge: Cambridge University Press, 1993.

Goode, William J. *World Revolution and Family Patterns.* New York: Free Press, 1963.

Goody, Jack. *The Development of the Family and Marriage in Europe.* Cambridge: Cambridge University Press, 1983.

Gordon, Sarah B. *The Mormon Question: Polygamy and Constitutional Conflict in Nineteenth-century America.* Chapel Hill: University of North Carolina Press, 2002.

Green, James N. *Beyond Carnival: Male Homosexuality in Twentieth-Century Brazil.* Chicago: University of Chicago Press, 1999.

Grandits, Hannes, ed. *Family, Kinship and State in Contemporary Europe.* 3 vols. Frankfurt: Campus Verlag, 2010.

Gullestad, Marianne, and Martine Segalen. *Family and Kinship in Europe.* London: Pinter, 1997.

Hahner, June E. *Emancipating the Female Sex: The Struggle for Women's Rights in Brazil, 1850-1940.* Durham: Duke University Press, 1990.

Hajnal, John. 'European Marriage Patterns in Perspective'. In *Population and History*, edited by D. V. Glass and D. E. C Eversley, 101–46. New York: McGraw-Hill, 1969.

Haney, Lynn A., and Lisa Pollard, eds. *Families of a New World: Gender, Politics, and State Development in a Global Context.* New York: Routledge, 2003.

Hareven, Tamara K. 'The History of the Family and the Complexity of Social Change', *American Historical Review* 96, no. 1 (1991): 95–124.

Harris, Alana, and Timothy Jones, eds. *Love and Romance in Britain, 1918-1970.* Basingstoke: Palgrave Macmillan, 2015.

Hartog, Hendrik. *Man and Wife in America: A History.* Cambridge, MA: Harvard University Press, 2000.

Harvey, Karen. *The Little Republic: Masculinity and Domestic Authority in Eighteenth-Century Britain.* Oxford: Oxford University Press, 2012.

Hegel, G. W. F. *Elements of the Philosophy of Right.* Edited by Allen W. Wood. Translated by H. B. Nisbet. 1820. Cambridge: Cambridge University Press, 1991.

Heilmann, Ann, and Margaret Beetham, eds. *New Woman Hybridities: Femininity, Feminism, and International Consumer Culture, 1880-1930.* London: Routledge, 2004.

Heinemann, Elizabeth D. *What Difference Does a Husband Make? Women and Marital Status in Nazi and Postwar Germany.* Berkeley: University of California Press, 1999.

Herzog, Dagmar, *Sex after Fascism: Memory and Morality in Twentieth-Century Germany.* Princeton: Princeton University Press, 2005.

Hetherington, Penelope. 'The Politics of Female Circumcision in the Central Province of Colonial Kenya, 1920–30'. *Journal of Imperial and Commonwealth History* 26, no. 1 (1998): 93–126.

Heuer, Jennifer N. *The Family and the Nation: Gender and Citizenship in Revolutionary France, 1789-1830.* Ithaca: Cornell University Press, 2005.

Higgs, David, and Luiz Mott. *Infamous Desire: Homosexuality in Colonial Latin America.* Chicago: University of Chicago Press, 2003.

Hirsch, Susan F. *Pronouncing and Preserving: Gender and the Discourses of Disputing in an African Islamic Court.* Chicago: University of Chicago Press, 1998.

Hodes, Martha E. *Sex, Love, Race: Crossing Boundaries in North American History*. New York: New York University Press, 1999.
Holden, Katherine. *The Shadow of Marriage: Singleness in England, 1914-60*. Manchester: Manchester University Press, 2010.
Hunt, Lynn. *The Family Romance of the French Revolution*. Berkeley: University of California Press, 1992.
Hyam, Ronald. *Empire and Sexuality: The British Experience*. Manchester: Manchester University Press, 1990.
Jean-Baptiste, Rachel. *Conjugal Rights: Marriage, Sexuality and Urban Life in Colonial Libreville, Gabon*. Columbus: Ohio University Press, 2014.
Joffe, Lisa Fishbayn, and Sylvia Neil, eds. *Gender, Religion & Family Law: Theorizing Conflicts between Women's Rights and Cultural Traditions*. Waltham, MA: Brandeis University Press, 2013.
Johnson, Christopher H., and David Warren Sabean. *Sibling Relations and the Transformations of European Kinship, 1300-1900*. New York: Berghahn Books, 2011.
Kertzer, David, and Marzio Barbagli. *The History of the European Family*. 3 vols. New Haven: Yale University Press, 2001–3.
Kholoussy, Hanan. *For Better, for Worse: The Marriage Crisis that Made Modern Egypt*. Stanford: Stanford University Press, 2010.
Kollman, Kelly. *The Same-Sex Unions Revolution in Western Democracies: International Norms and Domestic Policy Change*. Manchester: Manchester University Press, 2013.
Kuper, Adam. *Incest & Influence: The Private Life of Bourgeois England*. Cambridge, MA: Harvard University Press, 2009.
Langhamer, Claire. *The English in Love: The Intimate Story of an Emotional Revolution*. Oxford: Oxford University Press, 2013.
Lavrin, Asunción. *Women, Feminism and Social Change in Argentina, Chile* and *Uruguay, 1890-1940*. Lincon, NE: University of Nebraska Press, 1995.
Lind, Göran. *Common Law Marriage: A legal Institution for Cohabitation*. Oxford: Oxford University Press, 2008.
Loos, Tamara. *Subject Siam: Family, Law, and Colonial Modernity in Thailand*. Ithaca: Cornell University Press, 2006.
Maine, Henry. *Ancient Law: Its Connection to the History of Early Society*. 1861. London: J. M. Dent and Sons, 1917.
Majumdar, Rochona. *Marriage and Modernity: Family Values in Colonial Bengal*. Durham, NC: Duke University Press, 2009.
Mamdani, Mahmood. *Citizen and Subject: Contemporary Africa and the Legacy of Late Colonialism*. Princeton: Princeton University Press, 1996.
Mani, Lata. *Contentious Traditions: The Debate on Sati in Colonial India*. Berkeley: University of California Press, 1998.
Mann, Kristin. *Marrying Well: Marriage, Status, and Social Change among the Educated Elite in Colonial Lagos*. Cambridge: Cambridge University Press, 1985.
Mankekar, Purnima, and Louisa Schein, eds. *Media, Erotics and Transnational Asia*. Durham, NC: Duke University Press, 2012.
Mason, Karen O., Noriko O. Tsuya and Minja Kim Choe, eds. *The Changing Family in Comparative Perspective: Asia and the United States*. Honolulu: University of Hawaii Press, 1998.
Maynes, Mary Jo, and Ann Waltner. *The Family: A World History*. Oxford: Oxford University Press, 2012.
McMahon, Keith. *Polygamy and Sublime Passion: Sexuality in China on the Verge of Modernity*. Honolulu: University of Hawaii, 2010.

Metz, Tamara. *Untying the Knot: Marriage, the State, and the Case for their Divorce*. Princeton: Princeton University Press, 2010.
Midgley, Clare, ed. *Gender and Imperialism*. Manchester: Manchester University Press, 1998.
The Modern Girl Around the World Research Group (Alys Eve Weinbaum, Lynn M. Thomas, Priti Ramamurthy, Uta G. Poiger, Madeleine Yue Dong, and Tani E. Barlow, eds). *The Modern Girl Around the World: Consumption, Modernity and Globalization*. Durham, NC: Duke University Press, 2008.
Moeller, Robert. *Protecting Motherhood: Women and the Family in the Politics of Postwar West Germany*. Berkeley: University of California Press, 1993.
Montesquieu. *The Spirit of the Laws*. Edited by Anne M. Cohler, et al. 1748. Cambridge: Cambridge University Press, 1989.
Moran, Rachel F. *Interracial Intimacy: The Regulation of Race and Romance*. Chicago: University of Chicago Press, 2001.
Morgan, Lewis Henry. *Ancient Society, or Researches in the Lines of Human Progress from Savagery through Barbarism to Civilization*. London: MacMillan, 1877.
Morsink, Johannes. *The Universal Declaration of Human Rights*. Philadelphia: University of Pennsylvania Press, 1999.
Morton, Adam, and Helen Watanabe-O'Kelly, eds. *Queens Consort, Cultural Transfer and European Politics, 1550-1750*. London: Routledge, 2016.
Mouton, Michelle. *From Nurturing the Nation to Purifying the Volk: Weimar and Nazi Family Policy, 1918-1945*. Cambridge: Cambridge University Press, 2007.
Nautz, Jürgen, Paul Ginsborg and Ton Nijhuis, eds. *The Golden Chain: Family, Civil Society and the State*. New York: Berghan, 2013.
Nelson, Claudia, et al., eds. *British Family Life, 1780-1914*. 5 vols. London: Pickering & Chatto, 2013.
Newbigin, Eleanor. *The Hindu Family and the Emergence of Modern India: Law, Citizenship and Community*. Cambridge: Cambridge University Press, 2013.
Offen, Karen M. *European Feminisms, 1700-1950: A Political History*. Stanford: Stanford University Press, 2000.
Okin, Susan Moller. *Is Multiculturalism Bad for Women? Susan Moller Okin with Respondents*. Edited by Joshua Cohen, Matthew Howard, and Martha C. Nussbaum. Princeton: Princeton University Press, 1999.
Ozment, Steven. *When Fathers Ruled: Family Life in Reformation Europe*. Cambridge, MA: Harvard University Press 1983.
Parker, Stephen. *Informal Marriage, Cohabitation and the Law, 1750-1989*. Basingstoke: Macmillan, 1990.
Pascoe, Peggy. *What Comes Naturally: Miscegenation Law and the Making of Race in America*. Oxford: Oxford University Press, 2009.
Phegley, Jennifer. *Courtship and Marriage in Victorian England*. Santa Barbara, CA: Praeger, 2012.
Phillips, Roderick. *Putting Asunder: A History of Divorce in Western Society*. Cambridge: Cambridge University Press, 1998.
Pleck, Elizabeth H. *Not Just Roommates: Cohabitation after the Sexual Revolution*. Chicago: University of Chicago Press, 2012.
Pollard, Lisa. *The Family Politics of Modernizing, Colonizing, and Liberating Egypt, 1805-1923*. Berkeley: University of California Press, 2005.
Probert, Rebecca. *The Changing Legal Regulation of Cohabitation: From Fornicators to Family, 1600-2010*. Cambridge: Cambridge University Press, 2012.

Probert, Rebecca. *Marriage Law and Practice in the Long Eighteenth Century: A Reassessment*. Cambridge: Cambridge University Press, 2009.
Robcis, Camille. *The Law of Kinship: Anthropology, Psychoanalysis, and the Family in France*. Ithaca: Cornell University Press, 2013.
Saada, Emmanuelle. *Empire's Children: Race, Filiation and Citizenship in the French Colonies*. Translated by Arthur Goldhammer. Chicago: University of Chicago Press, 2012.
Sabean, David Warren, Simon Teuscher and Jon Mathieu, eds. *Kinship in Europe: Approaches to Long-term Development (1300-1900)*. New York: Berghahn Books, 2007.
Sabean, David Warren. *Kinship in Neckarhausen, 1700-1870*. Cambridge: Cambridge University Press, 1998.
Sabean, David Warren. *Property, Production, and Family in Neckarhausen, 1700-1870*. Cambridge: Cambridge University Press, 1990.
Saraceno, Chiara. 'Women, Family, and the Law, 1750-1942'. *Journal of Family History* 15, no. 4 (1990): 427–42.
Sarkar, Tanika. 'A Prehistory of Rights: The Age of Consent Debate in Colonial Bengal', *Feminist Studies* 26, no. 3 (2000): 601–22.
Scott, Joan W. *Gender and the Politics of History*. New York: Columbia University Press, 1988.
Seymour, Mark. *Debating Divorce in Italy: Marriage and the Making of Modern Italians, 1860-1974*. Basingstoke: Palgrave Macmillan, 2006.
Shadle, Brett L. *Girl Cases: Marriage and Colonialism in Gusiiland, Kenya, 1890-1970*. Portsmouth: Heinemann, 2006.
Shanley, Mary Lyndon. *Feminism, Marriage, and the Law in Victorian England, 1850-1895*. Princeton: Princeton University Press, 1989.
Shorter, Edward. *The Making of the Modern Family*. New York: Basic Books, 1975.
Simmons, Christina. *Making Marriage Modern: Women's Sexuality from the Progressive Era to World War II*. Oxford: Oxford University Press, 2009.
Sinha, Mrinalini. *Specters of Mother India: The Global Restructuring of an Empire*. Durham, NC: Duke University Press, 2006.
Skinner, Quentin, ed. *Families and States in Western Europe*. Cambridge: Cambridge University Press, 2011.
Sommer, Matthew H. *Polyandry and Wife-Selling in Qing Dynasty China: Survival Strategies and Judicial Interventions*. Berkeley: University of California Press, 2015.
Sreenivas, Mytheli. *Wives, Widows, and Concubines: The Conjugal Family Ideal in Colonial India*. Bloomington: Indiana University Press, 2008.
Stacey, Judith. *Unhitched: Love, Marriage, and Family Values from West Hollywood to Western China*. New York: New York University Press, 2011.
Stearns, Peter N. 'The Family in Modern World History'. In *The Cambridge World History*, vol. VII: *Production, Destruction and Connection, 1750-Present*, Part 2: *Shared Transformations?*, edited by J. R. McNeill and Kenneth Pomeranz, 58–83. Cambridge: Cambridge University Press, 2015.
Steinmetz, George. *The Devil's Handwriting: Pre-coloniality and the German Colonial State in Qingdao, Samoa and Southwest Africa*. Chicago: University of Chicago Press, 2007.
Stoler, Ann Laura. *Carnal Knowledge and Imperial Power: Race and the Intimate in Colonial Rule*. Berkeley: University of California Press, 2002.
Stone, Lawrence. *Broken Lives: Separation and Divorce in England, 1660-1857*. Oxford: Oxford University Press, 1993.
Stone, Lawrence. *Uncertain Unions: Marriage in England, 1660-1753*. Oxford: Oxford University Press, 1992.

Sturman, Rachel. *The Government of Social Life in Colonial India: Liberalism, Religious Law and Women's Rights*. Cambridge: Cambridge University Press, 2012.

Thane, Pat, and Tanya Evans. *Sinners? Scroungers? Saints?: Unmarried Motherhood in Twentieth-Century England*. Oxford: Oxford University Press, 2012.

Therborn, Göran. *Between Sex and Power: Family in the World, 1900-2000*. London: Routledge, 2004.

Thomas, Lynn M. *Politics of the Womb: Women, Reproduction, and the State in Kenya*. Berkeley: University of California Press, 2003.

Tilly, Louise, and Joan Wallach Scott. *Women, Work, and Family*. New York: Holt, Rinehart & Winston, 1978.

Traer, James F. *Marriage and the Family in eighteenth-century France*. Ithaca: Cornell University Press, 1980.

Tucker, Judith E. *Women, Family, and Gender in Islamic Law*. Cambridge: Cambridge University Press, 2008.

Vikør, Knut S. *Between God and the Sultan: A History of Islamic Law*. Oxford: Oxford University Press, 2005.

Vogel, Suzanne H., and Steven K. Vogel. *The Japanese Family in Transition: From the Professional Housewife Ideal to the Dilemmas of Choice*. Lanham, MD: Rowman and Littlefield, 2013.

Voorhoeve, Maaike. *Family Law in Islam: Divorce, Marriage and Women in the Muslim World*. London: I. B. Tauris, 2012.

Wallenstein, Peter. *Tell the Court I Love My Wife: Race, Marriage, and Law – an American History*. New York: Palgrave Macmillan, 2004.

Walsh, Judith E. *Domesticity in Colonial India: What Women Learned when Men Gave them Advice*. Lanham, MD: Rowman and Littlefield, 2004.

Wanhalla, Angela. *Matters of the Heart: A History of Interracial Marriage in New Zealand*. Auckland: Auckland University Press, 2013.

Weiss, Jessia. *To Have and to Hold: Marriage, the Baby Boom, and Social Change*. Chicago: University of Chicago Press, 2000.

Westermarck, Edward. *The History of Human Marriage*. London: Macmillan, 1891.

Willson, Perry, ed. *Gender, Family and Sexuality: The Private Sphere in Italy (1860-1945)*. London: Palgrave Macmillan, 2004.

Witte, John, Jr. *From Sacrament to Contract: Marriage, Religion and Law in the Western Tradition*. 2nd edn. Louisville, KY: Westminster John Knox Press, 2012.

Yack, Bernard. *The Fetishism of Modernities: Epochal Self-Consciousness in Contemporary Social and Political Thought*. Notre Dame, IN: University of Notre Dame Press, 1997.

Yalom, Marilyn. *A History of the Wife*. New York: Harper Collins, 2001.

Yan, Yunxiang. *Private Life Under Socialism: Love, Intimacy, and Family Change in a Chinese Village, 1949-1999*. Stanford: Stanford University Press, 2003.

Yount, Kathryn, and Hoda Rashad, eds. *Family in the Middle East: Ideational Change in Egypt, Iran, and Tunisia*. New York: Routledge, 2008.

Index

Abduh, Muhammad   134–6, 143, 146
Adenauer, Konrad, Chancellor of the Federal Republic of Germany   206
adoption   8, 11, 27, 35, 40, 42–3
adultery   12, 54, 56, 58, 60–3, 75, 84, 183, 195, 210. *See also* concubinage and bigamy
Albert, Prince of Saxe-Coburg Gotha   102
Albrecht VI of Austria   96
al-Bustani, Butrus   132
Allouba, Muhammad Ali   140–3
al-Nawawi, Muhammad b. Umar   131–2
al-Shaʿrawi, Huda   139
al-Tahtawi, Rifaʿa   132–4
al-Taymur, Aisha   133, 139
amicus curiae briefs   16, 44, 244–5, 248–9
Amin, Qasim   134–6
Amina Ilhami, wife of Khedive Tawfiq of Egypt   137–8
Anglicanism. *See* Church of England
Anna, Princess of Prussia   93
Anne I, Queen of Great Britain and Ireland   95
Anne of Austria, Queen of France   92
annulment. *See* divorce, annulment
anti-clericalism   13, 30, 109, 111–13
anti-semitism   6, 119
apostasy   6, 13, 93–6, 110–11, 114–15
Argentina   4, 103
atheism   4
Auersperg, Karl   109
August III, King of Poland   93
Australia   14, 98, 103, 173, 205, 238; New South Wales 177; Norfolk Island 173
Austria   6, 13, 27, 91–2, 95–6, 103, 109–28, 158, 195; 1848 Revolution in 110–11; Association of Catholic Separated Married Persons 116; Association for Marriage Law Reform 117–18; Austrian Civil Code (1811) 13, 109–11, 115–17, 120; Austrian Marriage Law Reform Society 111; Austrian People's Party 123; Catholic Imperial Women's Organization 118; Christian Corporate State 121–3; Christian Social Party of Austria 112, 118–19, 123; civil marriage in 112, 114–23, 125; Concordat (1855) 105, 111–13, 123; Concordat (1933) 121, 123; Cultural Policy Association 116; culture wars in 111–15; Democratic Republic of Austria 123; Dualism in 13, 115, 120–1; Federation of Austrian Women's Societies 116; General Austrian Women's Association 116; Law on Recognition of Churches (1874) (the 'Catholics' Act') 113; Marriage Act (1938) 122–3; Marriage Patent (1783) 109–10; May Acts (1868) 112; Pan-German Party 118, 120–1; Social Democratic Party of Austria 120–1; Supreme Court of Austria 114, 120
Austria-Hungary. *See* Austria

Bachofen, Johann Jacob   8, 76
Bahithat al-Badia. *See* Nasif, Malak Hifni
Banerjee, Gooroodass   154–6, 159
Barbara, Princess of Brandenburg-Kulmbach   94
Bauer, Helene   119
Belgium   90, 102–3, 158
Bellefeuille, Clarence de   198–9
Bengal   8, 149, 160, 174
Beviláqua, Clovis   31
bigamy   3, 12, 15, 54–6, 61–5, 98–100, 113, 115, 121, 177, 187–203
binational marriage. *See* mixed marriage
Bloom, Louis   198
Bonaparte, Napoleon   95, 172
Bongo, Omar   234
Bowring, Sir John   72
Braun, Ruth   214
Brazil   4–5, 11, 27–53; amicus curiae briefs in 44; Brazilian Association of

Family law 42; Brazilian Civil Code (1916) 27, 31–2; Brazilian Constitution (1988) 11, 27, 32, 35, 37, 39–44; Brazilian Federal Superior Court of Justice 43; Brazilian Federation for Feminine Progress 31; Brazilian National Judicial Council 43; Brazilian Supreme Court 11, 27; Brazilian Worker's Party 37; Christian liberation theology in 36; cohabitation in 28–9, 33, 35; Criminal Code (1830) 29–30; criminalization of homosexuality in 29, 32, 36; Estado Novo 32–3; Grupo Gay da Bahia 37, 52; homoaffective unions in Brazilian jurisprudence 11, 27, 41–4; Minas Gerais 42; National Labour Council of Brazil 33; patriarchy in 27–32, 35–6, 40, 44; same-sex marriage in 11, 33, 38, 40–5; Statute of the Married Woman (1962) 32; Rio de Janeiro 41–4; Rio Grande do Sul 33, 40–3; São Paulo 33–4, 38–9, 42; socio-affective family as a concept in Brazilian jurisprudence 40–1; Triângulo Rosa 37
bridewealth. *See* dower
Britain. *See* United Kingdom
British Empire 6, 8, 14, 168–85; cohabitation in 175; common law marriage in 168–83; *Countess of Limerick v. the Earl of Limerick* 173; *Dadaji Bhikaji v. Rukhmabai* 149–53; *Dalrymple v. Dalrymple* 175–8; *Kent v. Burgess* 172; *Latour v. Teesdale* 175–6; *Maclean v. Cristall* 178–9; *R v. Brampton*; *R. v. Millis* 175; *Ruding v. Smith* 173–6; *War v. Dey* 173; *Wingrove v. Wingrove and McPherson* 160. *See also* India
Brougham, Henry Peter 1st Baron Brougham and Vaux (Lord Brougham) 177
Buddhism 12, 55, 72, 74, 77–83, 85

Cabral, Sérgio 43
Caird, Alice Mona 158
Calvinism 94, 171
Campbell, John, 1st Baron Campbell (Lord) 177
Canada 3, 7, 15, 187–202; annulment in 188–90, 195, 198; Canadian Criminal Code 191, 199; Cape Breton 197; divorce in 188–90, 193–200; illegitimate children in 189–93, 199; Law Reform Commission of Canada (1985) 199; Montreal 193–5, 197–8; Morality Departments of the Police 194; Newfoundland 176; Nova Scotia 15, 187–202; Quebec 15, 182–202; Quebec Civil Code (1774) 188, 200; Society for the Protection of Women and Children 195; Toronto 194
canon law. *See* law and legal systems
Cape Colony 171, 173
Carlo di Borbone, King of the Two Sicilies 92, 96
Carneiro, Laura 43
Carneiro, Nelson 32
Caroline Mathilda, Queen of Denmark 101
Caroline of Braunschweig-Wolffenbüttel, Queen of the United Kingdom and Hanover 99
Catherine I, Empress of Russia 99
Catherine II (the Great), Empress of Russia 92
Catherine of Braganza, Queen of England, Scotland and Ireland 94, 100
Catholic Church. *See* Catholicism; concordats; Pius IX
Catholic Counter-reformation 28, 122
Catholicism 4, 11, 13, 15, 28–32, 36, 93–4, 98–9, 103–4, 109–28, 158, 169–70, 175–6, 178, 187–8, 193, 196, 199, 204–5, 212–13, 224–5, 228, 231, 233, 242. *See also* law and legal systems, canon law; marriage, as a sacrament in Christian theology
Chakrabongse, Prince of Siam 79
Charlemagne, Holy Roman Emperor 96
Charles I, King of England, Scotland and Ireland 94
Charles II, King of England, Scotland and Ireland 91, 94, 100
Charles VI, Holy Roman Emperor 94
Charles, Princes of Wales 101, 103
child marriage 8–9, 14, 77, 133, 139, 149–50, 152–4, 158–9, 225. *See also* marriage, age at
children 57, 75, 81–3, 91–2, 94–5, 99, 229–30; abandonment of 198; custody of 84, 97–8, 100, 207, 224, 229, 235;

illegitimacy of (out-of-wedlock children) 12, 28, 30, 72, 75, 82–5, 97–8, 168, 177, 189–93, 199, 207; legal rights of 15, 30, 35, 40, 43, 129, 174–5, 177, 235; rearing of 28, 31, 42, 57, 129, 131–4, 138, 194, 210, 245–6. *See also* adoption
China   54–70; Beijing 62, 65; Chinese Communist Party (CCP) 54–6, 63–5; Chinese Criminal Code (1928/1935) 60–1; Hebei 62; Henan 54; Hundred Days of Reform 55; Marriage Law (1950) 65; Marriage Law (1980) 64–5; Marriage Law Campaign (1953) 64–5; Mosuo 3; New Culture Movement 11, 60; patriarchy in 56, 59, 65; Qingdao 54; Shanghai 54, 58, 61; Shanghai Women's Circle (*Funü jie*) 61; Small family (*xiao jiating*) 54; Society of Women's United Voice (*Funü gongmingshe*) 61; Young Women's Christian Association of China (*Zhonghua jidujiao nü qingnianhui*) 60
Christian VII, King of Denmark   101
Christianity   3, 5–6, 13–14, 36, 61, 78–9, 83, 85, 96, 110, 112–13, 118–23, 130, 157, 168–9, 174, 179–80, 188, 204–7, 212–16, 223, 225, 231, 237. *See also* Christian missionaries; law and legal systems, canon law; marriage, as a sacrament in Christian theology
Chulalongkorn, King of Siam (Rama V)   79–82
Church of England   4, 14, 94, 103, 168–71, 176–9, 196
Church of Scotland   176, 178
citizenship   6, 9, 13, 35, 114–15, 120–1, 162, 205, 207, 210, 243; women's citizenship in marriage 207, 210–12, 216
civil codes: Austrian Civil Code (1811)   13, 109–11, 115–17, 120; Brazilian Civil Code (1916) 27, 31–2; Chinese Civil Code (1929/30) 9, 11, 55, 60–2; Civil and Commercial Code of Siam (1935) 12, 84–5; Code of Hammurabi 3; French Civil Code (1804) 6; Prussian Civil Code (1794) 4; Quebec Civil Code (1774) 188, 200; Swiss Civil Code (1912) 9; Turkish Civil Code (1926) 9

civil marriage   1, 4, 6, 27, 112, 114–23, 125, 223, 231–7, 242
civility, discourse about   2, 7–10, 73, 76–7, 116–17, 132, 153, 157–8, 161, 215
clandestine marriage   4, 47, 169, 178; Clandestine Marriage Act (1753) (Britain) 4, 169, 178
Clinton, William J., President of the United States   247
clitoredectomy. *See* female genital mutilation
cohabitation   1, 3, 6, 28–9, 33, 35, 63, 75, 84, 149, 175, 199, 250–1. *See also* concubines and concubinage
Colebrook, H. T.   155, 159, 161
colonialism   2, 5, 8–10, 12–15, 17, 28–30, 32, 71, 73, 77, 130, 139, 150–62, 174, 179, 187, 222–37; colonial modernity 13, 129; semi-colonization 73, 129
combined succession (*jiantiao*)   57
common law marriage   8, 119, 168–83
common law. *See* law and legal systems
concept of dignity in jurisprudence on same-sex marriage   11, 37, 40–1, 43–4, 248–50
concordats: Concordat (1855) (Austria)   105, 111–13, 123; Concordat (1933) (Austria) 121, 123
concubines and concubinage   9, 11–13, 28, 33–5, 40–1, 43, 54–70, 76, 116, 130, 136, 138, 177, 188, 235. *See also* adultery; bigamy; polygamy
Conference for the Codification of International Law (1930)   9
conflicts of law   111, 152, 156–7, 170, 175, 195. *See also* law and legal systems, forum shopping
Confucianism   11, 55–60, 65–6
Constitutions   3, 98, 110–11, 120–1, 162, 188; Austrian Constitution (1867) 112; Brazilian Constitution (1988) 11, 27, 32, 35, 37, 39–44; constitutional reforms in the Federal Republic of Germany 209; 5; constitutional reforms in Gabon 16, 228, 234–6; Egyptian Constitution (1923) 130; Egyptian Constitution (1956) 5, 130; German Basic Law (1949) 206, 210; Republic of Ireland Constitution (1937) 5; Spanish Constitution (1931), United States

266 Index

Constitution (1789) 242–9; Weimar Republic Constitution (1919) 5
Convention on Elimination of All Forms of Discrimination against Women (CEDAW) (1979)   10, 16, 234
Coulanges, Numa Denis Fustel de   76
Council of Trent   28, 175
court cases: *Baher v. Lewin*   242; *Countess of Limerick v. the Earl of Limerick* 173; *Dadaji Bhikaji v. Rukhmabai* 149–53; *Dalrymple v. Dalrymple* 175–8; *Kent v. Burgess* 172; *Latour v. Teesdale* 175–6; *Lawrence v. Texas* 243–4, 248; *Loving v. Virginia* 246; *Maclean v. Cristall* 178–9; *Obergefell v. Hodges* 249–50; *R v. Brampton* 175; *R. v. Millis* 177–8; *Ruding v. Smith* 173–6; *US v. Windsor* 248–9; *War v. Dey* 173; *Wingrove v. Wingrove and McPherson* 160
courts: Bombay High Court   149; Brazilian Federal Superior Court of Justice 43; Brazilian Supreme Court 11, 27; customary and family courts in Gabon 231, 236; ecclesiastical courts 114, 190; Federal Administrative Court of Germany 210; Guomingdang (GMD) Supreme Court 62; Hawaii Supreme Court 242; Jewish tribunals 7; panchayats 153, 156; Sharia courts 7, 13, 130, 135; Supreme Court of Austria 114, 120; Supreme Court of Bombay 178; United States Supreme Court 243, 246, 248–50
coverture   7, 9, 247, 250. *See also* patriarchy
customary law   156, 162, 228–9, 231, 235; customary marriage law 162, 228

Darwin, Charles   159
Denmark   6, 90, 94–5, 101, 103
Déry, Philomène   187–8, 195
Días, Maria Berenice   41
disobedience of the wife in Muslim jurisprudence (*nushuz*)   14, 131
dispensations to marry. *See* marriage prohibitions
divorce   3, 5–7, 10, 12, 14–15, 32, 35, 43, 60, 64–5, 75, 77, 83–4, 90, 95, 98–104, 110–19, 122–3, 129, 131, 133–6, 140, 153, 157, 160, 188–90, 193–200, 204, 207–10, 216, 222–35, 243, 245, 248; annulment 84, 135, 153, 188–90, 195, 198; Catholic indissolubility of marriages 31, 110, 112, 118–19, 122; conditional 135; delegated 135; Hindu indissolubility of marriages 153; *khul'*, 129, 143; no-fault 32, 193; remarriage after 13, 113, 115, 116, 119–22; restitution of conjugal rights 149, 152–3; separation from bed and board 110, 113–7, 122; *talaq* (repudiation) 129, 135
Dollfuß, Engelbert   121
domestic violence   41–2, 213, 215, 235
domesticity or domestic ideology   13, 34, 44, 58, 129–38, 154, 160, 208. *See also* family, ideal of; husband, role of; wife, role of
Donaldson, Mary   103
dower (bridal gift)   29–30, 94, 97, 139–41; bridewealth 10, 15–16, 75, 222–37; morning gift 97–8
Dumais, Elisa   196
Durkheim, Emile   9, 34
Dynasties; succession of   12, 56–7, 90–9, 101, 103, 138; Han Dynasty 55; House of Bourbon 90, 92, 95–6; House of Guelph 90, 93–4, 100; House of Habsburg 13, 90–6, 103, 118, 121; House of Hohenzollern 90, 93–4, 103; House of Romanov 103; House of Stuart 90, 94–5; House of Tudor 90; House of Valois 90; House of Wittelsbach 90, 94; House of Wettin 90, 93–4, 96; Jakri Dynasty 74; Muhammad Ali Dynasty 133; Qing Dynasty 11, 54–5, 58–60, 65, 72; Song dynasty 58

East India Company   173
Eberhard Ludwig, Duke of Württemberg   99
Eddy, Assad   194
education   13, 38, 40, 55, 64, 111, 139, 141, 143, 149, 152, 211–12, 235, 250; of women 10, 13, 60, 130, 132–4, 136, 138, 208, 210, 215
Edward IV, King of England   94
Edward VIII, King of the United Kingdom   103
Egypt   5, 7–8, 13–14, 55–6, 71, 110, 129–48, 151, 173, 238; annulment

in 135; conditional divorce in 135; Constitution (1923) 130; Constitution (1956) 5, 130; delegated divorce in 135; divorce in 129, 131, 133–6, 140; family ideology in 129–33, 136, 138–9, 141, 143; khedival (viceregal) family in 130, 136–9, 143; *khulʿ* divorce in 129, 143; Muhammad Ali Dynasty in 133; maintenance of the wife in Muslim jurisprudence (*nafaqa*) in 14, 129, 134, 135; Muslim jurisprudence in 130–6; obedience of the wife in Muslim jurisprudence in (*taʿa*) 14, 129, 131; patriarchy in 140–1; press in 141; polygyny in 130–6, 138; *talaq* divorce in (repudiation) 129, 135; Urabi Revolution (1881–2) 139; women's education in 130, 132–4, 136, 138
Elisabeth Christine of Braunschweig-Wolfenbüttel, Holy Roman Empress 92–4
Elisabeth of France, Queen of Spain 92
Elisabeth Charlotte, Princess of the Palatinate 91, 94
Elizabeth I, Queen of England and Ireland 91
Elizabeth II, Queen of the United Kingdom 90–1, 98,
Eller, Cassia 41–2
England. *See* United Kingdom of Great Britain and Ireland
Enlightenment and post-Enlightenment thought 7, 13, 132
Ernst August, Prince of Hanover 98
ethnography 11, 73, 77, 157, 162
eugenics 6. *See also* procreation
extraterritoriality clauses 12, 71–2, 135,

familialism 5
family 1–11, 28, 31–2, 37, 42, 44, 54, 56, 77, 84, 129–31, 141, 190, 192, 205; conjugal 2, 9, 11, 13, 28, 33, 56, 59–61, 65–6, 71, 84, 129–43, 224–5, 233, 235–6; ideal of 129–33, 136, 138–9, 141, 143, 209; patrilineal 11, 29, 56–61, 65–7, 91, 95, 101, 130
Fawwaz, Zaynab 133–4
Felipe VI, King of Spain 104
female genital mutilation 8, 225

feminists and feminism 8–9, 11, 27, 31–2, 35–7, 42, 44, 60, 116–19, 132–3, 137, 139, 150, 158
First Vatican Council (1870) 113
Fitzherbert, Maria Anne 99
France 4–7, 13–15, 72, 90–5, 99, 130, 133, 135, 158, 171–3, 222–8, 235; French Civil Code (1804) 6; French law 4, 6, 13–14, 33, 130, 135, 171, 173, 225, 228, 235; French Revolution (1789) 5–6, 95
Franz Joseph, Emperor of Austria 109, 112–13, 115,
Frederick VI, King of Denmark 101
Fredrik, Crown Prince of Denmark 103
free love movement 119
Friedrich August I (August the Strong), King of Saxony / August II of Poland 93
Friedrich II (the Great), King of Prussia 92–3
Friedrich II, Elector of Saxony 96
Friedrich III, German Emperor and King of Prussia 96, 102
Friedrich III, Holy Roman Emperor,
Friedrich Wilhelm I, King of Prussia 92, 100
Friedrich Wilhelm III, King of Prussia 101–2

Gabon 10, 15–16, 150, 222–41; Bridewealth Law (1963) 230, 237; children's rights in 235; civil marriage in 223, 231–7; divorce in 222–35; domestic violence in 235; Fang minority 226–7, 229, 231, 233; forced marriage in 225; Lambaréné 231; legal pluralism in 224–8; Libreville 226, 229, 231–3; Ministry of the Family, the Protection of Children and the Advancement of Women 234; missionaries in 223; movement for a family code of law in 231, 235; Muslim family law in 231; *Observatoire de droits de la femme et de la parité* (ODEFPA) 234–6; patriarchy in 225–6, 229–30, 235; polygyny in 225; widows in 235–6; Woleu N'tem 226, 231
Gambia 173
gay pride parades. *See* LGBT movement

Gelli, Odoardo   79–80
genealogy   74, 95–7
Georg Wilhelm, Duke of Braunschweig-Lüneburg   99
George I, King of Great Britain and Ireland and Elector of Hanover   93, 95, 100–1
George II, King of Great Britain and Ireland and Elector of Hanover   98
George III, King of the United Kingdom and Hanover   99
George IV, King of the United Kingdom and Hanover   99
Germany   4–7, 15, 32, 90–1, 93, 97–8, 102–3, 122–3, 158–9, 204–21; Bavaria 90, 93, 103; binational marriage in 205; Christian Democratic Party (CDU) 206, 210; civil code in the Federal Republic of Germany 206; divorce in 204, 207–10, 216, 222–35; domestic violence in 213, 215; emigration counseling in 212–13; family ideals in 205, 209; Federal Administrative Court 210; Federal Republic of Germany (West Germany) 204–21; German Association for Home Economics 208; German Basic Law (1949) 206, 210; German East Africa 6; German Southwest Africa 6; *Internationaler Sozialdienst* (International Social Service) 213; marriage as a matter of public opinion in 204, 207–11, 214, 216; marriage between Catholics and Protestants in 205; marriage between Jews and non-Jews in 6; marriage between Muslims and non-Muslims 204–21; National Socialism 6, 10, 13, 15, 122–3, 205; Office of Emigration 212; patriarchy in 209–10; press in 207–11, 214, 216; Protestant Church in 212–14; *Protestant Diakonie* 212; *Protestant Diakonisches Werk* 213; Prussia 4, 6, 90, 92–4, 100–2, 111; Prussian Civil Code (1794) 4; Saxony 90, 92–4, 96, 99, 103, 158; Social Democratic Party (SPD) 210; *St Raphaels-Verein* (*Raphaels-Werk*) 212; Turkish guest workers 204, 208, 211, 213, 215; Weimar Republic Constitution (1919) 5; women's citizenship in marriage 207, 210–12, 216; Württemberg 214; Württemberg Association of the Friends of Young Girls 214
Gföllner, Johannes Maria, Bishop of Linz   119
Gidumal, Dayaram   150, 159–61
Girardi, Alexander   115
globalization   1, 11
godparentage   29
Grabmayr, Karl von   117–18
Grävenitz, Christina Wilhelmina von   100
Gray, Nelson   196–7
Gross, Eliza   191
guardians and guardianship   75, 131, 139, 162. *See also* patriarchy; children, custody of

Habsburg Empire. *See* Austria
Hamilton-Temple-Blackwood, Frederick 1st Marquess of Dufferin and Ava (Lord Dufferin)   150
harems   12, 76, 79, 133, 138–9; Inner Palace in Siam 73–4, 79, 81; in politics 138, 143
Harris, Townsend   76
Hegel, G. W. F.   2
Heinrich II, Duke of Braunschweig-Wolfenbüttel   92
Henry VIII, King of England   91, 99
Herbst, Eduard   109
heterosexuality   5, 15, 35–6, 40–2, 44, 74, 77–8, 151, 222, 223, 228, 231, 237, 245. *See also* homosexuality; same-sex marriage
Hindu 'revivalists'   151, 154. *See also* modernists and modernism
Hinduism   4, 8–9, 14, 149–67; Hindu caste system 14, 151, 153–4, 159–61. *See also* marriage, marriage as a sacrament in Hindu theology; divorce, Hindu indissolubility of marriage
HIV-AIDS   37–9
Hohenheim, Franziska von   99
homoaffective unions in jurisprudence   11, 27, 41–4
homosexuality   1–2, 5, 7, 11, 16, 27, 32, 35–45, 81, 91–2, 104, 237, 242–50; criminalization of 29, 32, 36, 237, 243–4; and non-consummation of

marriage 92. *See also* LGBT movement; same-sex marriage
Hong Kong   173
Hötzendorf, Franz Conrad von   116
households   29–30, 54, 56–9, 62–3, 123, 130, 132–4, 141; 'household government', 139; joint (multiple family) 141
housewives. *See* wife, role of
Hudal, Alois   119
human rights   9–11, 27, 32, 36–8, 40, 42, 153, 224, 234,
Hungary. *See* Austria
Hunt, James   192
husband, role of   5–9, 14, 29–32, 84, 129, 131–2, 191, 199, 206, 213, 215, 217, 229, 235, 246–7. *See also* family, ideal of; patriarchy

impotence   91, 135. *See also* procreation
incest   9, 28, 58–9. *See also* marriage, prohibitions
India   7–9, 14, 71–2, 77, 130, 142, 149–68, 173–4, 176, 178; Age of Consent Act (1891) 149; child marriage in 149–50, 152–4, 158–9; Child Marriage Restraint Act (1929) 9; divorce in 153, 157, 160; Hindu Code (1919) 156; Hindu Law Acts (1855–6) 162; Hindu Marriage Act (1955) 9; Indian National Congress 150, 152; Islam in 151, 153–5, 157, 161; legal pluralism in 157–62; Lucknow 150; Madras 175; Native Marriage Act III (1872) 156; panchayats in 153, 156; Phulmoni case 149; Rukhmabai case 149–52; widows in 149–50, 156, 159, 163, 166
infertility. *See* procreation
Ingeram Codex   96
inheritance   6, 8, 30–3, 39, 41, 45, 77, 83–5, 91, 93, 95–7, 97–8, 116, 129–31, 157, 197, 200, 203, 224, 228, 235–7, 246; and bigamy cases 192, 194, 197, 200, 203; in Muslim jurisprudence 129–31; and primogeniture 91; and rights of widows 39, 163, 235–6
Inquisition   28, 45
interconfessional marriages. *See* mixed marriages

international law: Conference for the Codification of International Law (1930) 9; Convention on Elimination of All Forms of Discrimination against Women (CEDAW) (1979) 10, 16, 234; Universal Declaration of Human Rights (UDHR) (1948) 10; United Nations International 'Decade of Women', 10
interracial marriages. *See* mixed marriages
Iqbal Hanim, wife of Khedive Abbas II of Egypt   137–8
Iran   10, 23
Islam   3–5, 7–8, 10, 13–15, 23, 77–9, 87–8, 129–48, 151, 153–5, 157, 161–2, 204–7, 210–17, 213–15, 225, 231, 237
Islamic law. *See* law and legal systems, Muslim jurisprudence
Ismail, khedive of Egypt   136, 138, 143
Israel   7
Italy   5, 94, 208

Jagiellonka, Katarzyna, Queen of Sweden   92
Jagiellonka, Zofia, Duchess of Braunschweig-Wolffenbüttel   92
Jains   14
Jakri Reformation   79
James I, King of England and Ireland / James VI, King of Scotland   94
James II, King of England and Ireland / James VII, King of Scotland   94
James V, King of Scotland   91
Japan   6, 11, 60, 76–7
Javidan (Djavidan) Hanim, second wife of Khedive Abbas II of Egypt   138
Jewish law. *See* law and legal systems, Jewish law
Jews. *See* Judaism
Jia Changxiu   64
Johan III, King of Sweden   92
Johann Georg I, King of Saxony   96
Johann Sigismund, Elector of Brandenburg   96
Johanna Elisabeth of Baden-Durlach, Duchess of Württemberg   99–100
Joseph I, Holy Roman Emperor   93
Joseph II, Holy Roman Emperor   13, 109–11, 114, 123
Juan Carlos, King of Spain   104

Judaism 6–7, 13, 19, 119–20, 122, 124, 130, 169–71, 205. *See also* anti-semitism
Judge-made law 34, 41–4, 62, 134, 168–9, 178, 191

Karl Eugen, Duke of Württemberg 99
Kemal, Namik 132
Kennedy, Anthony 248–50
Kenya 7–8, 226; polygamy in 7
khedival (viceregal) family of Egypt 130, 136–9, 143
Königsmarck, Count Philip Christoph von 100
Kopp, Josef 132
Korea 6

Landa, Alphonse 196
Law, Edward, 1st Earl of Ellensborough (Lord Ellensborough) 171
law and legal systems; Austrian 109–15, 120–3; Brazilian 11, 13, 27–35, 40–5; in the British Empire 14, 168–80; Canadian 14–15, 188–94, 199–200; canon law 3, 5–6, 13, 289, 109, 117, 169, 175, 178–9; Chinese 9, 54–6, 58–66; common law (English) 8, 14, 153, 168–9, 172–5, 177–80; common law (other forms) 119, 200; Egyptian 5, 7, 13, 130–43; forum (jurisdiction) shopping 13–14, 113–15, 120–1, 135, 195; French 4, 6, 13–14, 33, 130, 135, 171, 173, 225, 228, 235; Gabonese 10, 15, 222–37; German 4–6, 206–7, 215–16; Hindu jurisprudence 151–7; Indian 9, 14, 149–62; Jewish 7, 169, 171, 181; Muslim jurisprudence 3, 7, 13, 130–6, 153, 155, 161, 231; Roman 3; Salic 91; Scots 153, 175, 180; Siamese 9, 12, 71–2, 74–7, 82–5; Swiss 9; Three Seals Laws (*Kotmai tra samduang / KTSD*) 74; Turkish 9; in the United Kingdom 4; in the United States 6, 15–16, 242–51. *See also* international law; legal pluralism; legal transplants
Leblanc, Joseph Honoré 196
legal pluralism 157–62, 224–8
legal separation. *See* divorce
legal transplants (emulation) 9, 11, 13–14, 16, 29, 33, 55, 60, 69, 77, 87, 130, 133, 135, 158, 161, 231, 237

Leonowens, Anna 76
Leopold, King of Belgium 102
lesbian, gay, bisexual and transgender (LGBT) movement 2, 11, 27, 35–40, 44, 237, 242; gay pride parades 38. *See also* same-sex marriage
Levinson, Steven 242
Li Erbao 63
Louis XIII, King of France 92
Louis XIV, King of France 91, 99
Louis XVI, King of France 92
Luise Ulrike of Prussia, Queen of Sweden 94
Luise, Duchess of Mecklenburg-Strelitz 101
Luther, Martin 4, 99
Lutheranism 94, 188
Lutz, Bertha 31–2

M'ba, Léon, Prime Minister of Gabon 222–3, 227–31, 233–4
Maine, Henry Sumner 8, 76, 162
maintenance of the wife in Muslim jurisprudence (*nafaqa*) 14, 129, 131, 134; arrears of 135
Malabari, Behrami 149–50, 152, 159–61
Malawi 225
Malaya 77
Mali 231
Malta 173
Malthus, Thomas 4
Mandlik, Vishvanath Narayan 151–3, 158, 161
Marcotte, Arthur 192
Maria Amalia of Saxony, Queen of Spain, Naples and Sicily 92–3, 96
Maria Joseph of Poland, Queen of Poland 93
Maria Teresa, Queen of France 99
Mariana of Austria, Queen of Spain 91
Marie Antoinette, Queen of France 92
marital property 4, 8–9, 28–35, 39, 41, 43, 45, 64, 84, 95, 97–8, 130, 139, 149, 163, 194, 200, 202, 206, 228, 235–6, 246–7. *See also* inheritance; coverture
marriage and divorce advertisements 114
marriage prohibitions (impediments) 45, 91, 115, 120, 124; disability as 6; dispensation marriages ('Sever marriages') 120–2; *impedimentum*

catholicisimi 110; 'impediment of existing wedlock', 115, 120–1; incest as 9, 28, 58–9; mental illness as 6; unequal status as 12, 28, 48, 75–6, 96, 98–9. *See also* mixed marriage
marriage; age at 8–9, 14, 30, 77, 101, 130, 133, 139–40, 143, 147, 149–50, 152–4, 156–60, 171, 225, 243, 248; arrangement of 29, 56, 58, 74–6, 85, 91, 93, 102, 131, 139–41, 147, 149, 152; childless 100, 104; companionate 2, 9, 12–13, 16, 40–1, 90, 98, 101–4, 130, 132, 134, 136, 138, 140–1, 225; contracts of, 84, 94, 97, 131–2, 138–41, 143, 230, 233; as a contract in Muslim jurisprudence 131–2, 138–41; endogamous 9, 92; forced 74, 225; handbooks of 2, 13, 63, 131–2, 134, 149–50, 212–14, 235–6; morganatic 98–9; neo-local 141; parental consent for 30, 84, 171, 229–30; patrilocal 56, 141; prenuptial meetings 101–2, 133, 140–1; as a public good 2, 6, 16, 242; as a matter of public opinion 54, 59–61, 64, 79, 99–100, 143, 150, 158, 195, 204, 207–11, 214, 216, 228, 236; as a sacrament in Christian theology 4, 13, 31, 34, 99, 109–10, 117, 196, 208, 242; as a sacrament in Hindu theology 153; marriage as a form of slavery 13, 74, 76, 130–1, 136, 138, 208, 225; spousal choice 230; urban-rural divide in marriage patterns 119. *See also* child marriage; civil marriage; cohabitation; husband, role of; maintenance of the wife in Muslim jurisprudence (*nafaqa*); marriage prohibitions (impediments); obedience of the wife in Muslim jurisprudence (*taʿa*); patriarchy; wife, role of; war
Mary I, Queen of England and Ireland 91
Mary I, Queen of Scotland (Mary, Queen of Scots) 91
Mary II, Queen of England, Scotland and Ireland 95
Mascarenhas, João Antônio 37
McDonald, Mildred 198
McLennan, John F. 76
Meisel-Hess, Grete 117
mental illness 6, 91, 101. *See also* marriage prohibitions

Mexico 4, 10
Middleton, Catherine, Duchess of Cambridge 97, 104
Millis, George 177–8
missionaries 14, 183, 223; Baptist Missionary Society 176; Wesleyan Methodist Missionary Society 176
mistresses. *See* adultery; concubinage
mixed marriages 6, 15, 174, 179, 205; binational marriage 205; between indigenous populations and colonizers 6, 28, 168, 174, 181; between Jews and non-Jews 6, 122, 205; between Muslims and non-Muslims 15, 204–22; between Protestants and Catholics 6, 114, 205
modernists and modernism 9, 11, 13–14, 30–1, 54, 60, 65, 78, 117, 119, 130, 132–6, 138, 149–54, 156–9, 160, 187
modernity, discourses about 1–2, 7, 9–10, 29, 65, 77, 103, 130–2, 140, 143, 158, 161, 209, 222–3, 228, 230. *See also* civility, discourses about; modernists and modernism
modernization theory 11
Mongkut, King of Siam (Rama IV) 72, 76, 79
monogamy 1–2, 9, 11–13, 36–40, 55–60, 65, 71–85, 130, 136–9, 143, 187, 189–90, 199, 199, 225, 235. *See also* bigamy; polygamy
Montesquieu (Charles-Louis de Secondat, Baron de La Brède et de Montesquieu) 7
Morgan, Lewis Henry 9, 76
Morin, Julie 196
Mormonism 7, 201
morning gift. *See* dower
mothers and motherhood 57, 82-3, 133. *See also* procreation; wife, role of
Muan, Amdaeng 75
Mubarak, Ali 132–4
Muhammad Ali, governor of Egypt 133, 135, 140
Müller, Max 159, 161
Muslims. *See* Islam

Nafaqa in Muslim jurisprudence. *See* maintenance
Narayan, Shantaram 151, 157–8

Nasif, Malak Hifni ('Bahithat al-Badiya') 133–4, 140
Natal 173
National Socialism. *See* Germany
nationalism and nationalist movements 9, 11, 14, 113, 132, 139, 141, 150–2, 162, 205
Netherlands 7, 10, 72, 77, 90, 103, 171–2; Netherlands East Indies 77
New Zealand 173, 179
Nigeria 231
Noronha, João Otávio de 43
Norway 90, 103
novelas 39, 41, 51
nushuz in Muslim jurisprudence. *See* disobedience
Nzet Biteghe, Honorine 231, 234

obedience of the wife in Muslim jurisprudence (*taʿa*) 14, 131
Odilon, Hélène 115
Ofner, Julius 117
Orientalism 8, 76, 129, 151, 209, 213, 223. *See also* civility, discourses about; legal transplants (emulation)
Ottoman Empire 7–9, 13, 22, 130–9, 144

Padoux, Georges 77–8
Paine, Thomas 153
Pakistan 10, 23
Pamuk, Orhan 141
papal infallibility 113
patriarchy 6–7, 9, 27–32, 35–6, 40, 44, 56, 59, 65, 74, 140–1, 197, 209–10, 225–6, 229–30, 235, 247, 250
Penha, Maria da 41–3
personal status law 8, 13–14, 129–30, 143, 156–7, 162, 173. *See also* legal pluralism
Perth Agreement. *See* royal marriage
Peter I, Emperor of Russia (Peter the Great) 91, 99
Pfalz-Neuburg, Dorothea Sophia von, Duchess of Parma 96
Philip III, King of Spain and Portugal 96
Philip IV, King of Spain and Portugal 91–2
Philip V, King of Spain 96
Philipp I, Landgrave of Hesse 99

Philippe, duc d'Anjou 92
Philippe, duc d'Orléans 91
Philippine Ordinances 30
photography 79–80, 101, 137, 142
Phule, Jotirao 153–4
Phulmoni case 149
Piffl, Friedrich Gustav, Cardinal of Vienna 119
Pius IX, Pope 109, 112, 123
Poland 91–3
polygamy 7–9, 12–13, 55–6, 71–85, 119, 130–6, 138, 188, 191, 201–2, 225
polygyny. *See* polygamy
Portugal 28–9, 46, 72, 175
posting of banns 169–71, 189, 196, 202
Prajadhipok, King of Siam (Rama VII) 80, 83
press and periodicals 2, 15, 60, 83–4, 132, 138, 141, 207–11, 214, 216
primogeniture 79, 91, 138. *See also* inheritance
Prince Philip, Duke of Edinburgh 104
Prince William, Duke of Cambridge 97, 104
Prisdang Chumsai, Prince of Siam 80
procreation 1, 4–7, 57, 74–5, 84, 91–2, 99–100, 131, 137, 198, 223, 228, 230, 244–6; artificial insemination 57; eugenics 6; impotence 58, 91, 135; infertility 91–2, 100; pronatalism 5
pronatalism 5. *See also* procreation
prostitution 29, 83
Protestant Reformation 3, 5, 94, 99, 169
Protestantism. *See* Christianity

Quakers 19, 169–70, 181,
Qur'an and Qur'anic verses 3, 136, 171

Ranade, M. G. 153
Ranade, Ramabai 149, 153, 156–7, 161
Rao, R. Raghunath 154, 164
Rao, Sir T. Madhao 150
Rauscher, Cardinal Joseph Othmar von 109–11
reformers. *See* modernists and modernism
Reis, Toni 41
Renner, Karl 120
Republic of Ireland 5
restitution of conjugal rights. *See* divorce

Rhodesia   173
Roberts, John   249
Rocasolano, Letizia Ortiz   104
Roller, Julius   118
Roman law. *See* law and legal systems
Romania   114, 198
romantic love. *See* marriage, companionate
Rosenberg, Laura   198
Roy, Rammohan   150, 159
Roy, Sripati   156
royal marriage   13, 73–6, 79–83, 136–9, 90–108; Perth Agreement (2011) 98, 103; Royal Marriages Act (1772) 98–9
Rudigier, Franz Joseph, Bishop of Linz   112
Rukhmabai. *See* court cases; India
Russia   91–2, 94, 99, 103, 119, 158–9, 198. *See also* Soviet Union

Saale, Margarethe von der   99
Salic law. *See* law and legal systems
same-sex marriage   1, 5, 7, 11, 16; in the USA 16, 242–51; in Brazil 11, 33, 38, 40–5
Saowapha, Queen of Siam   79–80
Sarasvati, Pandita Ramabai   150
Saudi Arabia   10, 23
Scheu, Robert   116–17
Schulenburg, Melusine von der   100–1
Schuschnigg, Kurt   121
Schwarz, Olga   119
Scotland. *See* United Kingdom of Great Britain and Ireland
Scots law. *See* law and legal systems
Scott, Sir William, 1st Baron Stowell (Lord Stowell)   171–2
secularization   13, 30, 109
Seipel, Ignaz   118, 121
Seitz, Karl   121
Sever marriages. *See* marriage prohibitions
Sever, Albert   120–1
sex and sexuality   3, 5, 8, 14, 28–9, 32, 34, 37, 55–8, 60–2, 73–9, 82–4, 92, 99, 103–4, 117, 129, 131–2, 136, 150–2, 159, 161, 163, 187, 191, 198–9, 208–9, 225, 230, 234. *See also* homosexuality; procreation
Shadwell, Sir Lancelot   172
Sharia law. *See* law and legal systems, Muslim jurisprudence; courts, sharia courts

She Dusheng   57
Shen Fu   58
Siam (Thailand)   9, 11–12, 55–6, 71–90, 129, 130, 138, 142, 146, 151, 238; Bangkok 72, 79, 83; Bowring Treaty (1855) 72, 76, 78; Civil and Commercial Code of Siam (1935) 12, 84–5; 'family' as a concept (*khropkhrua*) in 74; Inner Palace 73–4, 79, 81; patriarchy in 74; Penal Code (1908) 73, 75; polygyny in 71–85; Three Seals Laws (*Kotmai tra samduang / KTSD*) 74
Sierra Leone   173
Sikhs   14
Silva, Luís Inácio 'Lula' da   38
Simpson, Wallace   103
Singapore   72, 173
slaves and slavery   5, 28–31, 46–7, 73, 75, 138–9, 143, 153–4; Anglo-Egyptian anti-slavery convention 138; marriage as a form of slavery 13, 74, 76, 130–1, 136, 138, 208, 225
social reformers. *See* modernists and modernism
social-security legislation   31–3, 35, 40–1, 189, 198, 243, 248
socio-affective family as a concept in jurisprudence   40–1
Sonneveld, Nadia   129
Sophie Dorothea of Celle, Queen of Great Britain and Ireland   93, 100
Sophie Dorothea of Hanover, Queen of Prussia   100
South Africa   7, 13, 19, 226; polygamy in 7; Recognition of Customary Marriages Act (1988) 231
Soviet Union   5. *See also* Russia
Spain   90–4, 96, 99, 103–4, 158, 208
St Lucia   14, 173
Stowe, Harriet Beecher   76
Strachan, Alex   195
Stremayr, Carl von   111
Struensee, Johann Friedrich   101
Su Shi   58
Sun Shumin   62
Svasti Sobhon, Prince of Siam   82
Sweden   90, 92, 94, 103
Syria   23

ta'a in Muslim jurisprudence. *See* obedience
Tanzania 6, 231
Tawfiq, khedive of Egypt 136–7
Thailand. *See* Siam
Thiphakorawong, Jao Phraya (Kham Bunnag) 78
Tilak, Bal Gangadar 151–2
Transylvanian marriages 114, 120, 126. *See also* law and legal systems, forum shopping
Turkey 9, 23, 141. *See also* Ottoman Empire

Uganda 173
United Kingdom of Great Britain and Ireland 98, 170; Act of Settlement (1701) 95, 98; Act of Supremacy (1558) 103; Act of Union (1801) 170; Clandestine Marriage Act (1753) 4, 169, 178; England 97, 149, 153, 158–60, 168–79; Ireland 5, 169, 177, 192; Marriage Act (1836) 4; Royal Marriages Act (1772) 98–9; Scotland 4, 169–70, 175, 178; Succession to the Crown Act (2013) 98, 103; Test and Corporation Acts (1828) 170; Wales 4, 168–71, 173, 175, 179
United Nations International 'Decade of Women' 10
United States of America 6, 16, 38, 208, 24, 242–51; American Civil Liberties Union 242; amicus curiae briefs in 16, 244–5, 248–9; *Baher v. Lewin* 242; California 6, 245; civil marriage in 242; cohabitation in 250–1; criminalization of homosexuality in 243–4; Defense of Marriage Act (DOMA) 247–9; divorce in 243, 245, 248; federalism and marriage in 243, 249; Gay and Lesbian Advocates and Defenders 242; Georgia 244; Hawaii 242, 247; Hawaii Supreme Court 242, 247; *Lawrence v. Texas* 243–4, 248; *Loving v. Virginia* 246; Maine 6; Massachusetts 244–5, 247–8; New York 194, 198; *Obergefell v. Hodges* 249–50; patriarchy in 247, 250; polygyny in 7; Reno 195; same-sex marriage in 240–51; Texas 243–4, 248; United States Congress 243, 247–9; United States Constitution 242–3, 249; United States Revolution (1776) 245; United States Supreme Court 7, 16, 243, 246, 248–50; *US v. Windsor* 248–9; 248–9
Universal Declaration of Human Rights (UDHR) (1948) 10
Uruguay 5

Vajiravudh, King of Siam (Rama VI) 79–83
Vargas, Getúlio 31
Venkatesh, Trimulrao 152
Victoria I, Queen of the United Kingdom 91, 102
Victoria, Crown Princess of Sweden 103
Vidyasagar, Ishwar Chandra 150
Viswanathan, Gauri 155

Wahrmund, Ludwig 117
Wales. *See* United Kingdom of Great Britain and Ireland
war 2, 199, 204–5; Austro-Prussian War 111; Cold War 32, 206, 233; First World War 5, 9, 103, 116, 118–19, 138, 140–1, 143, 194; Napoleonic wars 171; Second World War 10, 104, 123, 189, 193–4, 204–6, 216, 223, 226; War of the Spanish Succession 97
Webb, Frederick 197
Wekerle, Sándor 115
Westling, Daniel 104
widows: burning of (*sati*) 8, 150, 225; child custody rights of 97–8; inheritance rights of 39, 97, 163, 235–6; remarriage of 14, 98, 149–50, 156, 159, 163, 166
wife, role of 30, 32, 74, 116, 123, 129, 131, 133–4, 209–11, 213, 247. *See also* family, ideal of; patriarchy
Willem-Alexander, King of the Netherlands 103
William of Orange 95
Wittekind 96
women 4, 15–16, 28–32, 56, 72, 75, 85, 91, 99, 116–19, 123, 129–36, 158, 162, 171, 174, 177, 189, 191, 195–6, 198, 204–7, 225, 229, 250; citizenship in marriage 9–10, 31, 207, 210–12, 216;

education of 10, 13, 60, 130, 132–4, 136, 138, 208, 210, 215; Convention on Elimination of All Forms of Discrimination against Women (CEDAW) (1979) 10, 16, 234; seclusion of 13, 133, 159; suffrage of 31, 118, 243; surnames of 29–31, 35, 59, 68; United Nations International 'Decade of Women', 10; veiling of 133–4, 137; women's rights movements 9–11, 27, 31, 35, 43, 60–1, 133–4, 149, 208, 215, 222–4, 234–6, 247; and work 10, 31, 34, 117, 119, 131, 134, 206, 208–9, 215, 226, 246. *See also* bridewealth; coverture; harems; mothers and motherhood; patriarchy; polygamy; wife, role of; sex and sexuality; widows

Wood, William Page 1st Baron Hatherley (Lord Hatherley)   179
Wuermeling, Franz-Josef   206

Xu Yingkui   57

Zenker, Ernst Viktor   111, 117
Zhao Meibao   63
Zorreguieta-Cerruti, Máxima   103